THE CAMBRIDGE COMP

MW00785135

This newly commissioned volume p.......... .. ..view or Dante's masterpiece, the *Commedia*, offering Dante's readers of today wide-ranging insights into the poem and its core features. Leading scholars discuss matters of structure, narrative, language and style, characterization, doctrine, and politics, in chapters that make their own contributions to Dante criticism by raising problems and questions that call for renewed attention, while investigating contextual concerns as well as the current state of criticism about the poem. The *Commedia* is also placed in a variety of cultural and historical contexts through accounts of the poem's transmission and reception that explore both its contemporary influence and its continuing legacy today. With its accessible approach, its unstinting focus on the poem and its attention to matters that have not always received adequate critical assessment, this volume will be of value to all students and scholars of Dante's great poem.

Zygmunt G. Barański is Serena Professor of Italian Emeritus at the University of Cambridge and Notre Dame Professor of Dante and Italian Studies at the University of Notre Dame. Among his publications are *'Sole nuovo luce nuova'. Saggi sul rinnovamento culturale in Dante* (1996), *Dante e i segni* (2000), *'Chiosar con altro testo'. Leggere Dante nel Trecento* (2001) and, with Lino Pertile, *Dante in Context* (Cambridge, 2015).

Simon Gilson is Agnelli-Serena Professor of Italian at the University of Oxford and Fellow of Magdalen College. He is the author of *Dante and Renaissance Florence* (Cambridge, 2005) and *Reading Dante in Renaissance Italy: Florence, Venice and the 'Divine Poet'* (Cambridge, 2018).

THE CAMBRIDGE
COMPANION TO
DANTE'S *COMMEDIA*

EDITED BY

ZYGMUNT G. BARAŃSKI
University of Cambridge and University of Notre Dame

SIMON GILSON
University of Oxford

CAMBRIDGE
UNIVERSITY PRESS

CAMBRIDGE
UNIVERSITY PRESS

University Printing House, Cambridge CB2 8BS, United Kingdom

One Liberty Plaza, 20th Floor, New York, NY 10006, USA

477 Williamstown Road, Port Melbourne, VIC 3207, Australia

314–321, 3rd Floor, Plot 3, Splendor Forum, Jasola District Centre,
New Delhi – 110025, India

79 Anson Road, #06–04/06, Singapore 079906

Cambridge University Press is part of the University of Cambridge.

It furthers the University's mission by disseminating knowledge in the pursuit of
education, learning, and research at the highest international levels of excellence.

www.cambridge.org
Information on this title: www.cambridge.org/9781108421294
DOI: 10.1017/9781108367769

© Cambridge University Press 2019

First published 2019

Printed and bound in Great Britain by Clays Ltd, Elcograf, S.p.A.

A catalogue record for this publication is available from the British Library.

Library of Congress Cataloging-in-Publication Data
NAMES: Barański, Zygmunt G., editor. | Gilson, Simon A., editor.
TITLE: The Cambridge companion to Dante's Commedia / edited by Zygmunt G.
Barański, Simon Gilson.
DESCRIPTION: Cambridge ; New York : Cambridge University Press, 2019. | Includes
bibliographical references and index.
IDENTIFIERS: LCCN 2018042044 | ISBN 9781108421294 (alk. paper)
SUBJECTS: LCSH: Dante Alighieri, 1265–1321. Divina commedia. | Dante Alighieri,
1265–1321 – Criticism and interpretation.
CLASSIFICATION: LCC PQ4390 .C279 2019 | DDC 851/.1–dc23
LC record available at https://lccn.loc.gov/2018042044

ISBN 978-1-108-42129-4 Hardback
ISBN 978-1-108-43170-5 Paperback

For our children, Anna and Ed, Lauren and Sofia

CONTENTS

CONTENTS

ILLUSTRATIONS

MAP

CONTRIBUTORS

ZYGMUNT G. BARAŃSKI is Serena Professor of Italian Emeritus at the University of Cambridge and Notre Dame Professor of Dante and Italian Studies at the University of Notre Dame.

THEODORE J. CACHEY JR. is Professor of Italian Studies at the University of Notre Dame.

FABIO CAMILLETTI is Reader in Italian at the University of Warwick.

GEORGE CORBETT is Senior Lecturer in Theology and the Arts at the University of St Andrews.

SIMON GILSON is Agnelli-Serena Professor of Italian at the University of Oxford and Fellow of Magdalen College.

CLAIRE E. HONESS is Professor of Italian Studies at the University of Leeds.

LAURENCE E. HOOPER is Assistant Professor of Italian at Dartmouth College.

TRISTAN KAY is Senior Lecturer in Italian at the University of Bristol.

JAMES C. KRIESEL is Assistant Professor of Italian at Villanova University.

GIUSEPPE LEDDA is Associate Professor of Italian Literature at the University of Bologna.

SIMONE MARCHESI is Associate Professor of French and Italian at Princeton University.

PAOLA NASTI is Associate Professor of Italian Studies at Northwestern University.

ANNA PEGORETTI is Assistant Professor in Italian Literature at Università degli Studi Roma Tre.

LINO PERTILE is Carl A. Pescosolido Research Professor in the Department of Romance Languages and Literatures, Harvard University.

PRUE SHAW is Emeritus Reader in Italian at University College London.

MIRKO TAVONI is Professor of Italian Linguistics at the University of Pisa.

The following editions and translations are used throughout, unless otherwise stated.

Bible   *Biblia Sacra iuxta vulgatam versionem*, ed. R. Weber and R. Gryson, 5th edn. (Stuttgart: Deutsche Bibelgesellschaft, 2007).

The New Jerusalem Bible (New York: Doubleday, 1990).

Commedia   *La Commedia secondo l'antica vulgata*, ed. G. Petrocchi, 2nd edn., 4 vols. (Florence: Le Lettere, 1994).

The Divine Comedy, trans. J. D. Sinclair, 3 vols. (Oxford University Press, 1981); slightly adapted.

Conv.   *Convivio*, ed. F. Brambilla Ageno, 3 vols. (Florence: Le Lettere, 1995).

Dante's Il Convivio (The Banquet), trans. R. H. Lansing (New York: Garland, 1990).

Detto   *Il Fiore e il Detto d'Amore attribuibili a Dante Alighieri*, ed. G. Contini (Milan: Mondadori, 1984), pp. 483–512.

The Fiore and the Detto d'Amore, A Late 13th-Century Translation of the 'Roman de la Rose' Attributable to Dante, trans. S. Casciani and C. Kleinhenz (University of Notre Dame Press, 2000), pp. 509–39.

Dve   *De vulgari eloquentia*, ed P. V. Mengaldo, in Dante Alighieri, *Opere minori*, 2 vols. (Milan and Naples: Ricciardi, 1979–88), II, 1–237.

De vulgari eloquentia, trans. S. Botterill (Cambridge University Press, 1996).

ED   *Enciclopedia Dantesca*, 5 vols. (Rome: Istituto della Enciclopedia Italiana, 1970–78).

Ecl.   *Egloge*, ed. G. Albanese, in Dante, *Opere*, 3 vols. (Milan: Mondadori, 2011–), II, 1593–783.

P. H. Wicksteed and E. G. Gardner, *Dante and Giovanni del Virgilio* (Westminster: Constable, 1902).

Ep.   *Epistole*, ed. C. Villa, in *Opere*, II, 1417–592.

Dantis Alagherii Epistolae: The Letters of Dante, ed. and trans. P. J. Toynbee, 2nd edn. (Oxford: Clarendon Press, 1966).

Four Political Letters, trans. C. E. Honess (London: MHRA, 2007).

Fiore   *Il Fiore*, pp. 1–467.

The Fiore, pp. 35–499.

Inf.   *Inferno.*

Mon.   *Monarchia*, ed. P. Shaw (Florence: Le Lettere, 2009).

Monarchy, trans. P. Shaw (Cambridge University Press, 1996).

Par.   *Paradiso.*

Purg.   *Purgatorio.*

Questio   *Questio de aqua et terra*, ed. F. Mazzoni, in *Opere minori*, II, 693–880.

A Question of the Water and the Land, trans. C. H. Bromby, in A. Paolucci (ed.), *Dante beyond the Commedia* (New York: Published by Griffon House Publications for The Bagehot Council, 2004), pp. 1–32.

Rime   *Rime*, ed. D. De Robertis (Florence: Edizioni del Galluzzo, 2005).

Dante's Lyric Poetry, trans. K. Foster and P. Boyde, 2 vols. (Oxford: Clarendon Press, 1967).

Vn   *La vita nuova*, rev. ed. M. Barbi (Florence: Bemporad, 1932).

Vita nova, trans. A. Frisardi (Evanston: Northwestern University Press, 2012).

All translations from classical Latin authors, unless stated otherwise, are taken from the Loeb Classical Library. All other translations are noted in the individual chapters.

1250	Death of Emperor Frederick II.
1252	First gold florin coined in Florence.
1260	Battle of Montaperti. Banished Florentine Ghibellines defeat Guelfs.
1265	May/June Dante born in Florence. Charles of Anjou enters Italy
1266	Battle of Benevento. Manfred killed. Guelfs return to Florence.
1289	Florence defeats Arezzo at Campaldino
1270-73	Dante's mother, Bella, dies.
1274	May: first encounter with Beatrice.
1277	9 January: marriage contract with Gemma Donati.
1282	Dante's father, Alighiero di Bellincione, dies.
1283	Dante publishes first poem. Friendship with Guido Cavalcanti
1285	Marriage to Gemma Donati
1287	Dante in Bologna? Beatrice marries Simone de' Bardi
1286	Dante writes the *Fiore* and *Detto d'Amore* (?)
1287	Birth of first child, Giovanni (?)
1289	Dante at the battle of Campaldino against Arezzo. Son Jacopo is born (?)
1290	Death of Beatrice. Son Pietro is born (?)
1293	Ordinances of Justice. Dante writes *Vita nova*. Brunetto Latini dies in Florence.
1294	December, Pope Celestine V abdicates five months after his election. Boniface VIII becomes pope.

1295	Dante enrolls in the Guild of Physicians and Apothecaries and enters political life. From November he is a member of the Council of Thirty-Six.
1296	Dante member of the Council of the Hundred.
1299	Daughter Antonia is born (?).
1300	Easter week: Dante's fictional journey to the realms of the afterlife.
	April: Pope Boniface proclaims the Jubilee Year.
	May: Florentine Guelfs split into Blacks and Whites.
	May: Dante ambassador to San Gimignano on behalf of the Guelfs.
	15 June–15 August: Dante serves as Prior; signs warrant sending Guido Cavalcanti into exile; Guido dies in the Summer.
1301	April–September: Dante member of the Council of the Hundred.
	October: Sent on a diplomatic mission to Pope Boniface VIII in Rome.
	November: Charles of Valois enters Florence; Black Guelph coup d'état.
1302	27 January: While on his way back to Florence, Dante is fined 5000 florins and excluded from public office for two years; refuses to pay fine.
	10 March: sentence confirmed; if caught, Dante will be burnt at the stake.
	Dante joins exiled White Guelfs in a leading position.
	Boniface VIII's bull *Unam sanctam*, proclaiming supreme authority.
1303	Dante in Verona, guest of Bartolomeo della Scala. Probably visits Treviso, Venice, and Padua. Begins *Convivio* and *De vulgari eloquentia*.
	French troops humiliate Pope Boniface at Anagni. Death of Boniface. Benedict XI elected October 1303.
1304	July: Benedict XI dies.
	Dante in Arezzo. Letter to cardinal Niccolò da Prato on behalf of the Whites.
	Dante in Bologna, works on *Convivio* and *De vulgari eloquentia* (?)
1305	Bertrand De Got elected pope with the name of Clement V.

1306	Dante in Lunigiana, guest of Moroello Malaspina. He starts writing the *Commedia* and continues until 1320/1.
1307	Dante in Casentino: letter and canzone (*Rime* CXVI) to Moroello Malaspina.
1308	Henry of Luxembourg chosen to be next emperor. Dante in Lucca.
1309	Henry crowned emperor as Henry VII at Aix-La-Chapelle (Aachen) Clement V moves the papacy to Avignon, France, where it remains until 1377. Robert of Anjou, king of Naples.
1310	October. Henry VII in Italy. Dante in Poppi, near Arezzo, guest of Guido da Battifolle, writes an open letter to rulers and people of Italy urging them to welcome Henry.
1311	Henry VII crowned in Milan. 31 March: Dante writes letter urging the Florentines to open the city to Henry VII. 17 April: Dante writes to Henry VII exhorting him to attack Florence.
1312	Henry VII crowned in Rome, but not in St Peter's. Dante settles in Verona as guest of Cangrande della Scala. He writes or begins writing *Monarchia* (?).
1313	August: Henry dies of malaria in Buonconvento, near Siena.
1314	Pope Clement V dies. Dante writes open letter to Italian Cardinals urging them to elect an Italian pope. Conclave closes for two years.
1315	June: Amnesty offered to Florentine exiles; Dante rejects offer. October: Florence reconfirms Dante's exile and extends it to his children.
1316	Conclave reopens in Lyons. Frenchman Jacques Duèse is elected pope as John XXII.
1317	Dante writes or begins writing *Monarchia* (?).
1318	Dante leaves Verona and settles in Ravenna as guest of Guido Novello da Polenta.
1319–20	Dante writes two Latin eclogues to Giovanni del Virgilio and the *Questio de aqua et terra*.
1320	20 January. Dante reads the *Questio de aqua et terra* in a public lecture in Verona. Completes *Paradiso* between 1320 and 1321.
1321	Dante is sent on a diplomatic mission to Venice by Guido Novello. On his return, he dies of malaria on the night between

	13 and 14 September and is buried in Ravenna in the church of San Pier Maggiore, now San Francesco.
1322	Commentary to the *Inferno* in Italian by Jacopo, son of Dante.
1324	Commentary to the *Inferno* in Latin by Graziolo Bambaglioli, Bologna.
1324–8	Commentary to the full *Commedia* in Italian by Iacomo della Lana, Bologna.
1334	*Ottimo Commento*, full commentary in Italian.
1335–40	Commentary to *Inferno* in Latin by Guido da Pisa, Pisa (?).
1340	*Comentum* in Latin by Pietro Alighieri, Verona.

Map 1. Dante's Italy around 1300

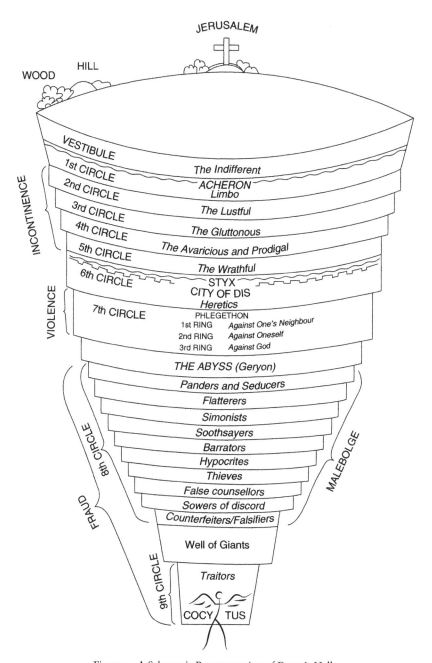

Figure I. A Schematic Representation of Dante's Hell

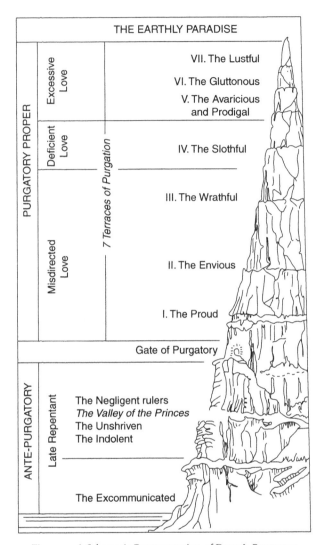

Figure 2. A Schematic Representation of Dante's Purgatory

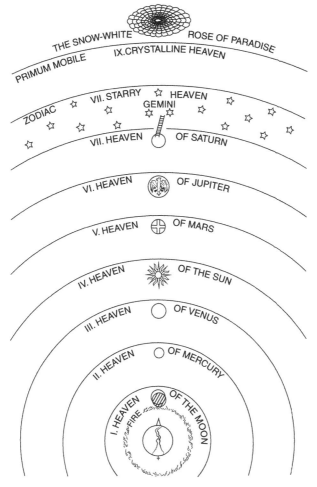

Figure 3. A Schematic Representation of Dante's Paradise

ZYGMUNT G. BARAŃSKI AND
SIMON GILSON

Introduction

Several good introductions, 'companions', and encyclopaedias on Dante have been published in English in recent years. The novelty of *The Cambridge Companion to Dante's 'Commedia'* is that, unlike *The Cambridge Companion to Dante* and the recent *Dante in Context*, also published by Cambridge University Press in 2015, its primary focus is Dante's masterpiece. This *Companion* aims to offer Dante's readers of today an accessible overview that gives a strong idea of the poem and its core features. We do this by exploring questions related to its structure, narrative and characterization, language and style, its handling of politics, the classics, vernacular writings, theology, philosophy and religious culture, and of various other major cultural issues, its relationship with Dante's other works, and its transmission and reception. As far as we are aware, no single study of this kind has ever appeared either in Italy or in the English-speaking world.

The book is divided into sixteen chapters that have been conceived in four broad blocks. The first four chapters study questions pertaining broadly to narrative, although the first chapter also offers a compelling overview of the *Commedia* as a whole. We were acutely aware that such 'narratological' features have been relatively understudied by Dantists, and that it has been especially difficult for readers confronting the poem to seek adequate orientation in this area. This group of chapters aims to address such omissions by offering new contributions on narrative structure, the relationship between poet and protagonist, characterization, and moral structure. The next three chapters are concerned with matters which can loosely be defined as literary, metaliterary, linguistic, and stylistic in character, from the poem's title and genre to Dante's choice of the vernacular, from the character of his Florentine to his syntactical and lexical choices, from the *Commedia*'s use of dialogue, similes and invectives to its complex deployment of allegory. The following five chapters turn to consider Dante's treatment of various kinds of cultural 'content': Latin culture, the vernacular, religion, philosophy and theology, and politics. In each case, these chapters examine the relevant context, but the primary emphasis remains, as throughout, Dante's poem, with discussion focused upon the artistic questions and complex cultural operations involved. This section is then followed by a single chapter that concentrates on Dante's 'other works' (still often – and unhelpfully we believe – referred to as his 'minor works'), examining their interconnections with the poem, as well as considering the *Commedia*'s genesis and processes of composition. The chapter is placed here rather than at the beginning of the volume out of a conscious concern to avoid it being read as having a programmatic status and as predetermining the treatment of the *Commedia*. The final three chapters address the poem's 'afterlife' and illustrate how richly and inextricably the *Commedia*'s reception is interwoven with its interpretation, and how deeply implicated Dante's poem has been and continues to be in the cultural sphere. One chapter explores the poem's complex textual transmission (a topic seldom summarized in English), and a further two illustrate its extraordinarily varied and influential afterlife, in its many forms across well over seven centuries, from the exegetical work of his first glossators and commentators to the poem's reverberations in our contemporary multimedia culture. We have used Cristoforo Landino's celebrated print edition and commentary, published in Florence in 1481 and a major watershed in Dante's presentation, in order to divide the discussion of the reception into two.

The volume has been designed so as to allow both individual chapters and broader blocks of chapters to be read in sequence in ways that allow crosscutting themes and issues to emerge. Several chapters can be read in especially close relationship with one another, such as the contributions by Cachey and Tavoni, Pertile and Corbett, and Gilson and Nasti. At the same time, however, a rich array of interconnections exists between all our chapters, although our readers will also note tensions and disagreements between chapters on important issues (for instance, the status of the Letter to Cangrande, Dante's attitude to his 'other works', etc.), as well as 'inconsistencies' regarding, say, the dates of certain works. Dante studies is a remarkably rich critical field characterized by competing interpretations, and we felt that it was only right that something of this energetically complex debate should seep into our volume. Furthermore, there is much that we do not know about Dante's life and career, hence, the discrepancies regarding the dating of his works. Indeed, alluring hypotheses are many about his time in Florence, his exile, his intellectual formation, and his emotional life, while hard facts are actually frustratingly few.

Our readers will also need and want to make use of the detailed name and subject index to explore topics of central interest, such as Rome, Virgil, and

Beatrice, but also sin, plurilingualism, and the body. We have used J. D. Sinclair's translation as our base text when citing the *Commedia*, although we have regularly adapted this in order to make the sense explicit.

Our hope is that the volume will be useful not only to students of medieval Italian literature and of medieval Italy, but also to those interested in literary classics. The book is intended to complement *Dante in Context*, which offers an exhaustive account of the historical, cultural, and intellectual context in which Dante lived. The *Companion* digests and synthesizes aspects of such knowledge, as well as the current state of criticism about the poem. Our volume is, however, intended to do more than summarize the state of play; its individual chapters also aim to make their own contributions to Dante criticism, by raising problems and questions that call for renewed attention. In these ways, then, we hope that *The Companion to Dante's 'Commedia'* – with its unstinting focus on the poem and its attention to several topics that seldom, if ever, appear in critical assessments of the poem – will also be of value to academic Dantists and other medievalists.

The Cambridge Companion to Dante's 'Commedia', unlike rather too many collaborative volumes, has been a relatively straightforward academic and editorial project. We are thus extremely grateful to Linda Bree, Anna Bond and Tim Mason at Cambridge University Press for their constant support, advice, and efficiency. Most of all we are thankful to our contributors for the timeliness with which they have sent us their chapters, and for the generous and understanding manner with which they have reacted to our editorial suggestions and interventions. Demetrio S. Yocum is an elegant and painstaking translator. The book has been enriched by his contribution. We are also very pleased to express our warmest gratitude to the Institute for Scholarship in the Liberal Arts at the University of Notre Dame for its generous financial support towards the costs of the translations. The Press's three anonymous readers gave us invaluable advice at a crucial moment of the book's development.

Working together has not simply been a source of intellectual satisfaction and enrichment. It has also been an act of friendship. As one of us is starting to bring to a close his career as a full-time scholar and teacher, collaborations such as this one stand out as among the most satisfying and happy experiences of his academic life. An opportunity, yes, to talk about Dante and medieval Italian culture, but perhaps more significantly, an opportunity to talk about much else, with our families always to the fore. It thus seems entirely appropriate to dedicate this book to our children, Anna and Ed, Lauren and Sofia.

I

LINO PERTILE

Narrative Structure

The *Commedia* is the story of a journey through Hell, Purgatory, and Paradise, which Dante says he made during Easter week 1300, when he was thirty-five. The poet finds himself lost in a dark wood on the evening of Maundy Thursday; his journey begins at dusk on Good Friday and ends six days later in the Empyrean, where God resides with the angels and the blessed. The purpose of the journey is to rescue the poet-character and bring him to moral perfection; the poet will then recount his journey with the aim of transforming the lives of his readers and of the entire world.

Dante: Character, Narrator, Author

The hero and true engine of the *Commedia* is the poet-character, protagonist, narrator, and author of the story. This is one and the same person, the poet Dante – as he explicitly declares at *Purg.* XXX, 55–66 – simultaneously at two different stages of his life: the stage of actual experience (the present of the narrative); and the stage of re-living that experience through the retelling of it (the present of the narration). The former takes place in Easter week 1300; the latter in an imprecise time, but one that certainly lasts 'many years' (molti anni; *Par.* XXV, 3) beginning in 1306, though the possibility that the *Commedia* may have been conceived and begun in some form before Dante's exile, as suggested by Boccaccio, cannot be categorically excluded.

One of the striking features of the *Commedia* is that, from its very beginning (*Inf.* I, 4), it not only tells a story, but it also makes the recounting of it part of the story itself. The narrator often comments on his present efforts to adjust his language to his experiences as poet-character, 'so that the telling may not be diverse from the fact' (sì che dal fatto il dir non sia diverso; *Inf.* XXXII, 12). He also inserts warnings to the reader, observations on the story's development, and comments on his own states of mind at the time of the narrative. Thus, in addition to being influenced by the reactions of Dante-character, the reader's responses are shaped by Dante-narrator who interrupts the narration to address the reader. These interruptions are far from rare – about twenty can be counted, but there are many more if we adopt a broader definition of the phenomenon. They can be as short as one line (*Inf.* XXII, 118) and as long as twenty-four (*Par.* XIII, 1–24). They occur at critical points in the narrative, when the expressibility, credibility, or interpretation of an event, sight, or statement is at stake. The narrator intervenes, calling the reader's attention to what is about to happen or has just happened, and in so doing creates suspense (as is the case at *Inf.* VIII, 94–6) or heightens the significance of the action. This dialogue has a didactic role but its chief purpose is to involve the reader in the character's experiences. Thus the narrator becomes another character, who is and is not the same as the protagonist, whose story he authenticates while bringing it closer to the reader.

To these two Dantes, some scholars add a third – Dante the author and man – who is responsible for every word the other two say and every move they make. According to this further distinction, the author Dante Alighieri is the only real person involved in the operation, whereas Dante-traveller and Dante-narrator are both characters created by him. Most importantly, the standard narratological distinction that applies to all first-person narratives is made in the *Commedia* as well. In the narrated story, the character becomes the narrator only after completing his journey, whereas, from the perspective of the actual poem (the plot), character and narrator coexist, but the narrator knows everything about the journey from its very inception, while the character needs to progress through the journey to acquire the same understanding of himself and the world as the narrator. This is a valid structural distinction, but it cannot be forced systematically upon the story without falling into substantial contradictions. Character, narrator, and author are indeed intertwined and often overlapping in the *Commedia*, but we cannot always treat them as one; nor can we assume that they are perfectly discrete. It is a structural ambiguity which the poet fully exploits.

Dante: Pilgrim and Exile

The poet-character performs another function in the *Commedia*, one that is intrinsic to the 'journey of life' metaphor. In Christian culture, life is understood, and experienced, as a journey back home, 'for here', Paul writes, 'we have no lasting city, but we seek the city which is to come' (Hebrews 13:14). Life is a state of exile in a land that was not meant for us. In this alien land we are pilgrims returning home, and our desire for fulfilment is the sign of a profound homesickness, the yearning for our lost paradise. The journey in the middle of which Dante suddenly finds himself lost at the beginning of *Inferno* is this universal journey from the human to the divine (*Par.* XXXI, 37–8); and it is because of this that Dante-character is referred to as 'the pilgrim'. However, there is something unique about the themes of journey and exile in the *Commedia*. When he wrote the poem, Dante was in exile from Florence, and it is to this double exile, from Heaven and from Florence, that we owe the poem. Sadly, while Dante-pilgrim reaches his heavenly home and beholds God, as an exile in life, he never saw his beloved Florence again. Thus, the theme of his desire for God, essential in the narrative of *Paradiso*, often mirrors the poet's longing for Florence.

Virgil and Beatrice

At the outset, Dante introduces two other fundamental and in different ways astonishing characters, both historical and yet both devised to interact with Dante-character, conferring on him the emotional and intellectual depth that makes his adventure plausible and compelling. The first is Virgil and the second Beatrice. Virgil is clearly the poet of the *Aeneid* – not a philosopher, an angel, or saint, but the pagan poet of the Roman empire and medieval classicism, who will lead Dante to Eden and Beatrice. But the lady who descends from Heaven to Hell to deploy the most venerated poet of the Latin tradition, saying to him 'I am Beatrice who bid you go' (I' son Beatrice che ti faccio andare; *Inf.* II, 70), who is she? There is something preposterous about this young, recently dead Florentine bidding Virgil to rescue her lover from the dark wood. The least that one can say is that, in imagining this story, Dante is immensely ambitious and self-confident. Only a reader of the *Vita nova* would know that the Beatrice of *Inferno* II is the same lady whose soul ascends to Heaven in the earlier work (*Vn* XXIII [14]). Such a reader would probably assume that the *Commedia* is Dante's promised work in honour of Beatrice (*Vn* XLII, 2 [31, 3]). But could Dante count on anyone knowing the *Vita nova* in the first two decades of the fourteenth century? And if not, how could he promote Beatrice to the role of heavenly guide, a role higher even than Virgil's?

Structure and Poetry

The autobiographical basis of Dante's multifaceted identity in the *Commedia* – character-poet, singer of Beatrice, exile longing for home and universal peace, pilgrim to the heavenly Jerusalem, intellectual in pursuit of truth, prophet of the regeneration of Italy and the empire – gives the poem's structure its extraordinary intensity and coherence.

There was a time when 'structure' was a rude word in Dante studies. Benedetto Croce, Italy's most influential philosopher, historian, and literary critic of the twentieth century, treated the structure of the *Commedia* as a necessary evil, 'the framework upon which the luxuriant vegetation of poetry is clambering, decorating it with pendulous boughs, festoons, and flowers'.[1] Dante's journey, with its physical and moral topography and its ethical-political-theological themes should be 'respected as practical necessity, while we go in search of poetry elsewhere' (p. 99). Croce was convinced that there is much poetry in the *Commedia*, but, as with all poetry, it is exclusively lyrical and is to be found in isolated characters, episodes, and passages that have little to do with the story of Dante's journey or its doctrinal content. For Croce, the poetry of the *Commedia* consists of 'the poetic representations in which the poet's multiform passion is condensed, purified and expressed' (p. 100).

While believing that a sharp distinction between structure and poetry is impossible, this chapter attempts to identify the 'structure' of Dante's great poem and show how essential it is in the generation of its 'poetry'.

The Three Otherworldly Kingdoms

Hell and Paradise, and to some extent Purgatory, already existed in the medieval imagination. Building on that existence, Dante maps out the three realms as an explorer charts a new continent; he gives them physical contours, psychological identities, and names. The three realms have – and this is new – parallel structures but distinct characteristics. Hell is a huge conical cavity extending to the centre of the earth; it is divided into the Ante-Inferno and nine concentric circles, sloping down towards the bottom. The damned are punished according to the gravity of their sin from the top to the bottom – the closer to the bottom, the graver the sin. Purgatory, topographically Dante's original creation, is a tall conical mountain arising from the ocean; it comprises the shore and Ante-Purgatory plus seven terraces and the Earthly Paradise. The penitents wait on the shore and lower slopes for a prescribed time and then enter Purgatory proper, where they purge themselves of their sinful dispositions in order of gravity from the bottom of the mountain to the top – the closer to the top the lighter the fault. Paradise consists of nine concentric translucent spheres rotating about the earth, plus a tenth heaven, the Empyrean, the domain of absolute rest outside time and space, which contains everything and is contained by nothing. The blessed appear to Dante in the sphere that influenced them most in their lives, from the sphere of the Moon to that of Saturn according to the degree of their blessedness – the closer to God the more intense their bliss. Thus there are ten major partitions in every realm, a structural symmetry that is matched by the highly symmetrical organization of the poem. This symmetry is not presented as an arbitrary choice, but as an objective requirement of the subject matter itself, a mirror of the reality of the afterlife. The three kingdoms and the symmetrical ways in which they function are the product of a unified, harmonious plan, which is presented as the work of God, witnessed by the pilgrim and related by the narrator.

The Poem: Form and Structure

Dante's claim is astonishing; however, the form in which he makes it renders it unique. The story is told in a 'comedy' (comedìa, *Inf.* XVI, 128; XXI, 2; for a discussion of Dante's decision to term his poem a 'comedy', see chapter 5) or a 'sacred poem' (*Par.* XXIII, 62; XXV, 1), divided into three books called *cantiche* (canticles) – *Inferno, Purgatorio,* and *Paradiso* – which are in turn subdivided into *canti* (cantos). As there are thirty-four cantos in *Inferno* (the first serves as general prologue) and thirty-three each in *Purgatorio* and *Paradiso*, their total is one hundred, a perfect number signifying the perfection of the universe and the poem. The cantos are made up on average of just under fifty interlocking units of three hendecasyllables each, called *terzine* or tercets. Each tercet consists of three lines of eleven syllables, for a total of thirty-three syllables per tercet. These numbers are not accidental. Three is the number of the Trinity, thirty-three the age of Christ, and the thirty-fourth of His life was the year when He died (*Conv.* IV, xxiii, 10).

This elaborate framework is highly self-conscious; once the poet has entered it, it cannot be modified in any major way; it can only be realized. In the poem, therefore, two interdependent movements or *journeys* co-exist: the journey of the poet-character from the dark wood to the Empyrean; and the journey of the poet-narrator from *Inferno* I to *Paradiso* XXXIII. The critical question is which came first: the idea of the journey; or the one hundred-canto structure? Most probably the great framework came into being gradually, as the vision of the journey gained clarity in the poet's mind. However, it is also reasonable to assume that it was only through the frame that that clarity was reached. It is no surprise then if, for Croce, the existence of the frame has 'a repressive effect on poetical inspiration' (p. 93). For us, however, it is the only form that an encyclopaedic, 'sacred poem to which both heaven and earth have set their hand' (il poema sacro / al quale ha posto mano e cielo e terra; *Par.* XXV, 1–2) could take, and in this form the frame or 'theological romance' (p. 65), as Croce calls it, is as inspired as the most passionate of its lyrical segments.

Textual and Narrative Units: The Canto

The canto – the word generally means 'song' – is the fundamental textual and metrical unit used to organize the story; and the way Dante employs it in relation to his subject matter is crucial to the narrative structure.

What strikes and intrigues the reader is the flexible length of the canto, from a minimum of 115 lines (*Inf.* VI and XI) to a maximum of 160 (*Purg.* XXXII). A difference of some forty lines can be extremely significant in narrative terms: it allows for ample creative freedom while the canto remains true to its form. Canto V of *Purgatorio* offers an interesting example of Dante's compositional strategy. The canto tells of the pilgrim's encounter with souls who died violently, repenting just before dying. After two public figures, Iacopo del Cassero and Buonconte da Montefeltro, have told the stories of their deaths (46–129), a third voice arises unannounced, the voice of a woman who condenses her life into six lines that are a masterpiece of suggestive restraint. The speaker is the mysterious La Pia, possibly Pia de' Tolomei from Siena. This episode prompts two observations. First, since Buonconte ends his speech on line 129, there was no compelling reason for adding a third figure; second, having decided to add a third figure, the poet had available much more space than the little he actually employed for the portrait of Pia. He could have used eighteen lines as he did with Iacopo in the same canto, or twenty-four as he did with another Sienese woman, Sapia, in *Purgatorio* XIII, 106–29. Instead, Dante concentrated Pia's biography into three lines, demonstrating that he uses the structure as it suits him and not vice versa.

This is even more apparent in *Purgatorio* XXXIII. Here Dante employs six precious lines (136–41) to inform us that, had he more space available, he would tell us more about the sweetness of the waters of Eünoè, but since all the sheets prepared for the second canticle are now full, 'the bridle of art' (lo fren de l'arte; 141) does not let him go farther. This is obviously a pretext. The poet could as easily have used those six lines to sing of the water; or, had he genuinely felt that six lines were not enough, he could have added six more, bringing the total for the canto to 151 lines, a reasonable length in the second canticle. In the event he did neither. Dante's narrative choices are determined by his desire to achieve a specific poetic effect rather than by the canto's length; his 'art' helps him attain his creative goal rather than constrain him.

There are many other ways in which the canto establishes continuities and contrasts between segments, characters, and episodes of the same or different canticles. A network of intratextual references, signalled by the repetition of the same word, image, rhyme, or structure enriches the *Commedia* with unsuspected and deeper meanings. Some episodes are illumined retrospectively by later passages. Thus only by completing the journey can the protagonist of the story – and the reader with him – gain the knowledge that the narrator has from the beginning; and only a second reading will begin to release the riches that otherwise remain buried under the surface of the text.

There is no space here to delve into the variety of effects achieved by this kind of intratextuality; one of the most prominent is the 'vertical' correspondence between the same cantos in different canticles to signal important topics or transitions in the journey. The three cantos VI concentrate on political issues in Florence, Italy, and the Empire; the three cantos IX signal a narrative and theological transition in all three realms and canticles; the cantos XIX of *Inferno* and *Purgatorio*, and the XXVII of *Inferno* and *Paradiso* are largely about the Church and the popes, one of Dante's foremost concerns; the final cantos, and the last sections of the three realms, echo each other by analogy or contrast: Cocytus, Eden, the Empyrean; three-faced Satan and triune God; finally, the last line of each canticle ends with the word, 'stars' (stelle).

Textual and Narrative Units: The Canticle
Inferno

At first sight the *Commedia* appears to be organized in a simple fashion, in which, textually and narratively, the canto works as the fundamental unit, and no action started in a canto remains unconcluded at the end of that canto. This is true of the first six cantos. The first two are introductory (one of Virgil, the other of Beatrice), the third tells of Ante-Inferno, and the last three are devoted, respectively, to the first three circles of Hell. Even canto VII, in which Dante describes the fourth and fifth circle, seems perfectly finished when we read its last, forward-looking line: 'we came at last to the foot of a tower' ('Venimmo al piè d'una torre al da sezzo'). Thus, if we had only the first seven cantos of *Inferno*, we might assume that Dante planned to organize the first canticle following the order of the seven capital vices, starting with lust and ending with pride. The canticle would have been less complicated and much shorter – ten cantos, perhaps twelve on the model of the *Aeneid*'s twelve books.

However, in the first eighty-one lines of canto VIII, Dante does something unexpected. He relates a series of thrilling events that happened just *before* he and Virgil reached the foot of the tower mentioned at the end of canto VII: namely, the arrival of the angry ferryman Phlegyas, their crossing the Styx on his boat, and their violent and morally problematic interaction with Filippo Argenti. This section of canto VIII is an amplification of the short segment devoted to wrath in VII, 100–30, so it could well be an addition that Dante, after seven cantos, might have deliberately devised to break the linearity and predictability of his narrative strategy up till now. However, there are other significant changes at this juncture that affect the shape and size of the canticle, and may reflect Dante's deliberate adjustments to his original plan. The question is how to interpret these adjustments. Were they made in the normal course of the composition of the poem, or do they signal an interruption of that process and its resumption at a later date with a substantially different working plan in mind?

The latter explanation would prevail if we could independently verify a story told by Giovanni Boccaccio and based on the first lines of *Inferno* VIII: 'continuing, I have to tell that long before we were at the foot of the high tower' (Io dico, seguitando, ch'assai prima / che noi fossimo al piè de l'alta torre). The critical word is 'continuing' – 'seguitando'. To explain this word, in his biography of Dante and commentary on *Inferno*, Boccaccio tells how Dante started the *Commedia* in Florence before his exile and, after a long interruption, resumed his writing in Lunigiana (a region between Tuscany and Liguria) in 1306, when the original draft of the first seven cantos was brought to him there: hence the word 'Continuing'. This story would explain the subsequent introduction of the episode of Filippo Argenti, as well as other anomalies that affect the narrative at this point. However, as Boccaccio himself acknowledges, it is difficult to see how Ciacco, in VI, 64–72, could prophecy events that took place in 1302 – namely, after Dante's exile from Florence – if Dante had written the first seven cantos before that exile.

Be this as it may, our problems are not finished. Once they are inside the walls of the city of Dis, Dante, and Virgil enter the sixth circle where the heretics, and specifically the Epicureans, are punished in their open, burning graves. This is puzzling. After the first five, we were expecting another capital sin; instead, we find a sin that does not belong to that series, the sin of those 'who make the soul die with the body' (che l'anima col corpo morta fanno'; X, 15). Sensing his readers' puzzlement, Dante has Virgil explain the doctrinal (and structural) change in the next canto (XI, 13–90). Hell, Virgil says, is divided into two major regions, Upper and Lower Hell, respectively outside and inside the walls of the city of Dis. Outside are the sins of incontinence, inside the sins of malice – a distinction which Dante borrows from Aristotle's *Nicomachean Ethics*. The incontinent fail to rein in their passions or desires for earthly goods (circles two to five); the malicious offend and injure others either by force (the violent, circle seven) or by fraud (the fraudulent, circle eight, and the treacherous, circle nine) – distinctions Dante borrows from Cicero's *De officiis* (I, 13). This sounds clear, but then where do we place circle six with the heretics? In his explanation, Virgil does not assign circle six to violence, and yet it would appear in line with the rule of *contrapasso* ('counter-penalty'; *Inf.* XXVIII, 142) that those who 'kill the soul with the body' should see their soul live forever and burn in a tomb where they expected it to lie dead and non-sentient.

This is not the only structural issue arising once we move inside Dis. The change in the moral organization of Hell has a spectacular effect on its physical structure. Whereas in Upper Hell sins and circles were coterminous, in Lower Hell the circles are partitioned into subcircles, and these become the new narrative units. Circle seven is divided into three *gironi* or rounds, in which three types of violence are punished: against others (tyrants and murderers, immersed in the Phlegethon, the river of boiling blood); against oneself and one's property (suicides and spendthrifts); and against God (blasphemers), nature (homosexuals) and art (usurers). Consequently, circle seven occupies cantos XII to XVII. Circle eight, known as Malebolge (Evil Ditches or Pouches), is subdivided into ten concentric ditches (*bolge*) where ten varieties of fraudulent sinners are found: panders and seducers; flatterers, simoniacs (corrupt prelates); astrologers and sorcerers; barrators (corrupt public servants); hypocrites; thieves; false counsellors; schismatics; and falsifiers, the latter in their turn subdivided into alchemists, impersonators, counterfeiters and false witnesses. These sinners are portrayed in cantos XVIII to XXX. Finally circle nine, named Cocytus after the frozen lake in which the treacherous are punished, is partitioned into four areas (Caina, Antenora, Ptolomea, and Judecca, for treacherous deeds perpetrated against, respectively, relatives, party or country, guests, and lords and benefactors) and described in cantos XXXII to XXXIV. In short, Dante devotes twenty-three cantos (XII to XXXIV) to the last three circles of Hell; the difference with the first five circles, occupying cantos IV to VIII, is staggering.

However, although the circles treated in the last twenty-three cantos are only three, the categories of sinners are seventeen – or twenty-two if we count the subdivisions of subdivisions. Thus sins in Lower Hell get on average the same amount of space as circles in Upper Hell, and quite often textual and narrative units are coterminous. This happens especially in the case of notable figures and episodes, such as Pier della Vigna (XIII), Brunetto Latini (XV), the simoniacs (XIX), Ulysses (XXVI), and Guido da Montefeltro (XXVII), though individual portraits are by no means the privileged focus of Dante's narrative. In fact, Dante appears to be equally interested in introducing interruptions and interferences between different places, episodes, and topics. To give a few examples: Geryon rises from the dark pit at the end of canto XVI (124–36) and 'docks' on the edge of circle seven at the beginning of the next canto (1–33); Dante's encounter with the usurers takes place while Virgil is negotiating with Geryon (XVII, 34–75); the episode of the Malebranche in the ditch of the barrators, one of the most lively and complex in the poem, takes place across two and a half cantos (XXI–XXIII, 57); while the meeting with Ugolino is artfully split into two parts (XXXII, 124–39 and XXXIII, 1–90), so that canto XXXIII may begin with a horrific close-up of Ugolino: 'La bocca sollevò dal fiero pasto' – literally, 'the mouth, (he) lifted it from his savage meal'. It is hardly possible to determine what came first to the poet's mind, the characters with their stories or the environment from which they emerge. Probably, there was no fixed process, and sometimes characters pre-existed the definitive design of their environment, while at other times the environment gave rise to the characters.

In canto XXXI, we come to the pit of the giants, and Antaeus takes Virgil and Dante in his hand – Phlegyas had ferried them on his boat, while Geryon had carried them on his back – and sets them down on the bottom of Cocytus. Finally, at the centre of the earth, planted in the middle of Cocytus, bat-like Lucifer/Satan, flapping his wings, tries in vain to lift himself out of his eternal prison: in an exquisite example of negative reciprocity affecting both moral and physical structures, the wind he generates keeps Cocytus frozen and him imprisoned. In his three mouths he chews forever the three worst traitors: Judas who betrayed Christ; and Brutus and Cassius who betrayed the Roman empire in the person of Julius Caesar. Here, hanging on to Satan's body hair, Dante and Virgil clamber down towards his legs. When they reach his hips, at the centre of the earth and of the universe, they turn upside down and continue their journey in an upward direction. Climbing up a dark and rough underground passage, they emerge on the other side of the globe 'once more to see the stars' (a riveder le stelle; XXXIV, 139).

Purgatorio

The second stage of the journey, Purgatory, is morally, and hence structurally, simpler. It begins as Dante and Virgil emerge on the shore of the island of Mount Purgatory, in the southern hemisphere, at a place diametrically opposite to where they entered Hell. The souls of Purgatory repented of, and received forgiveness for, their sinful deeds before dying. They now purge themselves of the bad inclinations that drove them to sinning. Unlike the damned, who are fixed in their earthly individuality, they move forward together, in peace with themselves, with each other, and with God. They suffer physical pain, of course. Yet their suffering is accepted and internalized; its very existence ensures that it will end, giving way to the joy of Heaven. This is why they are so eager to submit to it. What they feel with greatest intensity is their distance from God. This sense of separation and exile transforms their ascent into a pilgrimage towards their heavenly home. Dante climbs the mountain with them, pausing at night. A pilgrim among pilgrims, he understands and shares their memories of the past and their longing for the future.

In Ante-Purgatory, the excommunicates and the late repentant wait at the foot and on the low slopes of the mountain until they feel ready to enter the process of purification (III to IX). The structure of Purgatory proper is based on the traditional ordering of the seven capital vices. When the penitents enter it (X), they are made to progress through its seven terraces spending more or less time on each according to the degree of their need in respect of each sinful inclination. The seven faults are therefore rectified from the bottom to the top of the mountain according to their decreasing gravity. As Virgil explains at the centre of *Purgatorio* (XVII, 70–139), the first three (pride, envy, and wrath) are a perversion of love, or love turned to wrong objects; the fourth (sloth) consists of laggard or insufficient love for goodness; the last three (avarice, gluttony, and lust) represent excessive love for earthly goods. On the summit of the mountain is the Earthly Paradise, the place where Adam and Eve were innocent and happy, and where, after their fall and ensuing expulsion, human history began. The process of purification takes place gradually along the axis that unites the three crucial points in the history and geography of the world and of the human race: the centre of the earth, now occupied by the monstrous body of Lucifer; Earthly Paradise, the place of original sin in the southern hemisphere; and, at the antipodes from it, Jerusalem, the city of redemption. In Eden, Dante rejoins Beatrice, the lady he loved, while she lived, and betrayed after she died in 1290.

It should be noted that the structural parallel between Mount Purgatory and the other two realms is more apparent than real. If, on the one hand, the cone of Mount Purgatory seems to fit into the conical cavity of Hell, on the other, its three principal divisions hardly match those of either of the other two realms. The shore of the mountain (I–III), with its distinctive liminal atmosphere, has some parallels with *Inferno* III – just as the souls of the damned arrive at the river Acheron and are met by Charon, so the penitents, as they land on the shore of Purgatory, are met by another old man, Cato – but Ante-Inferno does not match Ante-Purgatory (III–VIII), nor is there anything like either in *Paradiso*. In fact, whereas in Lower Hell the narrative and textual divisions coincide and are sharply demarcated, Ante-Purgatory with its slow, long, and fluid ascent of the mountain, its ritualistic passages, its pervasive sense of wonder, and its double, elegiac nostalgia for both earth and Heaven, exudes a totally different feel. Undoubtedly, the three cantos IX share some common features, but the correspondence is superficial rather than substantive. *Inferno* IX signals the entry into the city of Dis and the sixth circle, the first of Lower Hell; *Purgatorio* IX signals the entry into Purgatory proper; *Paradiso* IX marks the end of the planetary space over which the earth still casts its shadow, and the transition to the fourth heaven, that of the Sun. The elaborate ritual at the gate of Purgatory with, among other notable things, the angel keeper tracing seven Ps on Dante's forehead signifying the seven sinful inclinations that the ensuing climb will have to erase, has no equivalent elsewhere in the poem. There is a contrastive correspondence between the cantos IX of *Inferno* and *Paradiso*, but *Purgatorio* is not included in it. The reason for this exclusion is that *Purgatorio*'s moral system is based on the seven capital vices, and, although in Purgatory the seven virtues opposed to these vices play an important role, it is not on these virtues that Paradise is ordered. As for Hell, the capital sins appear at the beginning, but Dante abandons that scheme in IX. If we believe that Dante wrote the poem in the order in which Dante the character proceeds in his journey, then we must deduce that he started *Inferno* following the model of the seven capital vices, abandoned that model at canto IX, but resumed it in *Purgatorio*, utilizing it fully from canto IX to XXVII. There is another compelling reason why Purgatory proper cannot have a parallel in either *Inferno* or *Paradiso*, and it is entirely structural. Dante's Purgatory is founded on the centrality of love 'as the seed of every virtue and of every action deserving punishment' (sementa . . . d'ogni virtute / e d'ogni operazion che merta pene; XVII, 104–5). But love is central to the entire poem, and Dante gloriously underscores this by placing the verbal enunciation of its centrality at the textual centre of both *Purgatorio* and the *Commedia*: an integrated, moral, and structural construct of this kind cannot by definition have parallels.

Dante's journey in Purgatory, contrary to that in Hell, is an ascent. After their encounters with Cato and Casella on the shore, and with Manfred at the foot of the cliff, Dante and Virgil's progress is marked by their climb first to the door of Purgatory and then from there to Eden. The task is physically exhausting, though less so as they get closer to the top. The narrative appears spatially and temporally structured in harmony with Christian liturgy, and the subject matter is evenly distributed. The first eight cantos tell the events of the first day; night falls at the beginning of IX, Dante falls asleep and has his first dream (1–33); the following nine cantos (X–XVIII) are dedicated to the events of the second day, Dante falls asleep at the end of XVIII and has his second dream at the beginning of XIX (1–33); nine cantos later (XIX–XXVII), at the end of the third day, Dante falls asleep and dreams for the third time (XXVII, 94–108). It can hardly be a fortuitous coincidence that, in

XXVII, after three days, three dreams, and three times nine cantos, Virgil takes his leave, announcing the coming of Beatrice's 'beautiful eyes' (XXVII, 137, the same eyes he saw full of tears in *Inferno* II, 116) for, as is explained in the *Vita nova*, Beatrice is intimately associated with the number nine, which symbolically confirms her miraculous status (XXVIII, 6 [19, 6]). Indeed Dante marks the ritualistic nature of the three dreams by opening the account of each with the same temporal formula: 'In the hour when' (Ne l'ora che; IX, 13; XIX, 1; XXVII, 94).

The three dreams are also perfectly spaced topographically, as the first takes place just before the gate and the first terrace of Purgatory, the second on the central and fourth terrace, and the third on the seventh and last. This even distribution of both textual and narrative spaces is underscored by the poets' regular ascent from terrace to terrace (cantos X, XII, XV, XVII, XIX, XXII, XXV, and XXVII). This becomes even more remarkable if we consider the pattern's regularity within each terrace. This pattern consists of seven narrative components: (1) arrival and general impression of terrace; (2) examples of virtue contrary to the vice treated on terrace; (3) penitents reciting a prayer, except on the terrace of sloth; (4) focus on individual penitents; (5) examples of vice punished; (6) removal of a P from Dante's brow by angel of reciprocal virtue; (7) angel singing the beatitude contrary to the purged vice. This structural grid is internally diversified by changing penance, prayer, and beatitude on each terrace, and also by the various ways in which the examples of virtues and vices are conveyed: carvings in marble for pride, disembodied voices for envy, ecstatic visions for wrath, and so on. There are also digressions (on Italy, VI, 76–151; on love, XVII, 91–139) and characters who play an extended role in Dante's journey, such as Sordello (VI–VIII) and Statius (XXI–XXII), who accompanies the pilgrim all the way to and through the Earthly Paradise. In conclusion, the structural order of *Purgatorio* contributes significantly to creating the shared sense of elegiac calmness and joy-in-suffering that is the hallmark of the second realm.

The last six cantos of *Purgatorio* (XXVIII–XXXIII) are hardly purgatorial, but they are not joyful, either. They give an account of the Earthly Paradise, a pivotal segment in the narrative, for it is here that the private story of Dante's salvation through Beatrice is firmly linked to the public theme of Dante's potential salvation of the world through the *Commedia*. It is also here that Beatrice – a Beatrice as hard on Dante in Eden as she was tender with Virgil in Limbo a mere week earlier – takes over from Virgil as Dante's guide. Structurally speaking, the first canto (XXVIII) presents Eden as a perfect *locus amoenus* or idyllic environment inhabited solely by the attractive and mysterious Matelda, while the last (XXXIII) reflects and draws conclusions on what happens in between. The four central cantos describe a surreal and partly enigmatic sequence of events orchestrated in three parts: (1) as Dante stands on one bank of the Lethe, an allegorical procession, personifying the books of the Bible, slowly advances on the other side; in the middle of the procession is an empty chariot (the Church) drawn by a griffin (Jesus Christ) (XXIX); (2) standing upon the chariot within a cloud of flowers scattered by singing angels, Beatrice appears; overwhelmed by love and fear, Dante turns to Virgil, but Virgil is gone, and Beatrice, far from comforting and reassuring her 'friend' (amico; *Inf.* II, 61), denounces and rebukes him for straying from her after her death; mortified and deeply ashamed, Dante confesses his guilt; dragged by Matelda across the Lethe, he drinks of its waters and joins Beatrice on the other bank (XXX–XXXI); (3) after an allegorical representation of the redemption, an apocalyptic dramatization of the degeneration of the chariot/Church follows from the time of the Roman persecutions to its imminent, sacrilegious kidnapping by the king of France (XXXII). When all this is over, echoing Virgil's promise of a liberating greyhound (veltro) in *Inferno* I, 100–11, Beatrice prophecies the coming of a heavenly avenger (mysteriously alluded to by the number 515, which in Roman numerals is DXV, the designation by which the celestial envoy is normally known; XXXIII, 43–4), who will kill those responsible for the corruption of the chariot/Church; she then charges Dante with remembering what he has seen and relating it for the benefit of the world 'that lives ill' (che mal vive; 70).

Beatrice's return to Dante at Easter-time 1300 re-enacts the wedding of Christ with the Church, as signified by the griffin drawing the chariot to the great tree of Adam which is revived by its touch. Modelled on the sacred narrative of the Song of Songs, this ritual gives meaning to Dante's individual story and to the history of the human race as a whole. As a result, Dante's soul is healed and renewed; his life, and potentially the life of every human being on earth, turns from tragedy to comedy. After being immersed in the waters of Lethe, which wash away his memory of sin, Dante now drinks from the other Edenic river, the Eünoè – the poet's invention – which revives in him the memory of his good deeds. He is now 'pure and ready to mount to the stars' (puro e disposto a salire a le stelle; XXXIII, 145).

Paradiso

On leaving Eden, Dante, now guided by Beatrice, finds himself almost instantly in Paradise. Theologically speaking, the journey should be completed, for, as the pilgrim will later be told, 'everywhere in heaven is Paradise' (ogne dove in cielo / è paradiso; *Par.* III, 88–9). Dante is now *in patria*: he has reached our true celestial homeland. Consequently, he should be capable of seeing God and the blessed immediately, embracing the whole of Heaven in one timeless instant. However, if this were indeed the case, what is the poet to do? How is he to portray a 'reality' that, not being subjected to the laws of time and space, is so radically different from what he has experienced and described so far? He could stretch his account of the ultimate bliss over the thirty-three cantos assigned to *Paradiso* by the poem's structure – a difficult, though not impossible, task for a poet of Dante's calibre. However, such a description would neither match the structure of the other two canticles nor respect the traditional spatial organization of Heaven; above all, it would not correspond to Dante's poetic intuition of Paradise.

Dante's stroke of genius was to conceive of, and depict, the pilgrim's experience of Paradise as still on his journey to God (what was termed *in statu viae*), namely, not as achieved fulfilment, but as a quest for fulfilment. In short, while affirming the theological notion of a true, inexpressible Paradise situated beyond time and space, Dante declares that, for his visit, Paradise made itself accessible to him in a gradual manner – one heaven at a time – just as the preceding two realms did. Thus, instead of appearing immediately and all together in the Empyrean, where they effectively reside, the souls of Paradise appear in the heavenly spheres most associated with their earthly lives, each perfectly, albeit differently, blessed according to his or her individual capacity to see God and partake of His bliss: in the Moon souls who were forced to break their monastic vows (II–V); in Mercury, seekers of glory (V–VII); in Venus, those inclined towards carnal love (VIII–IX); in the Sun, seekers of wisdom (X–XIV); in Mars, martyrs and crusaders (XIV–XVIII); in Jupiter, righteous rulers (XVIII–XX); and in Saturn, contemplatives (XXI–XXII). In the Fixed Stars, after witnessing the triumphs of Christ and Mary, Dante is examined on the three theological virtues by saints Peter, James and John, and he meets Adam (XXII–XXVII); while in the Primum Mobile he gazes at the nine angelic orders orbiting the dazzling point that is God (XXVII–XXIX). In the Moon, and to a lesser extent in Mercury, the pilgrim is still able to make out the evanescent features of the blessed; from Venus onward, however, the light that enfolds them is so bright that he cannot penetrate it. Only in the Empyrean does he see the blessed properly, with their resurrected bodies and individual features, in the glory of the celestial rose (XXX–XXXIII). This is also where Dante's journey ends as he reaches, in the last four lines of the poem, the supreme vision of God.

This accommodation of the heavenly 'reality' to human faculties makes Paradise poetically viable as a continuation of the pilgrim's journey. Nevertheless, the subject matter remains challenging, for the experience of 'passing beyond the human' (trasumanar; *Par.* I, 70) is neither perceivable nor describable in the physical terms of the journey's first two stages. The three principal narrative ingredients of the poem so far – the journey, the otherworldly landscapes, and the ever-changing individual souls with their particular stories and physical features – can no longer be seen. Gone are the lengthy and dramatic transitions between regions of *Inferno*, or the exhausting climbs of *Purgatorio*: Dante and Beatrice now ascend from heaven to heaven effortlessly and almost instantly. The landscapes are gone too, though the blessed produce some breathtaking light-and-sound spectacles for the benefit of the pilgrim: the dancing and singing crowns of philosophers and theologians in the Sun (X, 64–81 and 139–48; XII, 1–21); the cross of Mars (XIV, 91–139); the eagle of Jupiter (XVIII, 94–114; XIX, 1–12); the golden ladder of Saturn (XXI, 25–42); not to mention the river of light (XXX, 55–81) and the celestial rose (XXX, 82–132; XXXI, 1–24) in the Empyrean. Individual souls are few and become fewer as we ascend from heaven to heaven; moreover, after the dematerialized images of the Moon, they appear as blazing lights which can only be differentiated from one another by the intensity of their splendour. But it is particularly the lack of stories that marks the structure of *Paradiso*. Storytelling is very rare and, when it features, it is allegorical – the kind of allegory Dante elsewhere calls 'a beautiful lie' (*Conv.* II, i, 4), as is the case with the romance of Francis of Assisi and Lady Poverty. Yet, in theory, Dante could have told as many edifying and comforting stories in *Paradiso* as he told frightening ones in *Inferno*. Instead, he narrates Francesca's fall from innocence, but says nothing about Cunizza's repentance. Interestingly, he recounts the charming story of the good deed that saves the emperor Trajan in *Purgatorio*, and not in *Paradiso* where Trajan's soul is found. In *Paradiso*, historical, philosophical, scientific, and theological presentations replace the characters who, with the variety of their real-life experiences, animate *Inferno* and *Purgatorio*.

Nevertheless, *Paradiso* reserves its centre to earthly, rather than heavenly, concerns. Cantos XV, XVI, and XVII constitute a textual space devoted to the poet's complicated relationship with his beloved and detested city. XV looks back to the Florence of 150 years earlier, a model city, small but beautiful and pure, poor in money but rich in peace and goodness; XVI is about the good old Florentine families in contrast with the Florence of Dante's times, large and still growing, socially diverse but chaotic and insecure, wealthy but greedy, restless, and corrupt; XVII is about Dante's future exile, but also the vindication of his political stand, his duty and mission as poet, and his ultimate glory. As emerged from Farinata's and Brunetto's allusions to Beatrice (*Inf.* X, 130–2; XV, 88–90), Dante had originally assigned to his beloved the role of clarifying in *Paradiso* the prophecies of his exile. However, by the time the poet reached the third canticle, his need to affirm, albeit indirectly, the dignity of the Alighieri family as descendants of an imperial knight, as well as to confer authority to his searing indictment of contemporary Florence, became so overwhelming that he replaced the figure of Beatrice with that of his great-great-grandfather Cacciaguida. Having lived in the city during the first half of the twelfth century, Cacciaguida could legitimately stigmatize the city's current corruption, and having died fighting in the crusades, he had the authority to invest Dante with his prophetic mission. Thus, while Beatrice, a Florentine through and through, is exceptionally excluded from this autobiographical space, Cacciaguida, effectively Dante's *alter ego*, comes to play a fundamental role in the structure of *Paradiso* and, ultimately, of the whole poem.

However, what pervades *Paradiso,* giving it its special poetic and structural identity, is a new tension towards God as the source of all goodness, beauty, and truth – a desire for God that, not only because of their temporary dislocation, affects the blessed too. The concept of desire is central to the great Christian metaphor of earthly life as exile from and journey towards the heavenly homeland. Dante refers to desire several times in *Purgatorio*, but he develops the notion fully and originally in *Paradiso*, where it acts as a fundamental structuring principle, propelling Dante towards the Empyrean, while concurrently necessitating a series of important deferrals in his ascent. Desire is twofold in Paradise: there is desire as longing to see God face to face, and desire as appetite for knowledge. The latter is articulated by means of questions and doubts often explicitly formulated by Dante. Indeed, when desire is of an intellectual nature, the terms *dubbio* (doubt) and *disio* (desire) appear interchangeably. These two approaches to the Godhead correspond to two distinct forms of contemplation: the intellectual and the affective. Dante the narrator appears to favour a form of active approach to the beatific vision through knowledge, placing first, in Beatrice's words (XXVIII, 109–11), the act of vision ('l'atto che vede') and second that of love ('quel ch'ama'). However, the pilgrim's experience is lived through, and poetically portrayed, in affective terms. In fact, the two strands are strictly intertwined in the narrative as expressions of the same psychological tension, and Beatrice, as Dante's lover and teacher in Paradise, is their synthesis and embodiment.

The narrative structure of *Paradiso*, with its constant interweaving of the didactic with the affective, is an instrument perfectly attuned to Dante's quest for a God of knowledge and love. The heavenly journey is conceived and realized as an exhilarating progression that is both physical and psychological, and affects the pilgrim's eyes as much as his mind and heart. As Dante soars higher and higher, his heart is caught between opposite emotions. Each new step gives him what he longs for, yet it leaves him unsatisfied and anxious as his desire is at the same time fulfilled and intensified. Each doctrinal explanation (the spots on the moon in II; free will in V; the inscrutability of God's justice in XIX; predestination in XX–XXI), each appraisal of his earthly concerns (the history of the Roman empire in VI; the social, political, and moral degeneration of Florence in XV–XVII; the popes' greed in XXVII) is a stepping stone towards enlightenment. It is only by exercising his need to know that his desire to possess will be satisfied; hence the joy of knowledge is constantly expressed, outside the pilgrim, by an increase of light and, inside him, by an increment of his ability to withstand and penetrate that light. Light is indeed the external manifestation of this internal process. It, too, like desire, increases as the pilgrim ascends, and, as with desire, as soon as the pilgrim grows strong enough to take in the objects of his vision, those objects become more and more luminous. Light constantly surpasses (*sobranza*) the pilgrim's power to see (XXIII, 31–6), so much so that occasionally he feels blinded by it (XXV, 118–21 and XXVIII, 16–18). To the progressive intensification of light – the *sobranzare* (surpassing), the *trasmodarsi* (transcending) of the object, by which Dante is in turn *soprato* (surpassed) and *vinto* (defeated) – corresponds his adjustment to it through the process by which he *sormonta* (exceeds), with the help of ever-increasing grace, his own capacity to see. This is the long and highly dramatic 'struggle of the feeble eyelids' (battaglia de' debili cigli; XXIII, 78), and it matches, indeed it visually expresses, the internal, psychological drama of Dante's ever-increasing desire for God.

What we find throughout *Paradiso* is an expectation, more and more urgent, to come face to face with the ultimate goodness. It is a visionary tension, which already brings somehow a measure of reward, and yet acts as the constant reminder that fulfilment is still farther ahead. Dante's narrative strategy is to anticipate and simultaneously delay the final vision. Occasionally, God appears in reduced epiphanies, in fleeting manifestations, as in the cross of Cacciaguida in XV, or in the heavenly writings of the eagle of Jupiter (XVIII–XIX), or in the triumphs of Christ and Mary (XXIII). In fact, His appearance is put off till the very end of the poem, and even there, when Dante comes for a split second face to face with Him, we do not see God in His human likeness, but vertiginous geometric shapes that remind us of His mystery. Dante's quest is for a Deity beyond the anthropomorphic – a truly transcendent God, who can be approached only by pushing farther and farther the frontiers of poetic quest and experimentation. This narrative strategy has an inevitable theological consequence. *Paradiso* as a poem is all, and can only be, on this side of the journey's ultimate goal. It is the story of an approximation to a vision and a bliss that remain unsaid and unrevealed, for the pilgrim's true state of bliss can only begin where *Paradiso* as narrative ends, in the silence that follows the poem's last line: 'the love that moves the sun and the other stars' (l'amor che move il sole e l'altre stelle; 145).

Otherworldly Inhabitants

The account of Dante's journey is punctuated and enriched by his encounters with the inhabitants of the otherworld. These belong to two different categories: the functionaries (jailors and warders in Hell; angels in Purgatory and Paradise); and the human shades – damned, penitent, blessed – located, according to their deserts, where Dante 'finds' them, in Hell, Purgatory, and Paradise. Though ultimately impotent to stand in the way of God's will, functionaries and human shades have minds of their own; they interact with one another and with Dante and his guides, often telling their stories, but also obstructing, deceiving, assisting, instructing, squabbling, provoking anger and fear, compassion and contempt, pity and cruelty, gratitude and resentment. They are an essential element in the poem's narrative structure, providing variety, demarcating territories, creating suspense, inspiring questions.

Functionaries

The functionaries are the staff of the otherworld: mythological creatures and monsters, but also Christian devils and angels, appointed to take care of the management of the areas assigned to them; from Charon to Satan, they can facilitate or occasionally hinder the visitors' progress. Virgil has no problem in dealing with the classical figures. In Upper Hell, a short formula or a gesture is enough to quieten Charon, Minos, Cerberus, Plutus, and Phlegyas. In Lower Hell, Virgil can be contemptuous and sarcastic, as with the Minotaur (XII, 16–21) and the giant Nimrod (XXXI, 70–5), but also civilized and diplomatic, especially when he needs the cooperation of the infernal officers, as with Chiron the centaur (XII, 89–96), Geryon (XVII, 97–9), and Antaeus (XXXI, 115–29). In general he appears in control of the situation. However, there are two episodes in which his authority is seriously challenged. Not by chance, the challengers in both cases are Christian devils.

In canto VIII, 82–130, the devils who guard the city of Dis slam the door in Virgil's face, refusing to let in the two visitors. In one of *Inferno*'s most entertaining scenes, Virgil returns to Dante downcast but still determined to prevail. In fact, while he can shield Dante from the petrifying gaze of the Medusa and the Furies, he makes no headway with the devils, and only an angel from Heaven can open the gate, rebuking the insolent demons for their resistance to God's will (IX, 61–105). The second episode occurs in the fifth ditch of Malebolge, where the barrators are punished under the watchful eyes of the Malebranche (Evil Claws), a band of spirited devils with deliciously scary, vernacular names (Malacoda, Scarmiglione, Alichino, Calcabrina, Cagnazzo, Barbariccia, Libicocco, Draghinazzo, Ciriatto, Graffiacane, Farfarello, and Rubicante). Clearly enjoying their job, these devils play a game of cat and mouse with their wards, whom they keep under boiling pitch (XXI–XXIII). When Virgil and Dante appear on the scene, they get uncontrollably excited at the prospect of having them, too, as their playthings; their leader Malacoda (Evil Tail) can hardly restrain them. When they tell Virgil that a bridge to the sixth ditch is still intact, Virgil believes them, but soon, finding no bridge and frantically wanting to escape the Malebranche's grappling hooks, he is obliged to scramble on his backside down the bank, holding Dante tight in his arms. Hardly a dignified escape for 'the lofty poet' (l'altissimo poeta; *Inf.* IV, 80)! In the battle of wit and deception, a barrator-like Ciampolo turns out to be a better match for the Malebranche than wise Virgil. The two incidents have significant implications for Virgil, though his inability to deal with the crafty devils may well be meant to signify integrity and uprightness rather than weakness and gullibility. What is undeniable is their structural function, placed as they are one on the borderline between Upper and Lower Hell, and the other just half way through Malebolge, where all the bridges are down from the time of the earthquake that occurred when Christ died on the cross.

Exceptional in Hell, angels are at home in Purgatory where they have a variety of roles, from piloting the boat that brings the penitents to the mountain (II, 27–9) to chasing away the serpent from the valley of the Princes (VIII, 25 and 106), to guarding the gate of Purgatory proper (IX, 104), and etching the Ps on, and erasing them from, Dante's brow. They have loftier, though less structural roles in Eden, where they appear as 'ministers and messengers of eternal life' (ministri e messagger di vita etterna; XXX, 18), greeting Beatrice with flowers and sacred invocations, singing psalms (XXX, 82–4), and even pitying poor Dante when Beatrice is too hard on him (XXX, 94–6). In Paradise, where they are permanent dwellers, angels appear as dazzling lights without individual features. As movers of the heavenly spheres, they are responsible for governing the universe and directing the influence of the stars over human affairs (*Par.* II, 127–9). Dante sees them as nine sparkling circles rotating around the blinding light of the point that is God (XXVIII, 1–39 and 88–129). Closest to God is the swiftest and most ardent circle of the Seraphim, who are associated with the Primum Mobile; the other angelic orders follow the sequence of the Heavens from the Fixed Stars, associated with the Cherubim, to the Angels, associated with the Moon. They fly incessantly from God to the blessed as bees to flowers (XXXI, 4–18), and sing and fly around the Virgin in the Empyrean (XXXI, 124–38).

Residents

The human shades are the 'residents' of the otherworld: inmates in Hell; penitents in Purgatory; and blessed in Paradise. They are introduced, with varying degrees of detail, as Dante comes across, observes, or interacts with them. There are anonymous crowds, such as the neutrals (*Inf.* III, 22–69); individuals that are mentioned only by name ('Euripides, Antiphon, Simonides, and Agathon'; *Purg.* XXII, 106–7) or with some brief, emblematic qualification (lustful Cleopatra, *Inf.* V, 63; Caesar in arms with griffin-like eyes, *Inf.* IV, 123); individuals who make a short appearance (Lano from Siena, *Inf.* XIII, 115–23); finally, individuals who tell their own stories or whose stories are told by others. The great characters of the *Commedia*, especially *Inferno*, belong to this last category.

Occasionally, characters interact with each other: violently in Hell (Master Adam and Sinon in XXX, 100–29); calmly and compassionately in Purgatory (III, 79–93; VIII, 64–6, etc.). In some rare cases they become involved with Dante's journey. Virgil and Beatrice are macroscopic examples; however, Sordello, Statius, and St Bernard, too, leave more than a momentary impression on the pilgrim's progress. Conversely, Filippo Argenti's attack on Phlegyas' boat is an attempt to obstruct Dante's progress, and Virgil's exceptionally violent reaction to it is meant to underscore Filippo's arrogance. Dante-character is not excluded from this type of physical interaction with the damned. He unwittingly causes great pain to Pier della Vigna when, following Virgil's bidding, he breaks a twig from the great thorn that is Piero (*Inf.* XIII, 31–3). But there are also occasions when Dante seems to be intentionally cruel, as with Bocca degli Abati (XXXII, 103–5). Primo Levi notes this kind of 'useless violence' on the part of the pilgrim. The example he offers is one in which, at Dante's request, Friar Alberigo tells his story and then Dante, breaking his promise, refuses to clear the friar's eyes of the ice that locks them shut so that he is unable to weep (*Inf.* XXXIII, 109–50).[2]

These incidents are exceptional and they occur, understandably, in *Inferno*. Close contact is rare in Purgatory and is prompted by affection. Virgil and Sordello embrace most eagerly in the name of their common birthplace (VI, 75), though earlier Dante had unsuccessfully tried to clasp the insubstantial body of his friend Casella (II, 76–81). Generally, however, Dante's interaction with the souls is verbal. In every circle, terrace, or heaven, after describing wider scenes with large numbers of shades, Dante focuses on one or two and encourages them to tell him their stories or express their anxieties about what is happening on earth. They are often tales never heard before, and of which no independent evidence remains. Dante's journey fills the gaps left open by history, chronicle, and even legend. His exchanges with the dead shed light on their last days, hours, even instants, revealing secrets that the dead took to their graves. In *Paradiso* (XVII, 124–42) we discover that these stories are told so that we may learn from them. Nevertheless, what engages Dante-character, as well as the reader, is not necessarily the moral lesson they convey, but the extent to which they go beyond it. What persuaded Francesca to yield to her desires? How and where did Ulysses end the journey of his life? What happened in Ugolino's tower after its door was nailed shut? How did Buonconte da Montefeltro die, and where did his body go that it was never found? And what about Pia dei Tolomei and Piccarda Donati: what happened to them? And what was Florence like in 'the good old days'? Most of Dante's great characters tell the stories of their deaths. They satisfy the reader's desire to be taken back in time and see how the inevitable happened in Francesca's chamber, Ulysses' ship, Ugolino's tower, Buonconte's lonely plain of Campaldino. Dante's astonishing ability to give each of his characters a unique voice – or a silence that can be more disturbing than words, as in the case of Geri del Bello (*Inf.* XXIX, 1–39) – means that we willingly suspend our disbelief and fully identify with them, forgetting that the stories they tell are no more than poetic fabrications.

What makes Dante's characters so vivid and credible is, perhaps more than anything else, the poet's brilliant and pervasive use of dialogue. After one thousand years in which it had been virtually absent from literature, speech bursts out as one of Dante's most powerful tools in the *Commedia*'s narrative representation of reality. Direct speech is not rare in classical Latin literature or in the early Italian lyric, but in neither does it aim to reproduce ordinary conversation in all its subtlety and complexity. This is what Dante does, not just tentatively or experimentally, but with consummate self-confidence. Indeed his dialogue has the freshness of a new invention and the sophistication of a well-tested technique. The examples, especially in *Inferno*, are countless. Consider, for instance, how, as he traverses Styx, Dante replies to Filippo Argenti's challenge by picking up, and then turning against him, first one ('vieni') and then another of his words ('piango'), while at the same time carrying through the increasingly taunting theme of Filippo's muddiness/ugliness. Dante's counter-challenge is so effective that it enrages Filippo to the point that, frustrated by the verbal sparring, he resorts to physical violence only to be beaten back again. Eventually, Filippo finds that only against himself can he safely exercise his wrath (VIII, 30–63). Or consider in *Purgatorio* the lively three-way inter-action between Statius, Dante, and Virgil, when, still not knowing that Virgil is walking by his side, Statius sings the praises of the *Aeneid*, while Dante looks now at one and now at the other of his exceptional travelling companions, uncertain whether to hold his tongue or speak (XXI, 94–136). Even in *Paradiso* Dante instils unexpected freshness into the pervasive doctrinal and theological discourse, as in the conversation on the moon spots between Dante and Beatrice (II, 49–63) or the cut and thrust of St Peter's examination of Dante on faith (XXIV, 52–111).

The *Commedia* is one of the most fragmented and at the same time most unified of the great poems of the Western tradition. Fragmented in that so much of it is composed of the compelling stories of real as well as mytholo-gical and imaginary characters; unified in that the powerful macrostructure of Dante's journey is capable of absorbing and making sense, in both narra-tive and moral terms, of the multiplicity that threatens its very existence. In the end Dante's encyclopaedic project succeeds because the lost character at the beginning of the journey is able to reach total clarity at the end: in Longfellow's words, 'I saw that in its depth far down is lying / Bound up with love together in one volume, / What through the universe in leaves is scat-tered' (Nel suo profondo vidi che s'interna / legato con amore in un volume, / ciò che per l'universo si squaderna'; *Par.* XXXIII, 85–7).[3]

Conclusion

In the poetic preface to his translation of the *Divine Comedy*, Longfellow imagines himself approaching the poem with the same reverence with which 'a labourer, pausing in the dust and heat' (p. 2), approaches a cathedral door, and he continues:

> How strange the sculptures that adorn these towers!
> This crowd of statues, in whose folded sleeves
> Birds build their nests; while canopied with leaves
> Parvis and portal bloom like trellised bowers,
> And the vast minster seems a cross of flowers!
> But fiends and dragons on the gargoyled eaves
> Watch the dead Christ between the living thieves,
> And, underneath, the traitor Judas lowers!

This Gothic structure is not inert. Its statues, parvis, and portals are alive with leaves, bowers, and flowers; its gargoyles watch the mystery of the Son of God dead between the 'living thieves', the traitor Judas lowering under-neath. Here Benedetto Croce's 'luxuriant vegetation' does not spring from an external and separate source, but is produced by the frame itself. There is no separation here between structure and poetry; indeed structure is a direct, poetic expression of the poet's tormented mind and heart, of his 'exultations' and 'despair', his 'tenderness' and 'hate of wrong'. Needless to say, it is a 'romantic' reading of Dante's masterpiece; however, it captures the unity and singularity of Dante's wondrous invention.

Dante entrusts the *Commedia*'s structure with the task of creating differences throughout the three realms of the otherworld – topographical, psychological, moral differences. It is so fundamental that he needs to imagine and extend it even where, strictly speaking, it does not objectively exist, as in Paradise. Thanks to the structure, the souls appear on a graduated series of dramatically different planes and situations. Take, for example, the transition from the hustle and bustle of the ditch of the barrators to the eerie quiet of that of the hypocrites, or from the snake-infested *bolgia* of the thieves to the firefly valley of the fraudulent counsellors. Yet the structure is not a straitjacket; it never feels artificial nor does it overwhelm the 'natural' voices of the characters that inhabit it. Dante has the astonishing ability to identify what morally defines a character without reducing her or him to that definition. This is why souls can inhabit the same location without seeming similar, let alone the same. Cavalcante de' Cavalcanti lives next to Farinata (*Inf.* X) but the two Florentines could not be more different; and the same could be said of Ulysses and Guido da Montefeltro (*Inf.* XXVI–XXVII), Buonconte and Pia (*Purg.* V), Forese and Bonagiunta (*Purg.* XXIV), Carlo Martello and Cunizza (*Par.* VIII–IX), and so on. The invention of the narrative structure may even be more crucial than that of any 'lyrical' fragment of the poem. Although we know the poem was written over at least fifteen years, during which Dante changed and his views on the world evolved, the structure creates the illusion of verisimilitude and synchronicity, which in turn compels us to suspend our disbelief and experience the poem, seven centuries after the poet wrote it, on his terms as his travelling companions on his journey through the otherworld.[4]

Notes

1. B. Croce, *The Poetry of Dante* (New York: Henry Holt & Co., 1922), p. 93.
2. See L. Pertile, *Songs beyond Mankind: Poetry and the Lager from Dante to Primo Levi* (Binghamton: CMRS, 2013), p. 40. Levi mistakenly refers this episode to Bocca degli Abati (*Inf.* XXXII, 70–111).
3. *The Divine Comedy of Dante Alighieri*, trans. H. W. Longfellow (London: Routledge, 1890), p. 603.
4. I should like to thank Zyg Barański, Angus Clarke, Simon Gilson and my son Giulio Pertile for their comments on earlier drafts of this paper.

2

GIUSEPPE LEDDA

Dante Alighieri, Dante-poet, Dante-character

A First-person Narrative

From its very first lines, readers of the *Commedia* realize that they are dealing with a first-person narrative, where the identity of that first person shifts between the narrator and the protagonist. Moreover, the story's protagonist is characterized by the use not only of 'I' but also of 'we', so that it is a story about a specific historical person who is also an 'everyman', an archetypical individual common to many medieval narratives. The duality of the 'I' is also a declension of the duality distinguishing the poem's literal and allegorical meanings. During the course of the narrative, the protagonist is described in terms of his historical individuality. Yet, his is also a universal story – the story of someone who strayed from the true path in pursuit of 'false images of good' (imagini di ben ... false; *Purg.* XXX, 131) that led him into iniquity and made him forget the true purpose of life. His story is thus exemplary of a movement from sin to eternal joy through three stages: understanding evil; being cleansed of evil; and knowledge of the good. Nonetheless, throughout his experience, the protagonist never ceases to be an individual with his own identity and psychology.

At the narrative level, the *Commedia* is recounted by an 'extradiegetic' narrator who recounts the story 'from the outside'. However, in relation to the story, the narrator is 'autodiegetic', because he is also the protagonist of the narrative he tells. Moreover, in the *Commedia*, the narrator and the character share a common identity that underpins an overarching autobiographical structure. As in any autodiegetic narrative, there are many sentences in the first person. However, the reader must keep in mind the fundamental distinction between the two 'Is'. Consequently, narrator and protagonist, Dante-poet and Dante-character, the narrating and the narrated 'I' are some of the terminological pairs used by Dantists to distinguish the two 'Is' in the poem. The distinction was recognized, albeit vaguely, by the fourteenth-century commentators, but it became increasingly central to twentieth-century Dante studies, finding a particularly effective and influential systematization in the work of Gianfranco Contini.

In the *Commedia*, the narrator refers to himself by using the present or future tense, deictic expressions of time and place, and verbs of communication, writing, and memory. Consider, for example, *Inferno* I, 10: '*I* cannot really retell how *I* entered therein' (*Io* non so ben ridir com' *i'* v'intrai; emphasis added). The first occurrence of the pronoun 'I' is as the subject of a verb in the present tense that refers to the act of storytelling and writing; while the second 'I' is the subject of a verb in the past tense referring to what happened to the protagonist in the story that is being narrated. Furthermore, Dante the *narrator* often refers to himself as the work's *author*. As such, he is appropriately labelled 'Dante-poet'; while, as the protagonist of the poem, he is designated 'Dante-character'. Finally, 'Dante' or 'Dante Alighieri' is usually applied to the historical individual and actual author of the *Commedia*.

Dante-poet frequently interrupts the narrative to insert passages in which he represents himself remembering, imagining, writing, instructing the reader, and feeling emotions. He also emphasizes his being subject to the flow of time by highlighting that the poem took 'many years' (molti anni; *Par.* XXV, 3) to write. Dante-poet normally intervenes at the beginning of a canticle or of a new section, where he employs introductions, invocations, declarations of novelty, wonder, and ineffability. Almost every circle in Hell, terrace of Purgatory, and heavenly sphere in Paradise opens with a narratorial preface that quickens the reader's attention. These interpolations also serve as privileged spaces for metaliterary reflection.

A typical introductory element which is widely used in the *Commedia* is the invocation, a petition where the poet turns to the deity to assist him in writing his work. Medieval rhetorical taught that the invocation points to the importance of the matter at hand, thereby arousing the reader's interest, while also highlighting the humility of the author, who acknowledges his limitations and invokes the gods' help, thus obtaining the reader's goodwill. There are nine invocations in the *Commedia*. One opens each *cantica* (in *Inferno*, the invocation appears in the second canto: *Inf.* II, 7; *Purg.* I, 7–12; and *Par.* I, 13–36). Invocations also appear in the middle of a canto to mark a new section and stress significant events. In *Inferno* and *Purgatorio*, there is a second invocation that introduces the final part of each *cantica* (*Inf.* XXXII, 10–12; *Purg.* XXIX, 37–42). Finally, in *Paradiso*, after the opening appeal, there are a further four: the first introduces the souls forming letters in the heaven of Jupiter (XVIII, 82–7); the second announces the vision of the three highest heavens (XXII, 112–23); while the third and fourth precede the pilgrim's vision of respectively the Empyrean and God (XXX, 97–9; XXXIII, 67–75).

From Dante-character to Dante-poet

The *Commedia* not only establishes the distinction between Dante-character and Dante-poet, but it also reveals how Dante-character became Dante-poet, namely, how the protagonist became aware – first autonomously and then through prophetic investiture – of the mission entrusted to him: that of becoming the divinely ordained author of a poem which recounts what had been revealed to him during his journey through the afterlife.

After agreeing to undertake the voyage, the pilgrim then declares himself unworthy of the task, since the living are forbidden to travel from this world to the next. Indeed, God has only granted this privilege to very few individuals, most notably Aeneas and St Paul, who were successful because they had been invested with providential missions of great consequence for humanity. Not unreasonably, therefore, Dante-character ends up by asking Virgil two questions: 'But why should I go there? Or who allows it?' (Ma io, perché venirvi? o chi 'l concede?; *Inf.* II, 31). Virgil responds only to the second question: the authority comes from God, through the intercession of Mary, Lucy, and Beatrice. But what is the nature of his mission once he returns to earth? Virgil states on several occasions that the pilgrim must gain 'greater knowledge' of the condition of the souls in Hell (XVII, 37–9; XXVIII, 48–50) so as to arrive at an understanding of evil. Yet, he never suggests that his ward should then relate his experience. It is Dante-character who progressively realizes that he will need to tell others about his journey. Travelling through Hell, he receives information from the damned in exchange for the promise that, having returned to the world of the living, he will revive their fame. The intention to write about his otherworldly experiences emerges only once, when he asks an anonymous traitor to reveal his identity, so that, on his return, he can write his name 'among the others I have noted' (tra l'altre note; XXXII, 93). The sinner refuses, but his name is revealed by a fellow sufferer: 'What ails you, Bocca?' (Che hai tu, Bocca?; 106). At which point, Dante-character declares, 'to your shame I'll carry true news of you' (a la tua onta / io porterò di te vere novelle; XXXII, 110–11), thereby confirming he is already aware of his task to announce to the world the truth about the workings of divine justice. In *Purgatorio*, the protagonist reveals the further intent of propagating the doctrinal explanations he has learned from the souls. He asks Marco Lombardo to clarify the reasons for the world's sinfulness so that he may share this knowledge with others (XVI, 62). Equally, on the last terrace, shortly before arriving in the Earthly Paradise, he proclaims his intention to write an account of his journey: 'tell me, that I may again mark it on my pages' (ditemi, acciò ch'ancor carte ne verghi; XXVI, 64). Dante-character thus develops for himself the idea of composing a work in which he will present his experience of the afterlife.

Still, as ambitious a literary-didactic aim as the pilgrim's requires authoritative divine confirmation. In the Earthly Paradise, Beatrice announces Dante-character's first prophetic investiture: 'Therefore, on behalf of the world that lives badly, now keep your eyes on the chariot, and, having returned there, write down what you see' (Però, in pro del mondo che mal vive, / al carro tieni or li occhi, e quel che vedi, / ritornato di là, fa che tu scrive; XXXII, 103–5). In the following canto, Beatrice again orders the pilgrim to note and then repeat her words to the living (XXXIII, 52–3). Her commands clearly set out the fundamental parameters of his prophetic mission: the need for him fully to activate his senses, to rely on his memory, and to recount accurately his experiences, as well as the beneficial and salvific effects of his literary work. Furthermore, at the centre of *Paradiso*, in one of the *Commedia*'s key moments, the pilgrim encounters his great-great-grandfather Cacciaguida, who foretells his exile from Florence. At the same time, Dante-character reveals his fear that, if he were to tell the truth and write down everything he has seen and heard during his journey, this would cause him further misery as there would be those who would want to retaliate against him. Yet, he also recognizes that, if he holds back from speaking the truth, his work will fail and be soon forgotten. Cacciaguida's reply confirms and completes his descendant's prophetic investiture – 'But nonetheless, having put away all falsehood, reveal all your vision' (Ma nondimen, rimossa ogne menzogna, / tutta tua visïon fa manifesta; XVII, 127–8) – before concluding by stressing the poem's beneficial effect since it will provide 'vital nourishment' (vital nodrimento; 131). The pilgrim's prophetic mission is subsequently confirmed by several influential souls in the highest heavenly spheres: Peter Damian in Saturn (XXI, 97–9) and the apostles Peter, James, and John in the heaven of the Fixed Stars. In particular, James makes clear that Dante-character must see the reality of Paradise to 'strengthen' (*confortare*) first in himself and then in others the hope of eternal bliss (XXV, 43–7). In response, the pilgrim declares himself ready to 'shower' (*stillare*) on others the beneficial 'rain' (*pioggia*) of hope that the sacred writers had 'showered' on him (67–78). He is at last ready to fulfil his mission as he has now completely internalized his experiences and responsibilities. Finally, on reaching the Empyrean, to confirm that Dante-character has fully embraced his prophetic duties, he is compared to a pilgrim who has reached the end of his journey and is animated by the hope of returning home to tell his tale (XXXI, 43–5).

If the investitures conferred on the pilgrim shape the prophetic authority of Dante-poet as a *scriba Dei*, one of God's chosen mouthpieces, in the circle of simony, Dante-character, like a biblical prophet, delivers a harsh invective against the corrupt popes (*Inf.* XIX, 90–117). At the beginning of the canto a rather obscure autobiographical episode – Dante's breaking of a terracotta amphora used as a baptismal font in the Florentine Baptistery of San Giovanni (XIX, 13–21) – functions to confer prophetic authority on Dante-character so that he can legitimately attack the sinful clerics. Indeed, in some biblical passages, breaking an earthenware jug is a sign of the authority that God grants to prophets (Jer. 19:1–15; Ps. 2:7–9; Rev. 2:26–9).

A Political Autobiography

The prophecies that foretell the poet's exile from Florence in 1301–2 constitute a further important autobiographical element in the *Commedia*. Dante-character's journey through the netherworld takes place around Easter 1300. Thus, to speak of events occurring after this date, Dante uses a technique already employed by classical poets, the *post eventum* prophecy. The souls know the future, so they can talk about events that will happen *after* the pilgrim's otherworldly journey, but which were of course also known to Dante at the time he wrote the poem. For example, in *Inferno* VI, Ciacco foretells the upheavals in Florentine politics during 1300–2, but does not mention Dante's exile, which is instead announced by Farinata degli Uberti in canto X, and then by Brunetto Latini in canto XV. Elsewhere, Dante defends his reputation against the accusations of the city that had unjustly exiled him. In describing the ditch of barratry, he does not mention the same charge laid against him by the Florentine authorities and which led to his exile, but offers instead a reminder of his military exploits during the wars which in 1289 pitted Guelf Florence against the Tuscan Ghibellines (XXI, 94–6; XXII 4–6). After a series of further brief prophecies in the *Purgatorio* (VIII; XI; XXIV), the meeting with Cacciaguida in Paradise (XV–XVII) increases the focus on Florence's history and the autobiographical theme of Dante's exile and its impending hardships. Finally, in *Paradiso* XXV, Florentine politics are modulated in an autobiographical key. Thanks to his 'sacred poem' (poema sacro), the writing of which has been so all-consuming that it has made him 'lean for many years' (per molti anni macro; XXV, 1–3), Dante-poet expresses his wish to return home and receive the poetic laurel crown.

A Poet in the Making

The protagonist of the *Commedia* is a highly complex figure. The distinction between Dante-character and Dante-poet needs to recognize too that the character is also a poet and author of the *Vita nova* and other poems not included in that work or written later. During the journey, the pilgrim encounters many poets, writers, and characters associated with literary activity. These meetings are used to reflect on the literary experiences these figures embody in relation to the *Commedia*'s poetics. Given Dante's close association with some of these writers, the episodes represent a rethinking of his own literary journey.

In *Inferno* I, the first specific information provided regarding Dante-character's historical identity is that he is a poet who, imitating Virgil, has already obtained some 'honour' (onore; 87). Following on from this, the *Commedia* recounts the journey of a poet led by another poet. It thus comes as no surprise that the first characters with whom the pilgrim speaks are poets: the ancient poets in Limbo, who welcome him into their group as 'sixth amidst such wisdom' (sesto tra cotanto senno; IV, 102). This is an event of great metaliterary significance that highlights Dante's bold appropriation of classical poetry. The poet suggests that he is heir to that poetic tradition. Yet, while embracing it, he is also moving beyond it and even surpassing its achievements. These great poets can never leave Limbo, and Virgil will return there when he finishes guiding the pilgrim. Dante-character, on the other hand, will reach Paradise and will be granted the authority to write a poem in which, thanks to the divine inspiration that guides him, he will proclaim the highest truths of Christianity.

Romance vernacular literature is introduced as early as *Inferno* II, when Virgil explains that he has come to the pilgrim's rescue because Beatrice, the woman whom the poet had loved and celebrated in his writings, had descended from Paradise to go to her lover's aid. Virgil's account brings into play the *Vita nova*, which ends with 'a wondrous vision' (*Vn* XLII, 1 [31, 1]) of the blessed Beatrice that the poet feels incapable of putting into words. Instead, he declares that he will devote his time to study so as to be able to write a new work in which he hopes to 'write of her what has never been written of any other woman' (XLII, 2 [31, 2]). Since the *Vita nova* ends with the promise of a new work about Beatrice, her appearance in Limbo invites the reader to connect the *Commedia* to Dante's early work. Beatrice descended to Hell because Dante had 'loved her so much' (t'amò tanto; II, 104) that he left the 'vulgar crowd' (volgare schiera; 105) of ordinary mortals and poets.

Thus, before encountering in *Inferno* V a sinner who uses the language of courtly love, we are first introduced to a form of love poetry that has salvific force. Francesca is a passionate reader who is easily swayed by courtly love literature. She confuses fact and fiction with dire consequences: she sins, is murdered, and then damned. She begins her story declaring that 'Love ... is quickly kindled in the gentle heart' (Amor ... al cor gentil ratto s'apprende; 100), characterizing *Amore* through its close association with the 'gentle', namely, noble heart, which stilnovist poets, including Guinizzelli and Dante himself (*Vn* XX, 3–5 [11, 3–5]) had emphasized. Francesca thus justifies the love between herself and Paolo by using the same language as that used by stilnovist poets, thereby revealing that the 'first root' (prima radice; *Inf.* V, 124) of their love is to be sought in a literary experience, namely the reading of the Lancelot romance. On hearing her story, Dante-character is first overwhelmed by 'pity' (pietade; 140) and then faints – a symbolic death of that part of the pilgrim that linked him to the two doomed lovers.

The encounter with Cavalcante de' Cavalcanti among the heretics indirectly evokes his son Guido. Cavalcante believes that Dante-character is able to undertake his journey through Hell 'by height of genius' (per altezza di ingegno; *Inf.* X, 59). The pilgrim rejects this assumption, and adds that the person towards whom he is moving and to whom he owes that privilege had been rejected by his son Guido (61–3). That person is almost certainly Beatrice, the woman celebrated in the *Vita nova* for inspiring in Dante-character a love that leads to moral improvement and spiritual elevation towards God, and that persists even after her death. Guido Cavalcanti, instead, upheld a notion of love as an irrational and destructive passion, tied to the physical world, and lacking a spiritual dimension. In short, Guido denied what the love of Beatrice represented for Dante.

Towards the end of the *Inferno*, among the counterfeiters, the pilgrim witnesses an exchange of insults between two damned souls, Master Adam and Sinon the Greek. The verbal skirmish is in part modelled on the rhetorical structures of the *tenzone*, an exchange of scurrilous sonnets between 'comic' poets, a genre that Dante had used in his *tenzone* with Forese Donati. Virgil reproaches Dante-character because he is entirely absorbed by the sinners' altercation; and his condemnation, of course, also extends to the poet's insulting sonnets. Yet the *tenzone* is incorporated into the *Commedia*. The genre is thus not totally rejected but is included in the new pluristylistic 'sacred poem' (sacrato poema; poema sacro; *Par.* XXIII, 62; XXV, 1), since it too can be bent to salvific purposes.

In *Purgatorio*, reflection on literature increases. Already in canto II, Dante-character meets the musician Casella, who sings one of his friend's *canzoni*, 'Amor che ne la mente mi ragiona' (Love that discourses to me in my mind;

112). All those who gather to listen are transfixed, but are soon reprimanded by Cato for delaying their journey up Mount Purgatory. This poem was one of those dedicated to the love for a woman, who, in the *Convivio*, is identified as an allegorical representation of Philosophy. Despite the fact that the 'almost commentary' (*Conv.* I, iii, 2) was never completed and was left unpublished, Dante was well aware of that experience and of the fact that he had embraced the idea that, through philosophy, one can attain perfect knowledge and full happiness. Cato's reproach, therefore, seems to indicate that it is necessary to abandon the illusion that supreme truth is knowable through rational means. Once it is acknowledged that divine truth can only be reached thanks to grace, at that point the journey of faith, humility, and penance can begin.

The encounter with Forese Donati among the gluttons once more evokes their *tenzone* exchange. Dante-character reminisces about a wayward period of his life which he had shared with Forese. Dante here critically assesses another earlier poetic experience that had caused him to stray from the commitment to Beatrice that he had affirmed in the *Vita nova*. More important is the conversation, on the same terrace, with the poet Bonagiunta da Lucca, who asks the protagonist if he is the author of the innovative canzone 'Donne ch'avete intelletto d'Amore' (Ladies who have intelligence of Love; XXIV, 49–51). Dante-character responds by claiming his absolute fidelity to Love's inspiration in a language saturated with Scriptural and mystic overtones: 'I am one who, when Love breathes in me, take note, and in that manner that he dictates within go on to set it forth' (I' mi son un che, quando / Amor mi spira, noto, e a quel modo / ch'e' ditta dentro vo significando; 52–4). This assertion recalls the poetry in praise of Beatrice in the *Vita nova*, which is introduced by the canzone that Bonagiunta recalls. However, the pilgrim's use of the present tense suggests that, for him, the poetics evoked is the norm. Hence, the self-definition can be extended to the poetry that he intends to compose on his return to earth. Moreover, Bonagiunta reveals that he now appreciates that this poetic principle is what divides the 'sweet new style' (dolce stil novo; 57) from the previous lyric tradition. Indeed, on the following terrace of the lustful, the discussion of love primarily focuses on love poetry, as had been the case in *Inferno* V. Dante-character recognizes the Bolognese poet Guido Guinizzelli as the creator of a 'style' that he and others had followed. Guinizzelli avoids taking credit for his achievement, but instead indicates another soul who had been a better vernacular poet than him, the Occitan troubadour Arnaut Daniel. Guinizzelli then attacks Guittone d'Arezzo, a Tuscan poet of his generation, and his undeserved fame. Dante creates a new canon of Italian poetry: Guittone is snubbed and superseded by the 'sweet new style' of Dante and his companions, of which Guinizzelli is the 'father' (padre; *Purg.* XXVI, 97) and precursor. At the same time, and suggesting their subordination to Dante, Guinizzelli and Arnaut expiate in Purgatory the erotic lapses that were central to their poetry.

The return of Beatrice in Eden and their journey through the heavenly spheres represent the final triumph of salvific love over an imperfect and potentially sinful earthbound poetics of love. Beatrice's beauty now guides Dante-character to the divine beauty that is reflected in her. The encounter with Beatrice is also important for highlighting the literary implications of autobiographical events. Beatrice is severe with Dante-character, and immediately exhorts him to stop crying when Virgil departs, as he needs to weep for a different and more important reason (XXX, 55–7). This is the only occasion in the *Commedia* where the protagonist's name is pronounced, which prompts him to say apologetically, 'of necessity [it] is here recorded' (qui di necessità si registra; 63). Beatrice recalls that in his youth he had extraordinary potential for success. For a while she herself had guided him towards the good, but when she died, he deserted her and gave himself to others, 'pursuing false images of good, that make no promise whole' (imagini di ben seguendo false, / che nulla promission rendono intera; 131–2), which is in part an allusion to the literary experiences that drove him away from writing love poetry for Beatrice. All her attempts, through dreams and visions, to redirect him back to her were to no avail. Her last resort was to show him how sin is punished in Hell, so that he might understand the consequences of evil.

In *Paradiso*, encounters between Dante-character and other writers and poets, or with characters that reflect on literature, are more numerous than critics have generally recognized. Scholars have concentrated mainly on his relationship with classical and Romance authors. Yet, in Paradise, sacred literature is very much to the fore. Dante introduces authors and protagonists of the books of the Bible; authors of theological works; and figures associated with various kinds of religious literature, primarily hagiography.

In the heaven of Venus, Dante-character meets another famous troubadour, Foulquet of Marseilles, who after a libidinous youth, converted and became the bishop of Marseille. Another significant encounter is with Charles Martel, who greets Dante by citing one of his *canzoni* 'Voi che 'ntendendo il terzo ciel movete' (You who, by understanding, move the third heaven; VIII, 37). As with 'Amor che ne la mente mi ragiona', this is also a poem included in the *Convivio* exalting the love for the woman who in the prose commentary is allegorically identified with Philosophy. The other blessed in Venus succumbed in their youth to sensual and passionate love but then repented to devote their lives to virtue. After recalling the amorous folly of his youth, Foulquet comments on how now, rather than focusing on repentance, they smile at the providential order that foresaw their salvation (IX, 103–8). In Paradise all sins are forgiven: faults are forgotten and the souls delight in celestial joy thanks to divine grace that has helped them reject evil and turn to good. By citing his own earlier canzone, Dante alludes to and 'confesses' a false love, the exclusive love for worldly philosophical wisdom. Yet, in Paradise, guilt is completely removed, and Beatrice smiles reassuringly at the pilgrim.

Dante-character's other literary paradisiacal meetings do not engage with his past artistic experiences in order to transcend them, but serve to associate him with great authoritative models. The pilgrim's vision of the wise and contemplative souls respectively in the heaven of the Sun and that of Saturn, the hagiographic *canti* dedicated to Francis and Dominic (*Par.* XI–XII), and Peter Damian and Benedict (XXI–XXII), all belong to this latter strategy, as do the episodes centred on Scriptural figures, such as David, Peter, James, and John, and the regular allusions to St Paul. It is vital to recognize that the pilgrim's interactions with these figures are fundamental to the shaping of Dante-character, a poet in the making, who, to achieve this, meets fellow writers and other literary figures. Rather than occasions to meditate on the literature of the past, these encounters offer models for a future poetry and forge the identity of Dante-character, who, at the end of his journey, will become the poet ready to compose the 'sacred poem'.

Among the wise spirits in the heaven of the Sun, a special place is afforded to Boethius (*Par.* X, 124–9), whose sanctity is emphasized and who is presented in ways that sharply contrast with the treatment of Virgil and the great pagan philosophers in *Purgatorio* III, 34–45. Boethius is shown as rejoicing in his knowledge of 'every good' (ogne ben; 124), which clearly separates him from the fruitless desire to understand everything of the pagan philosophers – a desire that leaves them eternally grieving (42). The stress falls on the salvific nature of Boethius' contribution that reveals the fallacy of worldly goods. It is a lesson that, at the beginning of the next canto, Dante-poet reveals he has absorbed as he rails against the vanity of humanity's vain desire for earthly prestige, power, and wealth (XI, 1–12).

Failing to distinguish between the two 'I's in the *Commedia* can result in serious misunderstandings. The confusion between Dante-character and Dante-poet can, for example, lead one to attribute the emotions of the former to the latter. Hence, the pilgrim's compassion or sympathy for some of the souls in Hell may be erroneously attributed to Dante-poet or even the author. Dante-character, who is on a journey of knowledge, during which he progressively comes to understand evil and good, may give in to such feelings and partake in the sins through which he passes. However, such an attitude would be unacceptable in Dante-poet who has completed the journey and is now recounting what he has experienced in total conformity with divine justice. A further problem arises if we apply too insistently a metaliterary reading to Dante-character. Seen in this light, the pilgrim's journey corresponds to the voyage of writing the poem, with the difficulties the protagonist faces as equivalent to difficult stages in the *Commedia*'s composition. Not only does such an approach confuse the two levels of the 'I', but it also goes against Dante's propensity to deal explicitly with metaliterary themes, both through the character's encounters with literary figures and through Dante-poet's frequent metaliterary interventions.

Figures and Models of the 'I'

From its opening, the *Commedia* stresses the importance of biblical models behind the construction of the pilgrim-poet by transforming Isaiah's 'In the midst of my days I shall go to the gates of Hell' (38:10) into 'In the middle of the journey of our life' (Nel mezzo del cammin di nostra vita; *Inf.* I, 1). The first words spoken by the protagonist recall David's words, '"Have mercy on me", I cried' ('Miserere di me', gridai; 65), which translate the Vulgate's 'Miserere mei', with which Psalm 50, the most famous penitential psalm, opens. Although the formula was widely used, including in liturgy, the allusion to David is clear, since the king was the archetypal model of the sinner who asks for God's mercy and is willing to undergo a penitential process. This is confirmed by the repetition of the formula at the end of the *Commedia*, where the allusion is to David the 'singer, who grieving for his sin, said, "*Miserere mei*"' (cantor che per doglia del fallo / disse 'Miserere mei'; *Par.* XXXII, 11–12).

Similarly, in *Inferno* II, 10–36, Aeneas and Paul are presented as great exemplary figures – but also as precursors of Dante-character – divinely chosen to go on a journey through the afterlife, part of a providential mission that has a 'high consequence' (alto effetto; 17) for humanity as a whole: in Aeneas' case, his descent to the underworld marks the start of the historical process leading to the foundation of Rome and its empire; in Paul's, the affirmation of Christianity as the only faith leading to salvation is connected to his being taken up to the third heaven (II Cor. 12:2–4). Paul is described as the 'Vas d'elezïone' (chosen vessel; 28; cp. Acts 9:15), namely, the 'vessel' of God's free and unfathomable decision to transform certain people, beyond their individual merits, into instruments to carry out His will. From the *Commedia*'s beginning, Dante points to Paul as a key model for constructing his identity as both character and poet. Equally, Dante is alluding to the

Scriptural model of the person chosen by God who recognizes their limitations, as famously occurred to Moses (Ex. 3:11; 4:1–17).

In the Earthly Paradise, the pilgrim is granted apostolic connotations. On losing consciousness following the singing of a sacred hymn, he is awakened by Matelda intoning, 'Arise, what are you doing?' (Surgi: che fai?; *Purg.* XXXII, 72). The verb *surgere* reprises that used in the Gospel when Jesus addresses Peter, James, and John overwhelmed by his transfiguration: 'surgite et nolite timere' (arise and don't be afraid; Mt. 17:17). Dante proceeds by comparing in a lengthy simile the character's sleep and awakening to that of the apostles (71–82). Furthermore, once he awakes, Beatrice invests him with the responsibility to write down what he sees (104–5), which accurately repeats the order John receives at the beginning of Revelation (1:11).

The Pauline model is especially important in the third *cantica* where the saint is a constant point of reference. It is not surprising, therefore, that already *Paradiso* I, 5–6 should echo Paul's declaration of ineffability regarding his rapture to Paradise (II Cor. 12:4). Yet, if Paul remains silent about his heavenly experiences, Dante-poet promises to sing of the 'holy kingdom' (regno santo; 10) to the extent that he is able to understand and remember it, and human language to express it. For, after all, this is precisely his mission. Although *Paradiso*'s first invocation is dense with Ovidian allusions, when Dante-poet asks Apollo to make him 'such a vessel of your power' (del tuo valor sì fatto vaso; 14), he is again alluding to Paul, the 'vas electionis'. The apostle returns, too, at the start of the encounter with Cacciaguida, which is decisive for the shaping of the pilgrim's prophetic identity. Dante begins the episode by comparing the meeting to that between Anchises and Aeneas in the underworld and by having Cacciaguida ask whether anyone else has had the gates of Paradise opened to him twice (XV, 25–30). In the economy of the *Commedia*, the answer is obvious: only to Paul. Thus, the two models crucially present at the start of the otherworldly adventure emblematically return at this key defining stage of voyage.

The heaven of the Fixed Stars, where Dante-character is examined on the theological virtues, is heavily imbued with Scriptural references. Asked to define faith, he responds with reference to Paul by translating the definition found in the Epistle to the Hebrews (XXIV, 64–5; cp. Heb. 11:1). Dante emphasizes his source by highlighting Paul's 'truthful pen' (verace stilo; 61). Subsequently, when replying to James' question on the sources of his hope, Dante-character mentions David, first alluded to in *Inferno* I, then presented as an example of humility in Purgatory (X, 55–69), and finally seen in the heaven of Jupiter where he is termed 'the singer of the Holy Spirit' (cantor de lo Spirito Santo; XX, 38). David is thus a model not only for the penitent

Dante-character but also for Dante-poet, who is thus equated to the divinely inspired authors of the Bible.

Classical characters, too, offer several models with which Dante constructs his character and poet. Among the Virgilian ones, Aeneas obviously occupies a position of primacy. Indeed, throughout the *Inferno*, various moments of the pilgrim's journey recall Aeneas' otherworldly descent. Just as strikingly, myths taken from Ovid's *Metamorphoses* provide a range of characters whom Dante originally adapted to construct his character and sometimes his poet. For example, Dante repeatedly alludes to and reworks the Ovidian myth of Phaethon: the presumptuous, reckless, and ultimately tragic flight of the pagan hero is transformed into the flight of the Christian hero assisted by wise and capable guides on whom he humbly relies (*Inf.* XVII, 106–14; *Purg.* IV, 71–2; XXIX 115–20; *Par.* XV, 13–18; XVII, 1–6; XXXI, 124–9). In other instances, especially in *Paradiso*, Ovidian myths of flight and of contact with the divine that end tragically, as in the case of Semele evoked in *Paradiso* XXI, 1–12, prefigure contrastively the pilgrim's 'high flight' (alto volo; XXV, 50) and vision of the Empyrean and God.

In the two invocations that open the second and third *cantiche*, Dante reverses mythological instances of pride that irrationally and arrogantly challenge the divinity to construct an identity for himself as a humble poet conscious of his human limitations, especially given the lofty subject matter that he has been called to sing. In *Purgatorio* I, he invokes the 'holy Muses' (sante Muse; 8) and Calliope, the Muse of epic poetry, recalling their victory over king Pierus' daughters, who had foolishly challenged them to a singing contest (7–12; cp. *Metam.* V, 294–678). Similarly, in *Paradiso* I, the invocation to Apollo evokes another myth of punished hubris, that of Marsyas (*Metam.* VI, 382–400), which Dante ironically reverses (16–21): prideful Marsyas challenged Apollo, while Dante-poet humbly invokes the god's help so that, like Paul, he can be made into a 'vessel' of divine virtue. Similarly, once the narrative is resumed after the long invocation, the 'trasumanar' (70), the inexpressible soaring beyond the human of Dante-character is described through another Ovidian myth: Glaucus who was miraculously turned into a sea god (68–9; *Metam.* XIII, 917–59). Glaucus stands for the pilgrim, who, ascending to Paradise, transcends his humanity. This myth, too, is integrated with Paul's celestial vision. The saint is evoked when the poet wonders whether or not he experienced Paradise while still in his body (73–5; and cp. II Cor. XII, 2–4).

Among the otherworld's classical characters employed to forge the character's identity as a voyager and Dante's as a poet, Ulysses holds a special place. Inspired by accounts in classical and medieval texts, Dante invents the story of the hero's last voyage beyond the Pillars of Hercules as a warning to humanity not to exceed divinely instituted limits. Ulysses' final voyage serves as a negative model both of the character's journey beyond the limits normally granted to human experience, and of the challenges facing the poet, which are often indicated using navigational metaphors. Right at the beginning of the *Commedia*, alongside Aeneas and Paul, there emerges a negative model that subsequently merges with Ulysses. The phrase 'arduous passage' (l'alto passo; *Inf.* II, 12), that marks the start of the otherworldly journey, is later used when Ulysses sails beyond the Pillars of Hercules (XXVI, 132). Similarly, while the pilgrim fears that his journey may be 'mad' (folle; II, 35), Ulysses' journey is actually judged as such by the Greek hero himself (XXVI, 25) and by Dante-character when he considers it from the vantage point of the Primum Mobile (*Par.* XXVII, 82–3). Elsewhere, Dante has recourse to images of navigation (*Purg.* I, 1–3; *Par.* XXIII, 67–9), which were traditionally used to refer to literary composition, whereby writing was compared to a sea voyage. In *Paradiso* II's address to the reader, Ulysses' voyage hovers in the background: 'The water I sail was never sailed before' (L'acqua ch'io prendo già mai non si corse; 7). But this is immediately accompanied by the affirmation that the poet will receive divine assistance in completing his task (8–9). The *Commedia* is the fulfilment of the mission with which Dante has been entrusted; and so, at the start of the third and most artistically and intellectually arduous canticle, the poet, aware of his limitations, humbly seeks divine help. It is only with God's help that he can confront the uncharted waters without risking failure and shipwreck.

Metaphorical projections and models, both positive and negative, are also deployed in relation to other characters whom the pilgrim meets in the afterlife, and whose stories prefigure his biographical vicissitudes as these are presented in the poem. In particular, and in addition to the *post-eventum* prophecies, this type of identification is employed to address the question of his unjust exile. Thus, Pier della Vigna (*Inf.* XIII) and Romeo of Villanova (*Par.* VI) offer two alternative models of behaviour characterizing the honest and loyal politician who is unjustly and falsely accused of betrayal and then falls out of favour. Pier takes his own life, thereby committing a sinful and desperate act that transforms him from a positive into a negative model. Conversely, although poor and old, Romeo faces the shame and pain of exile with dignity and courage. The latter model culminates in Boethius, who already in *Convivio* was both a stand-in for the exiled Dante and an authority legitimating Dante's decision to talk about himself (I, ii, 13). In the *Commedia*, the persecution suffered by Boethius is defined as exile and martyrdom (*Par.* X, 128–9). The language of martyrdom connects Boethius to Cacciaguida, who went 'from being martyred to this peace' (dal martirio a questa pace; XV, 148). Cacciaguida, who dies during a crusade, represents a Christ-like acceptance of the need for personal sacrifice to accomplish a divine mission. Boethius is not simply an example of the righteous unjustly condemned and persecuted, but also of the sacred author who, in exile and suffering persecution, takes on the task of writing a work that will bring salvation to its readers.

The ties of both illustrious predecessors to the pilgrim-poet are more than self-evident; as is the extraordinary complexity of Dante's construction of his bifurcated first-person narrative distinguished into two 'I's: the narrating and narrated 'I', Dante-narrator and Dante-protagonist, Dante-poet and Dante-character, author and pilgrim. In addition, the second 'I' in each pairing not only has a precise individuality but also a universal meaning; equally, the narrative reveals how the character is progressively transformed into the poet. Finally, the poem's autobiographical dimension permits Dante to talk about himself and his historical circumstances. It is ultimately the complex interplay between the different, carefully modulated 'Dantean' self-manifestations that constitutes one of the *Commedia*'s richest and most satisfying sources of meaning.

Translated by Demetrio S. Yocum

3

LAURENCE E. HOOPER

Characterization

Characters in Search of a Reader

At first glance, the nature and meaning of the *Comedy*'s third-person characters seem fundamental to any interpretation of the poem. After all, the *Comedy*'s plot consists entirely of encounters between a first-person protagonist and a multitude of other figures comprising departed souls and non-human denizens of the afterlife. However, surprisingly little scholarship has addressed the question of characterization directly. There has been varied and penetrating discussion of related issues including allegory, autobiography, gender, and realism. But there remains a void on the two central aspects of characterization: the manner in which the *Comedy* depicts its characters; and the significance of the persons it depicts. The main exception is the narrator-character called Dante. Nonetheless, since a first-person narrative is no more than '[a] story told by one of its "characters"',[1] a considered discussion of the poem's protagonist requires a corresponding account of his interlocutors, which this chapter aims to provide.

Limiting ourselves to the figures directly encountered by the pilgrim, rather than mentioned in absentia, we can identify 364 third-person characters in the *Comedy*, of whom around a third (128) have speaking roles.[2] That gives an average of three to four new characters encountered per canto, and one, perhaps two, new voices that enter into dialogue with the pilgrim. Only two third-person characters, Virgil and Beatrice, are present for any significant proportion of the poem (63 and 37 cantos, respectively), while the vast majority appear only in passing. Meanwhile, the first-person narrator-protagonist is the poem's sole constant character. This ever-present figure is always on a journey, just as the words that describe him must follow the order of syntax to signify. The double progression of pilgrim and poet gives the work a structural dynamism that the third-person characters help to define via the counterpoint of their more limited motion.

As well as the concision with which the *Comedy* introduces and develops its characters, what is striking about them is their diversity. The damned, the penitent, and the blessed are all minutely divided and subdivided into a myriad of groupings: sins, vices, and virtues; natives of Italy and every other part of the Mediterranean world; contemporary and ancient figures; nobles and commoners; monsters, angels, and humans; guides who travel with the pilgrim and characters who appear in a single place. Each one of those categories then exhibits further diversity, with any principle of division tending to generate exceptions, until one is left with 364 categories of one.

Where scholars have examined characters other than the poetic 'I', they have done so in the service of illustrating the poet's intentions or praxis. Even Erich Auerbach, perhaps the twentieth century's most faithful exponent of literature's potential to express external reality, reduces the *Comedy*'s variegated cast of characters to an aspect of poetic style.[3] This determination to return everything about the *Comedy* to a function of the poet's expression bespeaks an anachronistic, post-Romantic emphasis on qualities such as originality and genius that overlooks the dramatically different understanding of such concepts in Dante's time.

In particular, received wisdom locates Dante's so-called genius in his ability to transcend medieval poetic tradition by creating a palpable realism *avant la lettre*. Ironically, scholars frequently express admiration for Dante's characters as concrete and historicized, without questioning their own ideological commitment to poetic subjectivity. Characterization is therefore a key issue that commentators on the *Comedy* must confront, if only implicitly. A brief survey of how they have reconciled these conflicting imperatives summarizes the main areas of debate and identifies some questions that remain unaddressed. Thereafter, this chapter sets out two modes of interpreting the *Comedy*'s characters: through history, drawing together notions of character from the literary theory of Dante's time; and through theory, applying to Dante relevant findings from the modern tradition of narrative studies. In light of this analysis, it proposes a consideration of the poem's third-person characters in terms of a static-dynamic axis – namely, the extent to which they accompany Dante-pilgrim on the journey represented by the poem.

The Romantic Character(s) of Modern Dante Studies

The modern tradition of studies on the *Comedy* dates back to the Romantic era (*c.*1770–1830). Readers like G. W. F. Hegel found in its characters one of the poem's prime attractions: 'these characters have produced their situation for *themselves*, as individuals, and are eternal in themselves, not in our ideas'.[4] The grisly story of Ugolino (*Inf.* XXXIII) first captured widespread interest with Heinrich Wilhelm von Gerstenberg's drama *Ugolino* (1768) and Sir Joshua Reynolds' painting *Count Ugolino and his Children in the*

Dungeon (1770–3). Soon after, the ill-fated love story of Francesca and Paolo (*Inf.* V) began to dominate the imagination of Dante's readers, generating a slew of representations by painters (e.g. Johann Heinrich Füssli in 1787; Ary Scheffer in 1835), poets (Leigh Hunt, *The Story of Rimini*, 1816), and dramatists (Silvio Pellico, *Francesca da Rimini*, 1818). Other favoured characters included Farinata degli Uberti (*Inf.* X), Brunetto Latini (*Inf.* XV), Pia de' Tolomei (*Purg.* V), and, naturally, Beatrice.

Despite this appreciation for Dante's characters among artists and thinkers of the Romantic period, literary criticism, then as now, concentrated its appreciation on the poet himself. Ugo Foscolo expounded the fascination of Dante's characters in English and Italian but as the creations of an inspired poet uniquely able to express Italian culture: '[Dante] condenses all his thoughts and feelings in the facts he relates – and expresses himself invariably through images often in what the Italian painters call *in iscorcio* ... [He never] stop[s] to fill up the design with minute or successive touches, but passes on hastily through the boundless variety of his subject'.[5]

Foscolo's secular, prophetic Dante influenced Italian critics during the Risorgimento (Italian unification, 1850–70), who made the *Comedy* the essential text of the new Italian nation. Chief among them was Francesco De Sanctis, for whom Dante's ability to render empathically a factional rival like Farinata exemplified the political renewal that post-unification Italy still lacked: 'Dante's man, the image of Farinata, the stuff of which the great characters of Shakespeare were made, has remained a unique and solitary example in Italian poetry!'[6]

De Sanctis' lament for Dante's lack of Italian successors paves the way for one of the two dominant approaches to characterization in the *Comedy* that continue to the present day. Both are, in truth, developments of the Hegelian vision of Dante's characters as eternal realizations of selfhood, albeit distinguished by their divergent genealogies. This first tradition might be called 'poetic expressionism': it was first enunciated by De Sanctis' admirer, the philosopher Benedetto Croce, and later developed by Gianfranco Contini to focus on questions of style and language. Poetic expressionism defines the *Comedy*'s characters as the prime conduit through which the poet manifests literary mastery and historical particularity, in contrast with the cold theological rigour of the afterlife. In Croce's terms, the characters bear the *poesia* that explodes the constraints of *struttura*: 'Over and above the many and diverse depictions of characters ... the image that rises is one of a robust will, a knowledgeable heart, a confident intellect, the image of Dante himself'.[7]

An alternative vision of Dante's characters that has found considerable success in Anglophone criticism on the *Comedy* is 'figural realism'. This view emphasizes the duality of figures such as Francesca or Cato of Utica

(*Purg.* I–II) as historically identifiable individuals who exemplify ethical and spiritual lessons for the reader. Dante achieves this figuration via his mastery of literary techniques drawn from medieval theology and exegesis. Figural realism was first propounded by Erich Auerbach, who reached back directly to the idealism of Hegel. Since then, it has been taken up by scholars, especially in North America.

The principal disputes between these approaches concern the place of theological learning in the literary processes of the *Comedy* and the importance of historical context. Poetic expressionist readings tend to see theology as antithetical to poetry, and privilege instead detailed historical and/or philological commentary that is taken to demonstrate the human aspects of the poem. Figural realism seeks to integrate poetry and Christian doctrine, often with a view to demonstrating the *Comedy*'s place in a transcendent canon of world literature, or as a harbinger of modernity. The shared idealist/post-Romantic framework is equally clear: both strands take for granted the notions that the *Comedy* is exceptional and its author a genius. This sublimation of poet and poem has helped to maintain the *Comedy*'s unrivalled reputation over nearly two-and-a-half centuries. However, it has also meant the consistent subordination of the *Comedy*'s third-person characters to the poetic 'I'. By contrast, this chapter adopts an integrationist position towards both doctrine and historicity.

Methodological Considerations: Characters in History, Characters in Theory

One challenging aspect of the *Comedy*'s characters is that they are highly incomplete. We rarely receive more than a proper name, sometimes not even that, plus a few salient details to identify the individuals and glean the reason for their placement in the afterlife. While many characters have distinctive voices, detailed physical descriptions are surprisingly rare, with notable exceptions (e.g. Brunetto Latini, Cato, Manfred). Indeed we know very little about the appearance of such famous characters as Francesca da Rimini or Ulysses. Small wonder then that the earliest manuscripts of the poem contain both the first commentaries and the first visual representations of the *Comedy*'s characters. Both types of paratext acknowledge the challenge that Dante's elliptical characterization posed, even for readers of his own era.

Medieval rhetorical and poetic theory can help us understand the incompleteness of Dante's characters without dismissing it. Rhetorical manuals recognized two primary forms of characterization: a brief *sketch* highlighting a few key traits (Latin *effictio*/Italian *mostramento*), and a more extended *description* (Latin *notatio*/Italian *disegnare*). It may surprise us that

46

rhetoricians deemed the sketch more definitive than its longer counterpart: a brief description was reserved for a person whose relevance to the overall discourse was unquestioned, while a fuller explanation implied a digression to exemplify a relevant quality, which thus took precedence over the character's identity.[8]

Many characters in the *Comedy* are depicted via sketches: they receive a brief mention in the narrative as representatives of a single vice or virtue. Longer descriptions, meanwhile, are reserved for characters that make more extended interventions in which they evoke multiple issues and often display diverse qualities. In certain cases, third-person characters speak uninterrupted for long periods and here we can evoke a further rhetorical figure, *dialogue (sermocinatio/informare)*: 'when the writer describes how a person who is not present would speak if he were present'.[9] Admittedly, descriptions often included direct speech; however, the existence of dialogue as a separate figure in its own right helps explain the distinction accorded to a character like Ulysses or Justinian, whose voice predominates for a significant portion of text.

The modern discipline of narratology offers an analytical framework for an account of narrative perspective that may remedy Dante scholars' overemphasis on the subjective elements of the *Comedy*. For example, Dante would have known the Ciceronian distinction between *natural* and *artificial* narrative order, namely, between a sequence of events narrated as they occurred in time and one reordered to suit the author's purposes.[10] This binary paradigm, still recognized today in technical terms such as the *flashback*, posits authorial agency as the sole determinant of narrative order. Gérard Genette, however, has proposed a threefold division of narrative levels, which allows for a more detailed analysis of narrative voices.

For Genette, *story (histoire*; the word also means 'history') indicates all the events and circumstances on which the narrative depends. The *Comedy*'s *story* is the totality of cosmology and salvation history referred to and implied. *Plot (récit)* is the underlying sequence of all events mentioned in the narrative. For the *Comedy*, this timeline begins at Creation and extends through history to 1300, where the poem is set; thereafter it continues up to the time of writing via pseudo-prophecies, about intervening events like Dante's exile, and beyond that through genuine prophecies like the *veltro* (greyhound) in *Inferno* I. Finally, *narration* is the continuum of events that the work presents to us, namely, the sequence that begins with the pilgrim's awakening in the dark wood in *Inferno* I and ends with his vision of God in *Paradiso* XXXIII.[11]

Armed with these narratological concepts, we can now explain how the structural dynamism of the *Comedy* intersects with its characterization.

The introduction of a middle term, *plot*, between the author's activities of imagination and expression reminds us that all narratives – fiction, history, myth, etc. – are necessarily representations of the temporal sequence of human experience. As the inhabitants of a notional timescape, literary characters are epistemologically distinct from the narrative author, who may intervene in his creation only by becoming another character. In the *Comedy*, third-person characters are especially important because they exemplify the limits on the trajectory of the protagonist, and hence of the reader. The third-person characters contrast with the pilgrim's progress in two ways: with regard to *plot*, because they are absent for some part of the protagonist's journey; and with regard to *narration*, because there are limits to their appearance within the poem.

What licenses us to talk of *static* and *dynamic* third-person characters is the fact that every character either joins with the protagonist's journey for a time or delays it while the two parties interact. Even *Paradiso*, where the nature of the pilgrim's interactions with the souls is uncertain, still obeys this broad narratological pattern: the protagonist journeys through the heavens, stopping to engage in dialogue with blessed souls whose virtues correspond to the location in which they temporarily appear. After the *cantica*'s first dialogue with Piccarda Donati, Beatrice describes the continuity of characterization practices as salvific, akin to the anthropomorphism of God and his angels that Scripture and other Christian writings use to render sacred truths comprehensible to believers (*Par.* IV, 37–48). By the time the pilgrim witnesses the 'triumphal vapours' (vapor triunfanti; XXVII, 71) returning to their eternal stations in the Empyrean, he has encountered static blessed characters across eight heavens and will soon be ready to confront infinity himself.

In sum, the Hegelian reading of Dante's characterization as eternalizing rests on the erroneous assumption that characters appear in the poem as they will remain forever after. This extrapolates to eternity a temporal and limited narrative perspective that is clearly defined as such by the poem's references to the Last Judgement. The punishments of Hell will worsen with the resurrection of the damned's bodies, just as the joys of Heaven will increase (*Inf.* VI, 103–11). Meanwhile, the penances of Purgatory are time-bound and cannot go past Judgement Day, even where atonement remains incomplete (*Purg.* X, 109–11). The only fully resurrected humans at the time of Dante's journey are Christ and Mary (*Par.* XXV, 122–9), whom the pilgrim glimpses from a distance. At no point in the poem, therefore, is there dialogue with a human person in its eternal aspect.

The early commentators were well aware of these issues and addressed them with commendable subtlety. Iacomo della Lana, author of the first commentary on the complete poem, notes without hesitation that there is no need to assume that a character named in the *Comedy* 'is in Hell or wherever else, because such a thing is unknown and hidden from mortals'.[12] Nonetheless, Iacomo does not therefore understand the work's characters as fictions devised solely by Dante. Instead, he believes that the poem's grouping of the souls by the vices and virtues they exhibited in life reflects the poet's insight into the pattern of divine justice in the world. The *Comedy*'s characterization is thus neither entirely personal to Dante nor a representation of divine omnipotence but a dialogue between those two possibilities.

At the beginning of *Inferno* XXIX, the pilgrim is moving towards Malebolge's tenth ditch where the falsifiers reside when Virgil mentions having seen Dante's cousin Geri del Bello in the prior *bolgia* with the schismatics. Iacomo finds poetic and spiritual positives in Geri's retrospective insertion into the narrative: 'That the reason for his damnation was for sowing havoc will be apparent since he [Dante] places him in the ninth *bolgia*. Still, because the author knew that Geri was also guilty of the vice of counterfeiting, he therefore treats of him in the present canto [sc. *Inf.* XXIX] in order that justice be fully satisfied both in open and in secret'.[13] Lana's sensitivity to the multiple levels of Dante's narrative allows him to reach a sophisticated analysis of Geri's characterization. He allows that Geri is a static character with respect to *story* – his damnation to the ninth *bolgia*. But, in delaying mention of Geri to the next canto, the *narration* departs from the underlying order of the *plot* (by referring to the moment when Geri gestured angrily at Dante, which his cousin failed to notice). The poem's journeying motif ensures that Geri's appearance in the same canto as the counterfeiters like the alchemist Capocchio insinuates his double condemnation without violating the doctrinal principle that each soul must receive a definitive judgement.

Versioning and the Question of Exemplarity

It is seldom noted that the characters of the *Comedy* had, without exception, already appeared in other books: the Bible; a classical or medieval source; the historical record; or the 'book of Creation'. The narratological term for the introduction into a work of characters who exist outside it is *versioning*. The technique naturally emphasizes a work's literary qualities by suggesting that its characters are not inventions *ex nihilo* but rather commentaries on and reworkings of prior texts. Even before the *Comedy*, the repeated appearances of a beloved lady are central to Dante's lyrics, *Vita nova*, and *Convivio*; the Beatrice of the *Comedy* continues this metanarrative.

The rhetorical figure from Dante's time that relates most closely to versioning was *exemplum*, 'which happens when we describe with our words some fair saying or deed of a wise and celebrated person'.[14] In accordance with medieval literary theory, an *exemplum* invokes individuals in order to present certain ethically salient actions; its characters are therefore necessarily *persons*, in the legal or theological sense of one who possesses an inalienable identity. The modern novel, by contrast, relies on the 'strong emotional appeal' of avowedly fictional characters that are 'haunted by no shadow of another person'.[15]

Dante's ancestor Cacciaguida, himself an exemplar of past Florentine nobility and virtue, uses *essempro*, the vernacular equivalent for Latin *exemplum*, in the poem's most detailed statement on characterization: 'For that reason have been shown to you, in these wheels, on the mountain, and in the woeful valley, only souls that are known to fame; because the mind of one who hears will not pause or fix its faith for an example that has its roots unknown or hidden' (Però ti son mostrate in queste rote, / nel monte e ne la valle dolorosa / pur l'anime che son di fama note, / che l'animo di quel ch'ode, non posa / né ferma fede per essempro ch'aia / la sua radice incognita e ascosa; *Par.* XVII, 135–41). Cacciaguida clearly intends his term to cover both positive and negative exemplarity, a diversity of attitudes more common in religious than secular accounts of *exempla*. Here we read that 'the fear of God ... is the first gift of the Holy Spirit',[16] namely, the spur to move from sin to beatitude. Still, the ethical value of the *exemplum* and the person presented therein remain inextricable. The totality of the description given, including positive assertions and anything left unsaid, contributes to its value for the reader or listener.

Accustomed to the conventions of medieval preaching, Dante's first readers immediately associated his depiction of the afterlife with an ethical and spiritual reflection on the fate of each character encountered. They thus reached a consensus that the persons encountered on the journey are the essential vectors of the poem's message. The epistle to Cangrande gives a typical summary: 'The subject, then, of the whole work, taken in the literal sense only, is the state of souls after death' (*Ep.* XIII, 8). The ultimate exemplary narrative was, of course, the Gospels, which were both a source of *exempla* and the historical fulfilment of Old Testament typology. This coexistence of type and antitype, source and symbol, allowed for a widespread recapitulation and expansion of biblical characters that formed part of every type of cultural expression in the Middle Ages. The *Comedy* clearly follows in this trend, building on the *exemplum*'s capacity to produce ethically fruitful narratives no matter their affective qualities – pleasure or fear, desire or repugnance.

The ancient commentators moreover observe that the *Comedy*'s use of sacred exemplarity makes it a hermeneutically complex text like the Bible. They therefore apply to the characters of the poem pluralistic modes of interpretation from Scriptural commentary – typically the fourfold senses of history, allegory, morality, and spirit. As with the multiple senses of the biblical text, the historical level is always primary and so the characters' identities are not effaced by any additional significances they bear. Indeed, the commentators expend particular effort in their exposition of the poem's many characters from the recent past. They appear conscious that these figures are receiving this kind of portrayal for the first time and that their analyses will carry the weight of primacy.

The philosopher-poet Cecco d'Ascoli also recognized the importance of Dante's use of examples from recent history, albeit less sympathetically. The *Acerba* (c.1324–7) contains a sarcastic prologue to his own consideration of the celestial spheres: 'Here one does not sing like a poet, inventing empty things in his imagination. No, here shines forth and glitters every kind of nature that brightens the mind of he who understands it. Here no one is wandering through a dark wood. Here I do not see Paolo or Francesca'.[17] Cecco's primary dispute is with *Paradiso* – whose encounters with blessed souls arrayed across the celestial spheres he deems inferior to his own, unmediated, appreciation of 'every kind of nature'. Nonetheless, he cites *Inferno* V's beguiling lovers as the *Comedy*'s characters *par excellence*, reinforcing Cacciaguida's lesson that compelling human exemplars, positive and negative, are essential to the poem's narrative ethics.

Static Characters: Virtue and Voice

The paradigmatic case of characterization in the *Comedy* is an encounter between the protagonist and a character located in a given zone of the afterlife who represents or exemplifies that place's moral virtue or vice. Already in Dante's time, readers like Cecco d'Ascoli saw such dialogues as microtexts in their own right.

The pilgrim's encounters with static characters follow an identifiable pattern with a number of stages, although not all are present every time and the order may vary. First there is a moment of recognition or acknowledgement, which can come from the pilgrim (Brunetto Latini, Nino Visconti), from the shade itself (Farinata, Casella), or from another character – Virgil, Beatrice, another soul (respectively, Ulysses, Adam, Bonagiunta). Next follows an initial dialogue that explores the historical identity and context of the shade in question, always with an eye on the relevance of these details either to Dante or to the speaker. Many encounters stop here and, with some licence, we can view such abbreviated exchanges as a character sketch (*effictio*).

On occasions, there are further interventions by the pilgrim, his guide, or the interlocutor. These exchanges tend to be of much broader scope than the initial conversation, and naturally give a more extended description of the character (*notatio*). Despite rhetoricians' privileging of *effictio*, these encounters tend to be the more memorable and influential ones in the poem: they include Francesca, Brunetto, Manfred, Guido Guinizzelli, Thomas Aquinas, and Cacciaguida, to name but a few.

Finally, certain static characters, including Ulysses, Ugolino, Justinian, speak uninterrupted for an extended period in the manner of the rhetoricians' *sermocinatio*. Much of their characterization occurs therefore through their own voice, in a manner similar to dramatic writing. Such characters are necessarily among those described at length and so tend to be doubly memorable.

After the encounter, there is often a moment of farewell, which can be mutual or internal to the pilgrim. Where this is present, it summarizes the encounter with the character in the focalization of the narrator. (*Focalization* is a narratological term indicating the person, if any, whose interior world a given narrative moment most closely represents).[18] Where there is no explicit leave-taking, the character's own words or actions take on a greater metaliterary significance as they become the keys to their own interpretation.

One static character who participates in all three stages of acknowledgement, dialogue, and dismissal is Marco Lombardo. In *Purgatorio* XVI, the fiftieth canto of the poem, Dante and Virgil are enveloped in black smoke on the third terrace of Purgatory. Dante keeps close behind his guide, who explains that the souls here are repenting the sin of wrath. Virgil's knowledge of Mount Purgatory has already been shown to be partial several times, forcing him to ask the penitents themselves for guidance. His resumption here of the role of an externally focalized 'omniscient narrator' sets up a strong contrast between his voice and the next to intervene. Directly after Virgil's speech, Marco Lombardo starts speaking unannounced and addresses the pilgrim: 'Who then are you that cleaves our smoke and speaks of us just as if you still measured time by calends?' (Or tu chi se' che 'l nostro fummo fendi, / e di noi parli pur come se tue / partissi ancor lo tempo per calendi?; 23–5). Marco's dramatic first intervention perfectly exemplifies Dantean characterization: it defines him in a way that is distinctive and yet intricately related to the broader context of the narrative. These interrelations immediately raise moral and hermeneutic questions that transcend the character's identity, even as his voice quickly carves out a particular role in the poem.

Marco's abrupt salutation naturally causes one to wonder if he remains guilty of the sin of anger purged on this terrace. The gambit 'Or tu chi se'?' echoes Paul's righteous condemnation of arrogant human judgement at Romans 2:1: a passage that moral treatises of the era invoked to urge restraint of angry speech: 'Who are you, that you want to speak to someone else? . . . the blessed Paul says in his Letter to the Romans: O you man who judges, you cannot excuse yourself, since in the act of judging another you condemn yourself'.[19] Marco is one of three characters, one in each *cantica*, to address Dante reproachfully using the phrase 'Or tu chi se'?': Bocca degli Abati hurls it at him from the ice of Cocytus after the pilgrim kicks the sinner's protruding head (*Inf.* XXXII, 88); the Eagle of Justice levels it as a challenge to the limitations of Dante's human judgement (*Par.* XIX, 79). Marco's brusque salutation thus links him both to the self-interested resentment of the treacherous and to the righteous anger of the just, without aligning him completely with either. Arguably, this is the one time where the character's angry tone is not immediately merited by the pilgrim's actions.

The suggestion of Marco Lombardo's volatile temper returns with his equally terse farewell: he is unable to finish explaining to Dante who is 'the good Gherardo' ('l buon Gherardo; 124) because he flees on glimpsing the brightness of the next terrace's guardian angel through the smoke (141–5). But within this apparently wrathful frame, Marco's speech takes on a different quality. The smoke of the terrace's punishment, which blinds both Marco and Dante, licenses the conversation between them as necessary in spite of human imperfection: 'if the smoke does not let us see, hearing will keep us together instead' (e se veder fummo non lascia / l'udir ci terrà giunti in quella vece; 36–7). Moreover, it is Dante, not Marco, who prolongs their dialogue after the penitent indicates that the travellers will escape the smoke if they continue ahead. Intrigued by the claim 'I knew the world and loved that worth at which all have now unbent the bow' (del mondo seppi, e quel valore amai / al quale ha or ciascun disteso l'arco; 47–8), Dante asks Marco to elaborate on the disappearance of virtue from the political sphere.

Marco then speaks at length (*sermocinatio*), raising vast issues that fit with his reputation for wisdom: political virtue; free will; the divine creation of the soul; the role of law; the need for separate temporal and spiritual powers; the recent history of North-Central Italy; and the damaging political primacy of the papacy. Without going into these questions in detail, we can characterize the voice in which Marco expounds them as one that expresses human anger rooted in a desire for justice.

Some commentators have described Marco Lombardo as an autobiographical representation reflecting the historical Dante's own ideology and emotional outlook. The political reform Marco desires is certainly reminiscent of that which Dante himself supports in his other writings (principally *Convivio* IV and the *Monarchia*). He is angry, indeed excessively so, and he expresses himself several times with the bitterness of a Cassandra: 'Laws there are, but who sets hand to them?' (Le leggi son, ma chi pon mano ad esse?; 97). Again, this tone is one that Dante himself adopts in his letters from the period of Emperor Henry VII's descent into Italy (1310–13). But, in fact, the character of Marco Lombardo illustrates the distinction between Dante the theorist and political thinker and the poet of the *Comedy*.

In a narrative, apparently ideological claims occur at the level of the *plot*, voiced by a character. Even a first-person assertion, such as the poet's bold claim to be writing 'the sacred poem to which both heaven and earth have set their hand' ('l poema sacro / al quale ha posto mano e cielo e terra; *Par.* XXV, 1–2), is not equivalent to the personal interventions Dante makes in the *Monarchia*. It is still more questionable to reduce a third-person character like Marco to a mere cipher for the poet's own concerns. Although Dante's beliefs undeniably inform Marco's speeches, we must account for their expression in the voice of a well-known figure: Marco's initial characterization is a sketch that evokes his depiction in *novelle* and chronicles as a wise courtier possessed of integrity and a sharp tongue.[20]

The character of Marco Lombardo incorporates a relevant *exemplum* in order to lend authority to a combination of views that is uniquely Dantean. A static character encountered on the terrace of wrath, Marco continues to purge that human flaw. He thus embodies a complex theological lesson: anger in response to political failure can be righteous sometimes and sinful at others; nonetheless, it can be repented. The literary process of characterization thereby makes a unique contribution to the poem's exploration of the connections between theology and politics that could not be replicated by a first-person intervention.

Dynamic Characters between Focalization and Voice

Dynamic characters are those that move through the different zones both of the poem and of the afterlife. They include the primary guides (Virgil and Beatrice), secondary guides (Sordello, Statius, Matelda, and Bernard of Clairvaux), and certain others who cross boundaries both textual and eschatological: e.g. the angel of *Inferno* IX, Geryon, Cato.

Dynamic characters have structurally significant roles in the poem, surpassed only by the narrator himself. This importance stems in many cases from the sheer quantitative prevalence of their voices in the poem. Moreover, the reader regularly gains access to the perspective of dynamic characters, with occasional exceptions, such as the monster Geryon. Even the angel that opens the gates of the city of Dis after Virgil has failed 'had the look of one pressed and spurred by another care than that of those before him' (fé sembiante / d'omo cui altra cura stringa e morda / che quella di colui che li è davante; *Inf.* IX, 101–3). Finally, these characters often personify exceptional or ineffable aspects of Dante's afterlife. For example, in *Inferno* IX Virgil acknowledges to Dante that it is possible, in rare cases, for the souls of Limbo to descend to the lower circles of Hell; however, the only precedent he cites is his own journey to Cocytus (23–4).

Dynamic characters generally receive extended descriptions and often deliver long speeches. Reference to accounts of these techniques by medieval theorists can help explain the seeming inconsistencies in the portrayal of dynamic characters that puzzle many modern readers. While the compact character sketch is easily confined to key qualities, it is more challenging to restrict an extended description to only '[those] features of a thing or a man [necessary] in order to prove something relevant to [the writer's] topic'.[21] Moreover, the depiction of a major dynamic character such as Virgil or Beatrice is, in effect, a great series of descriptions and speeches, spread across the shifting backdrop of places that are themselves eternal and unknowable. At times it seems justified to talk of 'recharacterization': when a dynamic character appears in a new and unexpected fashion, such as Beatrice's angry reappearance in the Earthly Paradise.

In the *Purgatorio*, the narrative gestures several times to Virgil's inexperience in this realm (*Purg.* II, 61–83; VII, 37–51). This seems appropriate since Virgil has never visited Mount Purgatory as he had the depths of Hell. On the other hand, Virgil continues to guide and teach Dante all the way to the top of the mountain, at times asserting quite confidently his ability to continue fulfilling his role (*Purg.* III, 22–45; XXVII, 19–32). If we insist on psychological realism, there can be no satisfactory explanation of the limits of Virgil's understanding of Purgatory. However, the early commentators found these seeming contradictions coherent with their interpretation of Virgil's character as the epitome of human reason: capable of great insight but subject to limits that are, by nature, mysterious. Uncertainties in Virgil's characterization were thus not flaws in the exemplary reading but rather challenges to the commentator's ingenuity in applying it.

Guido da Pisa's *Declaratio super Comediam Dantis* (*c.*1328) – a vernacular exposition in eight cantos of *terza rima* with Latin glosses – resolves the problem of Virgil's knowledge by declaring him 'no longer [the one] who guides Dante but rather his associate' in *Purgatorio*, with Cato of Utica his replacement.[22] For Guido, the poem's three parts each correspond to a human faculty: natural reason for *Inferno*; moral virtue for *Purgatorio*; and spiritual virtue for *Paradiso*. Since Cato unquestionably embodies moral virtue, Guido believes his example hovers over the ascent of Purgatory as complementary, metaphysical guide for Dante until he attains the summit. His pluralistic approach to characterization allows Guido to account for the manifest tensions in the character of Virgil without denying their existence.

As a representative of the dynamic characters, we will examine Matelda, who guides Dante in the short gap between Virgil and Beatrice in the Earthly Paradise (XXVIII–XXXIII). Matelda's characterization is unique in a number of ways, especially as regards the thorny question of her identity. Still, her participation in the poem shares much with other dynamic characters, especially other guides, who tend to appear unexpectedly and interact with their fellow characters in multiple ways.

Matelda's characterization shares the basic tripartite structure of Marco Lombardo's, although it is more complex given the greater number and variety of her exchanges with Dante. An initial encounter in *Purgatorio* XXVIII establishes Matelda as Dante's new guide in Eden. The *bella donna* then accompanies Dante throughout the six cantos of the Earthly Paradise, during which time her interventions include: advising Dante once the heavenly procession appears in canto XXIX; rousing the pilgrim twice after he faints in cantos XXXI and XXXII; mediating between Dante and the members of the heavenly procession, especially Beatrice; bathing the pilgrim in the two purgatorial rivers, Lethe (canto XXXI) and Eünoè (canto XXXIII). Matelda's farewell occurs just before the immersion in Eünoè, which also signals the end of the *Purgatorio* itself (135).

All the identifying information we receive about Matelda comes as she exits the narrative, leaving considerable uncertainty over how to integrate it with what has gone before. By comparison, the poem's final guide, Bernard of Clairvaux, appears unexpectedly, like Matelda, but soon volunteers his name. In the Empyrean, Dante turns to Beatrice and is shocked to find an old man in her place; but once he has explained Beatrice's absence, the poem's last interlocutor soon identifies himself as the twelfth-century reformer and mystic (*Par.* XXXI, 58–102).

Just as Bernard will fill the gap left by Beatrice, so Matelda helps Dante's transition away from Virgil. Bernard, however, acknowledges Beatrice's 'merits' (merti; 69), while the encounter with Matelda begins a series of events that highlight Virgil's limited understanding of Paradise. As he takes his leave of Dante, the Roman poet describes what awaits him: 'Take henceforth your pleasure for your guide ... See the sun that shines on your brow; see the grass, the flowers and trees ... till the fair eyes come rejoicing which weeping made me come to you, you may sit or go among them' (Lo tuo piacere omai prendi per duce. / ... Vedi lo sol che 'n fronte ti riluce; / vedi l'erbette, i fiori e li arbuscelli / ... / Mentre che vegnan lieti li occhi belli / che,

lagrimando, a te venir mi fenno, / seder ti puoi e puoi andar tra elli; *Purg.*
XXVII, 131–8). However, this account begins to unravel as soon as Dante
perceives Matelda (XXVIII, 38), a beautiful lady who is *not* Beatrice. From
this point forward, nothing in Dante's Eden coheres with Virgil's descriptions of it here or earlier in the *Purgatorio*. The promises of a joyful reunion
with Beatrice at the mountain's summit (*Purg.* VI, 46–8) prove especially
hollow when in fact she rebukes Dante bitterly.

Instead, it is Matelda whose initial characterization evokes the qualities of
a paradisiacal beloved: a young, beautiful, contented lady, who picks flowers
for a garland and sings beautifully. But there is no way to identify Matelda
positively from these traits; we know only that she is not Beatrice. In fact,
Beatrice is the only other character who knows anything about Matelda: she
alone uses her name (XXXIII, 119). Before then there is considerable doubt
as to whether Matelda has a historical identity at all.

Most early commentators identify Matelda with Countess Matilda of
Canossa (1046–1115), the powerful eleventh-century ruler of Tuscany
and papal ally. However, they are less concerned with Matelda's identity
than with her exemplary significance: she represents the active life,
Beatrice the contemplative. Since the early nineteenth century, critics
have proposed manifold alternative interpretations of Matelda, historical,
allegorical, and literary. But these debates typically distract from the
defining feature of her characterization: the exclusion of her name and
other identifying data until her role is all but over. In fact, Matelda
typifies the iterative characterization of dynamic characters discussed
above with regard to Virgil. Modern critics' painstaking interpretations
fail because they seek definitive conclusions free from logical impossibil-
ities like internal contradiction or equivocation. Instead, what is needed is
a theory of characterization that can incorporate the indeterminacy
intrinsic to Dante's portrayal of Matelda.

Iacomo della Lana gestures towards such a theory in his presentation of
Matelda, which refers the reader to his statement on Minos (*Inf.* V) in the
commentary's proem. Drawing on the fourfold senses of the Bible (historical,
allegorical, moral, and spiritual), Lana asserts that, while Minos may appear
'historically' in the poem as a 'demonic judge of souls', he is nonetheless
connected 'morally' to 'a king that once lived in Crete who was just and
virtuous in dealing out punishments to the wicked and rewards to the
virtuous'.[23] Lana's cross-reference implies that the connection between
the character Matelda and Matilda of Canossa is similarly labile. But, despite
the contingent nature of her identity, Matelda retains an ethically significant
role in the reader's journey through the text thanks to her exemplification of
the active life.

In fact, even Lana's interpretation of Matelda is arguably too restrictive. What she more properly exemplifies is true human fulfilment, which cannot be found exclusively in either the active or the contemplative life. This theme will return in the heaven of the Sun, with its ambivalent depiction of the mendicant orders. Already in the 1290s, Dante's *Vita nova* had confronted the relationship between vernacular poetry and medieval canons of learning, including the active life of communal politics and the contemplative life of religious devotion. The meeting with Matelda in *Purgatorio* XXVIII plays out a kind of *Vita nova* in miniature. Dante's initially erotic desire for this mysterious lady is sublimated when she evokes Psalm 92:4, which promises contemplative bliss via active metaphors applied to God: 'You have brought me joy, Yahweh, by your deeds, at the work of your hands I cry out'. In place of erotic fulfilment, Matelda offers knowledge via spirited disputation and, thereafter, access to Beatrice. In this, she reflects the *Vita nova*'s 'Ladies who have understanding of love' (*Vn* XIX [10]), who stimulate Dante's discovery of Beatrice's true praise.

The comparison is significant because Matelda's well-informed dialogue with Dante suggests her proficiency in contemplative speculation as well as action. In particular, her *corollary* (XXVIII, 135) offers a fulfilment that oscillates between the bodily and the intellectual. Matelda's term *corollario* brings into the vernacular for the first time a Latin word signifying the secondary conclusion of a philosophical argument. Etymologically, a *corollarium* was a garland (literally 'little crown'), which is what the lady was making when Dante first saw her. Matelda thus defines her long speech that closes canto XXVIII using an unprecedented term that fuses her distinctive action with the fruit of contemplation. Within this perfect hybrid of human endeavour Matelda praises pagan poets who wrote of the Golden Age, including Virgil in his *Georgics* and *Eclogues*, for capturing something of the bliss of Eden. *Purgatorio* XXVIII, and with it Matelda's initial characterization, ends with a momentary idyll only she could create: the delight of Virgil and Statius smiling in satisfaction at this ladylike, erudite validation of their craft, while Dante looks on admiringly.

The moment of bliss is just that, however: a moment. At the beginning of *Purgatorio* XXIX, a heavenly procession appears, transforming Eden from a joyous dwelling into a stage for Beatrice's entry into the poem and, with her, the pilgrim's conduit to divinity. Having helped Dante when Virgil's insight fell short, Matelda now becomes his mediator to Beatrice. Dante and Virgil share a dumbstruck look after glimpsing the candlesticks at the vanguard of the triumphal marchers, but Matelda chides Dante to look past this awesome first impression to the holy symbols that follow (55–63). The pilgrim obeys, not realizing as he does that the glance he just shared with Virgil was his final interaction with his first guide, whose powers of understanding do not extend past that initial dazzling vision.

In the remainder of the Eden cantos, it is Matelda, not Beatrice, who ministers to Dante's body: bathing him in the purgatorial rivers and awakening him when he faints. Again, this role is reminiscent of the *Vita nova*, where a 'Gentle lady of a young age' tends to Dante while he has a feverish premonition of Beatrice's death (*Vn* XXIII [14]); moreover, it again combines action and contemplation. Physical contact with the two rivers has an important mental effect – respectively, the forgetting of sinful memories and the restoration of virtuous ones – whereby the pilgrim becomes 'pure and ready to mount to the stars' (puro e disposto a salire alle stelle; XXXIII, 145). Matelda clearly understands this and, when Beatrice asks why Dante has forgotten the nature of Eünoè, she confidently asserts that Lethe is not the cause (115–26).

Still in the period after the pilgrim's immersion in Lethe but before that in Eünoè, Beatrice provides identifying details about Matelda: her name and the suggestion that her ministrations are not unique to Dante (119–29). However, our reinterpretation of Matelda in light of these details is complicated by one of the poem's most inscrutable instances of focalization. Beatrice addresses Matelda and the protagonist listens as they discuss the limitations of his memory. The narrative situation poses an awkward question: how did the pilgrim, still unrestored by Eünoè, retain this exchange with 'his weakened faculty' (tramortita sua virtù; 129)? If there is a moment where the *Comedy*'s poetic 'I' seems to evanesce in favour of a third-person, omniscient narrator, it is surely this discussion between the two enlightened ladies about the probable cause of the pilgrim's ignorance.

The examples of characterization considered in this chapter demonstrate the importance of third-person figures in generating the *Comedy*'s meaning. Its dialogical narrative structure creates a vast conversation between a multitude of voices, the significance of which is not reducible to abstract propositions or personal experience. The continuous presence of the first-person narrator gives this conversation its unity. But its hundreds of other participants are integral to the expressive variety that has captivated readers of the *Comedy* for seven centuries.

Notes

1. G. Genette, *Narrative Discourse* (Ithaca: Cornell University Press, 1980), p. 244 (emphasis in the original).
2. B. Delmay, *I personaggi della 'Divina Commedia'* (Florence: Olschki, 1986), p. xix.

3. E. Auerbach, *Mimesis: The Representation of Reality in Western Literature* (Princeton University Press, 1953), p. 190.

4. G. W. F. Hegel, *Aesthetics: Lectures on Fine Art*, 2 vols. (Oxford: Clarendon, 1975), II, 1104 (emphasis in the original).

5. U. Foscolo, 'Articoli della Edinburgh Review' in G. da Pozzo and G. Petrocchi (eds.), *Studi su Dante*, 2 vols. (Florence: Le Monnier, 1979), I, 1–145 (pp. 112, 114; November 1818).

6. F. De Sanctis, 'Il Farinata di Dante' (1869) in S. Romagnoli (ed.), *Lezioni e Saggi su Dante* (Turin: Einaudi, 1997), pp. 653–80 (p. 679).

7. B. Croce, *La poesia di Dante* (Bari: Laterza, 1921), p. 56. Contini finds an analogous unity in the *Comedy*'s 'composite expressivity' of poetic voices; see his ' Un esempio di poesia dantesca' in *Un'idea di Dante* (Turin: Einaudi, 1976), pp. 191–213 (p. 201).

8. See *trespas* (digression) and *demonstrance* (characterization), in Brunetto Latini, *Tresor*, ed. P. Beltrami (Turin: Einaudi, 2007), pp. 664, 666 (III, 13, 9–11).

9. Bono Giamboni, *Fiore di rettorica*, ed. G. B. Speroni (Pavia: University of Pavia, 1992), p. 51.

10. *Rhetorica ad Herennium* (Cambridge, MA: Harvard University Press, 1954), p. 184 (III, 9).

11. Genette, *Narrative Discourse*, pp. 25–32.

12. Iacomo della Lana, *Commento alla 'Commedia'*, ed. M. Volpi with A. Terzi, 4 vols. (Rome: Salerno, 2009), I, 117.

13. Ibid., I, 812, 814.

14. Giamboni, *Fiore di rettorica*, p. 44.

15. C. Gallagher, 'The Rise of Fictionality' in F. Moretti (ed.), *The Novel*, 2 vols. (Princeton University Press, 2006), I, 336–63 (p. 351).

16. Stephen of Bourbon, *Tractatus de diversis materiis predicabilibus*, ed. J. Berlioz, 3 vols. (Turnhout: Brepols, 2002–15), I, 16.

17. Cecco d'Ascoli, *L'Acerba*, ed. Marco Albertazzi (Lavis: La finestra, 2002), IV, 13, 2–7.

18. See Genette, *Narrative Discourse*, pp. 185–9.

19. Albertano da Brescia, *Trattati morali volgarizzati da Andrea da Grosseto*, ed. F. Selmi (Bologna: Gaetano Romagnoli, 1873), p. 5.

20. 'Marco Lombardo was a noble courtier who was very wise ... And this led to a witty remark [by Marco]': *Il Novellino*, ed. A. Conte (Rome: Salerno, 2001), p. 257. 'And then, what a wise and virtuous courtier called Marco Lombardo had prophesied to Count Ugolino would happen to him happened': G. Villani, *Nuova Cronica*, ed. G. Porta, 3 vols. (Parma: Guanda, 1990–91), I, 588 (VIII, 121).

21. Brunetto, *Tresor*, p. 664 (III, 13, 10).

22. Guido da Pisa, *Expositiones et glose; Declaratio super Comediam Dantis*, ed. M. Rinaldi, 2 vols. (Rome: Salerno, 2013), II, 989 (*Declaratio*, gloss to I, 43–63).

23. Lana, *Commento*, I, 114; and see II, 1524 for the cross-reference.

4

GEORGE CORBETT

Moral Structure

The epistle to Cangrande, purportedly written by Dante towards the end of his life as a commentary on his poem, classifies the *Commedia* as 'a work of ethics': its purpose is to lead people from the misery of sin and to direct them to the beatitude of Heaven (XIII, 15–16). In the poem itself, Beatrice commands Dante-character to write 'for the good of the world which lives badly' (in pro del mondo che mal vive; *Purg.* XXXII, 103). The *Commedia* is thus 'vital nourishment' (vital nodrimento; *Par.* XVII, 131) because, by depicting the state of souls in the three realms of the medieval Christian afterlife, it shows how a person – through the use of free will – may merit eternal happiness in Paradise, eternal damnation in Hell, or require temporary expiation for sin in Purgatory (*Ep.* XIII, 11). Dante projects these three realms onto the contemporary geocentric world view (the earth as the centre of the cosmos), creatively joining his original moral vision to the macro-history of salvation. Dante imagines that when Satan fell from Heaven, the earth in the northern hemisphere recoiled in horror, creating the spiralling funnel of Hell. This displaced mass of earth then formed the conical mountain of Purgatory in the southern hemisphere, humanity's way back to God. As the pilgrim descends into Hell, he encounters increasingly grave human evils until he reaches Satan at the earth's exact centre. As he ascends the mountain of Purgatory, he gets ever closer to God and ever further from Satan: the vices he travels through thus decrease in gravity. Likewise, as he ascends through the nine heavenly spheres on his way to the Empyrean, he meets blessed souls characterized by ever greater virtues and ever greater holiness. In short, the poem follows the simple, moral-geographical law that to rise up is good, to sink down is bad.

However, Dante's moral vision is especially innovative for its detailed and systematic ordering of saints and sinners. At a fundamental level, the number symbolism of three (the Trinity) and nine (creation) underpins the poem's moral structure. There are nine circles of Hell and, with the notable exceptions of circles one and six, there are three main categories of evil:

incontinence (circles two to five); violence (circle seven); and fraud (circles eight to nine). There are nine principal areas of Purgatory: the seven terraces that purge the seven capital vices (pride, envy, wrath, sloth, avarice, gluttony, and lust) are framed by the two regions of Ante-Purgatory and the Earthly Paradise. And there are nine heavens of Paradise, governed by the nine orders of angels. Although the moral structure is less explicit in Paradise, Dante does seem to allude to the three theological virtues (faith, hope, and charity) and the four cardinal virtues (prudence, fortitude, justice, and temperance) in the first seven planetary spheres. Furthermore, Dante-character is examined on the three theological virtues in the eighth heaven of the Fixed Stars.

Topographical markers are further delineators of moral structure. These are particularly clear in Purgatory (the seven terraces of the mountain) and in Paradise (the planetary heavens). The moral structure of Hell, however, is particularly complex. Dante divides up its multiple regions and sub-regions through a variety of topographical elements, drawing upon a range of sources from classical texts, such as Virgil's *Aeneid* and Statius' *Thebaid*, to Christian voyage and vision literature and preaching manuals. Upper Hell (circles one to five) is entered through a gateway; Lower Hell (circles six to nine) is within the city of Dis. A steep cliff divides the sins of violence (circle seven) from the ten 'evil ditches' (Malebolge) of simple fraud (circle eight), while a central well sets apart the treacherous (circle nine). Differing landscapes are used to subdivide regions: thus, a bloody river, a thorny wood, and a fiery desert segment the seventh circle of violence into violence against another, against self, and against God. Dante draws especially on Virgil's depiction of the pagan underworld in *Aeneid* VI, transforming this material in ingenious ways. He borrows four rivers to mark off groups of sinners: Acheron divides the 'neutrals' from the rest of the damned sinners (*Inf.* III); Styx contains the wrathful and the sullen (VII); Phlegethon the violent against others (XII); the icy lake of Cocytus the treacherous (XXXI). Similarly, Dante transforms mythological monsters to describe or nuance moral structure. For example, Dante gives Virgil's infernal judge Minos a monstrous tail that he grotesquely wraps around himself one to nine times depending on the circle of Hell allotted to a sinner's damnation (V, 4–12).

How original, then, is Dante's moral system, and what might it indicate about his wider political and theological outlook? What criteria does he employ to judge that some sins are worse than others, and conversely that some goods are more valuable than others? How, moreover, does Dante represent the moral structure of his afterlife in the poem? After all, Dante could have started his poem with a 'table of contents' outlining the moral structure of each of the three canticles. But he chose not to, deliberately withholding the kind of bird's eye view provided by later commentators, especially in the Renaissance, and by introductory visual diagrams in modern editions of the poem. It is only a third of the way through Hell (XI), half way through Purgatory (XVII), and two-thirds of the way through Paradise (XXII) that we find a gloss on the regions' moral structures. We should be sensitive, therefore, to the way in which Dante progressively builds a moral structure into his poem and to its narrative effects.

Inferno

One of many interpretations of the three beasts that Dante-character encounters at the beginning of his journey – the leopard, the lion, and the she-wolf (*Inf.* I, 31–60) – is that they represent the basic tripartite moral structure of Dante's Hell: incontinence, violence, and fraud. However, such symbolism is allusive at best, and the actual moral classification of sins occurs only after Dante-character has entered the city of Dis. Without the benefit of scholarly diagrams and maps, the first readers of Dante's poem would have been initially disorientated as surprise builds upon surprise: the pilgrim's first moral guide is not an authoritative Christian saint but the pagan poet Virgil; the first group of sinners encountered, the 'neutrals', are unknown to medieval theology and entirely Dante's own invention (III, 21–69); the first circle of Hell, Limbo, is radically revised by Dante to include virtuous pagans. Given that the second circle is devoted to lust, the third to gluttony, the fourth to avarice and prodigality, and the fifth to wrath, the reader might naturally suppose that the seven deadly sins (or capital vices) is an ordering principle. But Dante sets up this expectation only to frustrate it, for the system of the seven deadly sins then decisively breaks down. Although sloth may be implicitly condemned as a counterpart to wrath (VII, 115–26), there is no circle dedicated to either envy or pride, despite these two remaining deadly sins being referenced alongside avarice, in *Inferno* VI, 74. Boccaccio first claimed that the opening of *Inferno* VIII – 'Continuing, I have to tell' (Io dico seguitando) – represents Dante's return to writing after a decisive break, and some critics suggest that Dante changed his mind about the moral structure of Hell in the process of writing. It has been argued, for example, that Dante originally intended to embody envy in Cavalcante de' Cavalcanti and pride in Farinata, and only later salvaged the material in his masterly creation of the tenth canto of the Epicureans. Dante, of course, ultimately deploys the scheme of the seven vices to structure Purgatory. Whether or not he originally intended the scheme for Upper Hell, its suggestion remains strong, providing interesting points of parallel and contrast with its later development in the second canticle.

The delayed classification of moral evil is presented when the pilgrim and Virgil are unable to descend further because of the horrible stench cast up by the abyss of Lower Hell. They are forced to wait while they become accustomed to it and Virgil makes the time profitable by finally explaining Hell's moral structure (XI, 16–66). There is a threefold distinction: first, between incontinence (Upper Hell) and malice (Lower Hell); second, between malice through violence (circle seven) and malice through fraud (circles eight and nine); and third, between simple fraud like counterfeiting, which deceives a stranger who has no particular reason to trust us (circle eight), and treacherous fraud like betraying one's own father, which deceives someone who has a special reason to trust us, and thus breaks a special bond of love (circle nine). Many scholars have posited an inconsistency in Virgil's rationale that apparently derives from Dante's fusion of two sources. Where Cicero's *De officiis*, I, 13 subdivides malice into violence and fraud (XI, 22–4), Aristotle's *Ethics*, VI, 1–6 distinguishes between incontinence, malice, and mad bestiality (79–84). However, Virgil's rationale is arguably consistent. On such an interpretation, the Ciceronian and Aristotelian usages of the term 'malice' (22 and 82) both map onto the region of Lower Hell as a whole; the Ciceronian subdivision between 'violence and fraud' differentiates circles seven and eight; the Aristotelian 'mad bestiality' serves as a subcategory of the genus 'malice' to indicate extreme cruelty, thereby differentiating circles eight and nine. In this way, Virgil's rationale effectively demarcates the four main regions of Hell: the four circles of incontinence; the three 'rings' (*gironi*) of violence; the ten concentric 'pouches' (Malebolge) of simple fraud; and the pit of Cocytus consisting of four sub-circles of treacherous fraud.

The circles of incontinence follow the principle of 'counter-punishment' (contrapasso; *Inf.* XXVIII, 142) explicitly referenced by the Occitan poet Bertran de Born, according to which infernal suffering reflects the nature of the sin being punished. For Dante, human beings are rational animals: as incontinent sinners subject their reason to their desire (they know what the right moral action is but, despite this, do evil because of an overwhelming passion), they become – *in act* – like a beast or even like vegetative or inanimate matter. For the lustful sinners stripped of reason, the sensual pleasure of touch, shared by all animals, becomes their overpowering desire, and in Hell, in keeping with medieval bestiary lore, they are consequently compared to birds buffeted by the wind (*Inf.* V). For the gluttons, bodily nourishment necessary also to plant life becomes their overriding desire. In Hell, they appear human but in reality they have become indistinguishable from beasts and wallow in their own filth like dogs and pigs (*Inf.* VI). The avaricious make material goods, inanimate matter, their goal and become in Hell little better than the boulders they must endlessly push around (*Inf.* VII). Finally, according to the extent of their wrath, the sinners in the fifth circle are submerged by degrees in a river of blood (*Inf.* VIII).

As Virgil clarifies (XI, 28–33), the seventh circle of violence is divided into three rings: violence against one's neighbour (*Inf.* XII); against oneself (*Inf.* XIII); and against God (*Inf.* XIV–XVII). Modern commentators typically trace this triple division to Aquinas but, even if this is his source, Dante uses these categories in a very different way: for example, the classification 'sins against the self' includes, for Aquinas, the intemperate sins of gluttony and lust, whereas, for Dante, it is restricted to wilful self-destruction (suicide or a squandering of one's own possessions). More convincing, in my view, is that these three victims of man's violence (neighbour, self, and God) are connected to the parallel victims of man's hatred in Virgil's corresponding lecture on the moral structure of Purgatory (*Purg.* XVII, 104–14). Virgil explains there that one cannot hate God directly because God is the necessary cause of our existence. One can rebel against God indirectly, however, insofar as our disordered will hates God's effects such as His supremacy or His prohibition of sins. In this way, violence against God is possible. Similarly, we cannot hate ourselves directly but we can do violence to ourselves. Thus, for example, we may misjudge as good in some respect something that is, in fact, evil: the suicide may kill himself in order to end misery and suffering. From Virgil's lecture in Purgatory, therefore, we may understand why violence against self (our very existence) and against God (the origin of that existence) are – for Dante – not only possible but progressively more grave than violence against neighbour (who is outside our existence). Virgil's threefold division of violence against God into blasphemy (*Inf.* XIV), sodomy (*Inf.* XV–XVI), and usury (*Inf.* XVII) in the third ring of violence (a sterile desert battered by a rain of fire) requires, however, further comment and, in the narrative, provokes Dante-character's puzzlement (XI, 94–6). Citing Aristotle's *Physics* and, for further confirmation, the theological authority of Genesis, Virgil argues that Nature takes its course from the Divine Intellect, while human work takes its course from Nature. Where blasphemy scorns God directly, the sexual act of sodomy (whether between two men or between a man and a woman) disdains the principle of fertility in Nature and, consequently, indirectly scorns God. Usury – the lending of money at interest – scorns Nature because, as Aristotle argued, it is unnatural that money should beget money (*Politics*, I, 10). It also derides human work because the creditor does not add value and instead receives something (the interest) for nothing (the original sum of money is returned risk free).

Virgil allots only a single *terzina* to the ten species of simple fraud (circle eight): 'hypocrisy, flattery, divining, impersonators, theft and simony, panders, barrators, and like filth' (ipocresia, lusinghe e chi affatura, / falsità, ladroneccio e simonia, / ruffian, baratti e simile lordura; XI, 58–60). Virgil's list is in no apparent order, and two sins are missed out entirely. Is this accidental? Is it just for convenience of versification and rhyme? Does Dante, at this point of writing, not have a clear plan of how he will structure Malebolge? Whatever the reason, there is a clear narrative effect: the reader must discover those sins unnamed by Virgil – the counsellors of fraud (eighth *bolgia*) and the sowers of scandal and schism (ninth *bolgia*) – and also the respective gravity of the sins enumerated. Moreover, it may be that Dante is more concerned to stress the generic effect of simple fraud, which offends against the natural bond of love between human beings, than its degrees (and it is noticeable that no more detailed rationale is given). In this light, it is striking that half of Dante's *Inferno* (cantos XVIII–XXXIV) is concerned with the sin of fraud, whether simple (circle eight) or treacherous (circle nine). The moral weighting of *Inferno* arguably reflects Dante's profound concern with the way in which fraud perverts human reason and its expression through language. As Zyg Barański has demonstrated, Dante succeeds in integrating nineteen out of twenty-four of the 'sins of the tongue' listed in Peraldus' thirteenth-century preaching manual *De vitiis* in Malebolge.[1] Furthermore, all the sins of fraud undermine the very foundations of civil society, as Pietro Alighieri's gloss to *Inferno* XI, 52–60 highlights with its references to Aristotle's *Politics* and to Justinian's code, the *Corpus Juris Civilis* (the collection of fundamental works in jurisprudence, issued between 529 and 534 by order of the Eastern Roman emperor Justinian).[2] In the last pocket of Malebolge, this is emphasized by the punishment of the falsifiers: for their corruption of the 'body politic' through alchemy, impersonation, counterfeiting (especially of coinage), and lying, they must suffer eternally four horrific diseases: leprosy; insanity; dropsy; and a raging fever.

The social-political dimension of Dante's moral structure is reinforced in the pit of Cocytus (circle nine), where treachery is punished in four subcircles: Caina (to kin); Antenora (to country); Ptolomea (to guests); and Judecca (to lords and benefactors). In Dante's hierarchy, the first loyalty is to one's lord, the second to guests, the third to country, and the fourth to family. Dante thus considers it worse to betray one's lord than to betray members of one's own family. This reflects a key link between Dante's ethical theory and his imperial political philosophy. Where the Florentine state, keen to assert its independence, was soon to celebrate the republican Brutus,

Dante audaciously counterpoises Brutus and Cassius' betrayal of Julius Caesar with Judas' betrayal of Christ: the three sinners are endlessly chewed in Satan's three mouths. Dante considers Brutus and Cassius the very worst sinners precisely because, betraying their lord, they sought to frustrate the divinely ordained establishment of a universal ruler.

Although Virgil's rationale for the moral structure of Hell delineates the four principal regions of Hell that take up thirty of *Inferno*'s thirty-four cantos, it strikingly leaves out Hell's first section, where the 'neutrals' reside, and which lies inside the infernal gate but outside the circles of Upper Hell (*Inf.* III), as well as Virgil's own eternal resting-place, the Limbo of the virtuous pagans within the first circle (*Inf.* IV), and the very area in which Virgil gives his lecture, the sixth circle of heresy (*Inf.* X–XI). In a literal sense, these three categories are theological not philosophical, they do not concern moral evil as such, and they are not intelligible in pagan or purely rational terms. In an allegorical sense, however, these daringly original regions of Dante's Hell are the exceptions that prove the rule, arguably reinforcing the Aristotelian taxonomy underpinning the moral structure of Hell as a whole. The neutrals, who pursued neither good nor evil, may correspond to Aristotle's category of the pusillanimous: the river Acheron, on this reading, divides sins of omission (*Inf.* III) from sins of commission (*Inf.* IV–XXXIV). In the first circle of Hell, the exceptional virtue of the pagans may inversely parallel the exceptional degree of vice of the treacherous souls in the ninth circle (the pit of Cocytus). Aristotle, indeed, counterpoises incontinence with continence, malice with virtue, and extreme malice (or bestiality) with a rare superhuman level of virtue. Furthermore, where heresy is, conventionally at least, a specifically Christian sin, Dante singles out for special treatment the 'Epicureans' who are remarkable for their political and intellectual prowess, and are punished for denying the immortality of the soul rather than for any strictly moral fault.

What motivated Dante explicitly to privilege Aristotle as his primary ethical authority in Hell (in *Inferno* XI, Virgil directly cites Aristotle's *Ethics* (80), his *Physics* (101) and, arguably, his *Metaphysics* (97) within just twenty-two lines)? After all, as Alison Morgan has shown, most of the sins punished in Dante's Hell are found in popular Christian visions of the other world, or are listed in twelfth- and thirteenth-century confession manuals.[3] In major part, the cause was Dante's polemical ethical-political programme. Dante believed that the pagan Aristotle had given a comprehensive account of secular ethics, and this justified his insistence that philosophical principles were sufficient to guide humans to this-worldly felicity and to provide the basis for law in the political sphere. But why, in that case, did Dante choose Virgil, the poet of Roman empire (*Inf.* I, 73–4), and not Aristotle, 'the master of them that know' ('l maestro di color che sanno; *Inf.* IV, 131), as his moral guide? In the *Convivio*, Dante argues that, while imperial power without ethics is dangerous, ethics without political power is weak (IV, vi, 17). In *Purgatorio* VI, Dante bemoans the empty seat of empire: what use are laws if there is no one to enforce them (88–90)? Dante believed – against apologists for papal temporal power – that only a restoration of the Holy Roman Empire could lead to the establishment of moral order and therefore peace on earth. Arguably, then, one purpose of Dante's *Inferno* is to represent in the afterlife the moral justice which, in the absence of an emperor, Dante saw unfulfilled on earth.

Purgatorio

In the penultimate canto of *Purgatorio*, Beatrice glosses an allegorical representation of the Church's moral corruption (XXXII, 100–60). The final vision of the 'whore' (puttana; 149 and 160) almost certainly refers to the papacy of Boniface VIII (1294–1303) whom Dante vehemently opposed, while the detachment of the sacred chariot from the tree represents the transference of the papacy from Rome to Avignon in 1309. In opposition to a decadent Church in Babylonian captivity, Dante's *Purgatorio* presents a moral vision of the Church fulfilling its true divine mandate to lead sinners back to God. Dante draws on two important developments in the Church's ongoing reform. In response to a renewed emphasis on the practice of confession at the Fourth Lateran Council (1215–16), theologians mined the tradition of the seven capital vices as a convenient scheme for Christian ethical formation. As the doctrine of Purgatory gained more prominence in the life of the Church (it was only given the official stamp of doctrinal acceptance at the Second Council of Lyon in 1274), preachers sought to explain purgatorial suffering as, in part, an extension of earthly penance. In depicting the seven terraces of Purgatory (*Purg.* IX–XXVII), Dante thus fused this popular material on the seven capital vices with the emerging connection between earthly penance and purgatorial suffering. Dante's Purgatory is 'where the human spirit is purged and becomes fit to ascend to Heaven' (dove l'umano spirito si purga / e di salire al ciel diventa degno; *Purg.* I, 5–6).

There are, then, four key differences between infernal and purgatorial suffering. First, whereas Hell punishes sins or evil actions, Purgatory purges vices or evil habits. The seven capital vices are 'seven springs' from which 'all the deadly corruptions of souls emanate'.[4] Second, whereas corporeal suffering is unredemptive in Hell, it has a twofold purpose in Purgatory: according to its intensity, it punishes a sinner's guilt and, according to its duration, it corrects a sinner's vicious dispositions. Third, although all souls not in Paradise experience the lack of the divine vision (*poena damni*, namely, the pain of loss), this deprivation is perpetual in Hell but only temporary in Purgatory. Fourth, whereas evil is punished principally in accordance with natural ethics in Hell, the completely different moral order of Christian holiness emerges in Purgatory: 'here they make themselves holy again' (qui si rifà santa; *Purg.* XXIII, 66). Dante's treatment of wrath, avarice, gluttony, and lust is essentially different, therefore, in Hell and in Purgatory. For example, gluttony is punished in Hell as the failure of reason to moderate the appetite. By contrast, on the mountain of Purgatory (at the exact antipodes of Jerusalem, the place of Christ's crucifixion), the gluttonous souls' extreme fasting – their faces become dark, hollow, and wasted, and their eye sockets like rings without gems (22–33) – leads to spiritual union with Christ (70–5).

The moral structure of Purgatory is only articulated in the central terrace of Purgatory (*Purg.* XVII), and at the centre of the poem as a whole. Dante-character and Virgil arrive at the fourth terrace of sloth at nightfall and, as the mountain cannot be climbed without the light of the sun (symbolically without the grace of God), they are forced to wait. As in the corresponding episode in *Inferno* XI, Virgil makes the time profitable by explaining the region's moral structure. Its foundation is the universal relationship of love between the Creator and His creation: 'Neither Creator nor creature . . . my son, was ever without love' (Né creator né creatura mai . . . figliuol, fu sanza amore; XVII, 91–2). Virgil distinguishes, however, between two principal kinds of love: natural love and love of the mind ('naturale o d'animo'; 93). Natural love is shared throughout the order of creation: it is the love that makes any material body fall to the earth, fire to ascend, a plant to grow, or an animal to move towards food. As it is determined, this natural love is always without error. By contrast, rational love ('d'animo'), which specifies humans as 'rational animals', is subject to free will. As elective, this rational love may err, and such disorder is vice. For this reason, love is not only the seed of every human virtue, but also of every human action that deserves punishment (XVIII, 103–5). The function of Christian ethics, then, is the reordering of human love. As Augustine emphasizes, 'a brief and true definition of virtue is "rightly ordered love". That is why, in the holy Song of Songs, Christ's bride, the City of God, sings, "Set charity in order in me"' (*De civ. Dei*, XV, 22). Everything must be loved, including the self, insofar as it is ordered to God.

To describe this disordered love in terms of the seven capital vices, Dante adopts the moral framework provided by the Dominican friar William Peraldus in his treaties on the vices (*De vitiis*).[5] Dante divides disordered love into two main categories: love of an evil; and perverted love of a good through excess or deficiency (XVII, 94–6). The love of an evil must be directed against one's neighbour (106–14), as humans necessarily love their own existence and God as the cause of that existence. Dante defines pride, envy, and anger, therefore, as different ways by which we may hate our neighbour. The proud hope for excellence through the humiliation of others (115–17). The envious fear to lose their power, honour, or fame through the success of others, and thus desire that others be brought low (118–20). The angry, because of some injury, are desirous of revenge and are ready, therefore, to harm their neighbour (121–3). What, then, about the disordered love of the good? The unmeasured love by deficiency ('per poco di vigore'; 96) is the quiddity of sloth: the distinctive failure sufficiently to love God, the greatest good. Unmeasured love by excess ('per troppo . . . di vigore'; 96) is the genus of the three final vices of avarice, gluttony, and lust (136–9).

Virgil's doctrinal lecture may be represented poetically through the figure of the siren that appears in the pilgrim's second dream on the mountain (XIX, 1–33). As the opening metaphor of the canticle highlights (I, 1–2), our life is a sea-journey to God. The first triad of vices – pride, envy, and anger – concern internal spiritual blindness that sets us off on the wrong course leading to hatred of neighbour. This internal blindness is corrected on the three corresponding terraces: proud eyes are bent low; envious eyes stitched up; wrathful eyes plunged into impenetrable darkness. The second triad of vices concerns the disordered attraction towards external sensible things: the avaricious seek to possess all they see; the gluttons are possessed by the taste of foods and drinks; the lustful by the touch of sexual pleasure. Given where she appears, the siren arguably embodies a transition from the internal to the external triads of vices: she does not just distract the wayfarer from his true course and entice him to slow his oar (the specific vice of sloth), she seduces him to follow unworthy worldly cares and distractions. Indeed, in classical illustrations of the siren, her closed arms depict avarice; her fish's tail, gluttony; her virginal face, lust.

Dante only uses the noun 'Purgatorio' (VII, 39; IX, 49) to refer to the seven terraces of the mountain (*Purg.* X–XXVII), and Virgil's lecture just explains the moral structure of this region. As with his corresponding lecture on Hell, Virgil leaves out what are arguably the most theologically original parts of the canticle in terms of moral structure: an antechamber conventionally named Ante-Purgatory that stretches from the shore up a rock face to Purgatory's gateway (*Purg.* I–VIII); and the Earthly Paradise at the summit of the mountain (*Purg.* XXVIII–XXXIII). Dante condemns five groups of souls to Ante-Purgatory: the spiritually tardy (who must wait at the mouth of the river Tiber for their ferry crossing to the shores of Purgatory); the excommunicates (*Purg.* III); the lazy who delayed repentance (*Purg.* IV); those who repented at the last minute, even at point of death (*Purg.* V–VI); and negligent rulers (*Purg.* VII–VIII). According to a novel kind of 'counter-punishment', the souls in Ante-Purgatory – deprived temporarily of the purifying pain of sense (*poena sensus*) – are forced to wait to begin their journey of purification, and so experience exclusively the lack of the divine vision (*poena damni*). There is, in this way, a direct correlation between the souls in Ante-Purgatory and those in Limbo (who also do not suffer the *poena sensus*). There is also a key difference. The *poena damni* of the souls in Limbo is eternal: they 'live without hope in desire' (che sanza speme vivemo in disio; *Inf.* IV, 42); whereas the *poena damni* of the souls in Ante-Purgatory is temporary: they live, with hope, in desire for the beatific vision. And it is this hope that makes their waiting – for the excommunicates, thirty times the period of their contumacy; for the rest, the period equal to the duration of their earthly lives – bearable.

The emphasis in Ante-Purgatory on those who have delayed their penitence on earth and thus must wait, as a punishment for delaying, for the purifying pain of sense (*poena corrigentis*) highlights that Purgatory continues a moral process that should have started in this life. Ante-Purgatory is framed by the appearance of four stars symbolizing the cardinal virtues and three stars symbolizing the theological virtues that rise in their place (I, 22–7; VIII, 85–93). The region is characterized by a powerful nostalgia for the world left behind and, on reaching Purgatory, Dante-character is warned by the gate-keeper that 'whoever looks back must return outside' (di fuor torna chi 'n dietro si guata; IX, 132). In Augustinian terms, Christians must be in but not of this world: they are pilgrims (peregrin; II, 63) moving through a temporary dwelling place on their way to their true home, the celestial city (*De doctrina Christiana*, I, 4). In a thinly veiled allegory at the door of Purgatory (IX, 70–145), Dante-character undergoes the sacrament of penance and, on absolution, enters Purgatory to begin his satisfaction for his sins that are ritually marked as seven Ps (*peccata*) on his forehead. Through the seven terraces of Purgatory, Dante-character is purged of the seven sins and the seven Ps are miraculously erased.

The first terrace is of pride, the worst of the seven sins in the order established by St Gregory the Great. Pride and envy are both vices associated with the intellect and are graver, and thus lower on the mountain, than wrath and sloth (associated with the irascible appetite) and avarice, gluttony and lust (associated with the concupiscible appetite). The seven sins are, moreover, causally connected: thus pride begets envy as, in seeking an empty renown, the soul feels envy towards someone able to obtain it; the last vice, lust, may be caused by gluttony as the inordinate consumption of food may dispose the soul to sexual wantonness. Dante draws out different aspects of a given vice establishing, for example, a threefold division of pride in relation to time: Omberto Aldobrandeschi took pride in his ancestors (XI, 58–72); Provenzan Salvani in his present political power (109–42); and Oderisi in his future artistic fame (82–108). In keeping with popular tradition, Dante pairs each of the seven capital vices with one remedial virtue: thus pride with humility (*Purg.* X–XII); envy with charity (XIII–XV); wrath with gentleness (XV–XVII); sloth with zeal (XVII–XIX); avarice with poverty (XIX–XXII); gluttony with abstinence (XXII–XXV); and lust with chastity (XXV–XVII). These abstract vices and virtues are embodied in the vicious and virtuous actions of particular individuals in episodes taken from the Bible, from pagan myth, and from history. The narrative *exempla* are presented in contrasting ways from sculptured reliefs (humility and pride) and ecstatic visions (gentleness and wrath) to disembodied voices (envy and charity). The Virgin Mary occupies the most important role as the model *par excellence* of the path to Christian virtue, and prayerful meditation upon her life is presented as a remedy for the wounds of sin. The souls in Purgatory are also orientated to God through passages of Scripture, the beatitudes, liturgy, and major Christian prayers.

Where the pains of Purgatory as a whole were conventionally depicted as a refining fire, Dante specifically reserves fire for the seventh terrace. This has two advantages. First, Dante effectively evokes through fire the intense burning of sexual desire, whether natural (heterosexual), but potentially bordering on the bestial, or against nature (same-sex). Second, Dante brings together the final suffering of Purgatory with 'the fiery revolving sword' which guarded Eden after the Fall (Gen. 3:24), equating, thereby, the restoration of grace after ritual purgation with the recovery of a restored Earthly Paradise. However, Dante's syncretism is even more daring as he explicitly identifies Eden with 'the golden age and its happy state' dreamed by the pagan poets (l'età de l'oro e suo stato felice; XXVIII, 140). Strikingly, it is at this stage that Virgil nonetheless departs the scene. As is clear from the encounter with Statius (*Purg.* XXI–XXII), Dante conventionally believed that Virgil's fourth eclogue had prophesied Christ without the poet's awareness, so that Virgil himself had not benefited from its miraculous intuition. Although Virgil crowns Dante-character at Purgatory's summit with a will which is free, upright, and healthy (XXVII, 124–42), his role of guide is overtaken in Eden, first by Matelda and then, after a procession which allegorizes God's revelation through the books of the Bible, by Beatrice. The moral climax of *Purgatorio* is Dante-character's encounter with Beatrice, who is circled by handmaidens representing the three theological and four cardinal virtues. The pilgrim is forced to confess his sin in turning from her before having the memory of his sins washed away in the river Lethe and his good memories restored in the river Eünoè. Only then, and in the last line of *Purgatorio*, is the pilgrim finally 'pure and made ready to rise to the stars' (puro e disposto a salire a le stelle; XXX, 145).

Paradiso

With *Inferno* and *Purgatorio*, Dante combines moral schemes within invented topographies: the subterranean funnel of Hell in the northern hemisphere and the seven terraces of Mount Purgatory in the southern hemisphere. With *Paradiso*, by contrast, Dante starts with the actual universe as perceived in early fourteenth-century Ptolemaic astronomy: the seven planetary spheres; the eighth sphere of the Fixed Stars; the *Primum Mobile*; and the Empyrean. Dante informs us, however, that the souls in Paradise actually reside only in the Empyrean, the highest of the ten regions described. The blessed souls appear in the other celestial spheres just for Dante-character's benefit: in order to signify to him their different grades of beatitude (*Par.* IV, 28–39). As Scripture condescends to human faculties in attributing feet and hands to God, but means otherwise, so the blessed souls thereby condescend to Dante-character's human mode of knowing: from sense perception to intellectual cognition (IV, 40–8). There is in Dante's *Paradiso*, then, a clear distinction between what Paradise is (the ontological status of the blessed souls in the Empyrean) and how Paradise is conveyed (the illustrative appearance of the blessed souls and the angels in the nine celestial spheres). This distinction seems particularly appropriate to *Paradiso*, with Dante's insistent emphases on the limits of the human mind to comprehend divine realities and the even more limited capacity of human language to express them.

The simultaneous unity and diversity of the blessed souls – sharing the beatific vision but in different degrees – raises, however, a pressing theological question: how are degrees of beatitude compatible with the perfection of Paradise? Notably, the blessed soul to whom Dante-character addresses this question is Piccarda Donati, scion of one of the great Florentine families of the poet's time. In Purgatory, Dante-character had asked her brother, Forese, 'where is Piccarda?' (dov'è Piccarda; *Purg.* XXIV, 10), only to be informed that she 'triumphs joyous with her crown on high Olympus' (trïumfa lieta / ne l'alto Olimpo già di sua corona; 14–15). In the same encounter, Forese had prophesized the death and damnation of their brother, Corso, whom he foresees dragged 'towards the valley where guilt is never forgiven' (inver' la valle ove mai non si scolpa; 84). The hierarchy of Paradise is thus related to the central issue of divine justice in Dante's moral vision as a whole. Infernal pain, purgatorial suffering, and paradisiacal bliss are of different degrees in the afterlife because human beings are not equal in merit or fault on earth. But, as Piccarda explains, a lower degree of bliss in Heaven does not imply a lack of perfection because God's favour is proportionate to a particular individual's capacity to receive it. Repeating the word 'more' (più) thrice in two lines (*Par.* III, 65–6), Dante-character asks Piccarda, the 'least' of the blessed, if she desires a higher place. Smiling 'a little' (un poco; 67), Piccarda explains that were she to desire 'more' (più; 73) her will would be discordant with God's will: to be in God's will *is* the peace of Paradise (64–87). The pilgrim understands, thereby, both that everywhere in Heaven is Paradise *and* that the grace of the highest good does not 'rain' there in equal measure (88–90).

How, then, does Dante structure the celestial spheres to represent these different degrees of beatitude? In the *Convivio*, Dante had already used the Ptolemaic heavens to project his idea of the system of knowledge (II, xiii, 2–20), playfully connecting each discipline with a heaven by a shared characteristic: for example, the ninth sphere of the *Primum Mobile*, which sets the eight lower celestial spheres spinning in their diurnal rotation, is like ethics, which orders our learning of all the other branches of knowledge (14–18). For *Paradiso*, however, Dante rejects any straightforward analogy of this kind. Instead, alongside any symbolic significance, he insists upon the material effect of each of the heavenly spheres on the sublunar world. The discourses on free will at the centre of *Purgatorio* clarify that, for Dante, only the human intellect and will, as non-material, is free from astral influence (XVI, 67–130; XVIII, 49–75). All the human bodily organs and faculties including imagination, judgement, personality, and artistic gifts are influenced by the seven planetary heavens, an influence Dante considered to be more powerful than heredity.

As Charles Martel highlights (*Par.* VIII, 94–148), it is through these astral influences that Providence brings about the diversity in natural gifts necessary for society. Ascending through the seven planetary heavens, Dante encounters groups of souls, therefore, whose lives and missions were directly informed by the particular influences of the planetary sphere in which they appear. When we find lovers in the sphere of Venus, this is because Dante believed that the planet literally moved or disposed people under its influence to love. It is equally true, nonetheless, that the seven planetary heavens would have suggested to Dante the ethical schemes of the seven remedial virtues or the three theological and four cardinal virtues. As we have seen, the former scheme is adopted in the seven terraces of Purgatory, while the latter is anticipated by the stars in Ante-Purgatory and Beatrice's handmaidens in

Eden. For his vision of Paradise, the poet overlaps the scheme of the cardinal and theological virtues with the idea of astral influence on personality.

As the sun is the fourth planet orbiting the earth in geocentric astronomy, it was believed that the earth's shadow partly obscured the first three planets. Dante uses this 'shadowed' aspect of the heavens of the Moon (*Par.* II–V), Mercury (V–VII), and Venus (VIII–IX) to represent the three theological virtues – faith, hope, and love – tainted by earthly concerns. The equation between faith and the inconstant in vows (Moon), between hope and the glorious in earthly fame (Mercury), and between charity and the earthly lovers (Venus) is, however, no more than implicit. In fact, some scholars have interpreted these spheres in terms respectively of imperfect fortitude, justice, and temperance. Both interpretations are plausible. Piccarda was inconstant in her vow when seized from her cloister unlike, she says, St Clare of Assisi who persisted in her pledge of consecration despite threats (III, 98–9). Not holding to her vow even unto martyrdom, Piccarda thereby lacked both faith and fortitude. Justinian pursued justice on earth and consequently is presented as the ideal of the emperor-ruler. Yet he was overly motivated by the hope of earthly fame rather than by hope of eternal glory. The noblewoman Cunizza da Romano was compassionate in later life, and yet infamous for her serial lovers and marriages. Her love was intemperate and fell short of the perfect love of charity.

There is little doubt about the relationship between the next four planetary spheres and the four cardinal virtues. Prudence is clearly associated with the Christian intellectuals in the heaven of the Sun (*Par.* X–XIV), fortitude with the Christian crusader-martyrs in the heaven of Mars (XIV–XVII), justice with the just in the heaven of Jupiter (XVIII–XX), and temperance with the contemplatives in the heaven of Saturn (XXI–XXII). Yet, the scheme of the cardinal virtues is still subordinated to the primary consideration of astral influence. Thus, following Aquinas, it might have been more natural for Dante to pair prudence with temperance and justice with fortitude, as we need temperance to follow what prudence counsels, and fortitude to fulfil the social demands of justice. But Dante pairs prudence with fortitude and justice with temperance, and this is because – in terms of planetary influence – the human disposition to temperance is associated with the cold planet Saturn, while the virtue of fortitude is associated with the fiery planet Mars. Beyond the seven planetary spheres (II–XXII), the theological virtues reappear in the eighth heaven of the Fixed Stars, where saints Peter, James, and John become the shining *exempla* of faith, hope, and charity (XXIII–XXVII), and Dante-character is examined by them on each of these virtues in turn.

Although it is possible to draw out the moral structure of Dante's Paradise in this way, there is no parallel in the canticle to Virgil's lessons on the moral

order of Hell and Purgatory. There is, however, a backward glance at the
seven planetary spheres in *Paradiso* XXII, 133–5 and 151. This detached,
contemplative perspective on the world (in the tradition of the *contemptus
mundi* or contempt for all worldly concerns) is ethically significant, because
it is exactly what Dante believed was lacking in his own time, and particularly so in the Roman Church. The origins of the papacy in St Peter, of
western monasticism in St Benedict, and of the mendicant orders in St
Francis were all characterized by material poverty (88–93). But, where the
Church Fathers searched for God, the slothful modern prelates desire only
riches and worldly power: they have taken Cupidity not Poverty as their wife
(*Ep*. XI. 14–6), and their 'avarice afflicts the world, trampling the good and
raising up the wicked' (la vostra avarizia il mondo attrista, / calcando i buoni
e sollevando i pravi; *Inf*. XIX, 104). Dante's condemnation of the contemporary papacy reaches its climax in Peter's denunciation of his current
successors: in the eyes of the Son of God, the seat of the papacy is vacant,
and his burial place has become a sewer (*Par*. XXVII, 22–7).

An overarching moral theme of Dante's *Paradiso*, then, is Christian asceti-
cism and the Church's true mission to lead people to God. In the first, fourth,
and seventh of the planetary spheres, Dante places especial emphasis on
religious orders and the religious life. Piccarda and Costanza were
Franciscan nuns, 'Poor Clares', before being violently abducted from their
cloister. Thomas Aquinas and Bonaventure praise the founders of each
other's orders, St Dominic and St Francis, while denouncing the subsequent
degeneracy of their own. St Benedict, the founder of western monastic
orders, and St Peter Damian, a rigorous reformer, extol the ascetic contemplative life. Alongside a moral critique of the contemporary Church, Dante's
Paradiso also provides an ideal model for the empire and its relationship to
the Church. In the second sphere of Mercury, Dante upholds Justinian as an
exemplary emperor who reformed the civil law, he locates the corruption of
the papacy in the donation of Constantine, and he lauds pope Agapetus'
spiritual counsel of Justinian. In the sixth sphere of Jupiter, the dramatic
appearance of Ripheus and Trajan in the eye of the eagle highlights Dante's
belief in the providential role of the Roman empire to administer justice.
The heaven of Mars, moreover, celebrates the co-operation of the pope and
emperor in the liberation of the Holy Lands through the crusades, with Dante
presenting his ancestor Cacciaguida as an actual Christian martyr.
The glorious lives of the souls in Dante's Paradise not only illustrate particular aspects of virtue, therefore, but also provide models for the two
institutions of Church and empire, the 'the two suns' that, for Dante, should
make visible 'the two paths, of the world and of God' (due soli ... che l'una
e l'altra strada / facean vedere, e del mondo e di Deo; *Purg*. XVI, 107–8).

Given the sophisticated organization of evil in Hell, the school of ordered and disordered love in Purgatory, and the joyful celebration of human talents and virtues in Paradise, it is easy to lose sight of the binary division in Dante's moral universe which, from a Christian point of view, is the sole one that ultimately matters, namely, the division between those who are able and freely will to submit themselves to God's infinite love and mercy and those who, wilfully or not, are closed to God's love. The first category includes all those in Paradise and in Purgatory. The second category comprises all those in Hell. The primary condition of souls in Hell, after all, is not only the lack of the beatific vision but, crucially, the lack of any hope that they may ever attain it: on entering Hell's gate, they leave all hope behind (*Inf.* III, 9). In Purgatory, the souls are joyful – even in suffering – because of their living hope for the beatific vision. In Paradise, they enjoy this vision: 'light intellectual full of love, love of true good full of joy, joy that surpasses every sweetness' (luce intelletüal, piena d'amore; / amore di vero ben, pien di letizia; / letizia che trascende ogne dolzore; *Par.* XXX, 40–2).

This ultimate division between the damned and the saved strongly reaffirms the moral urgency of Dante's poem, written 'for the good of the world that lives badly' (in pro del mondo che mal vive; *Purg.* XXXII, 103), for those who live and, while alive, still have hope. As Manfred beautifully articulates in Ante-Purgatory, 'none is so lost that the eternal love cannot return while hope keeps any of it green' (non si perde / che non possa tornar l'etterno Amore, / mentre che la speranza ha fior del verde; III, 133–5). The poem's most powerful moral message, then, is God's love for those who turn to Him. As Manfred, smiling, confesses: 'Horrible were my sins, but the infinite goodness has arms so wide that it receives whoever turns to it' (Orribil furon li peccati miei; / ma la Bontà infinita ha sì gran braccia, / che prende ciò che si rivolge a lei; 121–3). Union with God is the fulfilment of all human desires as Piccarda, the first soul encountered in Paradise, explains: 'And in His will is our peace' (E 'n la sua volontade è nostra pace; *Par.* III, 85).

Notes

1. Z. G. Barański, *Language as Sin and Salvation: A 'Lectura' of 'Inferno' 18* (Binghamton, NY: CMRS, 2014), pp. 36–7, n. 46.
2. Pietro Alighieri, *Comentum super poema Comedie Dantis*, ed. M. Chiamenti (Tempe: ACMRS, 2002), gloss to *Inf.* XI, 52–60.

3. A. Morgan, *Dante and the Medieval Other World* (Cambridge University Press, 1990), pp. 108–43.
4. Peter Lombard, *The Sentences*, trans. G. Silano (Toronto: PIMS, 2008), II, d. 42, c. 6 (p. 210).
5. S. Wenzel, 'Dante's Rationale for the Seven Deadly Sins (*Purgatorio* XVII)', *MLR*, 60 (1965), 529–33.

5

THEODORE J. CACHEY JR.

Title, Genre, Metaliterary Aspects

Metaliterary Dante

Dante studies have dedicated great energy since at least the 1970s to investigating the metaliterary aspects of many of the *Commedia*'s main features. These include the poem's title and genre, formal characteristics such as its unprecedented *terza rima* verse form, and, in general, the self-conscious means by which Dante asserted, by virtue of the poem's transcendent subject matter and its divinely inspired artistry, the supreme authority of 'my comedy' (la mia comedìa; *Inf.* XXI, 2) vis-à-vis the previous literary tradition. Yet, while striving in the *Commedia* to provide access to a truth that transcended language and literature, Dante continually recognized and reflected not only on the limitations of the preceding literary tradition, but also on the inevitable failure of his own prodigious attempt to represent that truth: 'How incomplete is speech, how weak, when set against my thought! And this, to what I saw is such to call it "little" is too much' (Oh quanto è corto il dire e come fioco / al mio concetto! E questo, a quel ch'i' vidi / è tanto, che non basta a dicer 'poco'; *Par.* XXXIII, 121–3). At the same time that the originality and power of his poetry surpassed both secular and sacred precedents, Dante recognized the insufficiency of his own poem when measured against its transcendent subject.

His keen awareness of the intrinsic limits of human language was such that we find Dante inviting metaliterary reflection on the 'comic' literariness of his enterprise throughout the poem, and sometimes expressing an ironic, even wry self-consciousness about the inadequacy of language; for instance, as we will see, at the very moment when he first announced the poem's title, *Comedìa*, midway through the first canticle (*Inf.* XVI, 127–30). Indeed, the medieval literary theory of the doctrine of 'styles' (or *genera dicendi*) distinguished between 'high' ('tragic'), 'middle' ('comic'), and 'low' (elegiac) 'styles'. The 'tragic style' presumed a rigorous correspondence between elite subject matter, language, and style (*Dve* II, iv, 5–8). 'Comedy', on the other hand, the most wide-ranging and indefinite of 'styles', came to represent for Dante a kind of synecdoche for literature in general, in recognition of the ultimately insuperable incongruity that exists between language and truth. The metaphysical underpinnings of Dante's poem produced a literary artefact characterized by an acute metaliterary self-awareness that would remain unsurpassed in the Western literary tradition before the advent of literary modernism at the beginning of the twentieth century. Therefore, we should not be surprised that elements of Dante's reflection on the poem's status as literature, especially in connection with the fundamental question of the nature of the relationship between literary representation and truth, still remain to be recognized. For example, as will become apparent below, the role that geo-topographical similes play in the highly self-conscious poetic construction of the other world represents a hitherto little understood metaliterary feature of the *Commedia*.

Comedìa

The modern title, *Divina Commedia*, is not Dante's. It first appeared on the frontispiece of the 1555 imprint of the poem edited by Lodovico Dolce and published in Venice by Gabriele Giolito. There the adjective *divina*, frequently associated with the author Dante on the title pages of earlier editions ('Comedia del Divino Poeta Danthe': Venice: Stagnino, 1512 and 1520; Stagnino for Giovanni Giolitto, 1536), was transferred to the poem with the evident aim of increasing sales of the book. Giovanni Boccaccio (1313–75) had first referred to the work as 'la divina Comedia' in his *Treatise in Praise of Dante* (1351),[1] and it is probably no coincidence that Claudio Tolomei had reprised Boccaccio's expression in his *Cesano*, a linguistic treatise first published by Giolito in 1555, the same year as Giolito's *Divina Commedia* appeared. In any event, the title by which we know the poem today did not become standard before the middle of the eighteenth century. Until then the work had been known by various titles, including: *Commedia/Comedia*; *Commedia di Dante*; *Le terze rime di Dante* ('The tercet rhymes of Dante', titled thus by Pietro Bembo in his 1502 edition of the poem printed by the famous Venetian publisher Aldus Manutius); *Dante* (Venice: Pietro da Fino, 1568); *La Visione* (Padua: Leni, 1613; Padua: D. Pasquardi, 1629).

The instability of the title no doubt reflected uncertainties regarding the author's original intentions, doubts that date back to the earliest fourteenth-century commentators. In fact, Dante had explicitly given the title of the poem, *comedìa*, only twice, and only in the first canticle – *Inferno* XVI, 128 and XXI, 2 – albeit in highly charged metaliterary contexts. The success of the modern title, meanwhile, no doubt derived from its suggestive ambiguity.

'Divine' might refer to the subject matter or to the poetic quality of the work or both. Moreover, the contrast between the exalted attribute 'divine' and the humble genre status of 'comedy' is consistent with Dante's original intentions. Indeed, Dante wrote the poem in the tradition of the 'low style' (*sermo humilis*) of the Christian Middle Ages, that is an anti-'tragic style' inspired by Scripture that had overturned the doctrine of 'styles' by treating the 'sublime' subject of Christ's Incarnation and the redemption of humanity in a 'humble' or 'comic' register.[2]

Nonetheless, the title of the poem was the subject of controversy already among the earliest commentators. Petrarch reportedly opined that he could not understand why Dante had called it a 'comedy', and Boccaccio also questioned the title's appropriateness in the *accessus* or introduction to his *Expositions on Dante's 'Comedy'* (1373–4). However, Boccaccio concluded that, since the poem started in Hell and ended in Paradise, it could be considered to have ended happily and therefore to qualify as a 'comedy'. Boccaccio appears to echo in this explanation Dante's own rationale for the title as given in the epistle to the ruler of Verona, Cangrande Della Scala (1291–1329) (*Ep.* XIII; 1320?), whose attribution has been questioned, but which the most recent editor of the letter, Luca Azzetta, considers authentic,[3] a view with which I concur. In fact, Dante explained the title, as Boccaccio would later intuit, according to a commonplace notion of the genre, that is, in terms of the poem's trajectory from bad to good (*Ep.* XIII, 31).

For the early commentators, as for most modern critics, the issue has not been whether Dante intended to title the poem *Comedìa*; although some have argued that a secondary title, 'the sacred poem' (lo sacrato poema; *Par.* XXIII, 62, and poema sacro; *Par.* XXV, 1), introduced in two passages of the third canticle uncannily symmetrical with the two in which the title was first given in *Inferno*, should be given due consideration or even take precedence. Medieval exegetes of the Bible had assimilated the genre of 'comedy' to the biblical poetry of the Song of Songs as early as the ninth century, in light of what was considered to be the dramatic and dialogic mode of the Canticles, as well as their 'comic' theme and language, since love was traditionally considered a non-heroic or non-'tragic' subject. Based on the authority of the greatest Scriptural love poem, Dante's *comedìa*, originally conceived as a poem in praise of Beatrice: 'I hope to write of her that which has never been written of any other woman' (*Vn* XLII, 2 [31, 2]) could appropriately aspire to the sacred poetry of praise of the Canticles. Dante sought to underscore this connection by giving the secondary designation of 'sacred poem' in the third *cantica*, also in pointed emulation of Macrobius' characterization of Virgil's *Aeneid* as a *sacratus poema* (*Saturnalia* I, xxiv, 13).

Moreover, Dante appears to have derived from the Song of Songs his unprecedented formal term for the three major parts of the poem, the *cantiche* or 'canticles' of *Inferno, Purgatorio,* and *Paradiso*: 'this second canticle' (questa cantica seconda; *Purg.* XXXIII, 140). Nevertheless, the original and prior title Dante gave to the poem, and that he reaffirmed in the epistle to Cangrande, is *Comedìa*. Several years before Dante finished his poem, the poet Francesco da Barberino in his *Documenti d'Amore* (1313–14), had already referred to Dante's *commedia*, and Boccaccio would note in the *Expositions* that the title *Comedìa* 'is the one that everyone uses'.[4] Thus the critical question has mainly been – even for Dante in writing to Cangrande – what were his reasons for giving the poem the title of *Comedìa*?

In response to this question, one needs to turn to the passage in which the author's original title for the poem first appeared, *Inferno* XVI, 103–36, which ought to be considered the most crucial metaliterary passage of the first canticle and, arguably, of the entire *Comedy*. A mysterious metaliterary *corda* is introduced in connection with the announcement of the poem's title, and is retrospectively added to the details of the prologue scene of *Inferno* I: 'I had a cord around my waist with which I once had meant to take the leopard with the painted pelt' (Io avea una corda intorno cinta, / e con essa pensai alcuna volta / prender la lonza a la pelle dipinta; XVI, 106–8). Moreover, it is at this point in the poem that Dante addresses directly to the reader an emphatic claim for the truth of his *comedìa*, in direct anticipation of the imminent appearance of the monster Geryon, the symbol of fraud, who serves as the vehicle for the precipitous descent of the poet and his guide from the seventh circle of violence to the eighth circle of fraud: 'And by the strains of this comedy – so may they soon succeed in finding favour – I swear to you, reader, that I saw' (E per le note / di questa comedìa, lettor, ti giuro / s'elle non sien di lunga grazia vòte / ch'i' vidi; XVI, 127–30). From one perspective, Dante swears to the truth of the poem on its verses ('per le note'), as if swearing on the Bible, that is, as if already anticipating that his *comedìa* were indeed a 'sacred poem'. From another, more sceptical viewpoint, in making the truth claim conditional on the success of the poem with future readers, Dante appears to come 'perilously close to making a fraudulent deal'.[5] By giving a second title, the 'sacred poem', in the *Paradiso*, however, when the *Commedia*'s success with the public had already been established and on the eve of its completion, Dante, in effect, marked the satisfaction of the original vow sworn upon his *comedìa* in the first canticle.

All three elements – the *corda*, the title, and the truth claim – have been the focus of extensive scholarly investigation. In linking the *corda* to the question of the meaning of the three beasts of the prologue scene, Dante gave the commentary tradition plenty to ponder and debate. The *corda* clearly had for Dante a metaliterary valence, that is to say, at some level or other it referred to his imaginative and poetic powers. In fact, it is by means of the signal of the *corda* that Virgil casts into the abyss that one of the great inventions of Dante's prodigious literary imagination, the marvellous *monstrum* Geryon, is dramatically conjured up: '"Surely something new will answer", I said to myself, "this new gesture"' ('E' pur convien che novità risponda', / dicea fra me medesmo, 'al novo cenno'; XVI, 115–16). Likewise, at the end of the episode, Geryon departs, shot like an arrow from the *corda* of Dante's art: 'and, disburdened of our persons, vanished like an arrow from a string' (e, discarcate le nostre persone, / si dileguò come da corda cocca; *Inf.* XVII, 135–6). Moreover, in a highly paradoxical manner, the poem's title and the truth claim are announced in connection with the poetic invention of Geryon as the symbol of fraud.

To designate the poem by its genre corresponded to a standard type of medieval title (that based on a literary category rather than the name of the author or the subject of the work), and in calling the poem a *comedia*, Dante associated it with the most varied and fluid of all medieval literary categories, one that comprised a wide range of subgenres, including 'satire', and texts, including the Bible. Indeed, Dante stretches the flexibility of 'comedy' to its limits by including, in his *Commedia*, every 'style', register, language, and subject, a feature that modern scholarship has termed its 'plurilingual' or 'pluristylistic' character. The unusual form of the word *comedìa*, accentuated on the penultimate syllable in a learned Greek manner, was probably intended to call attention to its unique and unprecedented metaliterary significance.

In the epistle to Cangrande, the author notes that: 'comedy is a certain kind of poetic narration that differs from all others' (29). The unusual, not to say over-determined emphasis of the affirmation reflects Dante's awareness that he had effectively redefined 'comedy' in his *Comedìa*. Indeed, asserting the uniqueness of 'comedy' might otherwise have been taken to be banalizing in the extreme, since it was self-evident that each 'style' was unlike any other. Dante undertakes a long digression to explain his title in the epistle in a strained attempt to make more acceptable for contemporary readers the poem's revolutionary poetics. He cites key verses from Horace's *Art of Poetry* to justify the title, verses that suggest the radical redefinition of the category in the *Commedia*: '"Yet sometimes comedy her voice will raise, and angry Chremes [a comic character of Terence's] scold with swelling phrase;

and prosy periods oft our ears assail when Telephus and Peleus tell their tragic tale" [93–6]. And from this it is obvious that the present work is called comedy' (XIII, 30). These Horatian verses appear to have been quoted for their specific applicability to his *comedìa*, since they authorize the mixing of 'comic' and 'tragic' registers in contrast to the traditional strictures of the doctrine of 'styles' affirmed in the preceding verses of Horace's treatise: 'A theme for comedy refuses to be set forth in verses of tragedy; likewise the feast of Thyestes scorned to be told in strains of daily life that well nigh be fit the comic sock. Let each style keep the becoming place allotted it' (89–92).[6]

Indeed, while classical and medieval authors only cautiously indulged such liberty, Dante pushed it to its limits, going far beyond the preceding literary tradition in his blending of 'tragic' and 'comic' registers in his *comedìa*. The poet, in fact, radically reversed direction with respect to the conservative classicizing rhetorical principles that he had promoted in his *De vulgari eloquentia* in pursuit of an ideal 'illustrious Italian vernacular' (I i, 1) or 'high style'. Dante scholarship has yet fully to explain the motivations behind the poet's fundamental shift in rhetorical orientation in the transition from the unfinished linguistic treatise to the poem. In effect, Dante redefined the genre of 'comedy' in a completely original manner by bringing together in his epic poem (traditionally a 'tragic' genre *par excellence*) 'all the aspects of the "comic" that his culture recognized but which it had never actually conflated'.[7]

Among these, 'satire', which was, generally speaking, not considered one of the three 'styles' of the *genera dicendi* but rather a 'mode' of writing that could transcend their boundaries, is vital for an understanding of the distinctive character of Dante's *comedìa*, although it is not discussed in the *epistle*, probably because to have emphasized the 'satirical' nature of the poem would have been politically inexpedient given the courtly rhetorical context of the letter. In fact, the often violent invectives and polemics decrying the moral and political decadence of contemporary society that characterize all three canticles demonstrate the important role that 'satire' plays in Dante's *comedìa*, a role that did not leave unscathed members of Cangrande's family, including his father, Alberto Della Scala (*Purg.* XVIII, 121–6). Already in the Trecento, the commentator Benvenuto da Imola went so far as to suggest that Dante's poem might have appropriately been called a 'satire', since 'satire is that which criticizes audaciously and all kinds of vices nor is it intimidated by the dignity, the power of nobility of any individual'.[8]

Recent scholarship has accordingly emphasized the importance of 'satire' for Dante's conception of 'comedy', which found inspiration in medieval grammatical and rhetorical texts that associated the two (Isidore, *Etymologiae* VIII, vii, 6–7), and may also have found a source in Horace's conflation of 'comedy' and 'satire' in *Satire* I, iv, 1–7, 39–48, and 56–64. A Horatian genealogy for Dante's 'satirical' *comedìa* may explain the privileged position of 'Horace satirist' among the 'fair school' (bella scola) of poetry in *Inferno* IV (94), where Horace is the only non-epic poet celebrated and is placed second to Homer: 'he is Homer, sovereign poet; next comes Horace satirist; Ovid is third, the last is Lucan' (quelli è Omero poeta sovrano; / l'altro è Orazio satiro che vene; / Ovidio è 'l terzo, e l'ultimo Lucano; 88–90). Together with Virgil, Dante joins this exclusive cohort (101–2), implicitly for his modern Christian *comedìa*, a genre otherwise not represented among the poets of the 'bella scola'; and in figuring among the six poets of *Inferno* IV, Dante thereby transcended with his *comedìa* the classical 'comic' and 'satirical' authors, including Terence, Persius, Plautus, and Caecilius Statius, subsequently remembered in *Purgatorio* XXII, 97–108.

However, Dante's 'satirical' intent in the poem does not alone account for his radical departure from his culture's doctrine of the *genera dicendi* in favour of a biblically inspired conception of 'comedy'. Connections between 'comedy' and the Bible were widely recognized in Dante's culture. From a rhetorical viewpoint, Scripture was said to embrace all 'styles', including both the 'middle' and 'low styles', precisely those registers with which 'comedy' had been traditionally linked. Christian and biblical 'low style' (*sermo humilis*) came to coincide with the 'comic' 'low style' (*stilus humilis*). But what fundamentally distinguished 'comedy' in a Christian understanding from that of the classical literary system was the manner in which the 'lowly' and the 'sublime' were brought together in a paradoxical union whereby 'low' or 'humble' diction served a transcendent truth. Like the 'humble' Greek of the Gospels and the Latin of the Vulgate, Dante wrote his poem in a 'humble' vernacular language. His use of the *lingua volgare* (from *vulgus*, of the people) in a poetic *comedìa* of unparalleled literary ambition was unprecedented and controversial. Dante thus had to defend his choice of language in two *Eclogues* (1319), written in reply to the humanist Giovanni del Virgilio, a professor of classical literature at the University of Bologna, who had urged Dante to write in Latin rather than the vernacular. The 'comic' connotations of the use of the vernacular were also underscored in the epistle to Cangrande: 'As regards the style of language, the style is unstudied and lowly, as being in the vulgar tongue, in which even women-folk hold their talk. And hence, it is evident why the work is called a comedy' (31).

However, from a Christian perspective, the most important reason for terming the poem *comedìa* is the conventional motivation given in the epistle to Cangrande: 'For if we consider the subject matter, at the beginning it is horrible and foul, as being *Hell*; but at the close it is happy, desirable, and pleasing, as being *Paradise*' (31). The idea that 'comedy' begins badly and ends well was among the most commonplace definitions of the genre; yet, the notion is implicitly elevated to a 'sublime' level in light of the Christian connotations of the *Commedia*'s title, whose subject, as the poet states in the *epistle*, is 'man, either gaining or losing merit through his freedom of will, subject to the justice of being rewarded or punished' (34). In other words, the title 'comedy' implicates the author's position regarding an essential question, nothing less than the guilt or innocence of Dante Alighieri and of humanity before divine justice. Dante's 'divine' *comedìa* recounts both the salvation of one man ('my comedy') and of humanity in general. The title *Comedìa* points to what was for Dante the ineluctable happy ending to end all happy endings. For it was thanks to Christ's Incarnation and resurrection that the salvation of humanity was accomplished and the classical literary system superseded. Dante's shift from the classicizing vernacular humanism of the *De vulgari eloquentia* to the Christian *comedìa* thus has all the hallmarks of a Christian spiritual conversion: that of one individual, Dante Alighieri, who is also the representative of humanity, an Everyman, with revolutionary repercussions for the literary system.

Both Dante's preoccupation with justifying the title and the apparently conservative and anodyne rationale given for it in the *epistle* reflect the difficulty of Dante's personal situation at Cangrande's court when he wrote it close to completing the *Paradiso*. An anecdote recounted by Petrarch in his *Rerum memorandarum libri* (1343–5; II, 83) describes the poet's diminished standing at the court, reporting how that lord unfavourably compared Dante to a court jester, and the poet's tart reply. The fact that Dante decamped from Verona, without having delivered the letter to Cangrande, and headed to Ravenna and the more congenial court environment of Guido Novello da Polenta, where he eventually completed the poem, offers an idea of how salty had come to taste the bread Dante consumed at the court of Cangrande: 'You will experience how salty tastes the bread of another' (Tu proverai come sa di sale / lo pane altrui; *Par.* XVII, 58–9). Viewed from this perspective, the conservative and less-than-forthcoming character of the letter, which has led some scholars to doubt its authenticity, is symptomatic of the poet's difficult personal situation, and expressed his desire on the eve of publication of the complete poem that was still 'in progress' to conform as far as possible to the canons of his culture.

Similarly, Dante sought to establish his *bona fides* with contemporary natural philosophers who might otherwise have questioned the authority of the cosmology of the *Commedia* by writing in 1320, and hence around the same time as he wrote the epistle to Cangrande, the *Questio de aqua et terra*, about a relatively banal question of geophysics, namely, whether the lighter element, water, is universally higher than land. Moreover, Dante felt the need to clear up any ambiguity about the title that might have arisen once the first parts of the poem had begun to circulate a decade or so earlier. The fact that after *Inferno* XXI, 2, the work's title, *Comedìa*, is not mentioned again, and that, in *Paradiso*, Dante gave his poem a secondary designation may explain why he felt compelled to reaffirm and explain the original title as emphatically as he does in the letter to Cangrande. In fact, Azzetta considers the manner in which the question of the title constitutes a leitmotif running through its various parts as evidence in favour of the letter's authenticity.

Finally, a deeper metaliterary motivation for the title, not found in any grammatical or rhetorical repertories and unspoken in the epistle, accounts for the title's strategic emergence in conjunction with the appearance of Geryon, the symbol of fraud. In terming his masterpiece a *comedìa*, Dante acknowledged the inevitable and insurmountable distance separating language and the poem's status as *fictio* (*Dve* II, iv, 2; *Ep.* XIII, 27), namely as literature, however divinely inspired, from the truth of Christian revelation that is its ultimate referent but which, basically, was inexpressible. For Dante, the limitations of the classical and medieval *genera dicendi* transcended questions of literary propriety and efficacy. In fact, the doctrine of 'styles' had been superseded by the effects on the literary system of Christ's Incarnation and redemption of humanity. No language, whether in the 'tragic' or any other 'style', could adequately express revealed truth. In fact, Dante contrasts classical 'tragedy' and his Christian 'comedy' by evoking the designation *comedìa* for a second and final time at the start of *Inferno* XXI – 'speaking of things my comedy does not care to sing' (altro parlando / che la mia comedìa cantar non cura; 1–2) immediately after Virgil's proud self-citation of his 'high tragedy' (alta tragedìa; XX, 113), the *Aeneid*, and his guide's attempt to distinguish himself from the false prophets punished in the fifth *bolgia*. The poet pointedly pokes fun at Virgil by having his *maestro* contradict and ostensibly correct the account of the founding of Mantua that he had given in his *Aeneid* (97–102). In any event, the conventional limits of 'tragedy' and 'comedy' that are surpassed by Dante's unprecedented *comedìa* are later, tellingly, registered in connection with the praise of Beatrice's beatified beauty viewed beyond the borders of space and time in the Empyrean: 'At this pass I concede myself vanquished more than any comic or tragic poet has ever been surpassed by a point of his theme' (Di questo passo vinto mi concedo / più che già mai da punto di suo tema / soprato fosse comico o tragedo; *Par.* XXX, 22–4).

The truth claim at the end of *Inferno* XVI in connection with the presentation of Geryon is accordingly paradoxical in nature. In swearing on the notes of his *comedìa* that the monster Geryon is true, Dante implicitly acknowledges the impossibility of language to communicate truth except by means of a kind of aesthetic fraud or poetic lie. For Geryon, the marvellous figure of fraud, represents the anti-figure of the marvellous artistry of Dante's poem. In fact, the *Commedia* is the precise opposite of 'that foul effigy of fraud' (quella sozza imagine di froda; XVII, 7) whose 'face is that of a righteous man' (La faccia sua era faccia d'uom giusto; 10). Instead, the poem is 'a truth that has the face of a lie' (quel ver c'ha faccia di menzogna; XVI, 124). Dante's *comedìa* is, therefore, a 'true lie', the marvellous product of Dante's divinely inspired imagination, a poetic imagination so powerful as to produce the marvellous invention of the monstrous Geryon, an invention 'that has the face of a lie' but is nevertheless 'true'.

On the one hand, Dante claims that his poem is divinely inspired and that he is a *scriba Dei* or God's scribe (*Purg.* XXIV, 52–4), in the same sense that the authors of the Bible were not so much authors as faithful transcribers of the word of God *(Mon.* II, viii, 14). On the other, he calls attention to the limitations of human art and language 'to communicate the experience of non-contingent self-awareness ("truth") through spatio-temporal contingencies'.[9] Dante repeats this same metaliterary point throughout the poem: the *Comedìa* is a non-false error, a true lie, by continuously stressing the inadequacy of human language, including that of the divinely inspired poetry of the *Comedìa*, to communicate the truth. One way he indicates the limitations of language is by calling attention to a lack of correspondence between the vehicle and the tenor of his similes: for example, when he incongruously compares the pilgrim's successful salvific downward flight on Geryon to the failed ascents of the mythological figures Phaethon and Icarus (*Inf.* XVII, 106–11).

Generally speaking, Dante's use of simile in his representation of the otherworldly journey is designed to call attention to the poem's status as a true lie. Charles Singleton's famous dictum that 'the fiction of the *Comedy* is that it is not a fiction'[10] is not quite correct; or at any rate it does not go far enough in describing the metaliterary operation in which Dante is engaged. Rather than seek to persuade the reader of the truth of the poem's fictions in any conventional sense, the poet aims to destabilize conventional notions of the boundaries between fiction and truth. For, by regularly mixing the categories of history and myth, the fictional and the real, Dante seeks to awaken the reader to the relative nature of these categories, and to a divine truth that exceeds and is beyond time-bound notions of the real and of the true. Ultimately the metaphysical foundations of his *Comedìa* inspire both an unbounded freedom of poetic invention and an unprecedented level of metaliterary self-consciousness.

Metaliterary Aspects of Geo-topographic Similes

Geo-topographic similes and references play an important metaliterary role in the poetic *inventio* of Dante's other world. They mediate its construction in all three canticles, including the non-place of Paradise. In fact, descriptions of the Italian landscape, mistakenly considered to be primarily ornamental from a rhetorical point of view, present a metaliterary dimension that Dante systematically develops, beginning with the self-conscious manner in which he presents the third of Hell's rivers, the Phlegethon (*Inf.* XII–XIV).

Dante weaves the travellers' arrival at the third infernal river into the narrative fabric of the pilgrim's passage into and through the seventh circle of violence in a structurally complex manner. 'The river of blood in which boil those who by violence do injury to others' (la riviera del sangue in la qual bolle / qual che per vïolenza in altrui noccia; *Inf.* XII, 47–8) crosses the first ring of the violent against others who are immersed in it (*Inf.* XII, 124–32), and then circles the wood of the suicides (XIV, 11), only to re-emerge in the last ring of the seventh circle which features the violent against God. There, rather incongruously, Virgil claims that the still unnamed river is the most noteworthy thing yet encountered during the journey (XIV, 85–90). Finally, the river is described as exhaling a vapour that extinguishes the rain of fire that falls on the damned (XV, 1–3). As we will see, Virgil indirectly identifies the river as the Phlegethon when he explains the hydrological system of Hell in *Inferno* XIV. After loudly precipitating into the next section of Hell at the end of the circle of violence (XVI, 1–3; XVI, 91–105; XVII, 118–20), the Phlegethon disappears from the poem for the next thirteen cantos, only to resurface as lake Cocytus, the ninth and final circle of Hell (XXXI, 123). Like the 'coiled and knotted' (aggroppata e ravvolta; XVI, 111) metaliterary cord that Virgil removed from Dante's waist and cast down as a signal to evoke Geryon, Dante conjures up the river and entwines and interweaves it into the narrative of the seventh circle only to dispense with it.

At the beginning of *Inferno* XII, an elaborate Italian landscape simile describing the violent terrain of the seventh circle in terms of an Alpine rockslide (4–10) marks a heightened level of self-consciousness regarding the rhetorical construction of Hell as a plausible poetic space. This image is part of a series of landscape similes that cumulatively traces a map of the Italian peninsula against the background of Lower Hell, whereby the pilgrim's descent through its circles can be taken as a kind of 'journey to Italy'

(IX, 112–14; XII, 4–10; XVI, 91–105; XXVIII, 7–21). Moreover, *Inferno* XII links this Italian itinerary to Christ's harrowing of Hell, which provides a further structuring motif for the journey. The opening of the canto explicitly refers for the first time to the 'rockslide' (ruina; 4) caused by the earthquake that occurred at Christ's death. The *ruina* is a key structural and architectural feature of Hell that returns in *Inferno* XXI, 112–14, where it is used to date precisely the journey, and later as the means by which the travellers descend from the sixth to the seventh *bolgia* of the eighth circle (XXIII, 136–8). Dante's self-conscious and complex treatment of Phlegethon is in keeping with the heightened, geo-topographically inflected, narrative stakes of the river's immediate spatial context, especially the account of Hell's hydrological system presented in *Inferno* XIV. In fact, the poet introduces into his treatment of the third infernal river a sophisticated metaliterary reflection on the poem's broader representational strategies and its truth claims, a metaliterary reflection that begins in *Inferno* XII and culminates in *Inferno* XIV where the river's name Phlegethon is finally revealed.

Commentators typically identify the 'river of blood' (riviera del sangue; XII, 47) at its first appearance as the 'Phlegethon of Virgil', thus short-circuiting the rhetorical effect of Dante's delayed naming of the river, and eliding the critical question of why the river is explicitly identified only two cantos after its first appearance. Moreover, by asserting a straightforward relationship of equivalence between Dante's 'riviera del sangue', and Virgil's Phlegethon, commentators miss the opportunity to notice a point that the poet seems to have taken some pains to make, namely, that the third river presents features distinct from the Phlegethon of the classical tradition and Virgil's *Aeneid*. While the river of the *Aeneid* (VI, 549–51) is a great river of fire, Dante's river is instead a river of boiling blood, with all the corporeal and Christological associations that the liquid substance brings with it.

Dante deliberately distances his initially anonymous Phlegethon from Virgil's. His presentation of the 'riviera del sangue' thus appears designed to establish in the first instance the reality of Dante's infernal landscape above and beyond any literary precedents, that is to say, according to Singleton's famous dictum, it seeks to establish 'the fiction that it is not a fiction', and to stage the pilgrim's and, by extension, the reader's first-hand experience of the river. Accordingly, the next two allusions to the river denote without any reference to classical precedents that it is constituted of boiling blood and the site of the sinners' punishment. In both instances, Dante refers to the river as a *bulicame*, a vernacular coinage that makes its first documented appearance in Italian in *Inferno* XII. In the first, Dante describes the punishment of the tyrants who are submerged up to their necks in the 'boiling stream' (bulicame; 117). A dozen or so lines later, the centaur Nessus uses the same term to describe the river: 'Just as on this side you can see the boiling stream always diminishing' (Sì come tu da questa parte vedi / lo bulicame che sempre si scema; 127–8). In Dante, this kind of repetition is never accidental. Here it calls attention to the metaliterary reverberations of the poem's language; more specifically, it prepares for the return of the term *bulicame* as a proper noun in one of the *Commedia*'s most intriguing Italian landscape similes: 'As from the Bulicame flows out a rivulet that the sinful women then divide among them, so this ran down across the sand' (Quale del Bulicame esce ruscello / che parton poi tra lor le peccatrici, / tal per la rena giù sen giva quello; *Inf.* XIV, 79–81). At one level, the Bulicame hot spring simile functions like other Italian landscape similes that Dante uses to construct the landscape of Hell. The poet's evocation of the Bulicame of Viterbo, which medieval travellers would have come across on the via Cassia, the main road from Rome to Florence and to the north, is, in fact, contiguous both textually and territorially with the Maremma – the coastal area of western central Italy that includes much of southwestern Tuscany – that is evoked to portray the violent landscape of *Inferno* XIII, 7–9. By evoking a presumably familiar, albeit exotic, feature of the Italian landscape in his depiction of Hell, the poet makes the description of the river of boiling blood vivid, concrete, and realistic.

However, what is most striking about the Bulicame simile in the context of the complex narrative staging of the identification of Dante's Phlegethon are the metaliterary effects of employing the same word, *bulicame*, now transformed into a proper noun, in a simile after having previously used it twice as simple noun. By ostentatiously evoking different orders of semantic referentiality in his use of the word, ranging from the 'fiction' of the simile to the 'reality' of the proper noun, Dante brings into focus the metaliterary significance of the elaborate narrative artifice that he deploys in order to name the river over the span of several canti. On the one hand, the poet commands our assent to 'the fiction that the poem is not a fiction' in his initial presentation of the 'bulicame', and stresses the reality of his encounter with the Phlegethon, thereby transcending his literary precedents; on the other, he subtly exposes the literary nature of the operation in which he is engaged by 'fictionalizing' the reality of the Bulicame hot spring when he transforms it into a simile to describe the infernal river.

This complex double movement is typical of the *Commedia*, whose poetics are designed to destabilize conventional boundaries between reality and fiction. Indeed, by ostentatiously manipulating the poem's referential planes, one of Dante's fundamental strategies is to make fictional landscapes real while fictionalizing real landscapes, so that, in the switching back and forth, the reader can barely keep track of their difference (for example, *Inf.* XX, 61–99; XXVII, 28–54). While geographical description had always been a feature of epic poetry, Dante employed it with a metaphysical metaliterary purpose unknown to the classical tradition. By mixing the geo-topographic planes of referentiality, Dante ultimately aimed to lead the reader, like the pilgrim, 'to experience the sense in which finite reality is fiction'.[11]

This metaliterary aspect of the *bulicame*/*Bulicame* segment of the richly nuanced evocation of the river helps to explain the unusual emphasis that Virgil later attributes to the Phlegethon, when he claims that, since entering Hell, 'your eyes have yet seen nothing of such note / as is this river before us' (cosa non fu da li tuoi occhi scorta / notabile com'è 'l presente rio; XIV, 88–9). What is it that makes the Phlegethon more notable than anything yet encountered on the journey? Commentators are undoubtedly correct in observing that it is not the river itself that is the most noteworthy aspect of the journey but that this privilege goes to the explanation of the origins of the river system of Hell that immediately follows (91–3). Nonetheless, it is also certain that Dante is calling attention to the elaborate narrative staging of his river that prepares for a lesson in hydrology, which revealingly concludes dramatically with the Phlegethon's actual naming. Thus, at the end of his excursus on the source of the infernal rivers, Virgil calls attention to the issue of the designation of the third river and gently reprimands the pilgrim for not having recognized it from the outset as the Phlegethon of the classical tradition and described in his own poem (130–5). Virgil's rebuke constitutes the poet's knowing wink to the reader at the end of the extraordinary poetic tour de force that is the river's serpentine naming. On the one hand, Dante emphasizes his artistry and puts his signature on the Phlegethon, thereby overwriting that of Virgil and the classical tradition; while, on the other, he raises what was for him the fundamental metaphysical question of the relationship between literary representation and truth. In metaliterary terms, Dante's aim was to go further than simply foster the 'fiction that the poem is not a fiction'. By his elaborate staging of the third infernal river as the 'riviera del sangue', a 'bulicame', the 'Bulicame' of Viterbo, and finally the Phlegethon, Dante sought to undermine comfortable assumptions about the relationship between truth and fiction, and thereby to conform to the metaphysical grounding of the *Comedìa*'s truth that transcended the constraints of this world.

Conclusion

Dante made greater claims for the spiritual authority of his poem's truth than have been made for any work of literature before or since. At the same time, he revealed an awareness of the limitations of language and literature to express truth that was also without precedent. The critical tradition has been disoriented by the *Commedia*'s bold claim to an authority tantamount to that of the Bible and by the complexity of its metaliterary structures which both underscore that claim and appear to undermine it, beginning with the title *Comedìa*. By expanding the genre of 'comedy' to include all of literature, Dante sought to encompass the whole of reality explicitly challenging his culture's doctrine of 'styles', a literary system that had been rendered obsolete by the New Testament's spiritually radical and transformative combination of 'sublime' content articulated through a 'humble' or 'comic' 'style'. Accordingly, Dante reinterpreted the traditional trajectory of 'comedy' from bad to good in a Christian sense, so that his *Comedìa* became indeed a 'sacred poem', pointing beyond itself to the redemption both of one individual and of all humanity. While claiming a close affinity to Scripture, the poem also reveals its nature as artifice and representation. This complex metaliterary operation deconstructs and exposes the fictional nature of the poem and, by extension, of spatio-temporal reality: the *Comedìa* thus calls attention to the limits of representation (Geryon) in light of the transcendent truth of Christ, and seeks to trigger in the reader the experience of spiritual conversion that is its ultimate purpose, for, as the author stated in the epistle to Cangrande, 'the aim of the whole and of the part is to remove those living in this life from a state of misery, and to bring them to a state of happiness' (39).

Notes

1. G. Boccaccio, *Opere in versi, Corbaccio, Trattatello in laude di Dante, prose latine, epistole* (Milan: Ricciardi, 1965), p. 634.
2. E. Auerbach, '*Sermo humilis*' in his *Literary Language and Its Public in Late Latin Antiquity and in the Middle Ages* (New York: Pantheon Books, 1965), pp. 27–66.
3. D. Alighieri, *Epistola XIII*, ed. L. Azzetta in D. Alighieri, *Epistole. Egloge. Questio de aqua et terra*, ed. M. Baglio *et al.* (Rome: Salerno, 2016), pp. 271–487.
4. G. Boccaccio, *Expositions on Dante's 'Comedy'*, trans. M. Papio (University of Toronto Press, 2009), p. 41.
5. J. Steinberg, *Dante and the Law* (University of Chicago Press, 2015), p. 158.
6. Horace, *Ars poetica*, trans. H. Rushton Fairclough (Cambridge, MA: Harvard University Press, 1926), p. 459.
7. Z. G. Barański, '*Comedìa*. Notes on Dante, the Epistle to Cangrande, and Medieval Comedy', *Lectura Dantis*, 8 (1991), 26–55 (p. 38).

8. Benvenuto da Imola, *Comentum super Dantis Aldigherij Comoediam*, ed. J. F. Lacaita, 5 vols. (Florence: Barbèra, 1887), I, p. 8.

9. C. Moevs, 'God's Feet and Hands (*Paradiso* 4, 40–48): Non-duality and Non-false Errors', *MLN*, 114/1 (1999), 1–13 (p. 8).

10. C. S. Singleton, *Dante's Commedia: Elements of Structure* (Baltimore MD: Johns Hopkins University Press, 1977 [1954]), p. 62.

11. C. Moevs, *The Metaphysics of Dante's 'Comedy'* (Oxford University Press, 2005), p. 185.

6

MIRKO TAVONI

Language and Style

Dante's Language and Linguistic Thought from the *Vita Nova* to the *Commedia*

Dante wrote in Florentine, the language spoken and written by the Florentines of his generation, throughout his career. Indeed, the phonological and morphological system present in his work coincides with that documented in non-literary texts written in the city during the last quarter of the thirteenth century. However, this fundamental characteristic is affected and partly altered by Dante's experimentation with different literary genres and the evolution of his linguistic ideas. In fact, his activity as a poet and prose writer is often accompanied by acute and original linguistic self-awareness that runs parallel to the composition of his works, so that language and linguistic reflection complement each other. This is particularly true as regards vocabulary and syntax, which are influenced, more than phonology and morphology, by cultural factors, and are therefore affected more distinctively by the author's linguistic and stylistic preferences, which vary from his early works to the *Commedia*.

The *Commedia* – the culmination of Dante's entire intellectual and literary trajectory – is his most Florentine work, the one that incorporates unfiltered Dante's native vernacular. Dante exploits and simultaneously develops its resources and registers, while embracing and enriching the entire vertical range of lexical items, from the 'lowest' to the most sophisticated, and from the plain and natural syntax of the spoken language to the complexities of philosophical and theological argument.

Dante's early lyric poetry (dating back to the 1280s) was instead influenced by the poetic language that developed in the wake of the 'Sicilian School' at the court of Frederick II between 1230 and 1250, and therefore includes Sicilianisms, such as the verbal forms *aggio* for 'ho' (I have) and *saccio* for 'so' (I know), and Occitanisms, such as words ending in *-ore* like *dolzore* and *riccore* (sweetness; wealth), *-aggio* like *coraggio* and *paraggio* (heart; equal), and *-anza* such as *dottanza* and *orranza* (fear; honour). Such Sicilianisms and Occitanisms are drastically reduced in Dante's stilnovist

95

poetry and the *Vita nova*, resulting in a language that is both unified and Florentine. On the phonological level, instead of Florentine diphthongal forms such as *cuore, fiera* (heart; beast) there remain many non-diphthongal forms (*core, fera*) of Sicilian origin, that are also bolstered by Latin models and survive in Italian poetic language for centuries. On the morphological level, conditional forms in *-ia* such as *saria* and *faria* (would be; would do) are preserved, appearing in the doctrinal *canzoni* and the *Commedia*, alongside the Florentine conditional ending in *-ebbe*, which predominates in the prose of the *Vita nova* and *Convivio*. The same is true of imperfect forms in *-ia*, although these are much less present than the Tuscan forms in *-ava, -eva, -iva*. Dante retains these traditional forms of the poetic language also because they offer useful alternatives for the count-ing of syllables in verses and rhymes.

The poetry of the *Vita nova* is dominated by typically stilnovist words: the nouns *donna, amore, core, occhi, pietà, anima, mente, spirito, cielo, morte, pensiero, viso* (woman, love, heart, eyes, compassion, soul, mind, spirit, heaven, death, thought, face/sight); the adjectives *gentile, dolente, novo, dolce* (noble, sorrowful, new, sweet). The result is a rarefied lexicon, of the kind that in the *De vulgari eloquentia* Dante defines as *pexa* ('combed') for its phonic smoothness (II, vii, 2–5), as in the canzone 'Donne ch'avete intelletto d'amore' (Ladies that have intelligence of love) or in the famous sonnet 'Tanto gentile e tanto onesta pare' (So noble and so honest/beautiful appears).

In the *tenzone* – the poetic exchange – with his Florentine friend Forese Donati, which belongs to the genre of 'comic-realistic' poetry, Dante uses instead a concrete and 'low' vocabulary such as *foro, stecco, uncino* (hole, dart, hook; *Rime* CXIII, 4 and CXIV, 6), and vulgar *double entendres* (*nido*, 'nest', for the female sexual organ; LXXIII, 11). The poetry is experimental and in sharp contrast to the *Vita nova*, recalling rather the stylistic register of the *Fiore*, a narrative poem consisting of 232 sonnets that imitates the *Roman de la rose* and is written in a heavily French-inflected language, and whose Dantean authorship is still controversial. In the 'stony rhymes', another group of experimental poems written in the second half of the 1290s for a mysterious 'stony' woman and influenced by the *trobar clus*, the 'obscure style', of the Occitan poet Arnaut Daniel, Dante displays another type of experimentation: refined in style but harsh and dissonant in register as the programmatic canzone 'Così nel mio parlar voglio esser aspro' (So in my speech I want to be harsh) announces. The harshness is expressed semantically through 'hard' words like *pietra* (stone) and phonically via the combination of consonants that, in contrast to the 'combed' ones, the *De vulgari* characterizes as *yrsuta*, 'shaggy' (II, vii), since their phonic density offers resistance, like tugging at a knot with a comb. The effect of such words is especially pronounced in rhyme, as in 'Così nel mio parlar', where we find *cruda, diaspro, arretra, faretra, schermo, spezzi, prezzi* (cruel, jasper, retreat, quiver, shield, shatter, heed).

Furthermore, in the 'doctrinal' *canzoni*, written partly in Florence in the 1290s and then, after 1302, during the early years of his exile, Dante expanded his lexical range and enriched the complexity and toughness of his syntax. Abandoning the refined lexicon of stilnovist 'sweetness', Dante's new philosophical poetry required a 'harsh and subtle rhyme' (rima aspr' e sottile; LXXXII, 14) capable of conveying sophisticated rationalizing disquisitions. Dante's intention was to make the canzone stanza capable of sustaining a rigorous philosophical argument. Patrick Boyde has measured the increase of syntactic complexity that characterizes the poems written after the *Vita nova*;[1] and the best self-commentary on this poetic and philosophical interaction may be found at *De vulgari* II, vi, 5–7 which presents the 'supreme degree of construction', namely, the complex and highly rhetorical syntax befitting the 'tragic' style. In order to master it, Dante urges poets to follow the example not only of the great Latin poets, but also of the most prominent Latin prose writers.

The prose of the *Convivio*, compared to the 'fervent and passionate' one of the *Vita nova*, is 'temperate and mature' (I, i, 16). It abandons the emphasis on narrative and vision for the language and syntax of reasoned argument, characterized by long sentences made up of many subordinated clauses (hypotaxis) that develop complex syllogistic arguments. If the prose of the *Vita nova* participates in its poetic atmosphere, that of the *Convivio* reveals 'the outstanding goodness of the Italian vernacular' without the 'incidental embellishments' of rhyme and rhythm, namely, the ability of the vernacular to express 'the most sublime and original ideas aptly, fully, and attractively, almost as well as Latin itself' (I, x, 12). The lexicon of the *Convivio* is replete with scientific Latinisms, and receptive to the most varied disciplines, from geometry to medicine, from astronomy to philosophy.

All these previous literary experiences converge in the *Commedia*. The extraordinary breadth and expressive power of the poem cannot be fully understood apart from this rich linguistic apprenticeship. With regard to the theory of 'styles' (*genera dicendi*), the *Commedia* marks a break with Dante's previous works. The *De vulgari*, written in 1304–6, theorized, in line with classical and medieval rhetorical thought, the separation of 'styles' (II, iv). In keeping with Dante's primary contemporary interest in doctrinal poetry and philosophical prose, it focused on codifying the 'tragic' 'high' style reserved for lofty subjects, such as love and ethics, and left aside the lower 'styles', which Dante termed 'comic' and 'elegiac'. When, in 1307–8,

Dante began to write the *Commedia*, he embraced the radical idea of combining the different 'styles' and linguistic registers. This change is confirmed by the explicit statement that the poem is a 'comedìa' (*Inf.* XVI, 128; XXI, 2) in contrast to Virgil's *Aeneid* defined as 'tragedìa' (*Inf.* XX, 113). In *Inferno*'s opening canto, the pilgrim greets Virgil as his sole poetic 'teacher' (maestro; 85). In effect, Dante's poetic production before the *Commedia*, which he had valorized in the *De vulgari* and elevated to the status of model, had been exclusively in the 'tragic' style. Yet, already in *Inferno* IV, Dante included 'Horace satirist' (Orazio satiro; 89), namely a poet of the 'low style' in the group of five great classical poets who treat him as 'sixth among such wisdom' (sesto tra cotanto senno; 102). He does so to suggest that, to encompass the totality of his otherworldly experience, his *Commedia* will need more than one 'teacher', thereby necessarily embracing the 'low style' alongside the 'high' one.

The extreme breadth of subject matter, emotions, and types of speech that co-exist in the poem 'to which both Heaven and earth have set their hand' (al quale ha posto mano e cielo e terra; *Par.* XXV, 2) draws on all Dante's previous literary, linguistic, and stylistic achievements: the refined and rarefied language of the *Vita nova*'s stilnovist poetry and prose; the 'comic-realism' of the *tenzone* with Forese Donati; the virtuosity and *trobar clus* of the 'stony rhymes'; the 'harsh and subtle rhyme' of the doctrinal *canzoni*; and the philosophical syntax of the *Convivio*. The result is an all-encompassing language of an expressive power that is unrivalled by any other medieval Romance text. Accordingly, the *Commedia* has been considered the prototype of the multilingual, pluristylistic, and expressionist tradition in Italian literature that is opposed to Petrarch's *Canzoniere*, the archetype of the monolingual, monostylistic, and classicizing current.

To offer an idea of the *Commedia*'s linguistic and stylistic range, we might compare two antithetical moments, the predominantly 'comic' canto of barratry (*Inf.* XXI) and Beatrice's language in the *Paradiso*. In the first, we find a concrete, realistic, incisive, and expressive lexicon, from technical vocabulary relating to the shipyards of Venice, such as *arzanà, terzeruolo, artimon* (arsenal, jib, mainsail), where the workers are involved in *rimpalmare, ristoppare, rintoppare* (caulking, plugging, patching), to terms related to the body, which are anti-lyrical and reminiscent of the butcher's shop, the devil's *omero* (shoulder), the sinner's *anche* (haunches), *piè* (foot), and *nerbo* (tendon), before moving on to the lexicon of the kitchen with *cuoci* (cooks) and their *vassalli* (scullions) – an earthy vocabulary employed for debasing and expressionistic ends. In line with *De vulgari*'s idea of the phonically 'shaggy', we find consonantic clusters such as *sgagliarda, ghermito, addentar* (debilitates, clutched, to bite), and the rhyme words *graffi-raffi-accaffi* (scratches, hooks, and pilfer – the last a Florentine dialect verb) and *balli-vassalli-galli* (dance, scullions, float). In contrast, Beatrice's language in *Paradiso* is made up of an abstract, luminous lexicon: nouns that designate the soul and its motions like *animo, mente, pensier, intelletto, affetto, amore, disire, podere* (spirit, mind, thought, intellect, affection, love, desire, power); the human face, with its 'noble' parts and expressions, such as *viso* in the sense of 'visage', *volto, occhi, sorriso* (face, eyes, smile); light and related phenomena, such as *luce/lume, specchio, fulgore, secondo aspetto* (light, mirror, brightness, reflected glow), as well as *vista* and *viso* meaning 'sight', and *intento*, the focus of the gaze; *bellezza* and *piacere* meaning 'beauty', as in *piacere etterno*, namely, 'eternal beauty'. In *Paradiso* some very long sequences, even an entire canto, are devoted to monologues explaining cosmological, ethical, philosophical, and theological issues.

Elsewhere, opposing linguistic registers are juxtaposed, creating a clash of 'styles'; one that is particularly pronounced in Malebolge (*Inf.* XVIII–XXXI). For example, canto XXVIII begins with seven *terzine* that expressly allude to the classical epic by quoting Virgil and Livy. Thus, Dante bases the phrase 'd'aequar sarebbe nulla' (it could not equal; 20) on 'quis ... possit lacrimis aequare laboris?' (who can equal our pain with tears?) in *Aeneid* II, 361–2, but then immediately lowers the register by describing wounds and mutilations that include 'the loathsome sack that turns what one has swallowed into shit' (e 'l tristo sacco /che merda fa di quel che si trangugia; 26–7). Equally, in *Paradiso* XXVII, St Peter, in his invective against his successors, the degenerate popes, utilizes Latinisms as rhyme words – *concipio, pondo, fleto* (think, burden, weeping) for the purpose of rhetorical elevation, but then lowers the register by declaring that the pope 'has made my tomb a sewer of blood and filth' (fatt' ha del cimitero mio cloaca / del sangue e de la puzza; 25–6), where *cloaca* rhymes with the Latinism *vaca* (is vacant).

Phonology and Morphology

The accuracy of the lexicon, syntax, and in part morphology of Dante's vernacular works is generally not in doubt.[2] Instead, the graphic-phonetic and to some extent the morphological character of his written production is problematic, since not a single manuscript in Dante's hand has survived, so that it is impossible to establish his 'mode of writing'. In addition, parts of the *Commedia* circulated as early as 1314 in northern Italian circles where Dante lived after his exile. Thus, copyists of the poem from the Po valley almost certainly added a northern patina to the likely Florentine linguistic character of Dante's original. For instance, in *Inferno* I, manuscripts attest to northern

Italian modifications, such as double consonants becoming single, as in *camin, smarita, rinova, abandonai, matino, aquista, s'atrista, s'amoglia, trarotti, alor* (journey, lost, renews, forsook, morning, gains, laments, mates, I will lead you, then), and single ones becoming double, as in *doppo* (after), and protonic *e* replacing *i*, whereby we find *redir, delitoso, venesse* (retell, delightful, came). Additional philological-linguistic aspects are dealt with in chapter 14. I will only add here that editors of modern critical editions of the *Commedia* find themselves in a difficult position because the manuscripts closest to Dante's original intentions, and therefore most reliable when choosing between significantly different textual variants, are northern Italian and linguistically hybrid.

Given the uncertainties, only the forms guaranteed by rhyme are entirely reliable. For example, it is certain that, in *Purgatorio* XX, 134 and 138, Dante wrote the forms *feo* and *poteo*, and not *fé* and *poté* (did, could), because the two forms rhyme with *Deo* (God). Similarly, we know that in *Paradiso* XX, 134 and 138 he wrote *vedemo* and *volemo*, and not *vediamo* and *vogliamo* (we see; we will), because the two forms rhyme with *scemo* (lack). Therefore, on the basis of its rhyme words, we know that the language of the *Commedia* belongs to late-thirteenth-century Florentine, as the following forms demonstrate: *dimane, stamane, diece* instead of *domani, stamani, dieci* (tomorrow, this morning, ten); *tegghia, stregghia* instead of *teglia, striglia* (pan, curry comb); *dea, stea* instead of *dia* (may give), *stia* (may stay, be, rest); the second person singular, whether indicative and subjunctive, *gride* (cry out), *guarde* (stare at), *pense* alongside *pensi* (think); the first person imperfect subjunctives *io fosse* (I was), *io morisse* (I died), alongside *io udissi* (I heard); *poetaro* (they poetized), *saliro* (they ascended), *udiro* (they heard) used more frequently than with endings in *-arono, -irono*; and, with ninety occurrences, albeit not in rhyme, *sè* and not *sei* for the second person singular of the present indicative of *essere* (to be). All these features attest to the fact that the *Commedia*'s Florentine is quite archaic, namely, it is that of Dante's youth that remained fixed in his memory after his exile which interrupted his contact with the linguistic evolution that occurred in the early decades of the fourteenth century.

Lexicon

The lexicon of the *Commedia* combines and includes the various lexical developments evident in Dante's previous works. The poem embraces the everyday Florentine lexicon, including words such as *mamma* and *babbo* (mummy, daddy) that *De vulgari* downgraded as 'infantile'; *greggia* (flock) which was considered 'rustic'; *femina* and *corpo* (female, body) regarded as 'smooth' and 'unkempt' (II, vii, 4); and *manicare* (eat) and *introcque* (in the meanwhile) deemed 'provincial' (I, xiii, 2). In *Inferno*, especially in Malebolge, namely, the most 'comic' section of the poem, we find vulgar, plebeian, idiomatic words such as *grattare, porcile, sterco, tigna* (scratch, pigsty, excrement, mange); obscene ones such as *puttana, merda, fiche* (whore, shit, cunts); and others highlighted in rhyme for maximum expressiveness such as *incrocicchia-nicchia-picchia* (intersects, whimpers, beats) or else *scuffa-muffa-zuffa* (snuffles, mould, brawl). But such terms return elsewhere, even in the later parts of *Paradiso*.

At the opposite end of the *Commedia*'s linguistic spectrum, we find numerous Latinisms, which progressively increase, reaching their greatest deployment in *Paradiso*, in line with its philosophical and theological concerns. But Latinisms also permeate *Inferno*, from the 'secreto calle' (hidden path; X, 1) to Hell of Virgilian memory (*Aen.* VI, 443) to expressionistic three-line rhyme schemes where concrete words are used, such as *azzurro-curro-burro* (blue, chariot [Latinism understood as 'movement forward'], butter) and *sepe-epe-pepe* (hedge, belly [Latinism for liver], pepper). In *Paradiso*, we consistently discover 'lofty' Latinate three-line rhyme schemes such as *colubro-rubro-delubro* (asp, red, shrine). An interesting feature are those words that have remained in common use in modern Italian in a weakened meaning, while Dante uses them in a stronger and more physical way. Such words are closer to the original Latin denotation such as *pare* (appears), *affetto* (passion), *molesto* (unbearable), *offendere* (offend) in which the etymological value of colliding against or hurting is still preserved.

Scientific words, already present in the *Convivio*, are common, including terms from astronomy such as *emisperio, epiciclo, meridiano, orbita, plenilunio* (hemisphere, epicycle, meridian, orbit, full moon); geometry such as *circunferenza* and *quadrare* (circumference, to square); and medicine such as *complessione, idropico, oppilazione, quartana* (complexion, dropsy, obstruction, quartan fever), as well as common anatomical words for the groin, goiter, throat, and stomach (*anguinaia, gozzo, strozza, pancia*). We also find the learned Grecism *tetragono* (unyielding), of Aristotelian and Thomistic provenance, used proverbially in the expression 'tetragono ai colpi di fortuna' (unyielding to the blows of fortune; *Par.* XVII, 23–4). As well as Grecisms such as *archimandrita* (shepherd) and *baràtro* (abyss), Dante employed Arabisms, derived from Latin scientific translations, such as *alchimia* and *cenìt* (alchemy, zenith).

Alongside Latinisms, another large group is made up of Gallicisms. The poetic patterns of Occitan-Sicilian origin, which were expunged from Dante's early stilnovist poetry to achieve a more fluent and natural style, now reappear profusely, often in rhyme, in the omnivorous *Commedia* to elevate its style. Thus, we have *onranza-nominanza* (honoured-fame) in the encounter with the great classical poets in Limbo (*Inf*. IV, 74–6); and then, more expansively, in *Paradiso: amanza, beninanza, desianza, dilettanza, fallanza, fidanza, possanza, sembianza* (beloved, goodness, longing, delight, fault, confidence, power, appearance).

The striking presence of proper nouns is another feature of the *Commedia*'s impressive lexical concreteness. The main categories include the names of the inhabitants of the afterlife and others whom the poet evokes, be they public or private figures, historical or legendary, from Muhammad to fra Dolcino, Semiramis, Bertran de Born, and Aeneas), and place names (a very detailed toponomy of the Italian peninsula and the world known to Dante, from Vercelli to Majorca, Thebes to Troy). Together they constitute a rich collection of proper names that embraces chronicles, sacred and profane history, ancient and modern geography, Scripture, and pagan mythology. Of note too are the names of the infernal creatures that Dante borrows from the sacred and pagan traditions, or creatively develops, from Cerberus to Minos, and from Malebranche to Geryon.

Dante's lexical creativity leads him to coin new words. In *Inferno*, there are violent, expressionistic neologisms such as *stoscio* (drop), *arruncigliare* (to hook), *rinfarciare* (to swell); and, at the opposite end of the stylistic spectrum, in *Paradiso*, 'sublime' and highly innovative terms coined to describe the ineffable experiences and unprecedented transformations that the pilgrim experienced during his *trasumanare* (soaring beyond the human; *Par*. I, 70). These paradisiacal neologisms are the parasynthetic verbal compounds with the prefix 'in-', such as *indiarsi* (to en-god oneself), *intuarsi* (to en-you oneself), *intrearsi* (to en-three oneself), *insemprarsi* (to eternalize oneself).

Syntax

We now have a complete map of all the phrasal structures deployed in the three *cantiche* thanks to a comprehensive syntactic encoding of the *Commedia*, that is further distinguished between its diegetic, narrative sections and its mimetic parts, namely, the direct speeches and thoughts of characters.[3] Thus, direct speech takes up 53 per cent of *Inferno* and *Purgatorio*, and 63 per cent of *Paradiso*; but the number of exchanges totals 370 in *Inferno*, 335 in *Purgatorio*, and only 160 in *Paradiso*. These figures reveal that the first two *cantiche* are densely dialogic, with dialogues lasting an average of 7–8 lines, while *Paradiso* is much more 'monologic', with a smaller number of long speeches, whose average length totals 19 verses.

Moreover, in the cases of Justinian's history of the Roman empire (VI), Thomas Aquinas praising Francis (XI), Bonaventure celebrating Dominic (XII), Thomas again discussing wisdom (XIII), and Beatrice explaining the creation of angels (XXIX), their speeches constitute narratives or doctrinal treatises that occupy almost an entire canto. The dialogic component in *Paradiso* is thus reduced to a minimum: in the first two *cantiche*, the pilgrim's path to knowledge is developed dialectically, through dialogue; in *Paradiso*, he learns while listening silently to long 'lectures' given by authoritative figures.

Inferno is the most dramatic *cantica*, constructed out of sharply exchanged bursts of dialogue that leave little room for extended discussion. This, however, increases in *Purgatorio*, resulting in a 'horizontal', paratactic sentence structure; while, in *Paradiso*, sentences are 'vertical' and hypotactic, whereby the vernacular demonstrates that its syntactic efficacy is equal to that of Latin. The 'dramatic' syntactic force that erupts in *Inferno*, and which will be examined more closely in the next section, was the result of an extraordinarily creative initial phase of composition (1307–8). The rationative syntax that develops in increasingly large and complex structures in *Purgatorio* and especially in *Paradiso* builds on the doctrinal *canzoni* (as well as the prose of *Convivio*), a writerly experience which Dante had codified when referring to the 'most excellent construction' in the *De vulgari* (*supprema constructio*; II, vi, 5).

The increasing length and complexity of the *Commedia*'s sentences is confirmed statistically: *Inferno* has 1,700 sentences which average 3.4 clauses; *Purgatorio* 1,547 sentences with an average of 3.7 clauses; and *Paradiso* 1,203 sentences averaging 4.4 clauses. Furthermore, the number of subordinate clauses per sentence increases from 1.8 to 2.1 and then to 2.7, thereby confirming the increase in hypotaxis in *Paradiso*. Compared to the first two *cantiche*, in *Paradiso* there is a marked decrease in jussive clauses (phrases that express, in the form of an order, exhortation, advice, prayer, a request to act addressed to an interlocutor) and a dramatic drop in interrogatives. Jussive and interrogative clauses are a crucial tool for the interaction, verbal or otherwise, between characters, with a strong illocutionary effect, namely, they are speech acts that are intended to provoke a reaction in the interlocutor. It is significant that jussive and interrogative clauses are frequent in *Inferno* and *Purgatorio*, where there are strong dramatic interactions between characters, but decrease significantly in *Paradiso*, where souls appear together in a generally more static manner, and where the omniscient blessed do not need to ask questions. These are but a few examples, many others could be given, that help us understand how the distribution of sentence patterns highlights the distinctive 'cognitive style' of each of the three *cantiche*.

Mimesis, Deixis, Drama

The *Commedia* stages memorable dialogues between the pilgrim and the many souls that he meets, and between the souls themselves. A notable feature is Dante's almost theatrical ability to dramatize these encounters in ways that seem modern. Dante-character wanders through the netherworld, and especially so in Hell, like a traveller visiting an unknown city. He witnesses scenes in which characters, whom he does not know, interact; he hears exchanges without knowing what the interlocutors are talking about, and so on. Often, but not always, the identity of the speakers and the meaning of their words become clear during the course of their encounter with the pilgrim. Yet, the poet never feels compelled to provide all the information needed to understand, word for word, what has been said, or, ultimately, to offer all the information necessary to appreciate what he may have wanted to communicate by recounting those particular aspects that he did of what he saw and heard.

This 'theatrical' approach is primarily based on alternating, within the *terzina* and individual lines, the words of the narrator and those of the characters in an extremely fluid manner. In other words, Dante weaves a verbal fabric formed of narrative and dialogue, where the two elements merge while interrupting their respective syntactic constructions, which, after the interruption, restart precisely at the point where they had been disrupted. For instance, 'So [spoke] the master; and I: "Find a useful way", I said to him, "not to waste time". And he: "See I'm thinking about that"' (Così 'l maestro; e io 'Alcun compenso', / dissi lui, 'trova che 'l tempo non passi / perduto'. Ed elli: 'Vedi ch'a ciò penso'; *Inf.* XI, 13–15); and 'I was in doubt and said, "Tell her, tell her!", to myself, "tell her", I said, "to my lady, who slakes my thirst with her sweet drops"' (Io dubitava e dicea 'Dille, dille!' / fra me, 'dille' dicea, 'a la mia donna / che mi diseta con le dolci stille'; *Par.* VII, 10–12). Similarly there are cases of interrupted speech – 'I began: "Oh friars your evil deeds ... " but I said no more, for one caught my eye' (Io cominciai: 'O frati, i vostri mali ... '; / ma più non dissi, ch'a l'occhio mi corse / un; *Inf.* XXIII, 109–11) – and of inner speech: 'Like one who sees a thing suddenly before him at which he wonders, who believes and doesn't, saying "It is ... – it isn't ... " he seemed like that' (Qual è colui che cosa innanzi sé / sùbita vede ond'e' si maraviglia, / che crede e non, dicendo 'Ella è ... non è ... ' / tal parve quelli; *Purg.* VII, 10–13). Moreover, the *Commedia* displays a striking ability to represent the phenomena of language that modern linguists term 'pragmatic', namely, the ways in which a language is used, mainly in its spoken form, in actual communicative situations. This can be seen in the high use of deictic words, namely, words that are interpreted by characters in relation to the spatial-temporal context in which they are spoken. Such words are often accompanied by explicit or implied gestures, which form part of the lines spoken, strengthening or clarifying the deictic value – in terms of spatial positioning, near or far from the speaker or interlocutor – of the words constituting the lines. Thus, Virgil who names the lustful by passing them in review: '"See Paris, Tristan", and more than a thousand shades, he showed me and named for me pointing' ('Vedi Parìs, Tristano'; e più di mille / ombre mostrommi e nominommi a ditto; *Inf.* V, 67–8). Similar examples are found when Virgil describes, pointing at them, the two groups of the avaricious and prodigal (*Inf.* VII, 55–7), and when he draws the pilgrim's attention to his warning by raising a finger (*Inf.* X, 129).

In addition to these pragmatic and deictic signals we can discern in the mimetic sections linguistic features characteristic of speech. Take for example the interjective *come*: '*What?* did you say "he held"? Isn't he still alive?' ('*Come?* / dicesti "elli ebbe"? non viv'elli ancora?'; *Inf.* X, 67–8 italics added; and cp. *Purg.* XXVII, 43–4). The presentational *ecco* serves a similar function: 'From our bridge he said: "O Malebranche, *here* is one of Santa Zita's elders!"' (Del nostro ponte disse: 'O Malebranche, / *ecco* un de li anzïan di Santa Zita!'; *Inf.* XXI, 37–8 italics added; and cp. XXXIV, 19–21). The presentational *ecco* is also common in the diegetic sections, granting immediacy to the narrative: 'And *now*, near the beginning of the steep, a leopard light and very swift' (Ed *ecco*, quasi al cominciar de l'erta, / una lonza leggera e presta molto; *Inf.* I, 31–2 italics added; and cp. III, 82–3).

The language of the *Commedia* also reveals inserts from other languages, either entire passages or single words. These are predominantly in Latin, resulting in 'vertical multilingualism' given the prevailing diglossia in the Middle Ages, namely, the co-existence of the 'low' everyday vernacular alongside Latin, the highly codified language of culture. In the *De vulgari* (I, i and ix), Dante had lucidly theorized this diglossia as the opposition between *locutio vulgaris*, natural language, founded on *usus*, usage, and *locutio secundaria*, a learned 'artificial' language, based on *ratio* and *gramatica*, namely, a literary language governed by rules. In particular, the Latin titles of the Psalms and other gospel verses uttered by the penitents and guardian angels appear throughout *Purgatorio*. An especially notable instance is found in Eden given its deployment of the vernacular in both direct and indirect speech and its bold juxtaposition of a Gospel verse (John 12:13) with one from the *Aeneid* (VI, 883): 'All were saying: "*Benedictus qui venis!*" and, throwing flowers up and around, "*Manibus,* oh, *date lilia*

plenis!''' (Tutti dicean: '*Benedictus qui venis!*' / e fior gittando e di sopra
e dintorno, / '*Manibus, oh, date lilïa plenis!*'; *Purg.* XXX, 19–21).
By incorporating such Latin fragments into his vernacular text, Dante
abolishes the hierarchical distinction between the two languages.
Of a different order and of great significance is the *terzina* entirely in Latin
with which Cacciaguida begins his long speech that confirms the salvific
mission that God has assigned to his great-great-grandson Dante:
'*O sanguis meus, O superinfusa / gratïa Deï, sicut tibi cui / bis unquam celi
ianüa reclusa?*' (O my blood, o overflowing grace of God, to whom as to you
has the gate of Heaven been opened twice?; *Par.* XV, 28–30). Unlike other
Latin inserts, the tercet is composed by Dante himself, who, given the lines'
paradisiacal and prophetic solemnity, relies on the reverberations of Latin's
cultural superiority and sophistication when compared to the language of
normal communication to stress the importance of the encounter with his
ancestor.

Conversely, we find cases of 'horizontal' plurilingualism involving Occitan
and French, two sister vernaculars of Italian. A telling example are the three
terzine in Occitan (*Purg.* XXVI, 140–7) with which the troubadour Arnaut
Daniel is introduced as the 'better craftsman of the mother tongue' (miglior
fabbro del parlar materno; 117). The nickname *Ciappetta*, which is used to
designate the French king Hugh Capet (*Purg.* XX, 49), with its initial palatal
consonant is a phonetic Gallicism. Equally, the anonymous Florentine suicide, in fact the merchant Rucco de' Mozzi, employs the crude Gallicism
gibetto (from *gibet* [gibbet]) to reveal that he had hanged himself in his house
in Paris (*Inf.* XIII, 151). Finally, the verb *alluminar*, from Old French *enlu-
miner*, to illuminate, serves as a tribute to Bologna's university culture, with
its booksellers and illuminators strongly influenced by Parisian illumination
(*Purg.* XI, 81).

'Horizontal' plurilingualism is also established by Dante's recourse to
Italian vernaculars other than Florentine. Relying on a distinctive word or
phonetic feature, he uses these as markers of provenance in his character
portrayals. Thus, the adverb *issa*, 'now', is utilized to characterize the
Lucchese poet Bonagiunta, and also to belittle him as a 'provincial' versifier,
as Dante had already labelled him in *De vulgari* I, xiii, 1 (*Purg.* XXIV, 55–7).
The same word, in the variant form *istra*, characterizes as 'Lombard',
namely, as a northern Italian vernacular, the language spoken by Virgil
(*Inf.* XXVII, 19–21). This example confirms that, according to Dante, even
in Virgil's time, Latin was a *locutio secundaria* or *gramatica*, and the vernaculars were the languages of everyday use. Furthermore, Buonconte da
Montefeltro, hailing from the Marches, utters a non-Florentine *intento*
instead of *intinto* (darkened) (*Purg.* V, 117), a form that is confirmed by its

position in rhyme. Equally, the Sardinian word *donno*, from the Latin *dominus*, 'master', is used twice in connection with Sardinian figures (*Inf.* XXII, 83 and 88). Attacking Bologna, Dante twice introduces local terms. In the episode involving the Bolognese pimp Venedico Caccianemico, the pilgrim sarcastically addresses the sinner by employing the toponym *Salse*, indicating the place where the city abandoned the corpses of criminals and those sentenced to death (*Inf.* XVIII, 51), to allude to his infernal condition. Subsequently, Venedico himself, in condemning Bolognese avarice, utilizes the local affirmative particle *sipa*, 'yes' (60). In every case, these non-Florentine words are marked as provincial, and therefore as inferior when compared to the Florentine which overwhelmingly dominates the *Commedia*'s linguistic fabric, whether this be diegetic or mimetic.

Dante even incorporates into the poem phrases in nonsense languages, such as the one Pluto raucously voices in the opening of *Inferno* VII: '*Pape Satàn, pape Satàn aleppe!*'. The giant Nimrod, too, as the primary instigator behind the construction of the Tower of Babel, appropriately speaks in a tongue that nobody can understand: '*Raphèl maì amècche zabì almi*' (*Inf.* XXXI, 67).

In addition to such instances of linguistic characterization, there are more frequent and sustained instances of stylistic characterization. It is enough to recall Francesca da Rimini, who presents herself as a reader of courtly love poetry and prose, and whose speech is replete with quotations from Andreas Cappellanus, Guido Guinizzelli, Guido Cavalcanti, and even the lyric Dante (*Inf.* V, 100–8). Equally noteworthy is Farinata degli Uberti, whose life had been dominated by political controversy and clashes, and whose exchange with the pilgrim recalls the so-called 'vituperative' 'satirical style' (*Inf.* X, 40–51); as is Pier della Vigna, a refined courtier and sophisticated wordsmith, whose speech, in *Inferno* XIII, is a model of technically polished rhetorical artistry.

In *Inferno*, Dante-character is recognized because of his Tuscan or, more precisely, his Florentine speech, when Farinata remarks: 'O Tuscan who goes through the city of fire alive speaking so honestly' (O Tosco che per la città del foco / vivo ten vai così parlando onesto; *Inf.* X, 22–3). Ugolino too remarks: 'I don't know who you are nor by what means you've come down here; but you seem to me to be indeed Florentine when I hear you' (Io non so chi tu se' né per che modo / venuto se' qua giù; ma fiorentino / mi sembri veramente quand'io t'odo; *Inf.* XXXIII, 10–12). In *Purgatorio* the pilgrim is also called 'Tuscan' by Guido del Duca (XIV, 103 and 124) and Marco Lombardo (XVI, 137). This emphasis on his origins is very significant. A few years earlier, in *De vulgari*, while theorizing a supraregional Italian 'illustrious vernacular' that would be decidedly not provincial, Dante had presented himself as someone for whom 'the whole world is a homeland, like the sea to fish' (I, vi, 3). He had also dedicated an entire chapter (I, xiii) to dismantling the pretensions of those many Tuscans, 'who, rendered senseless by some aberration of their own, seem to lay claim to the honour of possessing the illustrious vernacular' (1). If, when writing *Convivio* and *De vulgari* (1303–6), Dante rejected the Tuscan vernacular, by the time he energetically launched into the *Commedia* (1307–8), he had fully embraced his native language. This was in part due to a change in personal circumstances. During 1303–6, Dante endeavoured to build a future for himself in northern Italy (either Verona or Bologna), but soon after, around 1307–8, he was animated by the hope of being pardoned and allowed to return to Florence.

From the Language of the *Commedia* to Modern Italian

Dante fully deserves the title of 'father' of the Italian language. Thanks to the *Commedia*, he so enriched the vernacular that he bequeathed to later writers a language which allowed them to deal with any subject. The basic vocabulary of Italian (the 2,000 words most frequently used in today's language, which in turn account for 90 per cent of everything that is said, read, and written) is already 80 per cent present in the *Commedia*. Little has been added in subsequent centuries. It can thus be said without exaggeration that when, as Italians, we speak our everyday language, we are speaking Dante's language. Furthermore, to this basic vocabulary, given the *Commedia*'s breadth of interests, Dante appended a wide range of specialized words, from astronomy to moral philosophy to science, thereby establishing the bases of our intellectual vocabulary. He also consolidated and structured Italian syntax, rendering it capable of expressing complex arguments, to the point that he laid the foundations for Italian to replace Latin as the language of culture.

Dante is also the 'father' of the Italian language in the sense that, after him, the literary language of all Italians could only be Florentine. Such an outcome was far from a given. In the Middle Ages, the poets at Frederick II's court in Palermo had written in a form of illustrious Sicilian; the *Storie de Troja et de Roma* was composed in Roman vernacular; religious literature favoured the vernacular used in central Italy; Bonvesin de la Riva wrote didactic poetry in Milanese; while the Anonimo Genovese penned civic and political poems in Genoese. It is true that Tuscan writers, and particularly thirteenth-century Florentine ones, had already accumulated an impressive body of writings both in prose and in poetry that surpassed that of other Italian regions and cities. However, it was Dante who, with the *Commedia*, wrote a work incomparably superior to anything that had been written before in any Italian vernacular – a work, indeed, that had no equal either in French or Occitan, the two established languages, until then, of European vernacular literature. In short, it was Dante's poem that assured the future of the literary language of Italy.

Translated by Demetrio S. Yocum

Notes

1. P. Boyde, *Dante's Style in His Lyric Poetry* (Cambridge University Press, 1971), pp. 155–208.
2. The online textual archive DanteSearch (www.perunaenciclopediadantescadigi tale.eu:8080/dantesearch/) presents all Dante's vernacular and Latin works annotated by grammatical categories, allowing searches by word form, lemma, and grammatical features to reveal a text's underlying morphology and syntax.
3. S. Gigli, 'La codifica sintattica della *Commedia* di Dante' in M. D'Amico (ed.), *Sintassi dell'italiano antico e sintassi di Dante* (Pisa: Felici, 2015), pp. 81–95.

7

JAMES C. KRIESEL

Allegories of the Corpus

Dante's Allegory: Body and Text

In the *Comedy*, Dante most overtly recalls contemporary ideas about allegory when he describes the obstacles that prevent the pilgrim and Virgil from entering the infernal city of Dis. In *Inferno* IX, while introducing the dangers that had threatened the travellers, the poet highlights the Furies who mutilate their own bodies, and observes that the pilgrim's body would have been petrified if he had gazed upon Medusa. Before a celestial messenger unblocks the travellers' path, the narrator addresses his readers: 'You who are of good understanding, note the doctrine that is hidden under the veil of the strange lines' (O voi ch'avete li 'ntelletti sani, / mirate la dottrina che s'asconde / sotto 'l velame de li versi strani; 61–3). We are instructed conventionally to search for meaning by looking under the 'veil' or garment of the text's verses, as though the poem were a covered object or a clothed body. The implied contrast between pilgrim and reader further establishes an analogy between the poem and a body: whereas the pilgrim cannot look at Medusa's petrifying figure, readers must peek under the veils of the textual corpus to find useful 'doctrine'.

The act of looking under the 'veil of the strange lines' of a textual corpus – *strani* had resonances ranging from 'strange' to 'unusual' – evoked standard medieval ideas about allegory. Allegory was defined as 'alien' or 'other speak' (*alieniloquium*): '[allegory] literally says one thing, and another thing is understood'.[1] Accordingly, allegory was a broad rhetorical trope that encompassed many kinds of transferred speech (metaphor, irony, personification, etc.), as well as a variety of categories of signs (images, figures, symbols, etc.). In addition, tropes like allegory were sometimes depicted as ornaments or colours on a garment covering a body.[2] Allegory was also intertwined with the exposition of Scripture and revelation: the veil and the disfigured bodies of *Inferno* IX may parodically recall Moses who hid the glory of his countenance behind a veil in contrast to Christ who fully revealed Himself (2 Corinthians 3:12–16). Finally, verses 61–3 underscore that allegory was related both to a kind of writing (sometimes called a weaving or covering) and to a manner of reading (sometimes termed a denuding or stripping; for instance, *Vn* XXXV, 10 [16, 10]). Medieval writers and readers, therefore, probably did not distinguish as clearly as modern ones do between an allegorical mode of textual composition (allegory) and an allegorical mode of reading (allegoresis).

Given the importance of allegory in medieval literary theory and poetics, several of the major debates about the *Comedy* – in medieval commentaries on the poem and in modern scholarship – have involved matters concerning the poem's relationship to allegory. These debates generally address three main areas: how Dante thought his poem signified meaning; how he developed new ideas about textuality and authorship by adapting classical-rhetorical and biblical-exegetical traditions; and how Dante intended that his text should influence readers, a major concern for all medieval writers since literature was classified as a branch of ethics, and a vital issue for a poet of a work meant to bring about individual salvation and social and political change.

What follows examines allegory's role in the *Comedy*, and does so, in part, by focusing on Dante's metaliterary and symbolic uses of the body. As is shown by *Inferno* IX, Dante introduced ideas about allegory by using the physical body as a symbol for the textual corpus. The body was a common metaphor for the textual corpus in the Middle Ages, in part because Christ at the Incarnation had presented the Word, or His 'text', in bodily form. Scholars have studied the many ethical, spiritual, and literary resonances of the body in the *Comedy*. For example, with respect to literary issues, critics have discussed how Dante drew on the body when developing ideas about signs and semiology. However, Dantists have not considered in similar detail how the poet used the body when reflecting on allegory, a question that is bound up with medieval ideas about signs in general. How Dante uses the corpus, whether body or text, to reflect on allegory in the *Comedy* comes into clearer focus when considered in light of ideas about allegory in medieval literary theory and his 'other works'.

The Critical Context: Medieval and Dantean

In the Middle Ages, ideas about allegory underwrote a key distinction between religious and secular writing. Christians thought that God signified through the things of creation and the events of providential history (*allegoria in factis*), which could foreshadow or prefigure other things and events (*figura, typus*). Regarding the Bible, elements in the Old Testament prefigured events in the New, especially as concerns the Incarnation and Christ's mission (Luke 24:44; Galatians 4:21–6). Like Christ's body,

Scripture was considered a historical corpus perfectly figuring meaning. Exegetes also recognized that, even though the literal sense of the Bible described historical events, it could contain metaphorical or figurative language: for example, the erotic metaphors and images of the Song of Songs were considered to embellish a narrative about the relationship between Christ and the Church or between the soul and God. Christian readers theorized that in Scripture there were three 'other' senses in addition to the literal one: the allegorical, often related to Christ's life; the moral, concerned with personal behaviour; and the anagogical, associated with the afterlife. The senses of *allegoria in factis* were regularly illustrated by reference to Psalm 113 that dealt with Israel's flight from Egypt. Thus, the author of a Latin epistle (*Ep.* XIII; 1320?), which features an exposition of *Paradiso* I and is addressed to one of Dante's patrons during his exile, Cangrande della Scala, lord of Verona, discusses the psalm's senses. Though the letter's attribution to Dante is disputed, the epistle nevertheless sheds light on contemporary ideas about allegory and 'polysemy', the fact that a text may have 'many meanings' (7). The author explains that the literal sense of Psalm 113 concerns the history of Israel; the allegorical, humanity's redemption through Christ; the moral, the conversion of the soul from sin to grace; and the anagogical, the soul liberated from bondage in this world (7). Moreover, medieval writers, including Dante, considered the universe as a book (Psalm 18:1–2; and *Par.* XXXIII, 86). In fact, creation as a whole was assessed for 'traces' (*vestigia*) that revealed truths about God. Reading creation allegorically was encouraged by the mystical theology of the influential sixth-century Christian Platonist, Pseudo-Dionysius, who maintained that God is present everywhere, even in worms,[3] and by Neoplatonic philosophers, who claimed that the world was a 'veiled' embodiment of the spiritual realm.

God's signifying in history was contrasted to human authors signifying exclusively through the words of a fictional literal sense (*allegoria in verbis*). Thus, Dante defined the literal sense of literature as a 'beautiful lie' (*Conv.* II, i, 4). Theologians and philosophers regularly dismissed literary fictions as falsehood, sometimes adding that literature afforded only superficial pleasures, although they did not deny that it had some didactic value. Even fantastic or erotic texts like Ovid's *Metamorphoses* and *Art of Love* were read in medieval schools to teach the structures of grammar, ideas about antiquity, and lessons about ethics. It was also thought that ancient writers had occasionally intuited Christian truths in an imperfectly analogous manner to God's writing in history. In the twelfth century, a group of philosophical poets at Chartres canonized the idea that one needed to look 'under the veil' (*sub velamine*) or 'under the wrapping' (*sub integumento*) of a fictional narrative to discover ideas about the world or ethics.[4] These

Chartrean proposals, coupled with the patristic commonplace that Scripture was a book with meanings 'written within and without' (Ezekiel 2:9–10), probably influenced Dante's appeal in *Inferno* IX to look for 'doctrine' under the 'veil' of the textual corpus (compare *Purg.* VIII, 19–21; XXXIII, 100–3; and *Par.* IV, 40–5). A few works, for example parts of Virgil's *Aeneid* and of *Eclogue* IV about the birth of Augustus, were also considered to be historically true, and even to have prefigured Christ's birth and life. In the *Convivio*, Dante implied that many 'writings' ('scritture') could be interpreted according to three 'other' senses: the allegorical was explained with Ovid's account of Orpheus taming the beasts (signifying the education of the ignorant); the moral with the example of Christ's transfiguration (one should have few confidants); and the anagogical with Psalm 113 about Israel's flight from Egypt (the soul liberated from sin; II, i, 2–7). Such ideas developed alongside the more systematic reading of ancient myths as imperfect intuitions of Christian truths, and the increasingly common practice of using pagan myths in literature to represent Christian notions. Everything in medieval culture could therefore be allegorical: a Christian could read any text or thing allegorically (allegoresis). At the same time, writers and critics discussed how an author ought to compose a text (allegory) as they endeavoured to vindicate the dignity of literature as a discursive mode in comparison to philosophy, theology, and history.

Dante discussed ideas about allegory in nearly all his texts. Nonetheless, his 'other works' provide only partial insights into how the *Comedy* signifies, mainly because the poem is unique with respect to his other writings and indeed with respect to any classical and medieval text. However, Dante himself encouraged readers to consider his 'other works' in light of the *Comedy* by evoking them, especially the *Vita nova* and his love lyrics, within the poem. As will be explained, he recalled these writings to help readers appreciate the uniqueness of the *Commedia*, a work boldly presented as a divinely inspired 'sacred poem' (sacrato poema, poema sacro; *Par.* XXIII, 62 and XXV, 1).

For their part, most late-medieval and Renaissance readers tended to downplay the *Comedy*'s prophetic, providential, and salvific claims – the exception being the Carmelite friar Guido da Pisa, who characterized Dante as God's scribe and the 'pen of the Holy Spirit'.[5] Other commentators concentrated on the poem's classical, doctrinal, and historical allusions, marvelled at the descriptions of the other world and its inhabitants, and interpreted the poem as an allegorical fiction about the growth of the human soul guided first by Virgil (Reason) and then by Beatrice (Theology). Only in the twentieth century did ideas about the poem's allegory begin to change, although not initially in Italy, where scholars, like the philosopher Benedetto

Croce (1866–1952), celebrated the aesthetic and lyric aspects of the *Comedy* as distinct from its ideological (and thus allegorical) dimension. In North America, Charles Singleton (1909–85) initiated discussion of the poem's allegory when he suggested that its structures of meaning approximate Scriptural ones. He noted that the *Commedia*'s literal narrative has a 'historical sense' that grounds its three allegorical senses. However, Singleton downplayed the poem's historicity by claiming that the 'fiction of the *Divine Comedy* is that it is not fiction', which amounts to saying that it is verisimilar, and thus like other human fictions.[6]

Singleton's German contemporary, Erich Auerbach (1892–1957), also made recourse to ideas about the Bible's modes of signification. In particular, he utilized the concept of prefiguration to contextualize one of the *Comedy*'s striking novelties: its realistic depiction of psychologically complex individuals in contrast to the stilted personification allegories found in Prudentius' *Psychomachia* (*c.*405) and allegorical-didactic poems like Alan of Lille's *Anticlaudianus* (1181–4). Auerbach suggested that the denizens of the afterlife were 'figural' fulfilments of their earthly selves, whereby their eternal existence reflected their earthly lives. Dante himself elucidated the notion of the *contrapasso*, the system of punishment that, in Auerbach's terms, 'figures' the reality of the souls' temporal existence, by programmatically referring to the body. In *Inferno* XXVIII, the Occitan poet Bertran de Born, who turned father against son (a grotesque inversion of the love binding the Father and Son), is punished among the sowers of discord. Bertran physically embodies his sin by having his head severed from his body: 'thus in me is observed the retribution' (Così s'osserva in me lo contrapasso; 142). In light of the *Comedy*'s 'figuralism', scholars have been encouraged to explore further how the poem might communicate through recourse to typology and analogy, in particular by including events, symbols, and persons that are modelled on biblical exemplars and passages: the pilgrim's otherworldly journey recalls Christ's descent to Hell and resurrection.

In the mid-twentieth century, Bruno Nardi (1884–1968), a historian of ideas rather than a scholar of literature, argued that Dante presents the *Comedy* as a true prophetic vision, an interpretation that also has had a profound influence on subsequent discussions of its allegory. However, like other contemporary Italian *dantisti*, Nardi did not consider the poem as allegorical, nor did he fully explore the implications of maintaining that it is a true prophetic vision. Readers have continued to interrogate the ways in which the *Comedy* can be considered 'true' in relation to reality and Scripture. Ideas about *figura* and typology, whereby something is true in so far as it accords with Scripture or theological concepts, only account for a part of the poem's veracity. Robert Hollander addressed this matter by arguing that ideas about *allegoria in factis* as described in the letter to Cangrande – though these overtly refer only to the Bible and not to the *Comedy* – were generally valid for the poem. However, the problem with relying on the epistle to understand the *Comedy* is that its author also terms one of the poem's 'modes of treatment' 'fictional' (9). Moreover, claiming that the *Comedy* signifies according to *allegoria in factis* does not explain what role tropes and *modi* typically associated with literary texts may have in the poem (for example, the personification of Lady Poverty; *Par.* XI, 55–75). More recently, scholars have studied the poem itself for clues about its signifying properties by analysing its metaliterary passages about allegory. Such passages often appear in the liminal parts of the *Comedy* – areas of a medieval text that typically foreground matters related to the formal, signifying, and genre properties of a literary work – and are located at the beginning and close of canticles, as well as in cantos that mark transitions between major groups of souls.

Allegorical Writing in the *Comedy*

Inferno I foregrounds matters related to the poem's allegorical *modi tractandi*, or 'ways a text treats' a subject and signifies meaning. The canto functions as a 'prologue' (*prooemium*) to the *Comedy*, and introduces ideas about the textual and connoting properties of the poem that later cantos address in greater detail. The first part of *Inferno* I (1–63) features a plethora of references to bodies, which prompted some medieval readers to conclude that the pilgrim had sinned by submitting his reason to the appetites. The pilgrim arrives at the foot (piè; 13) of a hill; the sun's shoulders are clothed with light (16–17); and the pilgrim's body may be deformed because his left foot is dragging (28–30; the left was associated with carnality and worldliness). Like the Furies and Medusa in *Inferno* IX, the beasts that block the pilgrim's way are described in fleshly detail: their skin, head, physical appearance, and desires are mentioned (31–54). The carnality of the opening seems to be associated with traditions of fantastic allegorical writing set in oneiric landscapes populated by beasts. The pilgrim's 'voyage' (vïaggio; 91) may evoke the allegorical–didactic journeys of learning depicted in texts like the *Anticlaudianus*. The violent beasts are reminiscent of a personification allegory such as the *Psychomachia*; while the narrator's sleepiness evokes allegorical dream visions, like the erotic *Roman de la rose* (c.1230 and c.1275). Such works featured beasts representing vices and personifications of the liberal arts, virtues, and emotions.

In the second part of *Inferno* I (64–111), the subject of the narrative changes, as does the nature of the bodily references. This section treats matters related to the pilgrim's biography and providential history, and dramatizes a purification of carnal desires. Dante-character meets the shade of Virgil, who is not described physically, but instead in historically precise and individualized terms. The pilgrim initially wonders whether the ancient poet is a 'shade or real man' (od ombra od omo certo; 66), and Virgil answers that he is no longer a man but once was (67). Moreover, Virgil does not simply represent Reason, but talks about his poetry, historical epoch, and political-religious milieu (67–75). He then treats the earlier, seemingly fictional, parts of the canto – and this is the key – as though they were both part of Dante-character's real experience and part of providential history. Virgil contextualizes the pilgrim's battle with the carnal she-wolf in light of the history of Italy: he prophesizes that a 'greyhound' (veltro; 101), which does not feed on earth or flesh (perhaps Christ or a universal emperor), will hunt the beast whose 'greedy appetite is never satisfied' (mai non empie la bramosa voglia; 98). This hound will restore the Italy of the chaste Roman heroine Camilla (107).

Inferno I introduces the poem as a historical and a true text – true because it is intertwined with the unfolding of providence and revelation. The *Comedy* thereby radically purports to signify in a manner akin to biblical *allegoria in factis*, but also – and this is just as significant – subsumes within itself other modes of signification like *allegoria in verbis*. At the same time, the references to the body in *Inferno* I point to the kinds of truths the *Comedy* depicts. They imply that, unlike allegorical-fictional fables, Dante's text does not 'veil' or 'block' any kind of moral or anagogical meaning. The fantastic portion of the canto features bodies that obstruct the pilgrim's ascent; its historical-prophetic part instead recounts that a Christ-like greyhound will chasten bodily desires, and Virgil advises the pilgrim to follow him through the afterlife. As noted, medieval exegetes thought that the moral sense concerned the soul's conversion from sin to grace, and the anagogical pertained to the soul being liberated from bondage in this world. *Inferno* I accordingly depicts a purification of sinful carnality, as well as a pilgrim who escapes from physical bondage into the spiritual afterlife. *Inferno* IX equally suggests that the *Comedy* 'unblocks' obstacles to anagogical truths, an idea again symbolized by the pilgrim's entering into the city of Dis, and hence passing (further) into the spiritual otherworld.

After cantos I and IX, in *Inferno*, Dante most overtly reflected on issues relating to allegory on the outer edge of the circle encompassing sins of fraud (Malebolge), an area that, once again, foregrounds matters related to textual signification and the body in order to challenge medieval ideas about literature as falsehood. The poet raises the issue of the truthfulness of the *Comedy* when the pilgrim encounters the monster Geryon, the 'foul image of fraud' (sozza imagine di froda; XVII, 7), whose physical presence dominates the action. The poet provides an extended description of the creature – a highly unusual rhetorical strategy in the *Comedy* – that focuses on its body. The beast is a hybrid: it has the face of a man; its trunk and limbs are comprised of bestial and reptilian elements; and its tail resembles that of a scorpion (XVII, 1–15). The narrator swears by the verses of the *Comedy* that he saw a 'truth that has the face of a lie' (ver c'ha faccia di menzogna; XVI, 124). The episode also features other key allegorical concepts introduced in *Inferno* IX; for example, the notion of reading 'beneath the veil' of a text is recalled when Dante mentions those who 'not only see the [external] deed but look with understanding into thoughts!' (non veggion pur l'ovra, / ma per entro i pensier mirano col senno!; XVI, 119–20). Moreover, Geryon's body recalls a textual veil: it is covered with drapes, weavings, and signs (XVII, 15–18), thereby appearing to demand interpretation.

Dante constructed Geryon as an analogue of the *Comedy* to reflect upon the novelty of its textual properties, including its relationship to the fraudulent or imperfect nature of human language and representation. The references to allegory underscore this point since allegory signalled that valid meaning was to be found beyond the 'letter' of a text. Dante, however, stressed the truthfulness of his poem by distinguishing its literal sense, symbolized by its 'carnality' or 'superficiality', from the literal sense of other texts. While fictional texts have a false literal sense, the *Comedy* has a literal sense that seems false but is true (XVI, 124). The paradoxical medieval wonder of a literary text being truthful and historical is symbolized, in part, by the 'marvellous ... figure' (figura ... maravigliosa) of Geryon's hybrid body (131–2). By creating a 'marvellous' body, a notion that can be extended to the whole *Comedy*, Dante likened his creation to God's work as the divine artist, the *Deus artifex*. God created the world, and therefore no body or object in it can be completely 'against nature', not even Geryon's corpus. Even though Dante's poem broke canonical rules about genre by integrating various styles and linguistic registers, the *Comedy*, like Geryon's body, is a natural part of God's creation. Accordingly, the literal sense of the poem cannot be discarded or looked past as in standard secular writing. In *Inferno* IX, the pilgrim must shield his eyes from Medusa and avoid the Furies, figures emblematic of secular writing and myth, because their bodies harm, petrify, and damn. Conversely, like Scripture, the *Comedy*'s corpus is directly connected to the unfolding of providential history and revelation. The pilgrim, therefore, must gaze upon and engage with Geryon's body, which physically impacts on his reality by transporting him forward on his divinely ordained journey. In other words, the creature's body, like the meaning it signifies, is immediately and directly present. Dante probably drew on the metaliterary resonances of the body to counter the criticism of literature as falsehood because, in the wake of the Incarnation, the body could be emblematic of truth and history. As Christ's body perfectly succeeded, so Dante – insofar as a human author could – attempted to embody truth and influence the course of history.

In the opening cantos of *Purgatorio*, Dante continued to highlight the formal properties and intended effects of his allegorical poem. He again distinguished the 'modes of writing' of his 'sacred poem' from those of classical myth and secular literature. *Purgatorio* I highlights matters related to the *Comedy*'s allegory by overtly evoking the images of the 'veil' and the (textual) corpus. Cato, the guardian of Purgatory, explains that he left the 'veil' (vesta; 75) of his body on earth by committing suicide to free himself from the tyranny of Caesar. On the one hand, Cato represents the best of classical culture since he is the first saved soul encountered by the travellers. On the other, he reveals how he and the ancient world were transfixed by the sensual superficiality, the carnal-literal 'veil', of creation and literature. Not only was Cato blinded by his experience of embodied reality to the point that he fatally harmed himself, but he was also bewitched by the kind of eroticism present in some of Dante's lyric poems, one of which is cited in the next canto. Indeed, as Cato was compelled by his wife Marzia's physical beauty to do whatever she willed (*Purg.* I, 85–7), so the pilgrim and the newly arrived penitents are sensually overwhelmed by the musician Casella's recital of one of Dante's pre-exile *canzoni*, 'Amor che ne la mente mi ragiona' (Love that reasons in my mind; II, 112). Cato subsequently criticizes the souls – and by extension (Dante's previous) love poetry – by declaring that the penitents are wasting their time and neglecting their spiritual purification (112–23). Cato commands that the penitents must strip off the carnal veil or 'slough' (scoglio; 122) that clouds their vision of God. Consequently, Dante questions the poetics and the signifying efficacy of pagan literature and his earlier love poetry. Whereas the 'veils' of those *corpora* confused Cato's and the penitents' search for valid meaning, the *Comedy* spiritually enlightens its readers and sharpens their perceptions of reality.

Purgatorio II further differentiates the symbolic properties of pagan and erotic literature from those of the *Comedy*'s signifying qualities by restressing that the poem should be interpreted using the conventions of *allegoria in factis*. The spirits arrive in Purgatory singing Psalm 113, thereby prompting some modern readers to turn to the epistle to Cangrande to clarify the *Comedy*'s allegory. However, given that the first two *cantiche* circulated before the letter was written, this means that clarification of its symbolic characteristics ought to be sought in the poem itself. In fact, the reference to Psalm 113 reveals that Dante carefully guided perceptions of the *Comedy*'s modes of meaning by evoking common ideas about biblical allegory. At the same time, the allusion does not imply that Dante intended to suggest that his poem communicated with three allegorical-spiritual senses throughout. In his *Monarchia*, Dante cautions against thinking that allegory is systematically present in every passage of a text (III, iv, 6–11). As the quotation of Psalm 113 confirms, it is only those parts of the *Commedia* that deal directly with providential history and with the pilgrim's divinely sanctioned journey that ought to be read according to *allegoria in factis*. The opening two cantos of *Purgatorio* thus develop issues first raised in *Inferno* I, thereby highlighting that the *Comedy* employs a biblically inspired 'figural' mode of signification: episodes, events, and persons acquire their full significance later in the poem when considered in light of subsequent episodes, events, and persons.

In *Purgatorio*, Dante also addressed matters related to allegory and ideas about semiology more generally. Since allegory was defined broadly as 'other speak', discussions of allegory encompassed and were influenced by notions about other categories of signs (*signa*), such as enigmatic symbols, visual images, and language. In the Earthly Paradise, Beatrice foregrounds semiological matters by discussing a range of signs, for example the 'enigma', 'words', and 'traces' (enigma, parole, vestigge; XXXIII, 50, 53, 108) left by God in creation. Tellingly, Beatrice deals with divine semiology, a crucial subject for an author purporting to be God's scribe, in Eden, the area situated between the terrestrial and celestial realms, because God's signs, as is the case with the *Comedy*, were supposed to mediate between the spiritual/divine and the carnal/human.

In the Earthly Paradise, the pilgrim sees the events and written record of providential history in bodily form. He witnesses a procession of human, animal, and fantastic figures which, at first glance, evoke the types of personifications and bestial representations of the emotions, virtues, and vices present in many late-antique and medieval allegorical fictions (*Purg.* XXIX, 43–154 and XXXII, 103–60). As the procession unfolds, however, it becomes clear that the pageant is a highly synthesized and detailed allegorical embodiment of salvation history as recorded in the books of the Old and New Testament (twenty-four elders symbolize the books of the Old Testament; four animals the four Gospels; a chariot the Church; the griffon Christ). Moreover, the sometimes enigmatic and fantastic nature of the imagery recalls John's prophetic dream-vision recorded in Revelation. Appropriately, in Eden, the apostle appears asleep (XXIX, 142–4), a detail that points not only to the inspired nature of the *Comedy*, but also to Dante's active role in its creation. The fact that the pilgrim is awake when he views the procession stresses the historical reality of his journey and the veracity of his poetic account.

The procession frames the pilgrim's reunion with Beatrice at the top of the mountain, helping to set up a complex contrast between the use and inter-pretation of verbal and embodied signs in the *Comedy* and in the *Vita nova*, the latter being explicitly recalled at *Purg.* XXX, 115. The *Vita nova* recounts the narrator's relationship with his beloved who has Christ-like attributes (for example, her greeting has salvific effects; *Vn* XI, 1–4 [5, 4–7]). In chapter XXV [16], Dante explains why he includes a personification of Love in an autobiographical narrative that should be distinguished from fiction, empha-sizing that he is imitating classical authors. The same section also fore-grounds similarities between signification in the *Vita nova* and in the Bible. In the previous chapter, the narrator has a vision of the lady of his friend and fellow-poet Guido Calvacanti, who is called both Primavera ('Spring' but also 'She who comes first') and Giovanna, because she preceded Beatrice, her name deriving from John the Baptist, who came before the 'true Light'. Dante thus establishes a figural relationship between Giovanna/John the Baptist, who announce the Word, and Beatrice/Christ, who (re)embody the Word (XXIV, 4 [15, 4]). In the Earthly Paradise, in keeping with the *Vita nova*, Beatrice recalls that she successfully guided her lover for a time thanks to her bodily presence, although, once she died – she continues – he abandoned her to follow false corporeal images (*Purg.* XXX, 109–45), a revelation that runs counter to the story told in the 'little book' (*Vn* I, 1 [1, 1]). She concludes that the decomposition of her body should have taught him to focus on spiritual rather than physical matters (XXXI, 49–57).

As in its opening, *Purgatorio*'s final cantos thus question a mode of signifying based vitally on erotic bodily signs. Beatrice's remarks offer a critique of the *Vita nova*'s symbolic 'mode', as well as its efficacy, for all its Scriptural allusiveness, as an ethical and salvific text. Beatrice charac-terizes the pilgrim as a writer who had concentrated on a single body and utilized just one 'genre' of signs, namely Beatrice's corpus and erotic secular literature. Conversely, the allegorical pageant, that is both a divine text and a record of God's writing, incorporates the complexity of signs present in creation by featuring different kinds of bodies (animal, elderly, female, male) and a diversity of signs (enigmatic, fantastic, historical, erotic). Accordingly, before the pilgrim ascends to Paradise, Beatrice enjoins him to remember as accurately as possible what has just been revealed to him (XXXIII, 73–8). Beatrice's command implies that the poet-scribe's representation will imitate not the personifications of human authors but the embodied symbols of God's divine 'writing'. The *Comedy*, therefore, endeavours to approximate the signifying range and properties of God's two 'books', Scripture and providential history. As the souls correct their previous sinful dispositions during their purgatorial ascent, so, in *Purgatorio*, Dante attempts to correct some of his misguided youthful ideas about allegory, signification, and embodiment.

In *Paradiso*, Dante returns to the subject of signs while reflecting on the ineffability of Heaven. In the opening canto, the narrator prays for help to make manifest 'the shadow of the blessed kingdom' (l'ombra del beato regno; I, 23), underlining that the *cantica* presents an approximate and analogic 'shadow' of the divine reality. Ideas about signification are also highlighted when Beatrice explains why the souls, who reside beyond space and time in the Empyrean, appear to the pilgrim in the lower celestial spheres. Beatrice clarifies that the souls experience beatitude in various degrees, and that this truth is revealed to the pilgrim by having the souls descend to the heaven that most closely approaches their paradisiacal reality: 'It is necessary to speak thus to your faculty, since only from sense perception does it grasp that which it then makes fit for the intellect. For this reason Scripture condescends to your capacity and attributes hands and feet to God, having another meaning' (Così parlar conviensi al vostro ingegno / però che solo da sensato apprende / ciò che fa poscia d'intelletto degno. / Per questo la Scrittura condescende / a vostra facultate, e piedi e mano / attribuisce a Dio e altro intende; IV, 40–5). On the one hand, Beatrice clarifies how God reveals the nature of eternal glory in Paradise to the pilgrim who is limited by his humanity. On the other, given the overt allusions to 'Scripture' and allegory ('altro intende'), her remarks also address how the poet should imitate divine modes of signification in order to communicate, of course indirectly, the immaterial-spiritual reality of Paradise. Thanks to Beatrice's reference to the bodily representation of God, it becomes apparent that *Paradiso*'s modes of signification are elucidated not in light of Geryon's monstrous physique, but in terms of a 'perfect', because divine, metaphorical human body. In contrast to disfigured infernal bodies, in Paradise the blessed form shapes, such as circles, letters, and even a symbolic eagle, that are untainted by earthly imperfection. Furthermore, in the heaven of the Sun, the pilgrim hears an allegory about Francis' love for Lady Poverty, an erotic personification narrative purified of unchaste carnal sexuality (X, 7–12, 61–81; XI, 55–84). The *Paradiso* thus models itself on signs and a love untainted by corporeal and symbolic imperfection so that it can offer a 'shadowy' glimpse of the divine truths that its author had been privileged to experience.

Allegorical Reading in the *Comedy*

While defining the properties of his allegorical writing, Dante concurrently reflected on allegorical reading. As noted, the two were intimately related in medieval culture, and they illuminated each another. It has been suggested that the whole of the *Comedy* dramatizes a journey of interpretation: the soul lost in the confusing wood of this world returns to the fullness of meaning in the presence of God. The nature of this interpretive journey is illustrated in several key episodes centred on the soul shedding its improper attachment to the self and the body. In particular, *Inferno* V and IX, that respectively feature the first carnal sin and the transition from the sins of incontinence to those of the intellect, dramatize the importance of reading and interpreting properly. In canto V, Francesca explains that she and Paolo were reading 'for delight' (per diletto; 127) about Lancelot and Guinevere and that the characters' erotic embrace prompted them to commit adultery (133–8). In *Inferno* IX, Dante invites his readers to look beneath the 'strange verses' of his textual corpus.

Both episodes have connections with Paul's affirmation that 'the letter kills, but the Spirit gives life' (II Corinthians 3:6), a biblical verse that inspired centuries of meditation on the nature of reading. For example, Augustine warned readers not to be mesmerized by the literal sense, the 'body' or 'veil' of a text, or by the superficiality of creation, but to look through the literal-carnal for allegorical-spiritual meaning.[7] Francesca and Paolo read 'superficially' about a kiss that they decide to imitate directly, thereby falling into adultery. In so doing, they misunderstand the moral warnings implicit in the story: the kiss was personally sinful and more broadly contributed to the destruction of the Arthurian court. Moreover, their reading exclusively 'for delight' violated classical and medieval precepts regarding the ethical purpose of literature. In the *Art of Poetry*, Horace explained that literature was for 'delighting and instructing the reader' (*AP* 343), and his proposal prompted medieval readers to classify literature under the philosophical category of ethics (*ethice supponitur*). Francesca and Paolo did not find any 'useful' or moral instruction in the text that they were reading, but focused solely on the erotic events recounted. They did not look under the literal-carnal 'veil' to discover an allegorical-moral meaning; rather they allowed the text to arouse them – indeed their superficial reading physically 'changed the colour of [their] faces' (quella lettura . . . scolorocci il viso; 131). Finally, the episode is a parodic reversal of Augustine's conversion. On reading biblical verses about drunkenness and lust (Romans 13:13–14), the saint, unlike Dante's sinners, was inspired to dedicate his life to spiritual and contemplative matters (*Conf.* VIII, xii, 29–30).

In *Inferno* IX, the pilgrim is cautioned not to gaze on the dangerous female body of the Medusa, as doing this would turn him into stone. When considered in light of the accompanying appeal to the reader to interpret correctly (61–3), the warning implies that we need to 'look' carefully to avoid being blinded by the literal sense of a text and equally by the superficial sensuality of creation. Outside the gates of Dis, the pilgrim avoids these pitfalls with the assistance of Virgil as the representative of human reason and, more substantially, of a heavenly messenger, who opens the gates for the two travellers (77–105). The celestial envoy's movements, appearance, and behaviour recall not only Christ's harrowing of Hell, but also the voyages of the ancient god Hermes, who was the son of Zeus and the messenger of the gods. Hermes was associated with crossing boundaries, especially between the divine and mortal realms, as well as with hermeneutics (as his name implies). Dante thereby suggests that readers aided by reason and especially by Christian revelation can deal with exegetical difficulties and moral obstacles. In the following canto, the pilgrim encounters heretics, namely those who persisted in maintaining false doctrinal beliefs, a sin that involved the wilful misinterpretation of reality and Scripture. He principally spends time among the Epicureans who believed that the soul dies with the body (X, 13–15). Like Francesca and Paolo, these sinners failed to understand the proper relationship between body and soul, ultimately becoming blinded by the physical 'veil' of creation. As their beliefs imprisoned the soul in the body, so they are eternally imprisoned in a tomb; as they failed to recognize an eternal spiritual life beyond the carnality of this world, so they see in a flawed way: they only know future and past events (58–72 and 97–105). Indeed, at the Last Judgement, they will lose all ability to 'open up' meaning: 'all our knowledge will be dead from the moment the door of the future will be closed' (nostra conoscenza da quel punto / che del futuro fia chiusa la porta; 107–8).

Other episodes deal with the question of how the *Commedia* should impact its readers, which is the issue at the heart of the poem's ethical concerns and reforming aims. For example, after the narrator describes each part of Geryon's body, the pilgrim rides the creature to the next part of Hell. The idea that descriptions of physical bodies could 'move' readers stems from medieval ideas about the emotions and passions. In treatises on rhetoric and poetic composition, writers were advised to employ detailed descriptions of beautiful and ugly bodies (*descriptio corporis*) to 'arouse' and 'motivate' (*movetur*) a person to behave virtuously.[8] Given Geryon's close association with explanations regarding the status of the *Comedy*, by describing and then travelling on the monster, Dante reveals that his poem too can affect its readers by depicting the process of moral and spiritual progress in terms of physical presence and movement. Furthermore, the pilgrim's aerial flight stands in contrast both to Phaethon's failed voyage to discover his celestial origins and to Ulysses' aimless wanderings. Phaethon, who did not believe that he was the son of Apollo, and Ulysses, who abandoned his family 'to gain experience of the world' (a divenir del mondo esperto; *Inf.* XXVI, 98), are both damned because they were poor readers. The former was a bad interpreter of his divine origins, while the latter of the spiritual purpose of humanity's terrestrial 'journey' since he focused his attention narrowly and exclusively on earthbound experiences. Unlike Phaethon and Ulysses, the pilgrim is moved by his 'reading', namely his encounters with the damned, the penitents, and the blessed, to search for truth in a morally appropriate and divinely sanctioned manner. His voyage, therefore, does not end in disaster; nor does he end up damned in Hell. Instead, close to the end of his experience of the Empyrean, he comprehensively reads 'in a volume that which is spread in leaves throughout the universe' (in un volume / ciò che per l'universo si squaderna; *Par.* XXXIII, 86–7).

In Purgatory, the pilgrim learns how to love others and the body properly. Indeed, Virgil's major exposition on love, which appears around the centre of the *Comedy* (*Purg.* XVII–XVIII), is followed by an episode in which the pilgrim gazes on an eroticized female body. As his dream of the siren reveals, Dante-character grapples with the difficulties of loving the body correctly (XIX, 7–24). By staring at her, the pilgrim transforms her hideous body into that of a sensual and attractive woman. Given the erotized context, it is likely that her body represents the seductions of the world and secular literature. Virgil must strip the 'clothes' (drappi; 32) from her body to reveal the fetid and corrupt nature of the material world if this is loved improperly (28–33). In Eden, Beatrice confirms that the pilgrim had, in fact, been drawn off course by the false pleasures of the sirens (XXXI, 34–46), and that he had been 'too fixed' (troppo fisso; XXXII, 1–12) on her physical body. After confessing his errors, the pilgrim peers beneath Beatrice's 'veil' (velo; XXXI, 82), and seven nymphs symbolizing the virtues purify his sight, which allows him to glimpse Christ reflected in Beatrice's radiant eyes (XXXI, 106–23). Nonetheless, the pilgrim still struggles to understand the meaning of Beatrice's prophetic, or 'dark' (buia; XXXIII, 46), discourse on the drama of salvation history. Recalling the Medusan threat evoked in *Inferno* IX, the pilgrim's intellect is 'petrified' (impetrato; 74), his intellectual obtuseness evidence that he is still prone to reading 'carnally'. Consequently, Beatrice must present providential history 'literally' by stripping her words 'naked' (nude; 100–1), thereby removing the 'veil' that has blinded her lover. Only then is the pilgrim ready to ascend to the spiritual light of Paradise where he will properly refine his abilities to 'read' spiritually which, in turn, will allow him to return to earth and compose the *Commedia*.

Conclusion

Immediately prior to his union with God, the pilgrim sees three coloured circles, one of which is 'painted [inside] with our likeness' (pinta de la nostra effige; *Par.* XXXIII, 131). A human form surrounded by three luminous circles contrastively recalls the pilgrim threatened by three carnal beasts in the dark wood. The opposition between the opening and the close of the poem further refines the function of allegorical writing and reading in the *Comedy*. God's recourse to the human form to 'paint' an 'image' (imago; 138) of a great divine truth, the Incarnation, confirms the centrality of the body in spiritual signification. The connections with *Inferno* I highlight how, in the *Comedy*, the literary corpus has been transformed to embody and allegorically reveal spiritual-anagogical truth. The bestial bodies that forced the pilgrim down to 'where the sun is silent' (dove 'l sol tace; 60) have been replaced by a figure aglow with divine radiance. By extension, this stark opposition reminds readers how, in composing his poem, Dante, as God's scribe, has incorporated and transformed the 'corpora' of various literary traditions, beginning with that of the secular allegorical texts evoked in *Inferno* I. Dante emphasizes that, as a human author, he imitates, however approximately, God's writing by employing every type of sign and mode of signification. The *Commedia* is thus both a divine 'image' and a 'trace' of divine 'traces', thereby transcending not only canonical literary distinctions and precepts, but also contemporary ideological biases related to historical versus fictional literature, religious versus secular writing, *allegoria in factis* versus *allegoria in verbis*. As a consequence, the poem establishes – in a bold and revolutionary fashion – the cultural import and the ethical-salvific value of the formal properties of literature in general. Finally, the ties between the first and the last canto offer an insight into how we as readers should understand the true nature of reality. Indeed, the links suggest that the carnal 'dark wood' is actually permeated with divine light – one's experience of the world depends on how one perceives it. In allegorical terms, the *Commedia* instructs us to see the divine 'Other' everywhere, to see spiritual light even in the darkness, as we make our way on our earthly pilgrimage towards God.[9]

Notes

1. Isidore of Seville, *The Etymologies*, trans. S. A. Barney *et al.* (Cambridge University Press, 2006), I, xxxvii, 22 (p. 63).
2. Alan of Lille, 'Anticlaudianus' in *Literary Works*, ed. and trans. W. Wetherbee (Cambridge, MA: Harvard University Press, 2013), III, 164–75 (pp. 304–7).
3. Pseudo–Dionysius, *The Celestial Hierarchy*, in *The Complete Works*, trans. C. Luibheid (Mahwah, NJ: Paulist Press, 1987), II (pp. 147–53).

4. A. J. Minnis and A. B. Scott (eds.), *Medieval Literary Theory and Criticism c.1100–c.1375: The Commentary Tradition* (Oxford: Clarendon Press, 1991), pp. 113–64.

5. Guido da Pisa, *Expositiones et glose; Declaratio super 'Comediam' Dantis*, ed. M. Rinaldi and P. Locatin (Rome: Salerno, 2013), p. 242 (my translation).

6. C. S. Singleton, *Dante's Commedia: Elements of Structure* (Baltimore, MD: Johns Hopkins University Press, 1977 [1954]), p. 62.

7. Augustine, *On Christian Doctrine*, trans. D. W. Robertson, Jr. (Upper Saddle River, NJ: Prentice–Hall, 1958), III, v, 9–x, 16 (pp. 83–9); and *Confessions*, VI, iii, 4–iv, 6; and VIII, xi, 25–xii, 30.

8. Matthew of Vendôme, *Ars Versificatoria*, trans. R. Parr (Milwaukee, WI: Marquette University Press), I, 57–60 (pp. 38–40).

9. I am grateful to Zyg Barański and Simon Gilson for their comments on earlier versions of this chapter.

8

SIMONE MARCHESI

Classical Culture

Terminology and History

As a bilingual Latin-vernacular writer, Dante's relationship to classical culture was significant and complex, so that describing it amounts to surveying his culture *per se*. The cultural system in which Dante operated and into which he inscribed the *Comedy* was predominantly defined by works either written in Latin or stemming, when composed in the vernacular, from a 'modern' engagement with Latin texts. His poem, too, has a special relationship with classical culture. Before becoming a classic, Dante's *Commedia* was, one might say, a 'classicist' poem: a work designed to enter into a close dialogue with classical texts.

For Dante, classical culture was multifaceted. In a general sense, it consisted of a body of knowledge, mediated by texts written at different times and places, organized along a broad historical continuum, conceptualized as a tradition unfolding in time and intersecting with other traditions and lineages defined by linguistic, thematic, and historical contrastive features. When applied to the late Middle Ages, the label 'classical' may be taken as meaning a cultural complex transmitted in and by 'non-vernacular', 'non-Christian', and 'non-modern' texts. These include works from the archaic age (and the relatively remote cultural space of Greece and Greek), like the Homeric poems, as well as literature from the present of pre-humanist circles around the poet and historian Albertino Mussato and the Bolognese professor of literature Giovanni del Virgilio.

Between these traditions, both of which make an appearance in the *Commedia*, there lies a body of writings with which Dante's poem also interacts usually in more sustained ways. It is a textual and cultural complex that encompasses philosophy (both theoretical and practical, Aristotle's *Ethics* and *Physics* along with Plato's *Timaeus* and Boethius' *Consolatio Philosophiae*); history (Livy's *Ab Urbe condita* as much as Orosius' *Historiae*, along with Valerius Maximus' *Facta et dicta Memorabilia*); Latin poetry (Virgil's complete works but also a school text like the *Ecloga Theoduli*); and poetics (Horace's *Ars poetica* and Geoffrey of Vinsauf's

Poetria nova); natural sciences (Pliny's *Naturalis historia* in the background of scholastic commentaries to Aristotle's works); political theology (Augustine's *De civitate Dei* and Giles of Rome's *De regimine principum*). Despite their differences, all these texts are part of Dante's classical culture.

In the *Comedy*, the presence of classical antiquity is felt in two main ways: directly, through characters, ideas, and texts portrayed and cited in the poem; and indirectly, as part of the horizon of expectation of Dante's audience: that is, of the cultural codes by way of which his readers would approach and interpret his text. In both cases, the line separating classical from non-classical was more blurred than might seem today. Thus, not all the characters constituting the classical canon presented in *Inferno* IV are uniformly non-modern, non-vernacular, and non-Christian. Averroës and Saladin are certainly non-Christian, but they are less ancient than the rest of their companions in Limbo, and, unlike the other figures, their status as 'authorities' is problematic. Equally, other key late-antique figures, such as Augustine and Boethius, are evidently non-modern and non-vernacular, and in chronological terms belong to the classical sphere, and yet, as Christians, they are less classical than their pagan counterparts. In addition, the ancient Latin poet Statius, who appears in *Purgatory* XXI, is uniquely presented as a Christian, a Dantean invention that substantially complicates his cultural identity, as do other Christianized classical figures, such as Cato of Utica in *Purgatorio* I and II, as well as the emperor Trajan and the Trojan soldier Ripheus in *Paradiso* XX. With the inclusion of these characters, Dante destabilized the cultural and historical expectations of his immediate audience.

Similarly, a concept and institution such as the Roman empire, the universal power that Dante treated as the cornerstone of his political vision, appears to contradict our earlier categorization of 'classical'. Dante's Holy Roman Empire was at once ancient, Christian, and vernacular. Although ancient in origin, the empire had not lost its key historical function. While secular in its workings, it was essentially Christian. While Latin in most of its legal and rhetorical manifestations, it had recently also begun to rely on the vernacular, as confirmed by the *Commedia* itself. For Dante, therefore, the Roman-ness of the Holy Roman Empire was no idle, vestigial qualifier of its past, but a crucial characterization of the monarchical institution, and a component of its claim to power in the present. Thus, in *Paradiso* VI, the emperor Justinian's recapitulation of imperial history is never divorced from a dissection of current Guelf and Ghibelline factionalism, presented as a vital contemporary political malady, a direct consequence of the failure of imperial authority in the present.

In sum, what we term today the 'classical past' was for Dante not a matter of archaeology but of actual and present relevance. His meditation on the relics of antiquity never emphasized the mutilations affecting its textual corpus and the status as ruins of its monumental architecture. As we will see, textual and architectural ancient monuments were viewed as surviving in his present. The same dialectical relationship affects the *Comedy*'s poetics (its narrative imagination and literary dialogue with ancient sources), the poem's hermeneutics (the interpretive frame in which that dialogue was intended to be read), and the relationship with the world outside the text that the classical elements establish (the active presence of the classical past in Dante's age).

Classical Elements in the Poem's Plot

Dante's decision to cast the Latin poet Virgil as the protagonist's first interlocutor and then his guide through almost two-thirds of the narrative represents an unexpected classicist move that has repercussions throughout the *Commedia*. The first two cantos of *Inferno* establish the complex nature of their relationship. Starting in *Inferno* I, 36, when Virgil first appears, the text coaxes readers into accepting that a poem on the Christian afterlife will entertain an open dialogue with the classical past. The speech in which Virgil explains how he was assigned the responsibility of rescuing the pilgrim (*Inf.* II, 43–126) combines elements of a clearly defined Christian afterlife, with souls in Heaven playing an intercessionary role, and classical ones, especially in the juxtaposition of the two proemial scenes of cantos I and II, the second being reminiscent of the classical epic convention of including a heavily dialogic prologue in Heaven after a prologue on earth. Thus, Virgil's *Aeneid* has a similar prologue (I, 227–96); Ovid's *Metamorphoses* features a council of the gods (I, 163–252); and Lucan replaces the transcendent setting of his predecessors with scenes of divination in *Pharsalia* I, 584–672. In each case, the narrative is halted to consider the larger forces at work in the poems' plots and, in Virgil and Lucan, to provide indications of the eventual outcome of the action. By staging a scene in the Christian Paradise, Dante indirectly evokes classical precedents while encouraging readers to measure the distance between his new poem and its ancient literary antecedents.

The rest of the *Inferno* confirms that the *Commedia* carefully negotiates between classical and Christian elements. It soon becomes evident that, while the metaphysical co-ordinates of Dante's afterlife are fundamentally Christian, characters, situations, and actions that are featured in it are imported from a culture that is not specifically Christian but classical.

The geography of Hell is, for instance, markedly classicizing and essentially derived from Virgil's account of Aeneas' descent into the underworld in *Aeneid* VI. Several of the monstrous guardians of the various circles of Dante's Hell are drawn directly from classical exemplars; Charon in canto III, Minos in V, Cerberus in VI, Plutus in VII, the Minotaur and centaurs in XII, the Harpies in XIII, and Geryon in XVII are all beings that are located in an eminently Christian metaphysical universe but do not actually originate from it. Each figure derives some traits from the literary tradition, but these are in turn balanced by Dantean innovations. Charon is explicitly termed a 'demon' (dimonio; III, 109), Minos acquires a devilish tail (V, 11), while Cerberus is fed a handful of dirt rather than a honeyed cake. The novelty of Dante's classicizing Christian poem lies in its interplay between adoption and adaptation.

Other distinctive elements in the *Comedy* are similarly dependent on a rewriting of classical antecedents. When the pilgrim wonders about the hydrological arrangement of the landscape he is traversing, Virgil offers a summary explanation that is closely aligned to the pagan otherworldly river system as conceived by him and other classical poets. All the tears shed in the world above, Virgil explains, flow down into Hell to form interconnected bodies of water. The names and qualities attributed to each match those that classical mythological lore had devised: Acheron, Styx, Phlegethon, Cocytus (XIV, 115–20; and cp. *Aen.* VI, 295, 439, 265, and 132 respectively). Any educated reader would have recognized the classical origin of the designations of the *Commedia*'s infernal rivers. As the exchange proceeds, it becomes clear that the pilgrim, too, appreciates the geography of Hell in classical terms. When, in line with *Aeneid* VI, 705, he asks about Lethe, Virgil clarifies that he had not mentioned it, because it is not found in Hell but in Purgatory. Lethe finally appears in *Purgatorio* XXXII, where Dante associates the classical river with one of his own invention, the Eünoè.

Classical antiquity also provides Dante with a significant portion of the *Commedia*'s personnel. Inventories of the poem's 'classical' characters usually include about two hundred names, ranging from the Greek hero Achilles to the philosopher Zeno. This canon is far from being a simple frequency index, since it includes as individual entries several characters who appear more than once in the *Comedy* or influence more than one passage in the text. Thus, Aristotle and Ovid (among the authors) or Narcissus and Ulysses (among the characters) recur regularly. There are scores of passages openly based on Ovid's poetry and dependent on Aristotelian philosophy; while Narcissus (*Inf.* XXX, *Purg.* XXX, and *Par.* III) and Ulysses (*Inf.* XXVI, *Purg.* II and XIX, and *Par.* XXVII) return across cantos in highly articulated structures of repetition. In comparison,

Scriptural figures appear less frequently: sixty-five names that range from Abel to Simon Magus. Hence, to judge from its personnel, the poem is strikingly more classical than biblical. While the *Comedy*'s horizon of reference is unabashedly Christian, its building blocks, especially but not solely in *Inferno*, are mainly classical.

Among classical characters, Dante grants one group an especially prominent position. The ancient poets, presented as a lineage, a 'fair school' (bella scola; *Inf.* IV, 94), appear together in Limbo, in the poem's most explicitly classicizing episode, where the pilgrim-poet is inducted into their company. A powerful metapoetic awareness characterizes the encounter. The scene narrativizes a moment of canon formation that transforms the traditional scholastic lists of authoritative authors (*auctores*) into an otherworldly encounter: 'that is Homer the sovereign poet; the other is Horace satirist who comes; Ovid is the third, and the last Lucan' (quelli è Omero poeta sovrano; / l'altro è Orazio satiro che vene; / Ovidio è 'l terzo, e l'ultimo Lucano; 86–90). It is significant that the movement from Homer to Lucan is not simply a matter of ranking, but also of articulating in chronological and spatial dimensions the canon of epic poetry to which the *Commedia* belongs: from Homer, through Virgil, to Lucan. The pilgrim-poet becomes the 'sixth among such wisdom' (sesto tra cotanto senno; 102). This is a central moment in the construction of the *Comedy*'s identity as a classicizing text, a moment that relies on the interplay between traditional values and innovation. In his short interaction with the poets of the 'fair school', the pilgrim is not only elevated to their rank, but he and the *Commedia* are also associated with a major cross-genre segment of Latin literature, the tradition of hexametrical poetry, thereby hinting at the poem's generic eclecticism. While all composed verse in hexameters, the poets chose different 'modes': epic (Homer and Virgil); love (Ovid); ethics (Horace); and history (Lucan). They thus also serve as standard representatives of different poetic 'styles'. Medieval genre theory divided literary works into three major categories: 'high' ('tragedy'); 'middle' ('comedy'); and 'low' ('satire'). The classical 'fair school' conventionally embodies 'tragedy' and 'satire', but it is Dante, the author of a new Christian 'comedy', who astonishingly completes and revolutionizes the generic triad. Indeed, his poem transcends the established distinctions between different 'styles' by synthesizing all of them in its pages, thereby going beyond the achievements of classical literature.

In addition to presenting the *Commedia*'s relationship to classical literature, *Inferno* IV reviews the 'great souls' (spiriti magni; 109) of antiquity, divided into exemplars of the active and speculative life: on the one hand, heroes of the past, whose deeds have been recorded in writing; and on the other, authoritative thinkers, whose writings have continued to influence later generations. The fact that it is the poets who grant the protagonist access to the noble castle in which the virtuous pagans reside reveals the primary role that poetry, one subset of that culture, plays for Dante as the means both for preserving the past and for diffusing philosophical doctrines. This same detail may also suggest how Dante had come to access classical culture as a whole. It was thanks to having read the ancient poets that he came properly to appreciate the achievements of the classical world.

A variety of attitudes, from warm appreciation to explicit challenge, defines the *Commedia*'s stance towards classical culture. One example from *Inferno* may be singled out to exemplify Dante's confrontational attitude: the direct poetic challenge that he levels at Ovid and Lucan when he describes the reptilian metamorphoses of the thieves in *Inferno* XXV, 94–9. It is an extreme case of literary interaction, in which the new text metaphorically silences its predecessors. Immediately after Virgil has finished correcting a passage from *Aeneid* VIII, 259–61 by recasting the death of the centaur Cacus by strangulation into death by clubbing (25–33), Dante tellingly recalls the signal with which he had caught his guide's attention: 'I held my finger up from chin to nose' (Mi posi il dito sù dal mento al naso; 45). This silencing gesture prepares for another, even more explicit silencing moment. In an extra-diegetic aside, now involving Lucan and Ovid, two other epic poets who had penned remarkable narratives involving snakes and transformations, Dante, as he is about to describe the exchange of features between a reptilian sinner and one who still retains his human shape, bids both poets to 'be silent' (Taccia Lucano ... / Taccia ... Ovidio; 94 and 97). The reason they must stay quiet is momentous: neither of them, unlike Dante, had to 'transmute' 'two natures face to face ... so that both forms were ready to exchange their matter' (due nature mai a fronte a fronte / non trasmutò sì ch'amendue le forme / a cambiar lor matera fosser pronte; 100–2).

The intertextual dynamics at work in this passage are based on a keen sense of the value the new text acquires in relation and in opposition to its classical antecedents. The *Commedia* directly evokes passages in its Latin antecedents only to stress its divergence and distance from them. The challenge levelled may be read both as a vindication of Dante's rhetorical and artistic prowess – the modern poet who outstrips his authoritative models by combining in a single work Lucan's historical truth with Ovid's imaginative vigour – and as a statement of his essential superiority as the divinely inspired poet to whom God has granted a direct and hence true vision of a marvel-filled afterlife. In either case, what is clear is that Dante constructs his identity as the poet of the *Comedy* through a dialogue with classical literature as much as through his association with Christian authorities. The next section explores the tensions between these two facets of Dante's poetics, as well as the means that medieval culture afforded him to elaborate and perhaps reconcile the two.

Tropes of Transmission and Translation

The opening line of the *Commedia* fuses Scriptural and classical elements. The midpoint of 'our life' (nostra vita) recalls both Isaiah 38:10 ('midway through the days of my life, I will go down to the doors of Hell') and the classical convention that epic poems ought to start in the 'middle' of the action. This syncretism raises two questions: What was the relationship between Christian and classical texts? More specifically, what were the functions of Dante's recourse to classical material in the *Comedy*?

Like any medieval reader, Dante's appreciation of classical literature was mediated through the scholastic commentary tradition that accompanied the texts of the 'major authors' and which offered standardized interpretations of events and characters. These interpretations were often allegorical in nature and stressed the moral and doctrinal implications of a text. Although Dante was influenced by such approaches to classical literature – for instance, his recourse to Horace's *Ars poetica* can only be understood in light of its commentary tradition – he normally avoided importing the most straightforward allegorizations into the *Commedia*, so as not to reduce or resolve a character or episode in terms of a banalizing extra-textual meaning. At the same time, like his contemporaries, Dante's recourse to the past was predicated on reframing the cultural contributions of antiquity in light of contemporary concerns: mining the ancient texts for meanings and values that would be consonant with the present.

Two distinct but related tropes of incorporation were dominant: the so-called 'gold of the Egyptians' analogy; and the concept of the *translatio studii et imperii* (transfer of learning and power). Both tropes forged strong ties between the classical past and the present. The first is effectively summarized by Augustine in *De doctrina Christiana* II, xl, 60: just as God ordered the spoliation of Egypt of its gold by the Jews when leaving for the Promised Land, so too classical culture should be treated as a treasure-house of knowledge that can be put to better use by Christians. A striking example of this approach is Dante's re-reading in Christian terms of Virgil's texts – the *Aeneid* as well as the fourth *Eclogue* – in his invention of the causes behind Statius' conversion to Christianity in *Purgatorio* XXI and XXII. While the idea that Statius had secretly converted to Christianity is uniquely Dante's, it conforms to the general paradigm of productive cultural reuse that underlies Augustine's trope of productive cultural reuse. The classical world thus offers the building-blocks of the Christian present, whose historical complexity and dynamism is captured in the notion of *translatio*. According to this understanding of the patterns of cultural and political domination, history is perceived as a precise, linear narrative, in which the centre of knowledge and power moves from one civilization to the next, specifically from east to west: the torch of civilization passes from Greece to Rome and then from Rome to Christian Paris in a development that conforms well to ideas of history as divinely ordained. Dante adapts the trope when organizing the canons of heroes, thinkers, and lovers in *Inferno* IV and V in terms of chronological and geographical transfer and of linguistic transferal.

The list of non-Christian thinkers detailed in Limbo, for instance, combines rank with historical succession. It moves from the internally ranked trio of Aristotle, Socrates, and Plato to the pre-Socratic school (Democritus, Diogenes, Anaxagoras, Thales, Empedocles, Heraclitus, Zeno, with the addition of the Romanized Greek Dioscorides), to a quartet of Roman poets (Orpheus and Linus) and philosophers (Cicero and Seneca the younger), to reach a 'modern' group of scientists and thinkers (Euclid followed by Ptolemy; then Hippocrates, Avicenna, Galen, and finally the great Aristotelian commentator, Averroës). The taxonomy combines a criterion of importance, hence Aristotle is presented first as the 'the teacher of those who know' ('l maestro di color che sanno; 131), with one of geographical and temporal interconnection and succession: Greek culture is followed and succeeded by Latin culture, while Latin culture eventually yields – in this non-Christian canon – to Islamic culture. Equally, the catalogue of sinners in *Inferno* V moves from the ancient east with Semiramis, the biblical queen of Babylon, to the middle-eastern Dido (born in Tyre, as Virgil reports), to the North-African Cleopatra. In the second part of the catalogue, the movement is again from east to west and from past to present, beginning with Helen, Paris, and Achilles (Greek and Trojan characters of the Homeric and Virgilian epic), passing through Tristan (a knight of the Round Table), to reach the contemporary Italian lovers Paolo and Francesca.

Both tropes treat classical culture as distinct from, yet subsumed by Christian culture. Internally structured in light of the translation trope, the classical world is perceived as providentially hierarchized and temporally complex with a strong sense of historical continuity that dialectically links pre-Christian, pre-modern, and pre-vernacular texts to their later counterparts. Significantly, the classical world is not treated as monolithic. Dante's recourse to classical elements in the *Commedia*, as is evident from his presentation of Virgil (see below), depends and builds on these perceptions. Essentially, the poet assigns a double role to classical culture. On the one hand, it is treated as a self-sufficient cultural system whose views are accepted as valid, as is the case, for instance, with Aristotle's scientific theories. On the other, it is presented as partial and sectarian, and hence as limited, provisional, and potentially misleading when not actually erroneous. Dante's attitude to classical literature, with Virgil at its head, falls into this latter category.

A telling example of the first attitude may be found in *Inferno* VI, in the discussion of the degree of pain that the souls will endure once their bodies are restored to them at the Last Judgement. Virgil deals with the problem in Aristotelian terms: 'Go back to your science that wants, when something is more perfect, that it should feel the good more, and the same goes for pain' (Ritorna a tua scïenza, / che vuol, quanto la cosa è più perfetta, / più senta il bene, e così la doglienza; *Inf.* VI, 106–8). The pilgrim's 'science' is Aristotle's *De anima* and the principle it expounds is introduced as authoritatively sufficient. Elsewhere, too, especially on matters relating to the 'natural' workings of the world, and in keeping with contemporary attitudes, Aristotle's views are presented as definitive, as occurs when Virgil cites the *Physics* (*Inf.* XI, 97–105) in order to elucidate definitively that art is the daughter of Nature and Nature is the daughter of God. In contrast, Virgil's later explanation of the rockslide between the sixth and seventh circles is portrayed as problematic. He asserts that the earth trembled just before Christ descended into Hell, further qualifying that, when this occurred, he 'believed that the universe felt love', the same kind of love that 'according to some has several times made the world return to chaos' (pensai che l'universo / sentisse amor, per lo qual è chi creda / più volte il mondo in caòsso converso; XII, 41–3). Virgil appears to equate a Christian miracle with a classical scientific explanation. However, it is important to note the caution with which the ancient poet expresses his opinion, highlighting that his was a 'belief' and not a certainty, and that, in any case, only 'some' pagan thinkers concurred with the scientific elucidation propounded. Virgil's explanation is thus open to question and revision. While Virgil is correct about Christ's triumph over Hell, and implicitly the love that underpinned His sacrifice on the cross, this truth transcends and challenges the classical paradigm with which it is aligned. The love felt by the universe at the moment of the crucifixion was not the same that Empedocles and Ovid postulated in their philosophical and poetic cyclical cosmogonies, but an event that radically and permanently changed human history.

These examples afford a glimpse of the double role that Dante assigned to classical material in the *Commedia*. Ancient texts are treated as repositories of information on philosophical, ethical, scientific, mythological, and poetic questions. In addition, Dante evaluated classical culture both in its internal complexity (Aristotle is more authoritative than Empedocles; Rome inherited Greek culture and then transmitted it to the Christian world) and by comparing it to its non-classical – namely, its Christian, contemporary, and vernacular – counterparts. The ambivalent manner in which Dante handled his classical heritage is particularly marked in his attitude to Virgil.

Virgil's Roles

Virgil stands almost unchallenged at the centre of the canon of poets show-cased in the *Comedy*. As a key character and a major poetic source, his presence in the poem is deep and pervasive. In literary terms, only Ovid, whose *Metamorphoses* serve as a fund not only of mythological lore but also of transformation narratives used to mark the progress of the protagonist through Paradise, and Lucan, whose *Pharsalia* confirms the bonds between poetry and history and, together with the *Aeneid*, offers Dante a storehouse of epic material and of information on ancient Rome, bear comparison to Virgil. Neither poet, however, plays the same variety of interdependent roles as Virgil, to whom Dante assigns three main functions. First, he is a self-sufficient character, on a par with all the other characters in the narrative. His status is double: on the one hand, he is a historical personage, as the allusions to his medieval 'lives' in *Inferno* I, but also *Purgatorio* III and VI, make clear; while on the other, he is an inhabitant of the afterlife. Consequently, he helps illustrate the moral structure and workings of Hell, in particular, the special standing of Limbo. Second, together with Beatrice, Statius, and St Bernard, he is granted a special position as guide, a role that is logistical as well as didactic, and that extends for almost two-thirds of the journey. In this role, he represents either classical culture in general or his own achievements and views. On the one hand, he mediates classical wisdom, as when he cites Aristotle, while on the other, he draws on his writings, most notably when alluding to episodes and characters from these, and is even a privileged posthumous 'editor' of his own texts, revising his treatment in the *Aeneid* of Manto and Cacus. Finally, beyond his role in the narrative, Virgil is the author of a body of texts to which Dante has recourse as he composes the *Commedia* and whose presence is interwoven into the poem's verbal fabric.

A complete census of these Virgilian allusions in the *Comedy* is probably impossible and certainly would require continuous updating. It has recently been calculated that the poem includes around seven hundred Virgilian references (approximately one every twenty lines), of which a hundred and twenty-six are direct citations from the *Aeneid*, sixteen from the *Georgics*, and six from the *Eclogues*. These references, even if most numerous in *Inferno*, stretch across the three canticles, the last echo being heard in the final canto: 'and so, to the wind, on the light leaves, the Sibyl's meaning was lost' (così al vento ne le foglie levi / si perdea la sentenza di Sibilla; 65–6 and cp. *Aen*.VI, 74–5). In addition, Dante draws on *Aeneid* VI to construct his afterlife, in particular Hell, creatively reworking the Virgilian elements in order to highlight the superiority of his Christian vision of the afterlife (for instance, in *Inferno* XVI and XVII, Geryon is granted a complexity which is quite lacking in the *Aeneid*).

As has been noted, Virgil serves as a spokesperson for classical culture and values in general. In the circle of blasphemy, for instance, when he condemns Capaneus, a character from Statius' *Thebaid*, for his rebellion against the gods (XIV, 68–72), he expresses a view deeply rooted in classical ethics. In addition, his censure serves to align the classical worldview with Christian moral values: all rebellion against any god is a violation of the principle of divinity. More suggestively, and further highlighting Dante's strong sense of the providential continuities uniting pagan and Christian culture, as well as serving as a counterpart to Capaneus' hubristic attack on the divine, the poet invents the salvation of Ripheus, a minor figure in Virgil's *Aeneid*, who, thanks to God's grace, as Beatrice explains, believed in the coming of Christ and rejected paganism (*Par*. XX, 123–5). Dante's use of classical nomenclature for Christian realities – for instance, Christ being addressed as Jupiter (*Purg*. VI, 118) – equally reveals his belief in the fundamental interconnections between poetic accounts of both the classical and Christian worlds.

Dante forges a range of refined intertextual connections between the *Commedia* and Virgil's texts. These may take the form of a pointed displacement of a particular detail from Virgil's narrative to a non-Virgilian context in the poem: this is the case with Dante's decision, in stark contrast to the *Aeneid*, not to narrate the crossing of the Acheron, while at the same time recuperating a Virgilian element from this episode, the lowering of the keel mentioned at *Aeneid* VI, 413–14, in the non-Virgilian crossing of the Styx on Phlegias' skiff (VIII, 27). Similarly, Dante strategically introduces the same Virgilian phrase into two different parts of the poem, as occurs with the tag 'iam histinc' (even from there; *Aen*. VI, 389), which is rendered via the Italian adverb 'costinci', 'from there', in *Inferno* XII, 63 and *Purgatorio* IX, 85, a formula that connects two distant moments of traversing. Dante also revises some of Virgil's best-known *sententiae*: for instance, in *Purgatorio* XXII, 40–1, Statius reinterprets and adapts Virgil's original 'auri sacra fames' – 'the *accursed* hunger for gold' that the poet blamed for the criminal slaughter of Polydorus in *Aeneid* III, 57 – into a '*holy* hunger for gold' ('sacra fame / de l'oro'). A similarly radical reformulation occurs when Dante revises Virgil's 'agnosco veteris vestigia flammae' ('I recognize the signs of the old flame', said by Dido of her new passion for Aeneas in *Aeneid* IV, 23) into the pilgrim's 'conosco i segni de l'antica fiamma' that refers to his love for

Beatrice (*Purg.* XXX, 48). In both cases, the effect is a vindication of Dante's 'modernist' attitude towards ancient literature: meaning depends as much on the intention of the ancient author as it does on the active interpretation of the contemporary reader.

Classical Culture Outside the Text: Material Traces and Literary Relations

On several occasions, Dante imagines the *Commedia* as a work that will endure into the remote future, read by an audience that will call 'ancient' the time of its composition. The poet's concern for the afterlife of his work is striking, in particular the way he juxtaposes its contemporary negative reception to its future success (*Par.* XVII, 118–20). The problem is framed in exquisitely classicizing and material terms. Dante knows that a poet needs to achieve both immediate contemporary success and long-term appeal. The problem of cultural survival depends on combining the two: pursuing both in tandem rather than one at the expense of the other. Mixing and balancing immediately recognizable modern features (characters, situations, textual references) with long-established classical elements (characters, cultural paradigms, textual references) appears to be the strategy whereby the *Comedy* endeavours both to speak to its present and to attain future cultural permanence that the dialogue with the classics would seem to guarantee. Cacciaguida effectively summarizes this strategy when he clarifies that the protagonist has been privileged to meet exemplary figures belonging to both the past and the present (136–42).

We have noted that when Dante looks back at his cultural past, he does so with a strong sense of his position within it, so that his classicism is clearly oriented towards the present. Such an attitude is historically comprehensible. The classical world was not an alien, distant reality, irrelevant to the author and his contemporary readers. Classical buildings and other structures marked the cityscapes of the poem's present, and, on different occasions, Dante refers to these. For instance, the anonymous Florentine suicide mentions the ancient statue of Mars, Florence's wrathful pagan patron deity, who continues to haunt the city with his totemic power, demanding a tribute of blood from the divided citizenship (*Inf.* XIII, 143–50). On his visits to Rome, Dante had the opportunity to see other monuments of the classical past. Unlike the temple of Janus or the Tarpeian Rock (mentioned respectively in *Par.* VI, 81 and *Purg.* IX,136), of which only confused or no archaeological evidence survived, monuments like the Mausoleum of Hadrian (the Castel Sant'Angelo of *Inf.* XVIII, 32) and Trajan's Column (essential to the imagery and structure of *Purgatorio* X) were part of Rome's medieval urban landscape, and the poem registers them as such. Although these constructs enter the *Comedy* primarily as textual objects (as place names on a cultural topographical map), they were also real objects that existed outside the sphere of language and literature. Views such as that from Monte Malo, evoked to capture Rome's effect on a foreign traveller (*Par.* XV, 109) or the astonished gaze of the 'barbarian' looking at the Lateran basilica (*Par.* XXXI, 34) attest to Dante's interest in noting not simply the effects that a textual meditation on Rome's past could produce, but also those of its direct impact on his audience.

The strong sense of continuity between the Roman past and the present that is a feature of the *Commedia* recalls the historically stratified urban character of the city of Rome. Already in *Inferno* II, Rome's double identity, as both pagan and Christian, is foregrounded, when the pilgrim is equated with two 'Roman' predecessors who had also travelled through the afterlife: Aeneas and St Paul. When Dante protests to Virgil that he is not Aeneas nor Paul, and hence does not have the authority to undertake the otherworldly journey, he evokes the remote founder of Rome, Aeneas, and links him to the evangelizing mission of the apostle Paul in the same city. Dante's illustrious precursors collaborate, from the opposite ends of the historical spectrum, to establish Rome as both imperial capital and papal seat. The city never ceases to play a central role in God's providential plan for humanity. When, in Eden, Beatrice defines heavenly bliss as eternal citizenship in 'that Rome where Christ is Roman' (quella Roma onde Cristo è romano; *Purg.* XXXII, 102), she confirms the continuity between past and present that characterizes the idea and reality of Rome. The heavenly citizenship that Beatrice promises the pilgrim will be 'endless' (sanza fine; 101), and it is the same Roman citizenship that unites in one continuous historical and cultural trajectory not only Aeneas and St Paul, but also the protagonist and the poet of the *Comedy*.

9

TRISTAN KAY

Vernacular Literature and Culture

'So has the one Guido taken from the other the glory of our tongue, and he, perhaps, is born who shall chase the one and the other from the nest' (così ha tolto l'uno all'altro Guido / la gloria della lingua; e forse è nato / chi l'uno e l'altro caccerà del nido; *Purg.* XI, 97–9). On Purgatory's terrace of pride, the thirteenth-century manuscript illuminator Oderisi da Gubbio describes how worldly fame is as transient as a single gust of wind when seen from the perspective of eternity. Nonetheless, literary rivalry and succession remain intense preoccupations for Dante in the *Commedia*. The examples Oderisi gives derive from contemporary Italian art and literature. Where once Cimabue was lauded as the pre-eminent painter of his time, Giotto now overshadows him (94–6); and where the acclaim accorded to one poet named Guido gave him the glory of the Italian language, another Guido has wrested it from him, while a third poet will soon eclipse them both.

The *Guidi* are most likely the Bolognese Guido Guinizzelli and the Florentine Guido Cavalcanti, protagonists in the lyric tradition in which Dante began his literary activity, and two of his most decisive vernacular influences. Few critics doubt that the third, unnamed poet is Dante himself. Dante's engagement with this lyric tradition, and with its dominant theme of love, accompanies his entire career, and he thus gives it a highly visible place in his *Commedia*. In *Purgatorio* XXI–XXVI, no fewer than seven vernacular poets are encountered or named (with others implicated intertextually) in what is Dante's most sustained attempt to situate his poem at the apex of the Romance lyric tradition. Yet, while the lyric is the most privileged facet of medieval vernacular culture within the *Commedia*'s diegesis, the poet in fact tackled a tradition that was much richer than this one vibrant yet rarefied genre. Moreover, Dante dealt not with a single vernacular, but with different, competing Romance vernaculars and their associated cultural traditions: not just Italian, but also Old French and Occitan.

When Dante wrote the *Commedia*, the vernacular remained culturally subordinate to Latin: the dominant and prestigious written language of the learned elite, associated with cultural authority (*auctoritas*) possessed by a relatively small number of texts deemed worthy of study and commentary. In light of Latin's continuing hegemony, Dante's use and promotion of the vernacular in a work of the scope and sophistication of the *Commedia* was revolutionary and exceptional. However, it would have been unthinkable without a host of developments in vernacular written culture that preceded and coincided with Dante's emergence as a writer. Of particular interest with respect to the *Commedia* are: (1) the lyric tradition, in its Italian and earlier Occitan manifestations, encompassing moral, martial, and especially erotic themes; (2) narrative literature, especially in Old French, including *chansons de geste*, chivalric romances, and allegorical dream visions (such as the *Roman de la rose* and Brunetto Latini's *Tesoretto*); (3) the largely anonymous vernacularizations of Latin works, composed in northern and central Italian communes, which transmitted important texts to a wider public illiterate in Latin, as well as Italian vernacular translations and rewritings of French texts; (4) other vernacular prose traditions, from chronicles and *novelle* to encyclopaedic works (notably Brunetto's *Tresor*) and vernacular epistles; (5) vernacular religious texts, ranging from St Francis' *Cantico delle creature* and the *laude* tradition (associated especially with the Umbrian mystic Jacopone da Todi) to popular didactic poetry, sermons, and vernacularizations of religious and devotional texts originally composed in Latin.

While all these traditions helped shape and refine the cultural and literary landscape of Dante's time, they are not of equal prominence and importance in the *Commedia*. While some key vernacular authors, texts, and traditions are highly visible in the narrative (authors appear as characters; literature is explicitly discussed), others are submerged intertextual presences or implicit stylistic or structural models, whose impact upon the poem is harder to assess. Nevertheless, the *Commedia*'s engagement with vernacular literature and culture is extremely wide-ranging. This chapter explores the poem's multifaceted negotiation of its secular vernacular inheritance by focusing on six key issues: (1) the immediate presence of vernacular intertexts, alongside more prominent classical and biblical sources, in *Inferno* I–II; (2) the rich and ambivalent treatment of love literature in *Inferno* V and the poem's continuing engagement with key lyric debates; (3) the spectre of Guido Cavalcanti, a highly influential but systematically critiqued poet-philosopher and theorist of love; (4) Brunetto Latini, a major exponent of Florentine prose and an important mediating figure of both French and classical culture; (5) the decisive role of poetic encounters, especially in *Purgatorio*, as part of Dante's process of self-definition and self-authorization; and (6) the broad eclecticism of the poem's formal debts to medieval vernacular culture.

Inferno I–II: Vernacular (Anti-)Models and Lyric Commitment

Although the *Commedia* is written in Dante's Florentine language, its opening cantos give prominence to biblical and especially classical, rather than vernacular, cultural models. *Inferno* I immediately establishes a close bond between Dante and Virgil, as poets as well as characters. On coming to the pilgrim's rescue in the dark wood, Virgil is celebrated as 'glory and light of other poets' (de li altri poeti onore e lume; 82). The pilgrim then evokes his devoted study of the *Aeneid* and puzzlingly speaks of the exclusive debt he owes to the ancient poet for 'the style whose beauty has brought me honour' (lo bello stilo che m'ha fatto onore; 87). Explicit Virgilian echoes proliferate throughout *Inferno* and especially in its opening nine cantos, whose topography, similes, and narrative programme owe far more to *Aeneid* VI than to any medieval Latin or vernacular source.

So manifest are these classical features that we might initially regard the *Inferno* as a vernacular rewriting of key Latin (and biblical) models, with vernacular literature a peripheral concern. However, this would be to misread the poem's syncretic ambitions, and to underestimate the ways in which vernacular literature is immediately, if less visibly, at stake. Take the first *terzina*: 'In the middle of the journey of our life I came to myself within a dark wood where the straight way was lost' (Nel mezzo del cammin di nostra vita / mi ritrovai per una selva oscura / che la diritta via era smarrita). Widely noted is the echo of Isaiah 38:10 ('in the midst of my days, I shall go to the gates of the nether region'), while the 'middle' of life's journey refers to the midpoint of the allotted human lifespan of 'three score years and ten' (Ps. 89:10). Yet important vernacular resonances can also be heard. The first-person protagonist of Brunetto's allegorical dream vision, the *Tesoretto*, similarly finds himself in a 'strange wood' (190), having lost sight of the 'great path' (188).[1] The motif of the dark wood, associated with error, is also prevalent in Arthurian romance. These echoes raise the possibility of other narrative and formal affinities between these works and the *Commedia*. Equally, they invite us to consider their status as 'anti-texts', not least in light of the critique to which Arthurian romance and Brunetto are subjected in *Inferno* V and XV respectively. Later in canto I, the three beasts which impede the pilgrim's path, and which stand for three categories of sin, recall the allegorical representations of vices, virtues, and other abstract qualities in the *Tesoretto* and its primary influence, the *Roman de la rose*, as well as other vernacular dream visions.

In *Inferno* II, Dante recuperates his identity as a lyric love poet, except that this lyric dimension is now wedded to classical and medieval narrative traditions. Virgil famously appropriates the language of the *Vita nova* to recount how Beatrice, a 'lady so blessed and so fair' (donna ... beata e bella; 53), descended from Heaven to Limbo to command his intercession, and his words stimulate the pilgrim's desire to embark upon the journey. The audacious presence of a secular *donna* in a 'poema sacro' (sacred poem; *Par.* XXV, 1) indicates Dante's enduring connection to the Romance lyric and to the idea of redeemed eros, alien to Virgil, at his poem's heart. Indeed, Virgil's and Beatrice's roles as guides point eloquently to Dante's sense of simultaneous affiliation to traditions epic and lyric, Latin and vernacular.

Indeed, *Inferno* II not only inscribes the *Commedia* into the vernacular lyric tradition, but also subtly evokes his most fraught vernacular rivalry, with his fellow Florentine Guido Cavalcanti. Echoes of Guido's poetry have been identified at several junctures in *Inferno* I, while in *Inferno* II Dante reworks elements of Guido's sonnet 'I' vegno 'l giorno a te 'nfinite volte' (When countless times I come to you each day), in which Guido had reproached Dante for his dissolute lifestyle and squandering of his poetic gifts.[2] As in Guido's poem, the pilgrim is rebuked for his 'cowardice' (viltade; 45 and 122); however, this time the reproachful figure is Virgil, under the command of the heavenly Beatrice, who successfully persuades Dante to voyage through the afterlife. The original sense of Guido's words is inverted to underline the unimpeachable moral and spiritual authority that underpins the journey (and the poem). Thus, even in the opening two cantos, generally not associated with Dante's close interaction with Romance sources, we find a sustained and intricate engagement with diverse strands of vernacular literary culture that establishes key elements that are more fully developed elsewhere in the *Commedia*.

Inferno V: Love Literature and Lust

The circle of the lustful presents the poem's first direct instance of its highly complex response to vernacular literature. *Inferno* V returns to issues central to the *Vita nova* and to the Romance texts – from Occitan and Italian lyric poetry to the *Roman de la rose* – with which it dialogues: the threshold between love and lust; the role of reason in the face of love; the compatibility of love and the 'noble heart'; and the association between love and death. These were dominant and contentious questions in Romance literature. The connection between lyric poetry and love was especially strong, with lyric authority and authenticity often predicated upon the poet's submission to *Amor*. But the legacy of love literature in *Inferno* V is not merely one of thematic congruence. Dante's description of the 'hellish storm' (bufera infernal; 31) that torments the lustful sinners recalls imagery associated with erotic passion in lyric and Arthurian traditions. Following the catalogue of great literary figures that succumbed, often fatally, to lust (which tellingly culminates with the Arthurian figure of Tristan), the tale of the doomed lovers, Paolo and Francesca, also richly alludes to vernacular traditions.

While Francesca's portrait contains classicizing elements, including reminiscences of the depiction of Dido in *Aeneid* IV, she speaks the language of medieval lyric poetry, nowhere more than in her celebrated emphasis on love with its triple initial repetition of the word *Amor* (100–8). Francesca's words echo Guinizzelli, Cavalcanti, Cino da Pistoia, and Dante himself and their theorization of love as an inexorable carnal force. Arthurian literature also plays a vital role in the canto. Francesca famously describes her and Paolo reading the popular Old French romance of Lancelot and Guinevere (most probably in the version of the thirteenth-century *Lancelot en prose*). Her account confirms Dante's detailed knowledge of the work. She describes how reading about the chivalric lovers' kiss prompted her and Paolo to do the same: 'but one point alone it was that mastered us' (ma solo un punto fu quel che ci vinse; 132). Scholars disagree as to whether Dante is criticizing the *Lancelot*'s notion of love and lack of edifying spiritual content, or else the lovers' narcissistic response to the work, which they read only 'for pleasure' (per diletto; 127) and partially, failing to reach the subsequent condemnation of adultery. Nonetheless, it is clear that Dante contrasts the Old French romance and Paolo and Francesca to the *Commedia* and its readers. The story of the chivalric lovers inspires a profane *Amor* that leads to damnation, while Dante's poem describes a divine *Amor* that saves. The disparity between the *Commedia*'s famous pairings – Paolo and Francesca, Dante and Beatrice – and their respective loves is all too evident.

Inferno V implicates a broad spectrum of erotic literature in its condemnation of lust, which is the category of *Amor* that this tradition ultimately celebrates and defines. Yet, the *Commedia*'s relationship to the epic, lyric, and chivalric currents – and indeed to 'love poetry' taken more broadly – cannot be reduced to one of hostile opposition. While the *Commedia* evidently surpasses the fatalism and carnality associated with the Romance love lyric, *Inferno* V, like *Inferno* IV with its double-edged treatment of the ancient world, betrays an enduring affection, as well as antagonism, towards its achievements – an affection that returns in *Purgatorio* XXVI. Francesca embodies conventional erotic poetry in all its beauty and moral inadequacy, so that a rigidly binary or dogmatic reading of this highly ambiguous figure underplays the complexity of the *Commedia*'s response to the traditions and tensions that her canto explores. As in *Inferno* II, the secular *donna* is not rejected but retained in the *Commedia*; equally, the poet's allegiance to love is not severed but redeemed. The divinely inspired character of the poem, together with the 'miraculous' figure of Beatrice, enable Dante to reformulate positively what had led others astray.

Guido Cavalcanti: Poet-philosopher and Theorist of Love

It is unsurprising that Guido Cavalcanti should be evoked in the *Commedia*'s opening two cantos, while also finding himself heavily implicated in *Inferno* V. Guido was regarded as a poet and philosopher of considerable authority in Dante's Florence, especially on account of his great doctrinal canzone 'Donna me prega' (A lady asks me). His standing was probably higher than Dante's at the turn of the Trecento. Indeed, Dante's relationship with Cavalcanti was profoundly complex. Guido was one of his early formative influences, his so-called 'first friend' (*Vn* XXIV, 3 [15, 3]) and the dedicatee of the *Vita nova*. Yet, the 'little book' (I, 1 [1, 1]) ultimately challenges Cavalcanti's pessimistic theory of love in formulating its notion of redemptive love for Beatrice. Nonetheless, the lyrics Dante wrote after the *Vita nova* reveal Guido's enduring stylistic and ideological influence. Considering Dante's combative treatment of Cavalcanti in the *Commedia*, it is thus important to remember the older poet's dominant stature as a vernacular poet and philosopher, as well as the prehistory of their textual relationship in Dante's 'other' works.

As regards the ideological dissent between the two poets concerning love, the *Commedia* is largely consonant with the *Vita nova*, though the latter's ambivalent affection for Guido has been replaced by palpable hostility. Having been an important but unnamed presence in cantos II and V, Cavalcanti features more prominently, albeit still as an 'absence', in the circle of heresy in *Inferno* X, where the pilgrim meets his father Cavalcante. Guido would not die until August 1300, during an exile sanctioned by a ruling Florentine council that included Dante. Cavalcante mistakenly locates the motivation for Dante's journey in his 'height of genius' (altezza d'ingegno; *Inf*. X, 59), and therefore asks why it is Dante and not his son who has been afforded such a privilege. The pilgrim underlines in response that he is not, in fact, embarking on this journey alone and, in a much-debated passage, declares that he is led by Virgil 'to one whom your Guido held in disdain' (cui Guido vostro ebbe a disdegno; 63). The ambiguity derives from the 'cui', which could be interpreted as 'whom' (in which case the pilgrim is referring to Virgil) or 'to one whom' (in which case he is referring to Beatrice and/or to God). If the pilgrim is alluding to Beatrice (the interpretation a growing majority of scholars regard as the most plausible), Dante is returning to the polemic at the heart of his *Vita nova*, and its proclamation of a redemptive love – recuperated in the *Commedia* – that challenges the fatalistic vision of love, associated inexorably with death, presented in Guido's treatment of *Amor* in 'Donna me prega'. Dante evokes the canzone intertextually through the rhyme-words *nome:come:lume* (X, 65–9; 'Donna' 16–19). Moreover, it has been widely claimed that Dante renders Guido guilty by association of not believing in the immortality of the soul, the heresy punished in the sixth circle, on account of the canzone's philosophical materialism.

Yet 'Donna me prega' remains an important touchstone for Dante, not only as an ideological anti-text, but also as a crucial example of philosophical poetry in the vernacular. Italian lyric poetry, from its inception in the first half of the thirteenth century, quickly took on a more philosophical emphasis than the Occitan tradition from which it had developed. Sicilian poets used scholastic formulae and the science of optics to interrogate the workings of love, while Guido Guinizzelli incorporated natural philosophy as well as theological motifs into his poetry in praise of an angelic beloved. The *Roman de la rose*, composed in two parts by Guillaume de Lorris and later by Jean de Meun, was a vernacular milestone in its encyclopaedic and doctrinal digressions and its application of scholastic philosophy to its secular 'art of love'. Medieval Latin works were also of considerable importance for Dante in this respect, especially Alan of Lille's twelfth-century allegorical-didactic poems, *De planctu naturae* and *Anticlaudianus*, which similarly describe journeys of knowledge and serve as key models for the *Roman*. Yet no lyric poem in a Romance vernacular had revealed greater philosophical sophistication and intellectual density than 'Donna me prega', and the canzone, immediately recognized as a substantive philosophical work, was soon subjected to detailed exegesis. A number of doctrinal passages in the *Commedia*, particularly in *Purgatorio* and *Paradiso*, are informed by Guido's valuable precedent.

Yet, as ever when Dante responded to Cavalcanti, poetic and intellectual debt is offset by ideological dissent and correction. Two examples are especially pertinent. In *Purgatorio* XVII and XVIII, Virgil's disquisition on love at the structural centre of the poem (and at the very heart of Dante's Christian ethics) evokes Guido's definition of love in 'Donna me prega' through the use of analogous modes of argumentation and via intertextual connections. Yet Dante borrows Cavalcantian language to elaborate a very different thesis. The notion of love Virgil presents is diametrically opposed to that defined in the canzone. His account challenges the erotic fatalism of the 'blind who make themselves guides' (ciechi che si fanno duci; XVIII, 18), one of whom is certainly Guido, whose analysis of love had seen him established as a philosophical authority. Above all, Virgil's emphatic affirmation of the unwavering influence of reason in the ambit of desire can be seen as a powerful riposte to the earlier poet's insistence on love's estrangement from the rational soul, as Dante again returns, albeit in a radically expanded intellectual and narrative context, to the ideological discord documented in the *Vita nova*. *Purgatorio* XXV, where the classical poet Statius explains to the pilgrim the origin and working of the souls' aerial bodies, has also been read in light of 'Donna me prega'. While a number of lexical, structural, and thematic similarities have been identified between the two texts, it is ultimately the profound disjuncture between the materialism of Guido's poem and Statius' exposition of the miraculous integration of the spiritual and the material in the human form that is key to Dante's polemical rewriting of the canzone in this canto.

But if these episodes can ultimately be interpreted in terms of Dante's strong ideological opposition to Guido in the *Commedia*, others betray a lasting ambivalence. In the Earthly Paradise, for instance, a space that can in part be associated with the orchard found in Guillaume's *Rose*, the pilgrim beholds the enigmatic figure of Matelda, often seen to embody prelapsarian beauty and innocence. Dante's representation of this figure, and of the pilgrim's sexualized response to her, draws upon several literary sources, from Ovid to the Romance lyric. Most striking, however, is his evocation of the erotic genre of the *pastorella*, and especially Cavalcanti's 'In un boschetto trova' pasturella' (In a little wood I found a shepherdess). The presence of the *pastorella* raises the ambiguous spectre of Dante's fellow Florentine, and indeed of the vernacular erotic tradition more broadly, while also hinting at their continuing influence, even as the pilgrim crosses into the most spiritually exalted region of the first two *cantiche*.

Brunetto Latini and Tuscan Prose Culture

For all Cavalcanti's importance, it was Brunetto Latini, encountered among the sodomites in *Inferno* XV, who, at the end of the thirteenth century, was the key figure in Florentine vernacular culture. His *Tesoretto* served as an important narrative antecedent to the *Commedia*. Equally, his encyclopaedic *Tresor*, composed in Old French during his exile from Florence in the 1260s, expanded the intellectual horizons of the vernacular by mediating classical and medieval Latin doctrinal traditions. Brunetto's importance, however, went beyond these two texts. He also meaningfully contributed to the new interest in 'vernacularization', translating Cicero's *De inventione* and several Ciceronian speeches into Florentine; and played an important role in the city's political life, undertaking a number of notarial and diplomatic roles. Dante presents him as embodying a significant, if problematic, proto-humanist yearning for cultural and political renewal. Brunetto was thus a figure of major and multifaceted cultural importance, whose legacy, as he sought to establish his own cultural status, Dante had deftly to negotiate.

As with Francesca, Dante's portrayal of Brunetto among the sodomites is suspended between earthly affection and eschatological censure, encapsulated in the contrast between the pilgrim's memory of Brunetto's 'dear and kind paternal image' (la cara e buona imagine paterna; *Inf.* XV, 83) and the present sight of his 'scorched features' (cotto aspetto; 26). Dante depicts Brunetto as a father and teacher, most likely for his intellectual influence and standing in Florence rather than for any kind of formal educational capacity. While damning him for his sexual proclivities – sodomy was deemed a sin of violence against nature – Dante also associated Brunetto with the sin for having committed acts of cultural, intellectual, and political perversion and sterility. Scholars have highlighted Dante's disdain for Brunetto's 'unnatural' rejection of his Florentine mother tongue when composing the *Tresor*; for his work as a 'vernacularizer'; and for his opposition to 'natural' imperial authority. Furthermore, Dante's presentation of Brunetto has been read as a critique of his 'sterile' pre-humanist pursuit of eternal life through fame. Certainly, the pilgrim's ironic reference to his teacher's lesson of 'how man makes himself immortal' (com l'uom s'etterna; 85), and Brunetto's parting exhortation that Dante remember his 'Tesoro', 'through which I live on' (nel qual io vivo ancora; 120), would accord with this last interpretation.[3]

Yet, as with many of his cultural influences, Dante did not dismiss Brunetto unequivocally. The intellectual breadth of the *Tresor* and the narrative sweep of the *Tesoretto* were valuable precedents for the *Commedia*, which borrows significantly from both works. However, debts and parallels are offset by significant divergences. The allusion to the *Tesoretto* in the *Commedia*'s opening lines immediately invites comparison between the two texts, hinting at the limitations of the earlier work. In light of Brunetto's infernal speech, which several times betrays a misdirected fixation on worldly goals, we may surmise that Dante regards the acquisition of temporal knowledge celebrated in the *Tesoretto* as ill-considered and disconnected from salvation. Equally, the *Tresor*'s eclectic and earthbound encyclopaedism is at odds with the *Commedia*'s ambition meticulously to represent the gamut of the created universe, 'bound by love in one volume' (legato con amore in un volume; *Par.* XXXIII, 86) as a celebration of the divine. The *Tresor*, furthermore, strongly promotes an autonomous, republican model of governance for the Italian city-states grounded in the civic and rhetorical teachings of the classical world, and especially Cicero, thereby standing in manifest opposition to the divinely sanctioned imperial vision promoted in the *Commedia*. Nonetheless, the lasting importance for Dante of Brunetto's example as a Florentine Guelf vernacular author whose work addressed a substantial range of moral, philosophical, and political questions cannot be overestimated.

Significantly less studied than Brunetto's impact on the *Commedia* is that of late-thirteenth-century vernacular, and especially Tuscan, prose culture. 'Vernacularizations' of classical and medieval works were numerous. Taddeo Alderotti, for instance, a Florentine who taught medicine at the University of Bologna, was notable as the vernacular translator of a Latin version of Aristotle's *Ethics*. In *Paradiso* XII, 82–4, Dante criticizes Taddeo (he had also disparaged his translation of the *Ethics* in *Convivio* I, x, 10) for the earthly motivations underpinning his approach to learning. Despite Dante's attacks, 'vernacularizations' had a substantial impact on his cultural formation (traces of Taddeo's work have been identified in the *Convivio*). As well as classical and medieval Latin works, texts were also translated into Italian from other vernaculars, ranging from Italian rewritings of French romances, such as the *Tristano Riccardiano* of the late Duecento, to a widely circulating Italian version of Brunetto's *Tresor*, attributed to the Florentine judge Bono Giamboni. Other important prose contributions of the late-thirteenth century include the *Composizione del mondo*, a vernacular cosmological treatise by Ristoro d'Arezzo, vernacular city chronicles, and short stories (*novelle*). One of the morally instructive *novelle* included in the anonymous *Novellino* features the figure of Marco Lombardo, who appears in *Purgatorio* XVI. Dante presumes a certain familiarity with this figure on the part of his readers, probably through this popular vernacular collection. The Duecento also saw the growth of vernacular letter writing thanks to the Bolognese rhetorician Guido Faba, who, around 1220, formalized instruction on basic vernacular epistolography, and to the letters of the lyric poet Guittone d'Arezzo. Whether in increasing the rhetorical and narrative malleability of the Italian vernacular or in transmitting different forms of philosophical, historical, and scientific knowledge, these various strands of prose culture almost certainly made important contributions to Dante's linguistic, literary, and intellectual development.

Poetic Debate and Self-authorization

If vernacular prose culture is a relatively concealed facet of Dante's vernacular cultural inheritance, the *Commedia*'s most intense form of engagement with vernacular models comes in its representation of Romance lyric poets. These encounters, dealing with some of Dante's most decisive influences as well as some discarded models, are important not simply in terms of Dante's evaluation of the poet in question. Taken together they form a sustained and

highly strategic vernacular literary history, underlining the moral and stylistic shortcomings of previous authors, and, by implication, how in the
Commedia such shortcomings are uniquely overcome. As such, these are
not impartial evaluations of poets but rather key sites of self-definition and
self-authorization. The *Commedia*'s historiography and judgements, however, from the label 'sweet new style' (dolce stil novo; *Purg.* XXIV, 57) to the
dismissal of the important figure of Guittone d'Arezzo, have nonetheless
proved extremely influential, often shaping critical responses and modern
histories and anthologies of early Italian poetry.

While not the only vernacular poetic encounters in the *Commedia* (the
Sicilian poet and senior bureaucrat Pier della Vigna appears in *Inferno* XIII,
the troubadours Bertran de Born and Sordello in *Inferno* XXVIII and
Purgatorio VI–VII respectively, and Dante's brother-in-law and occasional
lyricist Forese Donati in *Purgatorio* XXIII–XXIV), I shall focus here on the
aulic love poets of *Purgatorio* and *Paradiso*, beginning with the pilgrim's
brief but highly significant dialogue with Bonagiunta degli Orbicciani da
Lucca among the gluttons of *Purgatorio* XXIV. Bonagiunta was a largely
conventional lyric poet of the so-called Siculo-Tuscan school, notable for
taking issue with the overly philosophical bent of Guido Guinizzelli's love
poetry in an exchange of sonnets in the 1270s. He asks if Dante is the poet
who, in writing the canzone 'Donne ch'avete intelletto d'amore' (Ladies who
have intelligence of Love), poetic centrepiece of the *Vita nova*, inaugurated
the 'new rhymes' (nove rime, 50). Dante replies, rather obliquely, that he
simply acts as Love's scribe: 'I am one who, when love breathes in me, take
note, and in that manner which he dictates within go on to set it forth' (I' mi
son un che, quando / Amor mi spira, noto, e a quel modo / ch'e' ditta dentro
vo significando; 52–4). Bonagiunta says in response that he now understands
the 'sweet new style' he hears and the 'knot' (nodo; 55) that restricted his
own poetry, along with that of his Sicilian and Tuscan forerunners, Giacomo
da Lentini and Guittone (the latter notable for his dense and highly rhetorical
style), from achieving such a form of expression and such a fidelity to its
source of inspiration.

The relationship of Dante's poetry to 'Love' that the pilgrim describes has
been extensively debated. His brief response raises a number of specific
questions whose implications are far-reaching. Is the pilgrim referring to
the *Vita nova*, the *Commedia*, or both? Is the Love he describes erotic, divine,
or both? Where do these lines place Dante in relation to the Romance lyric of
his time? While it is impossible to do justice here to the breadth of critical
responses that this textual crux has elicited, I will address two particular
matters arising from the pilgrim's response to Bonagiunta. First, whether he
is alluding to the *Commedia* or to a past lyric phase that he continues to

endorse. The account of his transcription of Love's dictates powerfully recalls the process of divine inspiration affecting human authors of Scripture, and thus, like other passages in the poem, fashions Dante as a divinely sanctioned scribe. However, by grounding his poetry in *Amor*, Dante also evokes the vernacular lyric maxim, belonging to the troubadours as well as to contemporary Italian poets, that poetic authority and authenticity are predicated upon an inner experience of love. Rather than choosing between these competing forms of inspiration, we might once again stress Dante's own emphasis on integration and his continuing association with vernacular lyric modes of expression. A second ambiguity is created by the use of 'vostre' (your) in line 58 – 'I clearly see how *your* pens follow' (Io veggio ben come le vostre penne) – which can be interpreted as honorific or plural, with the latter reading suggesting a group or 'school' of 'stilnovist' poets. Again, the ambiguity may well be intended. As elsewhere, Dante is concurrently emphasizing the tensions between generations of Italian poets, between the old guard and the new, while also insisting on the singular properties and achievements of his own verse.

Dante's indebtedness to particular vernacular models and continuing affiliation to the erotic tradition come into sharper focus on the terrace of lust in *Purgatorio* XXVI, as the connection between Romance literature and lust is again interrogated. The pilgrim first meets the shade of the Bolognese poet Guinizzelli, whose poetry for an angelic beloved paved the way for the 'praise' poetry of the *Vita nova*, where he is termed a 'saggio' (wise one; *Vn* XX, 3 [11, 3]). Reinforcing the idea of a 'stilnovist' community, inaugurated by Guido, Dante refers to him as 'my father and of others, my betters, whoever have used sweet and light rhymes of love' (il padre / mio e de li altri miei miglior che mai / rime d'amor usar dolci e leggiadre; 97–9), evoking the 'sweet' rhymes of love described two cantos earlier. Guido's status as a 'father' to Dante positions him as the vernacular lyric counterpart to Virgil. Certainly, Dante's poetry for Beatrice in the *Paradiso*, as well as in the *Vita nova*, can be traced back to Guinizzelli's laudatory love poetry, as well as to the Song of Songs and mystical and Marian literature of the later Middle Ages. Dante is nonetheless eager to draw a distinction between his love for Beatrice, which emerges as compatible with his love for God, and Guido's love, which, as this canto reveals, remained contaminated by lust. Guido thus served as a decisive influence on Dante, while failing to formulate a redeemed form of love poetry such as that found in the *Commedia*.

Alongside Guido, we find Arnaut Daniel, the most privileged of the poem's troubadours, who is described as the 'better craftsman of the mother tongue' (miglior fabbro del parlar materno; 117) and accorded the privilege of speaking in his native Occitan in lines 140–7. Dante's treatment of Arnaut, as with the other troubadours, was informed by the biographical *vidas* and expository *razos* that accompanied his verse in medieval songbooks, as well as by a detailed engagement with his poetry. Arnaut is important for influencing a very different phase of Dante's lyric evolution: the harsh rhymes of the technically dazzling but thematically fraught lyric sequence of the *rime petrose*, or 'stony poems'. Rather than as the narrowly technical and formalistic poet he has often been considered by Dante studies, Arnaut stands out in the Romance lyric tradition for his highly individual forms of expression and his revivification of formulaic courtly themes. His powerful association with Love, his sole creative source, is suggested not only in his poetry, but also in Dante's *De vulgari eloquentia*, where he is cited as the leading Occitan exponent of erotic verse (II, ii, 9). If Arnaut's identification with love was profound, the love his poetry describes is exclusively carnal and often debilitating, which accounts for his place in Purgatory among those guilty of following bestial appetites (84). In a poem that prizes linguistic clarity, some scholars have identified a critique of Arnaut's stylistic obscurity in the character's plain and humble Occitan speech that now lacks the verbal extravagance associated with his poetry, while others have emphasized its spiritualization of courtly language. Yet, despite their moral failings, Guido and Arnaut appear as contrasting masters of vernacular expression – the one synonymous with verbal 'sweetness', the other with 'harshness' – now doing penance for their common inability to transform their poetic eroticism into a redemptive form. Their respective lyric registers continue to resonate in the *Commedia*'s poetics, from the final cantos of *Inferno* to the upper reaches of *Paradiso*.

In introducing Arnaut, Guido evokes two negative models: Guittone (whom Guinizzelli had addressed while alive, perhaps ironically, as a 'father')[4] and the twelfth-century ethical troubadour Guiraut de Bornelh. While Dante's evaluation of these important poets is, as always, complex, their relationship to love poetry is a matter of particular interest. In the *De vulgari eloquentia*, Guiraut had been deemed pre-eminent among Occitan poets, as the leading exponent of poetry of rectitude, considered in the treatise as the most illustrious form of vernacular song on account of its association with the rational part of the human soul (II, ii, 6–9). Now, however, Guiraut is demoted and declared inferior to the *De vulgari*'s privileged poet of love, Arnaut. The two pairings in *Purgatorio* XXVI – the eulogized but penitent love poets Guido and Arnaut on the one hand, the disparaged moralists Guiraut and Guittone, on the other – can be related to Dante's renewed commitment to love, and specifically to Beatrice, that characterizes the *Commedia*, while simultaneously pointing to the moral inadequacy of pre-existing erotic poetry. Guittone and Guiraut are associated with a non-erotic, ethical mode similar to that espoused by Dante in the moral *canzoni* he composed following the *Vita nova*. Guittone's corpus, in particular, is notable for its stark rejection of love and its exclusively moralizing focus following a mid-career conversion. Critics have highlighted the enduring influence of Guittone's moral and political poetry on the *Commedia*, but, in severing the bond between vernacular poetry and love, and prizing its stylistic obscurity, his verse emerges as decisively at odds with key tenets of Dante's poetics in the *Vita nova* and in his masterpiece. While Guido and Arnaut's love poetry is thus deemed morally insufficient by Dante, in light of their location on the terrace of lust, it is nonetheless to their work that the poet declares his indebtedness.

It is significant that the one vernacular love poet found in *Paradiso*, besides Dante, is the twelfth-century troubadour Folco of Marseilles in *Paradiso* IX, noted for his abandonment of courtly poetry in becoming a famous bishop and crusader. He subsequently penned a pair of surviving crusade songs, which, like Guittone's post-conversionary poetry, strongly renounce earthly love and distance him from his former poetic identity. Folco appears in the heaven of Venus, home to those who overcame a lustful tendency to become passionate servants of God. Before turning his attention to the avaricious Church, in a fervent invective that resonates with his crusade poetry and Latin sermons, Folco recalls the eros of his youth, when he burned with passion like Hercules, Phyllis, and Dido (98–102). It is interesting to contrast Folco, whose identification with Dido in Paradise is confined to his sinful lyric past, with Dante, who appropriates the identity of Dido upon beholding Beatrice in Eden (*Purg.* XXX, 46–8). Where Folco renounced his identity as a love poet in order to reach Heaven, Dante's erotic 'flame' remains lit: his redeemed love for Beatrice remains his conduit to salvation, and he insists upon the poetic continuity between the erotic love he first felt for her on earth and her celestial apotheosis in the Empyrean (see, for example, *Par.* XXX, 28–33). It is evident from Dante's rich catalogue of Romance lyricists that there is no prior vernacular poet, and certainly no prior vernacular love poet, whose verse is not found spiritually (and probably aesthetically) wanting, underlining the success and originality he claims exclusively for the *Commedia* and for the love at its heart.

Stylistic Eclecticism

While the previous section may imply the primacy of the Romance lyric – the tradition tackled most systematically in the poem's diegesis – the *Commedia*'s range of debts to vernacular literature and culture should ultimately be understood in terms of its extraordinary breadth, eclecticism, and syncretism. The poem's rhetorical approach, informed primarily by the Bible's mingling of 'styles', is radically inclusive. Its allegiance is not to a pre-existing rhetorical mode but to the purported reality of Dante's vision, whose content must be described unflinchingly. Just as it exploits an extraordinarily broad lexical range, the *Commedia* can thus be seen to draw upon a plethora of vernacular cultural traditions, 'high' and 'low', religious and secular, poetic and prosaic. Dante's intent is not only to maximize his poem's expressive capacity, but, in many cases, also to subject existing literary traditions to critique, redeploying their rhetorical conventions in his work of infinitely greater spiritual substance and literary sophistication. The use of any given 'style' or register in the poem normally pertains, therefore, not to an endorsement of the tradition with which that 'style' is associated, or to a form of textual homage, but rather to an expressive choice made out of ethical, poetic, and narrative expediency.

A telling example of Dante's formal eclecticism is the cantos of Malebolge (*Inf.* XVIII–XXXI), the eighth circle of Hell and home to various categories of fraudulent sinners. In addition to the classical *auctores* (especially Virgil, Ovid, Statius, and Lucan), whose influence is strongly felt throughout the *Inferno*, Dante draws upon an array of vernacular traditions in articulating the unspeakable horrors of lower Hell. The *bolgia* of barratry, for instance, is home to the Malebranche, a troop of sadistic devils charged with ensuring the barrators remain submerged in boiling pitch, who dupe Virgil and the pilgrim into following a wrong path to the *bolgia* below. The crude, corporeal representation of the snarling demons, often seen as paradigmatic of the 'low' poetics of the nether regions of Hell, has been associated with medieval jongleurs, whose performances in urban centres sought to titillate through vulgar language and obscene gestures. Another 'low' register on which Dante draws in Lower Hell is the 'comic-realist' one which he had previously utilized in the abusive *tenzone* with Forese Donati. In Purgatory, Dante and Forese recall with regret this past misdeed (XXIII, 115–7). Yet, if their remorse concerns the *tenzone* of the 1290s, the later cantos of *Inferno* remind us that Dante nevertheless profited poetically from that experience. This is most explicit in the abusive exchange between Master Adam and Sinon in *Inferno* XXX, 103–39, an episode interpreted as palinodic in light of Virgil's firm rebuke of the pilgrim's absorption in the sinners' unedifying dialogue. Indeed, a number of the testy exchanges between the pilgrim and the sinners throughout the opening *cantica* (notably those with Filippo Argenti in *Inferno* VIII and Bocca degli Abati in *Inferno* XXXII) owe something to this 'low' vernacular dialogic model. But while the offensive *tenzone* is implicitly cast as a frivolous misuse of poetry, the *Commedia*'s deployment of an analogous 'low style' emerges as a necessary consequence of its theme, of its endeavour to use language uncompromisingly in harmonizing language and reality, 'so that the telling be no different from the fact' (sì che dal fatto il dir non sia diverso; *Inf.* XXXII, 12). Thus, Dante does not employ the 'comic-realist' and jongleur traditions passively or mechanically, but rather redimensions these morally discredited vernacular literary models, formerly dedicated to gratuitous abuse or obscenity, faithfully to describe the purported realities of his salvific journey.

The strategy of adapting morally defective expressive modes in Malebolge is also apparent in Dante's engagement with the war poetry of Bertran de Born, a troubadour praised in the *De vulgari eloquentia* as the consummate Occitan poet of warfare (II, ii, 9) but condemned in *Inferno* XXVIII among the sowers of discord for his inflammatory verse. The bloody opening seven *terzine* of the canto, prefacing Dante's presentation of the dismembered sowers of discord, including the decapitated Bertran, are widely seen as rewriting the troubadour's *canso* 'Si tuit li dol' (If all the grief). Dante thereby dons the mantle of Italian poet of arms that the *De vulgari* had considered unclaimed (II, ii, 9), but does so not by fomenting earthly discord. Instead he documents the brutal scenes of the ninth *bolgia* in the context of a poem with profoundly unitive political ambitions. In Lower Hell, and especially in Cocytus, Dante also exploits the 'harsh rhymes' (rime aspre; XXXII, 1) previously refined in the violent eroticism of his *rime petrose*, a sequence whose formal extravagance and lexical harshness are especially informed by the troubadour Arnaut, but also by lesser Guittonian poets such as Monte Andrea.

The *Commedia*'s stylistic eclecticism cannot be reduced to an exploitation of 'low' vernacular models in *Inferno* and 'high' ones in *Paradiso*. Just as Dante's ancestor Cacciaguida deploys a harsh, corporeal idiom in exhorting the pilgrim to make his reader 'scratch where there is the itch' (grattar dov'è la rogna; *Par.* XVII, 129), we find 'high' registers in the depths of Hell, for instance in the tale of Ugolino with its unmistakably Virgilian prologue (XXXIII, 4–6), as well as in the continued evocation of epic classical figures, from Ulysses to the giants of canto XXXI. Indeed, alongside the reworking of Bertran's bloody poetry of arms and the crude jongleur and 'comic-realist' traditions, we find evocations of more prestigious Old French models. In canto XXXI, Dante evokes the *Chanson de Roland*, as he compares the thunderclap he hears on entering Cocytus to the sound of Roland's horn, who in vain summoned Charlemagne and his troops after they had been betrayed to the Saracens by Ganelon (XXXI, 16–18). We also find Ganelon named among the traitors of Cocytus in XXXII, 122, along with Mordred, who, according to chivalric legend, killed (and was simultaneously killed by) King Arthur with a single blow (61–2). In light of Dante's apprenticeship as a lyric poet, his engagement with Old French narrative traditions has tended to be seen as subordinate to his lyric debts and allegiances. Nevertheless, in spite of the anti-French sentiments powerfully voiced in the *Commedia* (notably in Hugh Capet's invective in *Purgatorio* XX and the vitriolic critique of the French monarchy in *Purgatorio* XXXII) and Dante's desire to promote Italian as the pre-eminent Romance vernacular, such references again suggest a close acquaintance with texts whose narrative scale renders them important models.

The *Purgatorio* not only displays debts to political poetry in the vernacular (the work of Guittone and Sordello resonates in cantos VI–VII), to doctrinal and philosophical verse, and to popular piety (consider the vernacular 'Our Father' of *Purgatorio* XI), but also stages the radical recuperation and reformulation of Dante's past identity as a lyric love poet, consolidating the fusion of eros and theology first witnessed in *Inferno* II. The intensely intertextual episode of Beatrice's arrival in Eden, along with the departure of Virgil, beautifully exemplifies the syncretism of literary and cultural traditions – Latin and vernacular, sacred and secular – so characteristic of the *Commedia*. Dante cites the Song of Songs and Virgil's *Aeneid*, Mark's Gospel and his own *Vita nova* and erotic canzone 'Io sento sì d'Amor la gran possanza' (I feel so much Love's mighty power). While Beatrice's Christological function is clear, she retains her historical identity, and she herself evokes in the Earthly Paradise the memory of Dante's 'vita nova' (XXX, 115). As such, the continuing presence of this lyric *donna* as the fulcrum of Dante's poetry reflects the incorporation of lyric discourse into the *Commedia* and his enduring connection to vernacular literary traditions.

Paradise might at first be regarded as the realm least concerned with vernacular literature and culture. Yet the theologizing poetry of the third *cantica* is largely mediated through the expressly vernacular female figure of Beatrice, as accepted cultural oppositions – Latin/vernacular, male/female, religious/secular, poetry/theology – are again eroded. We find in *Paradiso* a host of intensely lyrical passages. These articulations of ardent subjective desire can be understood in terms of manifold traditions, encompassing medieval mysticism, Marian literature, *laude*, and the Song of Songs, while also remaining strongly rooted in the lyric poetry of the *Vita nova*. The continuing presence of Beatrice and Dante's redeemed submission to *Amor*, from the Earthly Paradise to the end of the poem, stands in opposition to the stark abandonment of love witnessed in the lyrics of poets such as Folco and Guittone, and points to his more nuanced and ambivalent relationship to the vernacular literary tradition as a spiritually engaged author. Indeed, even when Beatrice is no longer present in the closing two cantos of *Paradiso*, the importance of vernacular culture continues to surface. St

Bernard's prayer to the Virgin in *Paradiso* XXXIII fuses the rhetoric of medieval mysticism and emergent popular piety with the expressive modes of the vernacular lyric. The white rose containing the blessed souls of the Empyrean, meanwhile, has been read as a sublimated version of the sexualized rose that is the dominant symbol and object of the lover's quest in the *Roman de la rose*. While the *Roman* serves as an important narrative and philosophical vernacular model, the thinly veiled erotic allegory of its ending renders it an apt profane anti-text for Dante, a negative image of the *Commedia*'s uniquely redemptive quest of desire.

The *Commedia* offers a window onto many aspects of a relatively young yet vibrant vernacular literary culture. Dante's endlessly rich and multifaceted response to this culture is never neutral or passive, but always critical and selective, aimed at highlighting his poem's novelty and surpassing of the moral, ideological, and expressive limitations weighing down other texts. As with many aspects of Dante's handling of his cultural and intellectual inheritance, his relationship to vernacular literature in the *Commedia* is best understood in terms of its radical syncretism: its absorption and harmonization of a rich variety of modes and traditions. Dante's genius lies in creating a poem that is at once deeply embedded in the debates and complexities of medieval vernacular literature and culture and yet – in its response to these debates and tensions, as well as in its remarkable thematic, philosophical, and linguistic scope – wholly new.

Notes

1. B. Latini, *Il tesoretto*, ed. and trans. J. B. Holloway (New York: Garland, 1981).
2. G. Cavalcanti, *Complete Poems*, ed. and trans. A. Mortimer (London: Oneworld, 2010), pp. 98–9.
3. Brunetto may refer in this passage to his French *Tresor* or to his Italian *Tesoretto*, which he had termed 'this rich Treasure' [*Tesoretto*, 75]).
4. See G. Guinizelli, *Rime*, ed. L. Rossi (Turin: Einaudi, 2002), pp. 68–72.

IO

PAOLA NASTI

Religious Culture

Defining the Field

There is no agreement on what religion is or does. Likewise there is no consensus on how to study it. Both the object of and the approaches to religion vary in time and space. Dante's understanding of the notion of religion differs considerably from our own. In the *Convivio,* describing the many virtues that ennoble humanity, he defined religion as a moral virtue and good disposition (IV, xix, 5). The same understanding of the notion can be found in Thomas Aquinas, the most important scholastic theologian of the thirteenth century, who broadly defined *religio* as our relationship to God and his worship, while also affirming that 'religion is a moral virtue distinct from piety, both of which are about operations'.[1] Like all virtues, Aquinas explains, religion has interior and exterior acts, having both contemplative and active dimensions. Devotion and prayer are interior acts; while adoration by means of the body, offerings such as sacrifices, oblations and tithes, and finally vows and praise are all external ones. In line with Aquinas' ideas on religion, this chapter seeks to answer questions such as: How is devotion portrayed in the *Comedy?* Is prayer a theme in the poem? Is sacrifice part of Dante's understanding of worship and the religious life?

Biblical Literacy and Prophetic Identity

At the core of every medieval Christian community was the Bible, which was considered to be God's word and the font of all truth. Unsurprisingly, in the *Comedy,* Dante quotes Scripture more than any other text. Indeed, as Beatrice declares in *Paradiso* V, in order to live well and achieve salvation, the believer must simply follow the teachings of the Old and New Testament (73–8). Yet, Dante regularly felt compelled to lament the contemporary ignorance and misuse of the Bible, vehemently attacking clerics, as he does in *Paradiso* XXIX, whose duty it was to elucidate the Gospels but who, to satisfy their own intellectual vanities, instead distracted the faithful with misleading claims (94–6). According to

Dante, the 'inventions' (invenzioni; 95) and 'idle tales' (ciance; 110) that had led clerics to marginalize the Bible were an excessive fascination with philosophical and theological debates ('filosofando', namely, philosophizing; 86) that were the focus of attention at the universities of Paris and Oxford, as well as in local cathedral schools and monastic *studia*.

Dante's negative portrayal of the status of Scripture in his world runs counter to the surviving evidence regarding the centrality of the Bible in medieval religious culture. In fact, the Bible provided daily guidance to the faithful as a result of its ubiquitous presence in liturgy, prayers, and sermons, as well as in the frescoes and mosaics that decorated the walls of churches and public places. The Bible also guided Christians in their private spiritual meditations. Additionally, in lay grammar schools, the Psalter was used as a basic text-book for instruction in Latin. Why, then, was Dante so worried about the Bible's contemporary standing? In spite of its universally acknowledged pre-eminence, the study of the Bible among intellectuals had increasingly been overshadowed by a focus on philosophical texts, predominantly Aristotelian, and theoretical discussions regarding matters of doctrine. Indeed, although a conflict had existed for nearly a century between those who considered philosophy as a discipline ancillary to divine wisdom and those who sought to establish its independence, by the late thirteenth century, rationalist scholastic theological reflection had largely supplanted biblical exegesis. Dante reacted to this situation by taking a very clear stance in the battle of contrasting epistemologies. As the pilgrim declares to the three apostles examining his religious beliefs in the heaven of the Fixed Stars, no philosophical proofs are needed to confirm the truths taught by the Bible (*Par.* XXIV, 130–8).

At the same time as he reproached the clergy, Dante claimed that the *Commedia* could teach its readers how to shape their relationship to God through a correct understanding and use of the Bible. In this regard, the poet presented himself as someone who 'approaches it [Scripture] humbly' (umilmente con essa s'accosta; *Par.* XXIX 93), namely someone who practises a method of reading the Bible that avoids error by respecting both the literal meaning of the text and the views of authoritative past interpreters. Indeed, the *Comedy* offers a wealth of examples that confirm Dante's profound knowledge of the Bible which he quotes, translates, paraphrases, glosses, rewrites, and imitates. Yet, when Dante drew on the Bible, this was always in conjunction with the exegetical tradition on the passages and stylistic registers that he was utilizing. A telling example of this process occurs in *Purgatorio* XXX. Having entered the Earthly Paradise, the pilgrim is finally reunited with Beatrice whose appearance is announced by an elderly figure who intones a Latin verse from the Bible: 'Come, bride, from Lebanon'

('Veni, sponsa, de Libano'; 11). The line is a direct quotation from Solomon's Song of Songs (4:8), a poem about the love of the king for his betrothed, which, since early Christianity, had been read as an allegory of the loving bond between God and his Church. Exegetes also interpreted the bride as the faithful soul that is united in mystic marriage to Christ, or as Mary who loves her son and saviour. Furthermore, the Canticle was read as the celebration of the final resurrection and union of body and soul in Paradise. Equating Beatrice with the bride of the Song of Songs, Dante granted his beloved the same values as the exegetical tradition had bestowed upon the *sponsa*. Equally, by imitating the biblical lovers, the pilgrim and Beatrice function as re-enactments (or *figurae*) of the Song's divine truths, thereby becoming part of salvation history.

If the Bible is an essential subtext to understand the way in which the *Comedy* creates meaning, the poem also serves as an invitation and guide to reading the word of God. In contrast to the contemporary clergy, Dante encourages his readers to consult Scripture if his message is to be fully understood. Again, a telling example occurs in the Earthly Paradise, where the pilgrim sees a symbolic procession representing providential history. Dante explicitly indicates the biblical sources of his vision, exhorting his 'reader' (*Purg.* XXIX, 98) to consult the prophecies of Ezekiel and John's Apocalypse in order fully to appreciate what he saw (97–105). He then claims that he is able to confirm a controversial detail of John's vision, which contradicted Ezekiel's account of the four winged beasts: 'but read Ezechiel, who paints them ... they were like that here, except that for the wings John is with me and departs from him' (ma leggi Ezechïel, che li dipigne / ... / tali eran quivi, salvo ch'a le penne / Giovanni è meco e da lui si diparte; 100 and 104–5). In other words, Dante not only interprets and discriminates between the two biblical accounts, but also momentously claims that John, a writer inspired by the Holy Spirit, agrees with him! In doing so, the poet enacts a strategy that includes him and his *Comedy* in a genealogy of biblical writers and texts and establishes the sacredness of his poem.

Indeed, to authenticate his own divinely ordained poetic authority, throughout the *Comedy*, Dante associates himself with major Scriptural authors (*scribae Dei*), such as David and Paul. Like David, the pilgrim, when morally lost in the dark wood, asks for help by calling out, 'Miserere' (*Inf.* I 65, and compare Ps. 51:3), thereby initiating a Davidic penitential journey. Later on, Dante defines the prophet as 'the singer of the Holy Spirit' (il cantor de lo Spirito Santo; *Par.* XX, 38) and author of a 'tëodìa' (*Par.* XXV, 74), namely a poem in praise of God. He invents the term *tëodìa* to establish, among other things, a sharp contrast between

David's writing and his own 'comedìa' (*Inf.* XVI, 128; XXI, 2). While presenting himself, too, as divinely inspired (for instance, *Par.* I, 19), Dante stressed his own artistic ascendancy over David. Indeed, instead of simply praising God, he describes himself as the author of an all-encompassing 'sacred poem' (poema sacro; *Par.* XXV, 1). In other words, though Dante never claimed that the *Comedy* was somehow superior to Scripture, in line with contemporary ideas about the role played by human authors in the Bible's composition, he was clearly keen to establish that he was a better writer than David.

Dante's strategy of self-identification with fundamental figures from Scripture underpins his message of urgent reform, since, for his voice to be authoritative, it needed to be recognized as prophetic. It is thus not a coincidence that some of the *Comedy*'s most intense biblical moments occur when the poet attacks clerical figures. Thus, in *Inferno* XIX, the pilgrim lambasts the simoniac Pope Nicholas III by alluding to a series of events in the New Testament, such as Peter's investiture as the first pope, that stress poverty as the defining feature of the apostolic life (88–97). At the same time Dante-character's attack on the contemporary Church increases in ferocity when he adopts apocalyptic tones drawing on John 'the Evangelist' (106) to describe the corrupt popes as a whore (106–11), before comparing them to the idolaters of the Old Testament (112–14).

Dante's regular and apposite recourse to Scripture explains why some fourteenth-century commentators considered the *Comedy* an *imitatio Bibliae*. Indeed, Dante introduced clear signposts in this regard. In *Paradiso* IV, for example, he underlined how his poem's symbolic modes of signification imitate those of Scripture which presents God with hands and feet so that humans might appreciate concepts that otherwise would be too complex or abstract (40–5). Dante also highlighted that the *Commedia* is a divinely willed *reportatio*, a 'record' of the events he witnessed and of things he heard. Consequently, as Beatrice specifies, what he writes is divinely inspired like the words of the *scribae Dei*: 'You take note; and just as these words are borne by me, so mark them for the living' (Tu nota; e sì come da me son porte, / così queste parole segna a' vivi; *Purg.* XXXIII, 52–3).

Equally, the places and events that the pilgrim 'records' are pervaded by or based upon biblical narratives. The Bible resonates throughout the realms of Dante's afterlife: it is perverted by the damned and solemnly recited by the saved; it also affects the punishments inflicted on the souls of Hell and Purgatory. The second realm, in particular, resounds with Scriptural elements: God's word is whispered to the penitents; biblical events appear in visions and are sculpted on the rock of the mountain. Imagined as an ideal earthly Church, Dante's Purgatory is presented as a community where the Bible plays a determining role in Christian education. In *Paradiso*, the relationship between the blessed and Scripture is even more intense: in fact, the two are identical, since Heaven and its inhabitants are both considered as God's books. This is most clearly expressed in the heaven of Jupiter, where the souls of the just metamorphose into the letters of the alphabet in order to compose the opening verse of the Book of Wisdom (*Par.* XVIII, 76–93). The celestial world-book, where God's words and creatures are one, where humans, like Christ, are incarnated words, constitutes divine art – art that Dante, God's *scriba*, has been chosen to reproduce for his readers 'to bring comfort from there to that faith that is the beginning of the road of salvation' (per recarne conforto a quella fede / ch'è principio a la via di salvazione; *Inf.* II, 29–30), thereby fulfilling that process of self-identification with Paul that had begun in the *Commedia*'s opening.

Liturgy

The pilgrim's voyage through the afterlife is a privilege that, as Dante never tires to declare, can only be compared to the experience of Paradise granted to Paul (II Cor. 12:2). Yet, for all the supposed exceptionality of his journeying, Dante draws on culturally established features to represent his afterlife: Hell is imagined as a perverted community (*ecclesia carnalis*; the carnal Church); Purgatory is represented as a congregation of souls who willingly perform acts of penance (*ecclesia in via*; the Church penitent); while Paradise is a luminous assembly finally united with God (*ecclesia triumphans*; the Church triumphant). Like the earthly Church (*ecclesia militans*; the Church militant), the saved souls of the Dantean afterlife establish their relationship to God through acts of worship and devotion that follow the same patterns established by the earthly Church's liturgical calendar. In the *Commedia*, liturgy is a bridge between this world and the other.

Crossing the threshold of a church, often inscribed with promises of salvation and decorated with figures from sacred history, a medieval Christian heard the almost incessant, and often incomprehensible, sequence of readings, prayers, hymns, and antiphons that constituted the liturgy. Likewise, every time the pilgrim enters a new area of the afterlife or passes through a door, he immediately hears sounds produced by the souls. At the gate of Purgatory, for example, such sounds are identified with those heard by worshippers listening to polyphonic music accompanied by organs (*Purg.* IX, 130 and 139–44) and to hymns sung by clerics. In this instance, the pilgrim is overwhelmed by the sounds of the *Te Deum laudamus* (We praise you God; 140). Alluding to a well-known liturgical hymn such as this would have had immediate resonance for contemporary readers who shared Dante's religious culture. It is therefore essential to grasp the ways in which liturgy affects the poem's narrative and ideological structures. The *Te Deum* is one of the Church's oldest hymns and serves as a blueprint for all acts of praise. It offers a vision of Heaven and earth joined in worship; it touches on the most important points of Christian doctrine (in particular the Trinity); and retells Scripture by recounting providential history from the creation to Christ's resurrection. Marking the start of Purgatory proper with this most potent hymn, termed a 'tuono' (thunder; 139), Dante defines it not only as a realm of praise and devotion, but also as a community that trusts in a merciful God to deliver it from pain. The *Te Deum* is also chosen to fix the time of the pilgrim's journey in religious terms. In the Liturgy of the Hours, the hymn was sung at Matins (dawn); thus, on the threshold of Purgatory, it announces that this is the dawn of a unique Easter for the pilgrim, when he will return to God while still alive.

As in *Purgatorio* IX, references to the liturgy and its calendar are introduced throughout the poem to elucidate different moments of Dante-character's internal and external movements, as well as the condition of the souls he encounters. The penitents who miraculously arrive on the shores of Purgatory sing Psalm 113, a text read during the Easter liturgy to announce the spiritual liberation brought about by Christ's resurrection (*Purg.* II, 46–8). The souls intone 'in one voice' (ad una voce; 47) a text that fulfils and activates the promise of a new life, which the pilgrim too is about to experience, albeit temporarily. This is the first hymn heard by Dante-character on his journey, and it is also the first time the reader is expected to recognize the polyphonic nature of the otherworldly liturgical celebrations. The fact that the penitents freely and unanimously choose to participate in the rituals of communal worship is one of the most significant aspects of Dante's wide-ranging utilization of liturgical materials. As the poet carefully stresses, acts of devotion occur throughout *Purgatorio*. Thus, the penitent wrathful recite in unison the liturgical formula 'Agnus Dei' (Lamb of God), which is usually sung during the Eucharist (*Purg.* XVI, 19–21). In Heaven, the pilgrim also hears the blessed and the angels harmoniously chant songs of praise such as the *Ave Maria* (Hail Mary; *Par.* XXXII, 94–9) and the *Hosanna* (133–5). He also experiences liturgical hymns 'of lofty praise' (d'alta lode; *Par.* XIV, 124) that either are unknown on earth or are performed so sweetly and perfectly to become unintelligible to the living: 'a melody ... which rapt me, without understanding the hymn' (una melode / ... che mi rapiva, sanza intender l'inno; 122–3).

Whatever the hymn or prayer, in both Purgatory and Paradise, the poet's emphasis is always on the importance of shared worship – a perspective that merits additional clarification. Our assumptions about the religiosity of people in the Middle Ages often obscure the reality of their formal devotional practices. The laity attended religious services, including the mass, rather less frequently than is generally believed today. People often only went to church at Easter when attendance was compulsory. Even when they did attend, the faithful would rarely have had contact with the clergy, who performed the liturgy mostly in the quire or behind screens. Instead, in Dante's otherworld, liturgy is shared and familiar to all, whether dead or alive. Most importantly, it becomes personalized through the voice of the pilgrim and of the first-person narrator. Hence, we can postulate that by integrating the intricate medieval liturgical system with the vivid representation of the pilgrim's first-hand experience, Dante conceived the *Comedy* as a means through which to engage the laity in the world of religious worship. In this respect, the poet's concern echoes that of the many lay Florentines who, in the thirteenth century, had formed dozens of confraternities to foster popular devotional cults and to express their own religious zeal.

The influence of popular religious trends is also visible in the impact that the medieval cult of the dead had on Dante. Belief in the Last Judgement and the resurrection of the body was accompanied by a powerful preoccupation with the care and commemoration of the dead. Liturgical rituals, such as the Office of the Dead, preserved the memory of the deceased, and fostered the idea that prayer could ease the pain of souls in Purgatory. The *Comedy*, too, subscribes to this sense of the relationship between the living and the dead. To a certain extent the entire poem can be considered as an extended *memento mori*; in fact, the personal history of each character erects a monument to the memory of the dead, as Pia de' Tolomei's words attest: 'Ah, when you'll have returned to the world and rested from the long way ... remember me who am Pia' (Deh, quando tu sarai tornato al mondo, / e riposato de la lunga via, / ... / ricorditi di me, che son la Pia; *Purg.* V, 130–1 and 133). Equally important is the *Commedia*'s focus on the recipro-cal relationship between the living and the dead through prayer. Dante's penitents often declare their gratitude for the prayers and charitable actions of the living that improve their condition in the afterlife. A famous case is that of the Sienese Sapia whose otherworldly condition is positively affected by the 'devout prayers' (sante orazioni; *Purg.* XIII, 128;) of Pier Pettinaio, a holy layman and fellow citizen.

Nonetheless, in the *Comedy*, prayers spoken by the dead are as important as those said on earth. In contrast to standard theological positions regarding the status of prayer after death, the communities of Dante's otherworld are frequently seen performing prayers not only as a mark of their devotion to God, but also as forms of service to the living. The most memorable example of this double function of prayer is the vernacular version of the Our Father intoned by the penitent proud in *Purgatorio* XI. Probably following an approach developed by preachers, Dante translates and interprets Catholicism's most important prayer in such a way that clarifies the meaning of each phrase so as to help the reader-believer achieve a fuller understanding of its message, thereby allowing her to participate more fully in its spiritual benefits. This strategy is clear from the prayer's opening:

> O Padre nostro, che ne' cieli stai, (translation of original line)
> non circunscritto, ma per più amore (Dante's exegesis)
> ch'ai primi effetti di là sù tu hai. (Dante's exegesis)
> (*Purg.* XI, 1–3; Our Father who are in Heaven, not circumscribed, but by
> the greater love that you have for the first effects up there)

To the glossed translation of the Our Father Dante adds a final tercet that, as the penitents aver, only applies to the living: 'This last prayer, dear Lord, is not made for ourselves, because it is unnecessary, but for those who remain behind us' (Quest' ultima preghiera, segnor caro, / già non si fa per noi, ché non bisogna, / ma per color che dietro a noi restaro; *Purg.* XI, 22–4). Presenting the dead praying for the living, Dante expressed his belief in the mutual exchange and reciprocity between this world and the next – a belief founded on the conviction that there is no separation between communities that worship God and act for the common good. If the living do good when praying for the dead, in their turn, the dead act as mediators between earth and Heaven, as Beatrice's, Lucy's, and Mary's intervention to support the pilgrim reveal at the beginning of the *Comedy*.

Devotion to Mary and the Cult of Saints

The idea of the permeability between this world and the next also lies at the heart of the medieval devotion to the saints and to the Virgin Mary. In the 1200s, thanks to the efforts of the mendicant orders and the confraternities, the cult of Mary had vigorously blossomed. She became a major object of devotion and a very large number of sermons, prayers, hymns, frescoes, and altarpieces were dedicated to her. Likewise liturgy had taken on a Marian flavour with the introduction of the Little Office of the Blessed Virgin into the Liturgy of the Hours, as well as the adoption of Marian hymns into the order of the Mass. At the same time, theologians continued in their efforts to develop a sustained doctrine of Mary (Mariology), namely, a theoretical explanation, supported by biblical evidence, of the role and meaning of Mary, both as a person and as the mother of Jesus, in providential history.

Once again, the *Comedy* reflects the interests of its time. No other Dantean figure plays as crucial a religious function in the poem as Mary. In keeping with tradition, she is the protector and intercessor *par excellence*, the exemplary believer, and the supreme example of religious virtues, such as humility and obedience to God's will. She is the heroine of the earthly battles between good and evil on behalf of those who, like Buonconte da Montefeltro (*Purg.* V, 85–129), invoke her name before shedding a 'lagrimetta' (little tear; 107) that saves them from eternal damnation. She also actively intervenes in the afterlife to protect the rulers in Ante-Purgatory from the attacks of a snake that serves as a reminder of the dangers of temptation. The importance of liturgy and prayer in this salvific process is underscored by the princes asking for Mary's intercession by singing a hymn, the *Salve Regina* (Hail Queen), in her praise (*Purg.* VII, 82–4). Discovering penitents who appeal to 'Mary to pray for them' ('Maria, òra per noi'; *Purg.* XIII, 50) is, of course, particularly apt in Purgatory. In Paradise the Virgin's role as *mediatrix* is no more than a memory, as is evident when Cacciaguida recalls how his birth occurred under Mary's protection (*Par.* XV, 133). Instead, the Virgin is now celebrated as an enthroned queen exalted by the angels and the blessed (*Par.* XXXI, 115–17).

In addition to her roles as intercessor and queen of Heaven, Dante presents Mary as the supreme example of virtue for the penitents to imitate on their journey of spiritual renewal. Since Mary was considered a perfect model of conformity to Christ, and since *imitatio Christi* was traditionally deemed the end of purgation, Dante introduced a Marian *exemplum* on each terrace of Purgatory to provide instruction on the Christian virtues. A noteworthy instance of this strategy is found in the cornice of pride on which God has wondrously and realistically carved the angel visiting Mary at the Annunciation (*Purg.* X, 34–45). In a few tercets, Dante offered a poetically condensed theological reflection on the most important moment of Mary's life, illuminating the fundamental providential significance of her humble acceptance: the utterance of 'Ecce Ancilla Dei' (44; Behold the handmaid of God). The annunciation of the Incarnation marks the moment of reconciliation between God and humanity thanks to which the possibility of eternal salvation was re-established (35–6).

The significance of this brief theological lesson on an otherworldly bas-relief needs to be understood in the context of the importance that representations of this and other episodes of Mary's life had acquired in popular devotion, especially in Tuscany, where cities claimed a special relationship with the mother of Christ. Dante was thus writing for readers who had increasingly become involved in the worship of Mary and who flocked in large numbers to adore what were considered miraculous images of her motherhood. Two significant examples of this Marian cult are the image of Mary of the Graces in the Florentine wheat market of Orsanmichele and the great fresco of the Annunciation in the Basilica of the Servi di Santa Maria, which attracted so many pilgrims that the commune was forced to open a new road (via dei Servi) to facilitate access to it. Assimilating such key aspects of popular devotion and using images, sounds, and tropes that belong to a shared vocabulary of devotion, Dante could appeal to his readers' imagination while at the same time instructing them in the more profound doctrinal significance of commonly performed acts of worship. Explaining worship, Dante stresses that it is the sum of exterior acts, which his readers must also understand intellectually in order that they might undergo the same process of knowledge and understanding that both the penitents and the pilgrim willingly experience.

The importance of Marian devotion in the *Commedia* is also reflected in Dante-character's participation in the cult. The pilgrim advances on his journey thanks to the support of the community of saints who aid his moral and intellectual development. However, it is Mary who intervenes at the most important moments of his otherworldly adventure: his safe escape from the dark wood and his final union with God. Although Mary offers succour without being asked (*Par.* XXXIII, 16–18), the pilgrim needs to pray for her help so that he may enjoy the beatific vision at the end of his journey. The prayer, nevertheless, is not intoned by Dante-character. Instead it is formulated by the greatest Marian authority of the medieval tradition, St Bernard of Clairvaux, who had been among the most prolific writers of sermons, homilies, and prayers dedicated to the Virgin. The prayer, which follows the precise structure of a Christian *oratio* (invocation, praise, and appeal; *Par.* XXXIII, 1–39), incorporates major themes of Marian doctrine, such as the relationship between the Incarnation and the resurrection (7–9), which are accompanied both by a catalogue of traditional Marian attributes – 'In you mercy, in you compassion, in you great bounty, in you is joined all goodness that is in a creature' (In te misericordia, in te pietate, / in te magnificenza, in te s'aduna / quantunque in creatura è di bontate; *Par.* XXXIII, 19–21) – and by the imagery of medieval hymnology: Mary as the 'noonday torch' (10) and as a 'gushing fountain' (12). As well as providing a good example of Dante's learned approach to prayer, this Marian piece can also be read as a testament of the poet's belief in worship as the most effective way for humanity to establish a relationship with God. There is no better evidence of the importance that Dante attributed to prayer and devotion than beginning to bring his masterpiece to a close with an appeal for grace and intercession.

Alongside the cult of Mary, the late Middle Ages saw an increase in the veneration of saints as intercessors and miracle workers, especially in urban centres where there were large gatherings of the faithful. As in the case of the Virgin, this system of popular devotion took many forms: devotional prayers, pictorial cycles, series of sermons, local rituals, biographies, and legends. All these cultural appreciations of sainthood can be discerned in the extensive parade of saintly figures that the pilgrim encounters or learns about during his paradisiacal ascent towards God.

Together with the confraternities, the other vital factor in the rise of this devotion was the establishment and spread of two mendicant orders, the Franciscans and the Dominicans, whose founders, Francis of Assisi (*c.*1181–226) and Dominic Guzman (*c.*1170–221), became the most revered saints in Christendom. It is no surprise, therefore, that Dante's most memorable hagiographic representations are those dedicated to St Francis and St Dominic in the heaven of the Sun. The pilgrim does not converse with the two saints as he does with St Benedict of Norcia (*Par.* XXII), the most significant medieval monastic figure, or with St Peter Damian (*Par.* XXI), a monk from Ravenna whose local cult must have become familiar to the poet during his time in the city. Much like the final prayer to Mary, the heaven of the Sun's diptych on the founders of the greatest mendicant orders is presented as 'reported speech', as biographies, or better, as hagiographical narratives recounted by the leading representatives of the two mendicant orders: the Dominican Thomas Aquinas, who praises Francis; and Bonaventure of Bagnoregio, who extolls Dominic. Once again this technique allowed the poet to adopt the forms of a popular religious genre familiar to his audience, thereby suggesting that his poem was intended to have a similar effect on and place in their lives as other forms of worship.

In addition, Dante's treatment of Francis and Dominic also proposed new material for the cult of saints. One of medieval hagiography's most striking characteristics was its constant and often direct reuse of material of biblical, hagiographical, and classical origin. Following the rules of the genre, Dante composed his biography of Francis by primarily drawing on Bonaventure's *Legenda major*, the official biography of the saint. However, the poet carefully selected the linguistic and thematic elements he borrowed from his source. He ignored both the miracles that the *Legenda* attributed to Francis and the details of his acts of self-abnegation, but instead distilled the saint's life to one overarching event: his mystical marriage to Lady Poverty (*Par.* XI, 58–63). This allegorical union, modelled on the Song of Songs, had already been used by other Franciscan writers, including Bonaventure, and inspired a magnificent fresco in the Basilica of Assisi by Giotto's pupil, the Maestro delle Vele. Dante, however, elevates the marriage to the key defining event of

Francis' ministry. The choice is significant, especially as the poet also utilizes the model of the mystic marriage to retell the life of Dominic in *Paradiso* XII ('le sponsalizie', 61) and that of St Claire of Assisi and her followers in *Paradiso* III, 97–102. It would seem that Dante chose this biblical archetype to underline the central role of charity in humanity's search for holiness. Furthermore he wanted to suggest that, since, according to the exegetes of the Song of Song, every soul is created to become God's bride, everyone can potentially become the companion of the 'the bridegroom who accepts every vow' (sposo ch'ogne voto accetta; *Par.* III, 101). In Francis' case, the marriage between the saint and Poverty, a figure for Christ, also expresses the transformational power of *caritas* – their love affair is the force that drives the new Franciscan family to choose poverty as their guiding value (*Par.* XI, 76–87).

Dante's attack on the corruption of ecclesiastical leaders and religious orders, as in *Inferno* XIX, as well as his call for a major reform of the Church, is predicated on his conviction that contemporary Christianity had largely rejected poverty. And yet poverty is the religious disposition needed to imitate Christ's sacrifice, given that, as the poet puts it, 'she wept with Christ up on the cross' (ella con Cristo pianse in su la croce; *Par.* XI, 72). Another form of sacrifice that Dante identifies as a mark of holiness is a commitment to proselytizing. The poet recalls Francis' brave attempt to convert Muslims not with weapons like the crusaders, but through preaching (100–5). Love, preaching, and poverty are the humble sacrifices that Francis offered to his Lord and that Dante stresses from among the ample apologetic material on the saint that he would have known. These are the religious acts, interior and exterior, that define Dante's ideal of holiness and which, for him, justify the final sign of Francis' exceptionality: the gift of the stigmata. Francis' stigmata were one of the most unique and controversial miracles accepted and defended by the Church, which ought to be understood in light of a heightened popular devotion to Jesus' Passion that had resulted in granting value to suffering as a form of worship and imitation of Christ. Even though Dante leaves little, if any space to the exaltation of Francis' pain in *Paradiso* XI, the popular veneration of Christ's blood is a regular feature of the *Commedia*. Equally, as we shall see, his portrayal of Christ is persistently focused on the Passion.

Penitence, Suffering, and the Imitation of Christ

Ancient representations of Christ as King (*pantokrator*) presented Him as peerless. However, from the twelfth century onwards, the faithful strove to discover the human face of their saviour, and found consolation in the devotion to and imitation of his humanity. Emphasis fell in particular on Jesus' suffering, on the crown of thorns, his martyrdom on the cross, and his wounds that had opened the doors of Paradise to fallen humanity. The adoration of the suffering Christ was primarily practised by the Franciscans, beginning with Francis himself, whose total dedication to the Saviour led to a veneration of the most humble aspects of His life, such as the manger and the cross.

In the *Comedy*, Dante seldom refers to the life of Christ. However, when he does, he concentrates on the Passion, the sacrifice of the cross, and the salvific effects of the blood Jesus spilt. Christ's death serves as a historical and spatial marker. For example, it defines the chronology of Statius' life and conversion (*Purg.* XXI, 82–7). It also provides the geographical and temporal co-ordinates for dawn in Jerusalem: 'As when [the sun] vibrates its first rays where their maker shed blood' (Sì come quando i primi raggi vibra / là dove il suo fattor lo sangue sparse; *Purg.* XXVII, 1–2). What is evident is that, regardless of the context in which the poet evokes the Passion, he invariably mentions the blood that Jesus shed to save humanity. Thus, Christ's blood is compared to a wedding gift (*Par.* XI, 33; XXXI, 3) given by the Messiah to his beloved Church, both triumphant in Heaven (*Par.* XXXI, 1–3) and militant on earth (*Par.* XI, 32–3).

The devotion to Christ's sacrifice and suffering had developed alongside the strong penitential emphasis that informed late-medieval Christianity especially after the Lateran Council of 1215, which had affirmed the importance of penance as a key element in the religious life of the faithful, while also calling for stricter practices of control and correction of behaviour. The widespread success of these policies is confirmed by the proliferation of Latin penitential manuals and guides on the vices and virtues for the use of parish priests and friars in their interactions with their flocks. In addition, vernacular didactic texts, often written by laymen such as Dante's fellow-citizen Bono Giamboni (*Libro de' vizi e delle virtudi*), addressed to those who could not read Latin spiritual literature, also became popular. In its extreme forms, however, the impulse to embrace the sacrificial example of Christ led to harsh customs, such as bodily self-punishment (the confraternities of *disciplinati*) and death in the name of God (the crusaders). At the heart of all these practices was the conviction that suffering was necessary for spiritual improvement and essential if one aspired to be Christ-like. The most obvious manifestation of this preoccupation with pain and discipline in the *Commedia* is Dante's sophisticated elaboration of the popular belief in Purgatory as an actual physical place, rather than merely as an interim state after death, where human beings, having asked God to forgive their wrongdoing, are able to rectify their sinful earthly dispositions through pain.

In *Purgatorio*, all forms of penance and suffering are productive. Pain is imposed by the divine Judge because it transforms the penitent souls and perfects them to saintly standards: 'All these people who weeping sing for having followed appetite beyond measure, in hunger and in thirst here again become holy' (Tutta esta gente che piangendo canta / per seguitar la gola oltra misura, / in fame e 'n sete qui si rifà santa; *Purg.* XXIII, 64–6). Dante clearly reveals the relationship between penance and *imitatio Christi* in the second realm in his description of the gluttons' torment. They suffer perpetual hunger and are reduced to skin and bone. However, their emaciated appearance reminds the pilgrim of the suffering and humiliation that Pontius Pilate inflicted on Jesus after the scourging (22–33). To be like Christ, however, pain needs to be embraced willingly and with joy (72), since, like Jesus' death, it leads to freedom in God: 'that led Christ gladly to say "Eli",when He freed us with His own vein' (che menò Cristo lieto a dire 'Elì' / quando ne liberò con la sua vena; *Purg.* XXIII, 74–5). The end result of purgatorial suffering is of course celestial bliss, a joy so ineffable that the pilgrim can only describe it by recalling the brightness of the cross formed by the souls in the heaven of Mars: 'Here my memory defeats my ability; because that cross flamed forth Christ' (Qui vince la memoria mia lo 'ngegno; / ché quella croce lampeggiava Cristo; *Par.* XIV, 103–4).

Conclusion

In his discussion on religion, Thomas Aquinas noted that religious people are all those who worship God (*Summa theologica*, II II, q. 81, art. 1, ad 5). However, he also added that only those who totally dedicate themselves to God's service, by renouncing the world, practise religion perfectly. The theologian thus created a scale of values distinguishing between secular devotion practised by lay people and a contemplative religiousness that characterized the life of the clergy. This distinction mirrored and justified the existence of different orders in society and the inequalities that arose from such hierarchization. Clerics not only had access to all the necessary resources to pursue the daily worship of God, but, most importantly, they also had a greater appreciation of the Latin texts that were at the heart of the Christian religion: the Bible; and the writings of the Fathers and Doctors of the Church. The majority of the lay population was unable to understand, read, or write Latin, and had minimal access to the texts available to clerics. In the *Convivio*, Dante challenged this state of affairs and emphasized that lay persons, too, could achieve a state of religious perfection if pure in spirit: 'St Paul says to the Romans: "He is not a Jew who is one outwardly, nor is that circumcision which is outwardly manifested in the flesh; but he is a Jew who is one inwardly, and circumcision is that of the heart, in spirit and not in the letter, whose praise comes not from men but from God"' (IV, xxviii, 10). This is a key point when endeavouring to comprehend the poet's attitude towards religion. It is not unlikely that Dante's devotional zeal paralleled that of many members of late-medieval lay communities. At the same time, he also believed that the religious experience and practice of the laity needed to be augmented as a result of better competence in fields which normally were the preserve of learned clerics, most notably theology and biblical exegesis. Among his greatest challenges when composing the *Comedy* was to create a mirror of and a dialogue on contemporary religious culture that could engage clerics as well as ordinary believers, while at the same time presenting the poem as an act of praise of and of sacrifice to God, thereby becoming part of Christian worship, and hence an apt means through which its readers could achieve salvation.

Note

1. Thomas Aquinas, *Summa Theologica* (New York: Benziger Bros., 1947–8), I II, q. 60, art. 3.

11

SIMON GILSON

Doctrine

Tradition, Innovation, and Syncretism

Dante's poetic rendering of physical, ethical, and religious doctrine is one of the most remarkable features of the *Commedia*. As poet, he deals openly with a multifarious body of teachings, above all in a series of doctrinal 'discourses', delivered by various speakers, and which form a core part of the poem's narrative, beginning just before the midpoint of *Purgatorio*. These speeches are, at one level, building blocs in a carefully fashioned vision of God, the cosmos, and the sublunar world, and of the nature and place in the created universe of inanimate bodies, living creatures, the celestial orbs, and their motors. The poem's first readers were quick to celebrate the poem's rich doctrinal offering, frequently presenting the work as a *summa* of knowledge; and generations of later readers have argued over the significance and status of its vast array of teachings, and puzzled over the poet's possible 'sources' and motivations. This chapter examines how, in the *Commedia*, Dante presents knowledge of all kinds, about God, the universe, and humankind, as well as about the place of humans in relation to one another, love, the cosmic order, and the divine. Its primary aim is to illustrate how Dante brings these and related concerns into the narrative, language, themes, and ultimate messages of the poem. 'Doctrine' is understood throughout in the varied acceptations by which Dante himself used the word, as pertaining not only to the Bible and Christian teachings, but also to the totality of knowledge encompassed by this term and related ones such as 'philosophy', 'wisdom', 'science', 'reason', and 'art'. Before we undertake our analysis of some selected passages and blocs of cantos across the entire *Commedia*, it may be helpful to set out three general sets of considerations regarding the poem's overall approach to doctrine that will underpin our discussion.

First, as in so many other areas of the *Commedia*, Dante is a remarkable innovator. No one before him, either in Latin or in European vernaculars, had written a narrative poem of such totalizing ambition and speculative depth, incorporating so much theology and philosophy, and so many different fields of knowledge, from optics and astronomy to medicine and animal lore, from cosmology and angelology to embryology and creation theory. What is more, Dante is extraordinarily radical in privileging vernacular poetry as his chosen medium of expression, and in creating his own poetic structure in which to express knowledge in all its forms. At the same time, however, his novelty consciously builds upon and responds to tradition. He is, in fact, acutely aware both of existing poetic works with a strong philosophical and/or theological content, and of how Latin poetry was glossed in learned ways. In the first category, some of the major interlocutors include: the lay intellectual poetry of earlier or contemporary Italian poets, such as Guido Guinizzelli and Guido Cavalcanti; the continuation of the narrative French poem, the *Roman de la rose*, by the bourgeois lay intellectual, Jean de Meun; and the earlier twelfth-century allegorical-philosophical epics, set in a cosmological frame and enlivened by contemporary scientific and theological problems, which were composed in Latin by Bernard Silvestris and Alan of Lille.[1]

The second category of erudite glossing is best understood as a mode of reading which is widespread amongst readers and commentators on ancient authors, and attempts to use their texts as a framework upon which to articulate moral lessons and encyclopaedic knowledge pertaining to all the arts and sciences. From the fourth century onwards, it was standard to treat Virgil in this way, as a poet learned in all disciplines whose *Aeneid* is a storehouse of knowledge.[2] Alongside the traditions of doctrinal poetry and of poetry that was subject to doctrinal reading, Dante's poem also evinces his familiarity with multiple, non-poetic sources of learning. Almost all the scientific, philosophical, and theological terms, concepts, and teachings we encounter in the *Commedia* are rooted in concrete sets of intellectual practices and mental habits, usually identifiable with the Latin-literate, learned environments of the late-medieval university and the convent schools or *studia* of the religious orders. A veritable intellectual revolution had been brought about in these sites by the recovery of Greek and Arabic scientific and philosophical texts, and, above all, by the rediscovery of first Plato's *Timaeus*, and then Aristotle's works, between the late eleventh and mid thirteenth centuries, and their difficult, often fraught, accommodation to Christian teachings. Of course, the precise ways in which Dante acquired such a body of knowledge, and related mental habits and practices, is anything but clear or straightforward, especially given his status as a lay outsider, the precarious conditions of his exile, and the deficiencies in our own knowledge. By the standards of his culture, he is most certainly not a professional philosopher, nor a theologian, nor even a systematic thinker. But neither is our poet an amateurish bricoleur. Indeed, quite the opposite is true: his use of doctrine in the poem reveals a consummate artificer, engaged in complex and multifaceted processes of intellectual and artistic selection, filtering, and construction.

This leads us to our second consideration, which is that the poem's teachings are not 'things' to be separated off and categorized in relation to particular sources, thinkers, schools, or –isms: they need rather to be located first and foremost within the poem itself, and understood in relation to its language, imagery, and narrative. All things in Dante need to be judged in the light of poetry and of the transformations effected by poetry. Within the narrative, the poem's teachings are rooted to Dante-character, to his own remarkable, divinely willed journey, and to the 'educational' experiences that unfold through his experiences in the afterlife, be they encounters and dialogues with guides and other interlocutors, or sights of various kinds. As we will see, the *Commedia* could not be at a further remove from any notion of versified doctrine, or even that prevalent early reading of the poem as a *summa* of doctrinal knowledge.

A third point, one closely linked to the preceding ones, is to signal Dante's consistent and highly innovative use of syncretism, as he presents, judges, and often synthesizes various kinds and forms of knowledge, and constructs his own teachings. Syncretism is often understood as the fusion of the classical and the Christian, but in Dante it extends beyond classical literature and myth, to include philosophy and theology, and indeed intellectual work simply speaking, including a range of non-Greco-Roman traditions. Rather than a portmanteau term associated with eclecticism or forms of conflation, then, it might best be regarded as a highly sophisticated cultural operation that lies at the heart of Dante's artistry. His Limbo is one emblematic case amongst many. Rather than being presented in more standard theological terms as comprising the Limbo of the Fathers (*limbus patrum*) for the righteous of the Old Testament awaiting the coming of Christ and the *limbus puerorum* for unbaptized infants, Dante fashions a complex imaginative construct. His Limbo is notable not only for its rewriting in a Christian key of the Virgilian Elysian fields and the romance motif of the noble castle, but also for its coupling of *elegantia* (refinement) and *doctrina* in the way it brings together ancient poets and philosophers, as well as for its inclusion of Arab polymaths and philosophers such as Avicenna (980–1037) and Averroës (1126–98). Understood as 'a highly sophisticated integrative process', Dantean syncretism brings together 'discrete and partial human truths to provide a potentially salvific intuition of absolute Truth'.[3] It bears directly on the poet's own imitative practices, ones which conform to the tradition of the *Deus artifex*, that is, the notion of God as maker whose script is written in the two 'volumes', the Book of the Universe and that of the Bible. The *Commedia* offers Dante's own 'comic' synthesis of all things within a harmonious structure in which he draws together diverse epistemologies and traditions to present what appears to be a complete map of knowledge that is set against the totality of creation.

Hell and its 'Partial' Lessons

It might be tempting to begin with the central bloc of cantos in *Purgatorio* (XV–XVIII), the point at which, as we have noted, lengthy poetic expositions on sundry matters start to punctuate the poem. But we should not neglect the place of *Inferno* in providing lessons, and the fact that such 'instruction' is rarely a matter of direct exposition. Openly doctrinal passages in the first *cantica* are relatively few, and are all voiced by Dante's guide, Virgil, whose intellectual credentials are made clear by early references to him as a 'celebrated wiseman' (famoso saggio; *Inf.* I, 89), as honouring art and knowledge (IV, 73), as the 'sea of all knowledge' (mar di tutto 'l senno; VIII, 7), and more technically and scholastically as a 'master' (dottore; V, 70, 123; XVI, 13, 48). As early as *Inferno* VI, 106–11, Virgil the guide answers Dante-character's question regarding the nature of infernal torments after the Final Judgement, by telling him, with a degree of frustration, to return to his 'scienzïa' (106) in order to understand whether such punishments will increase when the soul is united with its body.[4] The 'science' here is natural philosophy of a neo-Aristotelian kind, and one strong implication of the passage is that the pilgrim is himself presented to us as a sedulous student of such writings. Virgil, who clearly has some familiarity with Christian teachings, instructs Dante into how rationally derived philosophical knowledge might be applied to an understanding of Hell and Christian concepts.

Virgil's major discourses in Hell – on Fortune and on the moral order of the infernal realm – present intriguingly syncretic blends of philosophical, classical, and Christian concepts. The exposition of Fortune in *Inferno* VII, 67–96, for example, draws heavily upon Boethius' *Consolation of Philosophy* in offering a vision of the deity as swiftly wheeling and imperiously ruling over humankind. Yet Virgil's speech daringly sets such Boethian elements within a cosmological setting in a highly distinctive synthesis. Transcendent divine wisdom is presented as the creative principle within a cosmic system in which Fortune is an angelic minister of God's providential design. Fortune is, in short, a special motive force in the heavens that causes change in fortunes on Earth. The discourse nonetheless carries a degree of paganizing charge, as Virgil refers – not unproblematically – to Fortune as ruling her sphere like an imperious goddess (86) and as being driven by necessity (89).

Virgil's best-known infernal speech, his 'lesson' on the moral ordering of Hell, is a *tour de force* of rationalization. Precipitated by a forced pause in the journey as the protagonist adjusts to the stench arising from Lower Hell, the guide makes explicit use of Aristotle to instruct Dante-character on the moral and topographical order of a Christian Hell. In so doing, he deploys a battery of techniques identifiable from late-medieval scholastic teaching, utilizing divisions and subdivisions, providing definitions and distinctions, and answering the doubts raised by Dante within a master-pupil relationship. Virgil begins by explaining how the three lower circles of Hell (violence, fraud, and treachery) relate to injurious acts of malice that are carried out deliberately, and can be divided according to whether they are done by force or by fraud (22–4). The basic conceptual scheme here draws above all upon Aristotle's teachings in the *Nicomachean Ethics* (VII, 1–6, 1145a 15–1149a 20) with some additional elements derived from Cicero's *De officiis* (I, 13). Virgil then fills in this frame with definitions of each of the three sins, discussion of their respective gravity in relation to God, and details of their subdivisions (25–66). Dante-character replies by saluting his guide as teacher, and uses technical language of his own when he praises the clarity of the rational arguments and the distinctions he has just heard (67–9). The protagonist now raises a doubt, and asks for clarification on the upper circles. Virgil's impatient reply returns us directly to Aristotle's *Ethics*, a work that is so familiar to Dante that it is said to be his own: 'Do you not recall those words with which your Ethics treats the three dispositions that heaven does not want, incontinence, malice, and mad bestiality? And how incontinence is less of an offence to God and receives less blame?' (Non ti rimembra di quelle parole / con le quai la tua Etica pertratta / le tre disposizion che 'l ciel non vole, / incontenenza, malizia e la matta / bestialitade? e come incontenenza / men Dio offende e men biasimo accatta?; 79–84).

Declaring himself satisfied by the illumination provided by Virgil, Dante is assailed by another doubt regarding the place of usury within this classification. His guide again bases the explanation upon ancient natural philosophy as it is expounded in Aristotle's foundational work, the *Physics*, which is also identified as one of Dante's own 'books' whose very pages he is sent back to turn (97–111). Virgil's argument is subtle and ingenious: man-made art, which follows created nature, is an offshoot of divine art which produces Nature. Within the economy of Hell, such reasoning serves taxonomical purposes, allowing Dante to bring together in a single circle, the seventh, the sins of blasphemy (violence against God), sodomy (violence against nature), and usury (violence against art). In order to respond to the pilgrim's specific question, Virgil – again perhaps surprisingly for a damned pagan – then connects this chain of reasoning with well-known passages in Genesis

(2:15; 3:17–19) on the role of work in providing sustenance to humankind. The view that human art is an imitation of Nature follows the oft-repeated Aristotelian axiom that 'art follows nature insofar as it can' (*Physics*, II, 2, 194a 21). But more significant is the way Virgil interrelates human and divine artistry, a formulation indebted to a mediated reading of other Aristotelian texts and their medieval commentaries,[5] and which is a theme fundamental to Alan of Lille's philosophical poetry, and may well also be a pointed response to Meun's *Roman* (16,005–248), where the comparison is only made between humans and Nature and the linkage with God is avoided entirely.[6]

Aside from these Virgilian discourses, other passages in the first *cantica* illustrate the poet's concern to adumbrate themes that shape the poem's overall teachings in relation to knowledge and love, the nature of intellectual enquiry and error, and the use and misuse of reason. Three might be mentioned here, since they help to indicate how the poet uses dramatic encounter and dialogue for complex revisionist ends, and how he constructs his own character's spiritual and intellectual development within the unfolding narrative of the poem, presenting lessons in Hell that are 'partial' in both senses of the word. The meeting with Paolo and Francesca, our first example, is a good case in point. The protagonist initially understands the distorted relationship between reason and lust, by inferring from the punishment that these are sinners who have submitted their reason to carnal desire (37–9). But his subsequent dialogue with Francesca (88–138), which is so subtly constructed by the poet, quite intoxicates the protagonist – in 1300 Dante's renown was above all as a love-poet and author of the *Vita nova* – and draws its readers into his own empathy and confusion over her fate. The poet's ultimate teachings on love will only emerge in retrospect, as key words, concepts, and images present within the canto are recontextualized and re-semanticized, both at points when the voice of Virgil as *dottore* treats the doctrine of love in *Purgatorio* XVII–XVIII, and in later encounters with love poets whose lust is being purified or has been redeemed in *Purgatorio* XXIV and XXVI and *Paradiso* VIII–IX.

In the final *cantica*, further strategic recalls of Francesca's tale help to clarify, in specular or oppositional ways, her earlier presentation of love and the role of reading in her ultimate fate (*Par.* XXV, 19–24; XXIX, 7–9; XXX, 11; XXXIII, 87). As critics have shown, moreover, Francesca's own doctrine of love, which she presents as entirely instinctive and not controlled by reason, can be situated in relation to Cavalcanti's great philosophical canzone, 'A lady asks me' (Donna me prega), which puts forward these very themes and whose language is consciously echoed by Dante. Cavalcanti's philosophical poem is placed into an overall antithetical relation to Dante's own ideological position and is subject to radical critique at the very moment that its language is recalled. This is one of several passages where a strong implicit dialogue with other poets informs the presentation of teachings.

Related features inform our second example, that is, the pilgrim's meeting, in *Inferno* XV, with the shade of Brunetto Latini, a leading notary, intellectual, and civic figure in the Florence of the poet's youth. Poet, translator of Cicero, and author of a major vernacular encyclopaedia, Brunetto developed a programme of vernacularization aimed at training the laity to speak, behave, and govern well. To the pilgrim's great shock and surprise, however, Dante espies Latini amongst the sodomites in the seventh circle of the violent. The pilgrim himself confesses to having been taught by him how man becomes eternal (85). Eternity is here understood, as Francesca understands love, in restrictive, exclusively worldly terms, much as some ancient writers had viewed fame and glory (Cicero, *De inventione*, II, 55, 166; *De officiis*, II, 31–51; *Disputationes Tusculanae*, II, i). That perspective, which seems to be shared at this point in the narrative by Dante-character, is reaffirmed at the close of the episode when Latini reminds the pilgrim to keep in mind his major prose encyclopaedia, the *Tesoro*, a work of compilation originally composed in French but which was soon 'vernacularized' and covers topics of all kinds, especially ancient ethics, politics, and rhetoric. Brunetto's posthumous existence is, he believes, vouchsafed by this book 'in which I still live' (nel qual io vivo ancora; 124), even though his soul is in Hell and his shade moves frenetically between the fiery rains that afflict the sodomites in this subcircle (121–4). Brunetto's earthly, reputation-driven vision of fame will be revisited at several later points, and its partiality shown up in later encounters (*Purg.* XI, 79–108; *Par.* I, 22–30; XVI, 86–7) in ways that cast a revealing light on the *Commedia*, whose uncompromising message is to be broadcast directly, even at the cost of Dante losing earthly fame (*Par.* XVII, 112–20). Dante's is a 'sacred poem' (poema sacro; *Par.* XXV, 1) which fashions a new encyclopaedic form that is created under the aegis of heaven and earth. It is one not only richer in theological material than the *Tesoro*, but organized on entirely different principles, presenting knowledge in carefully articulated ways through narrative poetry and the first-person account of Dante's own journey.

The encounter with Ulysses in *Inferno* XXVI presents us at first sight with what seems a still more remarkable example of the value of human intellectual enquiry. Within the narration of his own speech to his crew, at the very moment when Ulysses recounts how he urged his sea-faring companions to continue on their journey outside the limits of the known world, his stress falls on that which differentiates humans from beasts – the ability to pursue 'virtue and knowledge' (virtute e canoscenza; 120). Though there are already some coded hints within the canto that Ulysses' ill-fated journey is a transgression of divine limits and requisite *pietas*, it is only in retrospect that the reader appreciates the implications of his eventual shipwreck, an image used by some Christian writers to refer to philosophers who are distant from true faith. As with Francesca and Brunetto, greater perspective is achieved through textually privileged later passages (*Purg.* I, 132; *Par.* II, 1–15; *Par.* XIII, 133–8; *Par.* XXVI; XXVII, 82–4; XXXII, 145–6) which evoke the Ulyssean journey through the use of shared rhyme words and echoes of key terms and motifs such as 'esperto', 'ardore', 'folle', and 'volo' (expert, ardour, mad, flight). Such richly allusive intratextuality is used to probe the very meaning of human intellectual enquiry in relation to the deity in ways that cast a contrastive light on Dante's own journey. As an unaided pursuit of worldly wisdom and knowledge, Ulysses' own navigation is a mad flight, one opposed to the pilgrim's own divinely aided 'flight' (volo; *Par.* XV, 54; XXV, 50).

Purgatory: The Limits of Earthly Knowledge

In a scene of remarkable emotion and pathos, at the beginning of *Purgatorio* III, the pilgrim believes himself to have been deserted by his guide, because he only sees one shadow cast by the sun. Dante-character does not realize that, as a spirit, Virgil has no body to impede the light. Virgil's response is to remind the pilgrim that his body is buried on earth, and that God or rather 'the Power' (la Virtù; 32) provides the souls in the afterlife with immaterial, aerial bodies that suffer torments in ways that are hidden to human understanding. Virgil develops the theme of the limits of human reason, by evoking the unfathomable mystery of the Incarnation and stressing how Plato and Aristotle could not 'see' everything, and that their desire to do so is vain and is felt by them as a loss in Limbo (*Purg.* III, 34–43).

Aristotle had acted as a major *auctoritas* in some of Virgil's discourses in the first *cantica*, and had been singled out in Limbo, as the 'master of those who know' (maestro di color che sanno; *Inf.* IV, 131), outshining Plato there. But now Dante places the 'Philosopher' in parallel with his teacher at the very moment when the stress falls upon the limitations of pagan reason in the face of divine revelation. Aristotle will not be named openly again (cp. *Par.* VIII, 120), even though his ideas, as mediated and enriched by late-medieval scholastics, continue to inform the poem's own teachings on the soul and perceptual theory, the ability of reason to regulate sensory perception, the formation of the human soul-body union, and aspects of its cosmological framework. More diffusely, throughout the poem, medieval Aristotelianism provides Dante with a deep philosophical understanding of the natural order

and the ethical realm, a set of intellectual tools and argumentative procedures, rich material for his lexical and stylistic choices, and even particular
kinds of imagery. In all these areas, however, as we have already begun to see
for *Inferno* XI, the Aristotelian underpinnings are blended, enriched, and
perfected by other elements, including Neoplatonic and Christian ones.

The opening twelve lines of the following canto reveal how the narrator on
occasion intervenes to correct 'doctrinal' errors. The authorial narrating
voice offers the reader an analogy to the pilgrim's experience of distraction
so as to elucidate the narrative moment, and, in so doing, a preference is
marked out for the scholastic-Aristotelian theory of the substantial unity of
the soul which is affirmed over theories, especially Plato's, that argue for the
existence of separate souls. Correction of intellectual error will become an
increasingly pressing theme as we move through the poem and one in which
the protagonist becomes intensely involved. The pilgrim, of course, remains
firmly in need of Virgil-character's assistance and explanations.

Virgil's role as 'dottore', as one who teaches through words, gains greater
prominence in the second *cantica*, even as he voyages into a realm to which
he will never return. Later in canto IV, at another moment of pause in the
journey, Virgil explains some basic matters of astronomy and the sun's
movement, and an indolent fellow Florentine, Belacqua, smiles at the boyish
intellectual curiosity of the pilgrim (119–20). The protagonist, however,
begins to interrogate Virgil-guide more closely on matters of Christian doctrine; and, crucially, in *Purgatorio* VI, he does so in relation to Virgilian
teachings, as set out in *Aeneid* VI, 376, a verse which openly states that
prayers cannot bend the divine will. Dante's questioning of Virgil is perfectly
consonant with the narrative moment: he has just freed himself from
a pressing throng of souls who solicited his intercession as a living man
able to ask relatives to say prayers for the dead. Virgil's reply to his own
text makes subtle, scholastic distinctions that place its limited truth claims in
relation to its temporal position. As a text written before the advent of Christ,
it is true – Virgil argues – that prayers cannot bend the divine will; but after
His resurrection such a claim no longer holds sway. For this reason, Virgil
refers to a higher jurisdiction, Beatrice, who is now explicitly named at line
46. As well as a Christianizing correction of the pagan belief in fate (one may
think afresh of the passages in *Inferno* VII in this light) and of the passage in
the *Aeneid*, critics have pointed to contemporary contextual factors in which
the Cathars had asserted the heretical position of the inefficacy of prayer.
The stress on the limits of Virgil's text is also notable here, as is the poet's
concern with questions of orthodoxy.

From *Purgatorio* XV onwards there is not only a veritable explosion of
technical 'scientific' language, but also further Virgilian discourses, steeped

in theological and philosophical concepts. The discussion of the nature of charity in this canto, which is elicited by the need to clarify an obscure earlier expression (*Purg.* XIV, 86–7), recalls teachings in Augustine (*De civ. Dei*, XV, 5). The following canto, the fiftieth and midpoint in the poem, develops major religious and political themes that are rooted in an understanding of the nature and inclinations of the human soul: the freedom of the divinely created human soul to choose what it loves without any determinism being exercised over its choices by astral influences (this is an important topic in Meun's *Roman*, 17,029–70); and, at the same time, the need for the divinely created human soul – naturally driven to pursue anything that attracts it – to be regulated in its desires and choices by clearly separated temporal and spiritual guides on earth.

The speaker who calls for allegiance to imperial authority is not Virgil but rather a plain-speaking contemporary courtier, Marco Lombardo. The following canto – another centre of sorts – presents us with a further pause in the journey during which Virgil sets out a discourse on love which is argued to be a creative, dynamic principle informing the entire universe, uniting God and His creatures and lying at the root of all human acts. It is here that we properly begin to gain a deeper perspective on the limitations of Francesca's words in *Inferno* V. Virgil's account of how love is central to all human deeds is again built upon discussions found in Augustine and in the rich twelfth-century theological literature on love. He asserts the role of elective acts based on natural desire as the 'seed' of 'every virtue and of every operation that merits punishment' (sementa in voi d'ogne virtute / e d'ogne operazion che merta pene; 104–5). In the light of this exposition, Virgil goes on to explain the moral organization of Mount Purgatory, dividing it into two sets of three vices – love as directed to the wrong object; and love as spiritually misdirected due to excessive intensity – positioned around a further vice, *acedia*, which consists in the lack of sufficient energy or zeal in loving the correct object of desire.

The first half of *Purgatorio* XVIII, which picks up where the discourse of the previous canto ended, offers a further rich example of Virgil's rationalizing proclivities. His speech in the previous canto is itself termed a 'discourse' (ragionamento; 1); he is the 'high master' (alto dottore; 2); and he is linked explicitly with the use of reason or 'ragion' (12, 46–8, 85–6). Dante-character uses technical terms for dividing up an argument, setting out its features and demonstrating the underlying causes (partire, descrivere, dimostrare; 12, 14). All these features recall prominently the language and procedures common in the scholastic method of teaching and argumentation. In Virgil's voice, Dante brings into the vernacular technical philosophical terms found in late-scholastic Latin ('apprensiva', 'intenzion', 'forma sustanzïal', 'vertute', 'appetibili'; apprehensive faculty, intention, substantial form, power, desirables; 22, 23, 49, 51, 57), as well as using imagery related to fire (28–30), wax (38–9), and bees (58–9), which is based upon Aristotelian-scholastic texts.

In line 18, Virgil reinforces the seriousness of the teaching that will follow, and the gravity of the error corrected, through a strong biblical reminiscence (Matt. 5:13): the pilgrim will appreciate the error of the blind who call themselves leaders. The first section of his discourse explains how the perceptions and passions of the human soul work in relation to desire and love (19–33), in line with a scholastic theory of perception built largely upon Aristotle's *De anima*. The following section (49–75) then expounds, on the basis of passages from the *Nicomachean Ethics*, how reason is capable of controlling such impulses. Love is a primary impulse in humans, and, as soon as the senses are awakened by beauty, it creates in them attraction towards all things that please. Reason is capable of controlling such impulses, by acting as innate principle of judgement, or discrimination that holds the threshold of assent according to whether humans choose good or bad objects of desire. In celebrated lines Virgil refers to this principle of freedom as having being discovered by those who reasoned thoroughly (67), that is, pagan moral thinkers who left ethics to mankind.

All this can and should be set squarely against Francesca's speech, which may well be explicitly targeted in lines 34–6. But the canto does not only look back: it marks one part of a complex statement on love and (free) will from a series of different vantage points (the city, the individual, love poetry, the status and origin of the soul), not only in a bloc of cantos in this part of *Purgatorio* (XV–XVIII), but elsewhere in the poem, including *Purgatorio* XXVI–XXVII and above all *Paradiso* I, where Beatrice discusses fire and the motion of the soul, its inclinations and relationship to God. Within *Purgatorio* XVIII, the shift from Aristotelian-scholastic perceptual theory to ethical doctrine is carried out in a close dialogue – one set up in the form of a series of precise textual recalls – with Cavalcanti's 'Donna me prega', whose own theory of love as a dark, turbid phenomenon of the sensory soul is rooted in an exclusively naturalistic reading of the *De anima*, in line with Averroës' own paraphrase (*De anima*, I, comm. 63–6). Dante's treatment of the relationship between reason and desire resolutely refuses to reduce the power of the rational and elective faculties.

In canto XVIII, the epistemological limitations of Virgil's intervention are underscored, especially at lines 46–8, where his 'reason' is counterposed with the 'faith' of Beatrice. Virgil's limited intellectual and spiritual jurisdiction is marked out even more prominently in the transition between him and the character Statius. The scene in which Virgil and Dante meet Statius anticipates this shift by presenting Virgil, in canto XXII, 67–9, as a light to 'make people learned' (fa le persone dotte; 69), but one which illuminates not his own path but that of others who come behind. Three cantos later, Virgil defers to Statius to explain what in *Purgatorio* III he could not, namely, how it is that the souls of the dead have bodies which react physically, mentally, and emotionally to their surroundings.

This seemingly narrow object of enquiry issues into a discourse that broaches fundamental issues about humans, their bodies and souls, the connection between natural and transcendent components in their being, and their relationship to the creator God. Like other great discourses in the poem, most notably *Paradiso* II, it brings together issues about the relationship between a world of natural causes that can be rationally understood and a divine order governed directly by God and which does not obey natural causes. The entire discussion has the form, like *Inferno* XI or *Purgatorio* XVIII, of a tightly organized scholastic disputation or *quaestio*, and is replete with medical and philosophical terms such as 'human members' (membra umane; 40, 60, 90), 'informative power' (virtute informativa; 41), 'foetus' (feto; 68), and verbs related to the development of the foetus ('constare', 'coagulare', 'organar'; appear, coagulate, form organs; 50, 57, 101).

Lines 37–60 deal with entirely natural processes, namely, reproduction and the development of the foetus and its capacity for movement and sensation: all this is presented largely in line with Aristotelian teachings in *De generatione animalium*. In lines 61–6, Statius refutes the error of Averroës, offering a further correction of a 'wise man' (savio; 63) introduced in Limbo, who had maintained that the human intellect was common to all humankind and located outside the body, thereby denying individual mortality. From lines 67–75, though technical terminology is still present, biblical language also becomes prominent (Gen. 2:7), as Statius considers the divine inspiration of the rational soul. Statius also suggests how the immaterial and the material meet by offering the pilgrim an analogy, one combining beautiful simplicity and deep eucharistic associations, to the way the sun makes wine (76–8). The remaining thirty verses discuss, with a flourish of metaphor and simile, how the aerial body is formed (79–108). When humans die and their material body fades away, the formative virtue that had originally made the body now radiates out a new body made up of the air that surrounds them. Not only does the passage offer a remarkable example of how Dante mobilizes complex patterns of alliteration and assonance, rhythmic variation, harsh and internal rhymes, unusual verb metaphors, and extended similes, it also shows his continuing, deep dialogue with other philosophical poets. As Zyg Barański in particular has shown, the discourse is carefully textured with echoes of Cavalcanti's 'Donna me prega', but also Jean de Meun and probably Alan of Lille.[7]

In the Earthly Paradise, Dante dramatizes still further the relationship between, on the one hand, the realm of created nature which can be understood through rationalizing, earth-bound explanations, and, on the other, a transcendent order of Christian truths governed by God. In a move that may well represent a reaction to Alan's and Bernard's poems and their presentation of allegorical goddesses at major transitional moments, we meet a beautiful, learned lady, Matelda. The 'bella donna' discourses on the cause (cagion; 89) of wind and water in Eden (*Purg.* XXVII, 85–133) and responds to Dante-character's puzzlement at the presence of such atmospheric phenomena at this altitude – once more the pilgrim's level of understanding is consonant with the rational dictates of Aristotelian science, here meteorology. Matelda clarifies the relationship between the earthly and the divine, explaining that such phenomena do not have natural causes because they are part of the creation of the 'supreme God' (sommo Bene; 91). With the advent of Beatrice in canto XXX, Dante-character is not only fiercely cross-examined on his failings, including intellectual ones, but subjected to a dream-like sequence of images in a great allegorizing pageant representing the history of the Church. The superiority of heavenly knowledge over earth-bound forms is here dramatically asserted by Beatrice who condemns Dante's overly terrestrial mode of understanding as he fails to appreciate her enigmatic words in relation to the parade. When Dante-character comments that her language exceeds his powers of understanding, he is reprimanded explicitly on the inadequacy of his 'doctrine' (dottrina; XXXIII, 86) based not on a divine 'way' (via; 88) but a 'natural' one, the path of natural reason rather than that of supernatural revelation (85–90).

Paradiso: Correcting Error and 'Seeing' Truth

In the *Paradiso*, the poet places still greater emphasis on teaching through the story of the pilgrim's education, on celebrating truth and correcting error, and on the need to balance up and discriminate between naturalistic, philosophical methods of enquiry, on the one hand, and truths based on the Bible and revelation, on the other. The third *cantica* shows the full extent and sophistication of Dante's experimentation with how doctrine enters into the form and structure of the poem. The very opening line, 'The glory of He who moves all things' (La gloria di colui che tutto move; *Par.* I, 1), bears all the hallmarks of Dante's syncretic stamp by setting the Aristotelian-scholastic topos of the unmoved first mover amidst echoes of the Bible (Ps. 18:1),

Boethius (*Consolation of Philosophy* III, 3), and the sixth-century Christian Platonist, the Pseudo-Dionysius (*On Celestial Hierarchy*, 1).

Explicitly doctrinal passages now permeate the poem in a large-scale manner and with increasing frequency. Well over twenty major discourses are voiced by characters at moments that are artfully articulated into the exigencies of the narrative and measured against Dante-character's state of knowledge in his astral flight towards ever greater understanding. The pilgrim journeys through the nine corporeal heavens and arrives in the Empyrean, stopping in each one to experience its sights and sounds and to participate in dialogues with the blessed. There are ten major discourses in the opening nine cantos alone; five of these are delivered by Beatrice in the first seven cantos. Compared to her speeches to Dante in the Earthly Paradise, Beatrice's voice is modulated quite differently but just as surprisingly. The beautiful young woman of the *Vita nova* speaks in Florentine vernacular, 'in her own language' (in sua favella; *Inf*. II, 57), yet one that is now saturated with the modes of expression and argumentative techniques of a male university teacher, a Latin-literate *magister*. Her learned disquisitions are directed at doubts expressed by the pilgrim regarding his own flight through the heavenly spheres (I), the causes of the moon-spots (II), the location of the blessed souls and the relationship between absolute and relative will (IV, 64–117), the nature of vows and how they might be commuted (V, 1–63), and the justness of the divine destruction of Jerusalem (VII, 19–148). In characteristically Dantean fashion each discourse, though examining a particular doubt raised by the pilgrim, offers a 'universalizing' treatment of it within a nexus of broader questions about matters such as the order of the universe and the place of all creatures within it, the cosmological system and how divine power is differentiated throughout it, the nature of creation, of original sin, and of immortality.

Remarkably innovative in linguistic and stylistic terms, rich in metaphor, simile, and other rhetorical figures, these discourses make prominent use of terminology, argumentative procedures, and examples drawn from contemporary philosophy and theology, transmuting into the vernacular the Latin expressions and teaching techniques of the schools. At a lexical level, Beatrice's speeches thus offer us, for example, Latinizing neologisms such as 'sempiternare' (make sempiternal; I, 76), rare scholastic terms such 'permotore' (driving force; I, 116), and other philosophical terminology such as 'principi formali' (formal principles; II, 71, 147), 'virtù informante' (informative virtue; VII, 137), and 'complession potenzïata' (potentiated complexion; VII, 140). She makes use of the argumentative techniques and procedures of the scholastic *disputatio* such as the use of proof and refutation ('provando e riprovando'; III, 3), the formulation of opposing views ('Or

dirai tu ... '; II, 91; 'Tu dici ... '; VII, 124), and the ruling-out of arguments
(' ... è l'argomento casso'; IV, 89). Once more, the examples and imagery
deployed by her – fire, arrow, wax, hammer, the three-mirror experiment –
are all present in scholastic writings.

The first two cantos present a Dante-character who continues to think in
naturalistic, neo-Aristotelian terms about both his own flight through the
heavens and the spotty patches on the Moon. In the opening canto,
the pilgrim receives a lesson (99–141) from Beatrice in how to think about
the created universe beyond a rationalistic understanding of movement as
governed by the laws of natural place in which the heaviest of the four
elements, earth, moves downwards and that of fire, the lightest, upwards.
However unnatural it might seem for the embodied pilgrim (cp. *Par.* XXVII,
64) to be flying through the sublunar spheres towards the Moon, Beatrice
teaches Dante that this is in fact a divinely implanted movement towards his
own allotted place. The 'naturalness' of Dante's own movement aloft stems
from the fact that his soul, as created directly by God (cp. *Purg.* XVI, 85–90;
XXV, 67–75), has Heaven as its own 'own true site' (proprio sito; 92).
In order to elucidate this, she presents a vision of a providentially ordered
universe in which all things in the great sea of being, both inanimate and
animate, move instinctively towards their good. Dante's soul is drawn
upwards (75) towards God by the kind of attractive force that Augustine
called the 'weight of love' (*pondus amoris*), and echoes of this Augustinian
teaching are but one of a cluster of Neoplatonic, mystical, contemplative,
and Biblical motifs – the music of the spheres (82–4), *admiratio* (97–9,
136–8), *deificatio* (67–71), *raptus* (73–5) – that lend the canto a markedly
Christian Neoplatonic patina.

Canto II opens with an address to the reader that develops the trope of the
poem as sea voyage and is studded with thematic and verbal recalls of
Ulysses' failed navigation. The poet warns his readers to be wary about
following his 'ship' (legno; 3; cp. *Inf.* XXVI, 101); for, were they to be
insufficiently equipped, philosophically and theologically, they might risk
being lost. After the pilgrim has ascended to the heaven of the Moon, the
remainder of the canto develops strongly the *quaestio*-style format as
Dante-character raises a doubt about the spotty surface of the Moon visible
from earth, Beatrice solicits his views, and then rebuts the naturalistic
explanation provided by the character. This first sequence of sustained
argumentation (61–105), resolutely asserts the limits of reason when it
relies solely on the senses, and includes further dialogue with earlier philosophical poetry, since the pilgrim's erroneous view is the very one found in
Meun's *Roman de la rose* (16,835–80). Beatrice then delivers the true
explanation for the moon-spots, by presenting a grandiose vision of the

cosmos as penetrated by light and divine virtue or power. The eighth heaven or Primum Mobile takes the imprint of the profound mind that turns it. Divine power is then distributed throughout the chain of being by means of the heavens which derive their own motion from their angelic intelligences. The concluding sequence, enriched with arresting metaphors that link the cosmos to the human body and soul, stresses how the angelic motors animate and control the heavenly bodies, as the human soul vivifies the body. The animation multiplies goodness throughout the cosmos; and each heavenly body participates in this distribution, which is manifested as light, in differentiated ways, creating different 'alloys' with the celestial orbs and revealing the joyous nature from which that light derives, just as joy shines out through the human eye (127–48).

Non-Beatrician discourses in the first three Heavens of Paradise are delivered by other blessed souls, a nun of the Order of Poor Clares, a Holy Roman emperor, and an Angevin prince. Their discourses deal respectively with the diversity of beatitude (III, 34–90), Roman history from its origins to the Republic and empire onto Charlemagne and beyond (VI), and the way human talents pass from one generation to the next (VIII, 85–148). Later speakers include near-contemporary theologians such as Thomas Aquinas, biblical figures (Solomon and Adam), contemplatives (Peter Damian, Benedict, Bernard of Clairvaux), and even an eagle made up of lights in the heaven of Jupiter. Their discussions concern matters related to the resurrected body (XIV, 34–60), the inscrutability of justice (XIX, 34–99), the status of virtuous pagans and the possibility of their miraculous salvation (XX, 82–148), predestination (XXI, 73–102), the length of time elapsed since the Fall, the time spent by Adam and Eve in the Earthly Paradise, the cause of their being cast out, and the first Adamic language spoken (XXVI, 97–142). The pilgrim, like a well-trained bachelor of arts undergoing a university examination (XXIV, 46–51), makes his own interventions regarding the three theological virtues in response to questions addressed to him by Saints Peter, James, and John (XXIV–XXVI).

Beatrice then returns prominently to her role as teacher when she delivers two more major philosophical-theological discourses on the angels in order to explain the pilgrim's sight of a point of light surrounded by nine concentric circles in the Primum Mobile. She first resolves Dante's doubt on the positions of the circles/angelic orders in relation to one another (XXVIII, 40–87), explaining their functions, and then she expounds their creation, faculties, and number (XXIX, 1–48). The final major discourse is delivered in the Empyrean by a Cistercian mystic and contemplative, Bernard of Clairvaux, who, as one endowed with doctrine through his relationship with Mary, speaks on the predestination of blessed infants (XXXII, 49–84).

The subject matter of these teachings is often, though not exclusively, theological, but more significant is the poetic and narrative context, the status of the speaker, the point reached in the journey, and the relationship with earlier episodes and cantos and surrounding imagery and narrative themes. As in the opening two cantos, we continue to find rationalizing modes of enquiry, as well as the content, terminology, and teaching strategies of late-medieval scholasticism. And yet, the extent of reason's power continues to be delimited. The heaven of the Sun (*Paradiso* X–XIV) shows how the poet intricately balances both the rationalist and non-rationalist currents, and how he maps diverse forms of knowledge and their relationship to the divine.

Beginning with a paean to the order and creative power of divine wisdom, the poet uses this bloc of cantos to orchestrate an intricate play of oppositions that he harmoniously reconciles. The sustained use of motifs of circling, concord, and dance emphasizes the harmony in this heaven, one which offers a pointedly bleak contrast to the ideological rifts and intellectual animosities found on earth. Twenty-four spirits, extraordinarily diverse in era, nationality, and approach to knowledge, appear to the pilgrim in two circles of lights. Some are organizers of knowledge in explicitly scholastic forms (Peter Lombard, Peter Comestor, Peter of Spain, Gratian, Hugh of St Victor); others are earlier collectors of information in encyclopaedic form (Orosius, Isidore, Bede, Rhaban Maurus); still others are intellectuals (Anselm, Albert the Great, Aquinas, Bonaventure, Siger of Brabant), who to varying degrees and over time either incorporated or reacted against the deployment of Aristotelian concepts and methods in theological enquiry. Alongside these figures, Dante also sees the lights of Boethius, the Pseudo-Dionysius, a mystic celebrated for his contemplative bent (Richard of St Victor), a grammarian, a historian, and an orator (Donatus, Orosius, Chrysostom), an apocalyptic prophet (Joachim of Fiore), and two humble Franciscans. Antagonists in life – Aquinas and Siger; Bonaventure and Joachim – are shown united in a common purpose to celebrate God.

In all these ways, Dante makes clear his deep awareness of contemporary intellectual controversies, displays his concern with harmonizing different positions, and affirms the unity of Christian thinkers in pursuit of truth. Methods and language familiar from the scholastic *quaestio* continue to be employed – disputation, the reconciling of diverse authorities, the use of distinctions, subdivisions, and refutation. However, the heaven of the Sun also displays an intense concern with metaphor, as well as with affective and non-rationalist currents; and the value of the poetic and divinely inspired voice is ratified in the choice of Solomon as the most learned light. Moreover, the need for humility in the face of a Truth that exceeds the human intellect is emphasized by recalls of Ulysses' navigation ('ardore' and 'sapienza'; ardour and wisdom; XI, 37–8; shipwreck, XIII, 136–8).

The cantos in which Dante-character himself is examined and speaks upon matters of Christian doctrine reveal a similar blending of rationalizing and non-rationalizing elements. This bloc offers powerful statements on Dante's poetic authority and religious orthodoxy, and it also provides us with strong indications of his ultimate sympathies, including his reliance on the Bible. The pilgrim's opening definition of faith (XXIV, 61–6), for example, translates the beginning of Paul's Epistle to the Hebrews (1:11). Throughout the first part of his examination, the pilgrim balances the language and associated techniques of scholastic theology, such as quiddity, syllogism, and demonstration, with declarations and prayers asserting his faith in God, the miracles, and Scripture (9–111). Later in the episode, when asked to set out specific doctrines of belief, his assertions draw on both the Nicene Creed and the Aristotelian doctrine of the unmoved mover (130–3) and refer to both philosophical and biblical proofs (133–8). The definitions of hope and charity in the second and third parts of the examination are equally rich in formulas from both scholastic theology and the Bible.

The pilgrim's own privileged access to truth is, then, strongly authorized in these cantos, and the poet's concern with ultimate verities and the correction of error pervades the cantos that follow, culminating in the *viator*'s final vision of the 'high light that is true in itself' (alta luce che da se è vera; XXXIII, 54). In the final *cantica*, the poet often condemns errors of certain Christian teachers, but his criticism of theological 'authority' is especially pronounced in the Primum Mobile. Here, Beatrice's discussion of angels marks out the deficiencies and wilful errors of theologians and preachers (XXVIII, 133–8; XXIX, 37–45, 70–5, 85–110), and it ends with an exquisite scene in which Dante presents Gregory the Great smiling at his own error in the ordering of the angels. Gregory only recognizes that the order proposed by the other major authority on angelology, the Pseudo-Dionysius, is the true one when he sees the actual hierarchies in the afterlife. It is difficult here not to think of the pilgrim and his multiple investitures as seer and writer of truth (*Purg.* XXXIII, 52–7; *Par.* XVII, 127–8; XXVII, 64–6). The *Comedy* becomes a space where conscious and unconscious errors are resolved and the authority of theologians (and popes) is delimited, and where the pilgrim emerges as a divinely anointed eyewitness, as one who sees truth and then writes it down, and whose privileged access to 'the truth that is confused on earth' (la verità che là giù si confonde; *Par.* XXIX, 74) is the very basis of the veracity of the poem and its messages.

Notes

1. We still lack sufficiently close studies of Dante's relationship with Meun, Silvestris, and Alan. Also of relevance is the fifth-century poem by Martianus Capella, *Marriage of Philology and Mercury.*
2. Macrobius, *Commentarium in Somnium Scipionis*, I, vi, 44: 'learned in all disciplines'; see also II, viii, 1; *Saturnalia* I, xvi, 12; Servius, *Aeneid* VI, pref; VI, 264–6 *ad loc.*
3. Z. G. Barański, 'Sulla formazione intellettuale di Dante: alcuni problem di definizione', *Studi e problemi di critica testuale*, 90/1 (2015), 31–54 (p. 49).
4. The principle that the soul is more perfect when joined with the body is axiomatic in late scholastic theology; see Aquinas, *De anima*, I, lect. 14, 208: 'the more the soul is perfect the more it exercises more perfect and diverse powers'.
5. E. Berti, 'Politica', in *ED*, IV, 585–7.
6. The interrelations between Nature and God as makers are fundamental to Alan of Lille's *De planctu naturae* and *Anticlaudianus.*
7. Z. G. Barański, '"Per similitudine di abito scientifico": Dante, Cavalcanti and the Sources of Medieval "Philosophical" Poetry', in P. Antonello and S. Gilson (eds.), *Science and Literature in Italian Culture* (Oxford: Legenda, 2004), pp. 14–52.

12

CLAIRE E. HONESS

Politics

A Political Poem?

'See our city' (Vedi nostra città; *Par.* XXX, 130): with these words Beatrice reveals to the protagonist of Dante's *Comedy*, his journey through the after-life now all-but-complete, the celestial rose of the Empyrean, the community of the blessed, the city of God. The journey of Dante's protagonist, which had famously begun in a dark wood, is thus configured as a journey from a wood to a city, from wilderness to civilization, and from a solitary place to one thronged with citizens. This chapter will examine the implications of this trajectory in relation to Dante's political context, his political thought, and – and most significantly – the status of the *Comedy* as a political poem.

This latter label requires a brief introductory explanation. What does it mean to describe the *Comedy* as a political poem, and how does understanding it as such impact on the way in which we might read it? To describe the *Comedy* as a political poem is not merely to suggest that it is a poem that touches on political themes, although it certainly does this, primarily in those episodes where characters – including the character of Dante himself – raise political issues close to their own hearts. Nor does it imply only that the poem has a political agenda – that it is in some sense a political manifesto – although it can certainly be read in this way. Rather, it proposes that Dante's text is to be read *throughout*, from dark wood to celestial city, as addressing its readers as citizens, as members of a community: as 'political animals'. And in doing this, it suggests that Dante makes of the political world that he knew, with its get-rich-quick merchants, its corrupt politicians, and its worldly churchmen, with its saints, sinners, and all those who fall somewhere in-between, with its individuals, families, communities, cities, and kingdoms,[1] the very stuff of poetry itself: its metaphors, its structures, its language.

From Politician to Political Thinker

To understand the broader significance of the *Comedy* as a political poem, however, it is important to have a clear understanding of Dante's own political views and of their development during his formative years in Florence, and then in the long and sometimes politically fraught period of his exile. The notion of development is key here. The *Comedy* was written over a roughly fifteen-year period, between about 1306 and the poet's death in 1321, years of turbulent change both for the poet and for the world around him, and it would be inconsistent to assume that a poem written against this unsettled backdrop would present a single unchanging political view. This chapter therefore describes a set of political views in flux (although not without some central convictions that remain unshakeably constant throughout), in line with Dante's own fluctuating political fortunes.

We know, then, that Dante was actively involved in politics from the age of about thirty, since records of the meetings of Florence's governing councils attest to the poet's contribution to debates on a number of issues from the year 1295 onwards. His political engagement culminated in the year 1300 with his election as Prior, the most senior role open to a Florentine within the city's government. In a system of government that extended voting and participatory rights to relatively few, this level of direct involvement in politics was not unusual for a mature male citizen of Dante's class in the final years of the thirteenth century. Nonetheless, this brief period of hands-on political activity must have opened Dante's eyes to the everyday challenges of governing a wealthy and growing city-state, riven with internal conflicts, at loggerheads with its neighbours, and in constant fear of losing its autonomy to some larger external force: all issues which reappear in the political discussions of the *Comedy*.

By the end of the thirteenth century, those Florentine conflicts were no longer centred on the old rivalry between the Guelfs (long the dominant faction in the city, and associated with support for the papacy) and the Ghibellines (traditionally supporters of the empire); the Guelfs had split into Black and White factions (distinguished from one another as much by family feuds and alliances as by opposing ideologies), and the city's primary aim was to preserve its independence by allying itself with whichever of the two greater powers of Church and empire appeared to pose the lowest risk to its autonomy. Although a Guelf by birth, Dante had no truck with the Church's appropriation of secular political power, and he was outspoken, in his contributions to council debates, in opposing the Blacks' proposals to bind Florence ever more closely to the papal cause. It was this stance that would ultimately lead to the great turning point of the poet's life, his exile from Florence. When the Blacks seized power in 1301, Dante was forced from the city on what appear to have been trumped-up charges of corruption; he would spend the last twenty years of his life in exile, and would die in

Ravenna without ever returning to the home for which his writings express love and hate in almost equal measure.

Already by the time of Dante's exile, the key elements of his mature political views were in place: above all, his commitment to engagement with and service of his community, and his deep scepticism about the role played by the Church in political life. Over the years of his exile, these fundamental political tenets would develop into a fully fledged political philosophy, first expressed in a coherent way in the fourth book of the *Convivio* (*c.*1304–6), and expounded most fully in the Latin political treatise, the *Monarchia* (*c.*1317),[2] but clearly traceable, as we shall see, also across the three *cantiche* of the *Comedy*.

Dante's political vision is grounded in the Aristotelian notion that human beings are 'political animals'; that is to say, that they are designed for and can only be properly fulfilled as human beings via life in a community. This understanding is tempered, however, by a conviction, derived from St Augustine's pessimistic view of human nature, that human beings are fundamentally corrupt, selfish, and greedy both for goods and for power. This self-centredness (in theological terms, *cupiditas*: a word often translated as 'greed', but carrying far more wide-ranging implications) inevitably stands in the way of the realization of successful communal life and leads, instead, to a political order characterized above all by conflict – that very same conflict which Dante saw tearing Florence apart and casting her citizens into the political void of exile. Dante came to believe that none of the smaller political units into which human beings tended to form themselves – and particularly not the bellicose and fractious city-states which he knew so well – was able to counter this tendency towards conflict, not least because they were themselves run through by the same insatiable desire for power, wealth, and domination that afflicted individuals: Florence's inability to build peace either with her neighbours or among her citizenry proved as much. Only, he suggested, by investing *all* power, *all* goods, *universal* domination in a single all-powerful ruler, who would thus be inoculated against *cupiditas*, could peace be brought to the world (*Conv.* IV, iv, 3–4).

But where was such an all-powerful ruler to be found? Not, to be sure, in the Church, whose remit was, for Dante, decisively *not* the political sphere. Rather, the poet placed his hopes of political redemption in an idealized emperor, based on the Roman emperors of the past, and, in particular, on Augustus under whom Roman power had reached its height, extending, indeed, almost to the whole known world. For Dante, it is no coincidence that Christ is born – that He *chooses* to be born – at the time of the census ordered by Augustus (Luke 2:1–7); in registering Himself as a citizen of Rome, Christ submits to Rome's secular authority, and endorses the

Roman right to rule over his kingdom on earth, that is, the whole world. The whole history of Rome and of the world builds towards this moment – conceived, in St Paul's terms, as the 'fullness of time' (Galatians 4:4) – and the exiled Dante's political goal (embraced with ever-increasing fervour, at least until about 1313) is to put in place the conditions necessary for its recreation, and specifically the establishment of a strong, universal empire, with its capital in Rome.

Such a goal, however, was significantly out-of-kilter with the political context of the time. The new, 'holy', Roman empire had been re-established under Charlemagne in 800, but by the end of the thirteenth century its power had been significantly diminished, held firmly in check by the increasing political power of the papacy, which traced its secular influence back even earlier than the time of Charlemagne, to the supposed 'Donation' of Constantine in the second decade of the fourth century.[3] It is against this backdrop that the individual who had perhaps the greatest single influence on Dante's political views in the period following his exile came to prominence. Elected emperor in 1308, Henry, Duke of Luxembourg (later Henry VII), vowed to restore the empire to its rightful seat in Rome, and, in the process, to unite the warring cities of Italy under the empire's jurisdiction. Some of Dante's most impassioned political writing dates from this period;[4] yet his support was of no avail. Henry was met with ever more intransigent opposition, bolstered by the not-inconsiderable forces of the papacy, in the traditionally Guelf cities, and most particularly in Florence; his coronation in Rome was held in secret and in the Pope's absence, and by 1313, within little more than a year of this coronation, Henry had contracted malaria and died. With Henry expired all possible hope for the realization of Dante's political vision, and he largely steered clear of any practical political engagement thereafter.

Dante's political activities and ideas have been summarized here with the hope of conveying both his broad political philosophy and its development over time on the basis of the real political events that touched the poet's life. In what follows, I highlight how the multiple threads of this developing vision are woven through the *Comedy*, making of it a fundamentally (even if not a straightforwardly) political text.

Community

We have seen that, for Dante, as for Aristotle, human beings are fundamentally and unavoidably 'political animals': they are designed for life in a community, and it is only in a community that they are able to flourish and – ideally, at least – enjoy true happiness. In the *Comedy*, this fundamental truth is presented most explicitly in the heaven of Venus, where the soul of the titular king of Hungary, Charles Martel, asks Dante's protagonist whether human beings would be worse off if they did not form socio-political associations: 'would it be worse for man on earth if he were not a citizen?' (sarebbe il peggio / per l'omo in terra, se non fosse cive?; *Par.* VIII, 115–16). To this, the answer is an emphatic affirmative: 'Yes ... and here I ask no proof' (Sí ... e qui ragion non cheggio; 117). Community is essential for happy, peaceful, fulfilled human existence.

Yet, it is no coincidence that Dante should wait until so far into his poem to share what for him is such a fundamental political truth. The inevitability of the tainting of earthly communities by that typical combination of greed and lust for power that makes up the political sin of *cupiditas* means that it is only in Heaven that a perfectly harmonious community, best epitomized in the image of the celestial city, can be envisaged, since it is only here that the selfishness that lies at the root of *cupiditas* can be definitively transformed into the selflessness that enables the prioritization of the common good, the good of the community as a whole, over the good of the individual.

The 'communities' which Dante's traveller encounters on his journey through the planetary heavens memorably illustrate this assimilation of the individual into the community, as they appear to him not in airy bodies as the souls in Hell and Purgatory had done, but as points of light, of varying colour and intensity, which collectively form symbolic shapes: circles, a cross, an eagle, a ladder. The most significant of these, from this point of view, is the eagle of the heaven of Jupiter, in which the individual souls are subsumed so entirely into their community that they speak with a single voice, using first-person *singular* pronouns where the plural would be expected: 'I saw and I heard the beak talk and utter with its voice *I* and *mine* when its meaning was *we* and *ours*' (io vidi e anche udi' parlar lo rostro, / e sonar ne la voce e 'io' e 'mio', / quand'era nel concetto e 'noi' e 'nostro'; *Par.* XIX, 10–12). And the blessed souls are able to speak with a single voice because, as Piccarda explains in *Paradiso* III, they also will with a single will. Where *cupiditas* turns one citizen against another, these citizens are utterly united in willing one thing only: that God's will be done, and 'in His will is [their] peace' (E 'n la sua voluntade è nostra pace; 85). Here we see Dante's imperial ideal writ large and viewed *sub specie aeternitatis*: individual wills are wholly aligned with the will of their lord (namely, of *the* Lord), who is thus able to hold in check all the conflicting demands and desires of all the individuals, ensuring no discord and no dissatisfaction.

How different the harmonious and united community of Heaven is from the discordant and fractious one of Hell. Yet Hell too, in its way, is a community for Dante, and his character's entry into this realm is marked by his passage through a gate, explicitly referred to as the gate of a city:

'Through me the way into the woeful city' (Per me si va ne la città dolente; *Inf.* III, 1). Like the gates of many medieval Italian cities, this gate bears an inscription, although, unlike those gates, which habitually praised the city to which they offered access, the gate of Hell bears only its famous chilling warning: 'Abandon every hope, you that enter' (Lasciate ogne speranza, voi ch'intrate; 9).

In a similar vein, the city of Dis, which Dante's traveller reaches in canto VIII, both is and is not a city. Presented from the outside in extremely realistic terms, with its tower (*Inf.* VII, 130; VIII, 2), moat (*Inf.* VIII, 76–7), walls (78), and gates (115), it is soon clear that this city is little more than an optical illusion. Once through the gates, Dante's protagonist finds himself not in a *polis* but a necropolis, among the open tombs of the souls guilty of heresy; and beyond this he is confronted with a landslide, a river of blood, a forest, a desert, a cliff, and the strange barren landscape of the Malebolge. This structure is echoed as the traveller descends into Hell's final circle where the bodies of the giants, standing guard over the frozen depths of the abyss – the ice-lake, Cocytus – are mistaken from far off for the towers of a city, like the Tuscan town of Montereggioni (*Inf.* XXXI, 20–1; 40–1). Once again, civic expectations are raised only to be overturned by the savage natural reality of the infernal landscape.

And this is no coincidence. Rather, the landscape of Hell reflects a more profound social reality that serves to teach the reader something of the nature of sin. Although punishment in Hell is a communal experience, in the sense that the souls suffer together in groups, a closer reading reveals that they are all fundamentally, and often aggressively, isolated from one another. Francesca appears to be unable to refer to her lover, Paolo, by name, instead speaking of 'this one who will never be parted from me' (questi, che mai da me non fia diviso; *Inf.* V, 135), a phrase which suggests that his constant presence at her side, far from being a comfort, only adds to her suffering. In other cases we see a violent rejection of community on the part of the damned souls, or a sly desire to do harm to their neighbours in punishment. An example is found in the *bolgia* of barratry, where the willingness of the devils to believe that Ciampolo would be prepared to deceive his fellow sinners into coming to the surface of the pitch in which they are punished seems to imply that it is not unusual for the souls to turn against one another (*Inf.* XXIII, 97–111). However, the most memorable example of this sort of violence is found in the case of Ugolino and Ruggieri, where the punishment of the two traitors, citizens of the same earthly city, frozen together eternally in the ice of Hell's lowest circle, recalls the eternal togetherness of Paolo and Francesca, but where Ugolino's insistent gnawing on the skull of his companion reveals the most extreme consequences of a rejection of earthly citizenship.

As if to remind his interlocutors of the status he had enjoyed in his life as a civilized and respected politician, Ugolino carefully wipes his mouth on Ruggieri's hair before speaking, in a grotesque parody of table manners (*Inf.* XXXIII, 1–3). The poet's description of him at the end of his speech, however, when he turns back to Ruggieri's skull with teeth 'which were strong on the bone like a dog's' (che furon a l'osso, come d'un can, forti; 78), leaves the reader under no illusions: the veneer of civilization is completely removed. And, in keeping with the natural landscape which they inhabit, Hell's citizens are frequently described in this way: the gluttons are compared to dogs (*Inf.* VI, 19), the wrathful are like 'swine in the mire' (porci in brago; VIII, 50) and like frogs (IX, 76–8), a comparison also used of the barrators (XXII, 25–33). Indeed, this latter group – significantly, political sinners one and all – is particularly characterized by animal imagery: the souls are also compared to dolphins (19–21), an otter (36), and a duck (130).

Hell, therefore, both is and is not a community. It inverts and perverts the normal rules of citizenship and belonging, existing not for the benefit of its citizens but to their detriment. Devoid of the unity of purpose that joins the souls of the blessed into a single community with a single voice, it is a mere agglomeration of angry and isolated individuals, more animal than human, punished in a wilderness-city. Human beings are, certainly, by nature political animals; but Hell shows that when *cupiditas* corrupts that most fundamental political inclination, the political animal is reduced to the level of a mere beast.

Florence

On the basis of what we have already learned about Dante's own political history, it should come as no surprise that a great many of the bestial citizens of the wilderness-city of Hell are Florentines. Probably written in the years immediately following his exile,[5] Dante's grief at the loss of 'everything loved most dearly' (ogne cosa / diletta più caramente; *Par.* XVII, 55–6) is translated, in *Inferno*, into an almost obsessive desire to understand the causes of Florentine sinfulness. And, in the context of the poem as a whole, the political corruption of the poet's own city, with its disastrous consequences for him personally, provides the motivation for a thoroughgoing examination of human political engagement.

In *Inferno* XIII, then, Dante has an anonymous Florentine suicide trace the city's political ills back to the substitution of the city's original tutelary deity, the Roman god Mars, for the Christian saint, John the Baptist. For this reason, the unfortunate soul suggests, Mars has ever since overshadowed Florence with his 'art', the art of war (145). Already in *Inferno* VI, Florence had been identified as a 'divided city' (città partita; 61), and the implications of these divisions are illustrated nowhere more clearly than in the episode of Farinata in canto X. Notwithstanding his magnanimity (73) in preventing the victorious Ghibellines from razing Florence to the ground following the battle of Montaperti (1260), Farinata is presented here as being inextricably bound up with the factional conflicts which, in 1300, are turning Florentine against Florentine. His tit-for-tat argument with Dante-character about whose ancestors better mastered the art of returning from exile functions almost as a microcosm of the city's factional conflicts, provoking Farinata to anticipate prophetically Dante's own politically motivated exile. Like Ugolino and Ruggieri, Dante and Farinata are citizens of the same city, irrevocably set against one another by an attachment to faction, rooted in a mere accident of birth.

Moreover, Farinata's arrogant disregard for Hell itself (36) and for his companions in suffering – seen in his failure to acknowledge the dramatic intervention of the soul of Cavalcante de' Cavalcanti into his conversation with Dante-character (73–5) – looks both backwards, to Ciacco's identification of pride, envy, and avarice as the three besetting sins of the Florentines (VI, 74), and forward to the episode of the Florentine sodomites, where it is the pilgrim himself who defines Florence as characterized above all by 'arrogance and excess' (orgoglio e dismisura; XVI, 74). In *Inferno* Dante begins to provide his reader with examples from which a practical definition of the fundamental political sin of *cupiditas* can be extrapolated: a sin which the proud, avaricious, and envious Florence of the *Comedy* epitomizes. For *cupiditas* involves a greed for possessions, but also, and more insidiously, a failure to recognize and to accept one's proper place in the order of things, leading to a desire to elevate one's own status at the expense of others and ultimately to conflict and corruption. In *Inferno* XVI, the blame for Florence's descent into just such a state of conflict and corruption is laid firmly on the *nouveau riche* mercantile class that had risen to prominence in the two centuries or so preceding the writing of the poem. Such 'new people' with their 'sudden gains' (la gente nuova e i sùbiti guadagni; 73) are seen as having fundamentally changed the character of the city, reducing it to a moral wasteland, which is reflected in the desert on which the sodomites are punished.

This image of the corrupt Florence finds its answer in the cantos of *Paradiso* that parallel (numerically) those of the sodomites in *Inferno*. Here, in the heaven of Mars, Dante re-appropriates Florence's first patron, but in a Christian context, as his interlocutor in these cantos, his great-great-grandfather, Cacciaguida, describes his own city, the Florence of the eleventh century, and compares it with the corrupt city of his descendant.

Significantly, however, when Cacciaguida describes the good Florentines of the past, he does not refer to the city's leading politicians – the eleventh-century equivalents of Farinata, or even of Dante himself – but to a category of Florentines who, politically, would not have been considered citizens at all: the city's women. In sharp contrast to the brash self-confidence and extravagant ostentation of the 'new people' of Dante's time, the women of the past are described as wearing plain clothing, eschewing make-up and jewellery, and living simple family-oriented lives. In an episode whose focus is on the deterioration of civic life and which prepares for the prophecy of Dante's own exile in *Paradiso* XVII, the focus on women is striking and unexpected. What can the women of Florence – debarred by their gender from active political agency – possibly have to teach the reader about matters of good government? With their focus on home and family, how can they hope to tame the city's bellicose nature? Cacciaguida's choice of examples is far from accidental, however. In the heaven of Mars, where the souls form a cross of light, and therefore under the sign not of Mars, the bringer of war, but of Christ, the bringer of peace, Cacciaguida suggests that the problems of Florence are not political, but moral. Florence cannot redeem herself simply through political reform; indeed, as Dante points out in his famous invective against Italy in *Purgatorio* VI, the more she changes her politicians and fiddles with her laws, the worse things become (145–7). In sharp contrast to the virtuous, active, engaged women of Cacciaguida's time, Florence herself, in 1300, is 'like the sick woman that can find no rest on her bed of down' (somigliante a quella inferma / che non può trovar posa in su le piume; 151–2).

Political reform has to happen elsewhere, and on a more global scale; and Florence will never resolve what is essentially a moral crisis by mere political tinkering. Unlike the 'brazen women of Florence' (sfacciate donne fiorentine) described by Forese Donati, who parade their bodies through Dante's city 'showing the breast with the paps' (mostrando con le poppe il petto; *Purg.* XXIII, 101–2), the women of Cacciaguida's time are exemplars of a virtue which – with rare exceptions, as in the case of Forese's widow, Nella – no longer exists in the city. As the episode of Farinata shows, the male citizens of Florence can all too easily be identified with the faction with which they were associated. But, as we have seen, Farinata's failure as a citizen is not that he is a Ghibelline, but that he lacks the basic communal instinct which should unite members of the same community; he ignores the suffering of Cavalcante not because the latter is a Guelf, but because he fails to see in him the humanity that unites them – the same humanity that unites members of all cities and kingdoms with the Christ who lived as a human being and died on the cross.

Empire

It should come as no surprise, therefore, that at the culmination of Cacciaguida's eulogy of the good Florentines of the past in *Paradiso* XV, we find a reference to the Florentine mothers telling their children stories 'of the Trojans, of Fiesole and Rome' (de' Troiani, di Fiesole e di Roma; 126). These are the stories that attest to Florence's importance by stressing the city's affiliation with the great Roman empire of the past. Florence's most important foundation myth asserted that the city had been founded in 59 BCE by Julius Caesar himself, and populated by Roman settlers after they had destroyed the neighbouring Etruscan city of Fiesole as revenge for its support for the conspirator, Catiline. As the 'daughter' of Rome, and, as it were, the granddaughter of Troy, whence Aeneas had sailed to Italy, Florence should have been destined for greatness; her current dividedness, her moral and political downfall is, thus, directly connected to her rejection of her Roman heritage.

This much emerges already in the encounter with Brunetto Latini in *Inferno* XV, where Brunetto laments the fact that 'that thankless and malignant folk who came down of old from Fiesole' (quello ingrato popolo maligno / che discese di Fiesole ab antico; 61–2) was ever allowed to mingle with and settle alongside Florence's Roman population: a population whose values have been almost irrevocably lost. Only in Dante, Brunetto implies, does enough Roman blood survive to represent a slim hope for the future – if only he can keep himself safe from his political opponents (73–8). Here Dante has Brunetto assert the 'holy', divinely willed, nature of Rome's mission, an idea which would come to form one of the unshakeable pillars of Dante's mature political thought.

At the time of writing *Inferno*, though, Dante's espousal of the imperial ideal had not yet developed this far. Here, more than with a systematic political vision, the reader is presented with a series of clues to the importance that Rome and its empire would come to take on for the poet. The most significant of these is doubtless the role played by Virgil, the great Roman poet of empire whose *Aeneid* had told the story of the founding of Rome by Aeneas, with the aim of justifying and bolstering the imperial authority of that same Augustus to whose authority Christ would submit Himself, in the 'fullness of time'. Similarly, the conclusion to be drawn from the presence of Brutus and Cassius, alongside Judas Iscariot, in two of the three mouths of Lucifer is never made explicit by Dante; yet their positioning within Hell's structure alone makes clear the seriousness with which their sin is to be considered. To betray the empire, Dante implies, is tantamount to betraying Christ himself. No sin is worse; and no further comment is necessary.

By the time he comes to write the invective against Italy which closes *Purgatorio* VI, however, it is clear that Dante feels the need to be much more explicit about the inevitable consequences of the *cupiditas* which drives the politics of his city and others like it. In sharp contrast to the profound peace identified by Piccarda as a characteristic of Heaven, in Italy peace is totally absent (82–4). The use of the verb *rodere* (to describe fellow citizens 'gnawing' each other; 83) invites the reader to recall the episode of Ugolino and Ruggieri, two Pisans who epitomize the politically pessimistic situation outlined in *Purgatorio* VI. But whereas Dante's earlier invective against Pisa (*Inf.* XXXIII, 79–90) focuses on the corruption of the city and its inhabitants, the later invective begins to suggest the causes of (and, by implication, the potential remedies for) this parlous political landscape.

The invective against Italy is shot through with references to emptiness, abandonment, and absence. 'What avails that Justinian refitted the reins on thee if the saddle is empty?' (Che val perché ti racconciasse il freno / Iustinïano se la sella è vota?; *Purg.* VI, 88–9).[6] The question is the same one posed by Marco Lombardo on the terrace of the wrathful (*Purg.* XVI, 97), but by this time the question is purely rhetorical; the answer has already been made abundantly clear. Abandoned by a series of emperors concerned only with events north of the Alps – the poet's reference to 'German Albert' (Alberto *tedesco; Purg.* VI, 97, my italics) could not be more pointed – Rome, the great imperial city, is left – like the Jerusalem of the Old Testament – 'widowed and solitary', weeping and crying 'night and day: "Caesar, my Lord, why dost thou deny me thy companionship?"' (Roma che piagne / vedova sola, e dí e notte chiama: / 'Cesare mio, perché non m'accompagne?'; 112–4; cp. Lamentations 1:1). It is no coincidence, then, that Dante accuses both Albert of Hapsburg (emperor 1298–1308) and his father Rudolph (emperor 1273–91) specifically of the sin of *cupiditas* (104), for it is this sin, above all others, which lies at the heart of all political corruption and stands in the way of a generous approach to political leadership, which puts the good of the community before the individual needs of the ruler himself.

Nor is it a coincidence that Dante's invective should set up the contemporary 'German' emperors in contrast to Justinian, for it is in the canto of *Paradiso* dominated, and entirely narrated, by Justinian that Dante's imperial ideal is, at last, most fully expressed. *Paradiso* VI is almost entirely devoted to a potted history of the Roman empire, told as the story of the eagle, Rome's sign and standard. Justinian's narrative is not, however, merely a chronological account of a sequence of historical events; rather, it is a lesson in salvation history, for the eagle whose story he tells is a 'most holy standard' (sacrosanto segno; 32), and the account of its adventures builds to a climactic moment, the moment when political and providential plans come together. The entire history of Rome is presented as mere preparation for the time when finally (and uniquely), under imperial authority, the world would attain perfect peace – a peace willed both by the political authorities and God (55–7, 80–1). As we have seen, it is this peace which creates the conditions necessary for the birth of Christ, marking history's most significant turning point.

Justinian's account does not stop here, though, for the peace achieved by Augustus is – and can only be, given humanity's frailty and propensity to sin – fleeting, a mere interlude in the history of a world tainted by *cupiditas*. As a result of human sinfulness, it is not enough for Christ to be born, He must also die; and if He is to take upon Himself the sins of the whole world, then He must necessarily be punished by a legally constituted authority with a remit that extends over that whole world whose sins are being punished. Justinian's account therefore praises not only Augustus, but also the much more problematic figure of Tiberius, who is granted 'the glory of doing vengeance for [God's] wrath' (gloria di far vendetta a la sua ira; *Par.* VI, 90). Now, at last, the true role and significance of the empire emerges: the empire is essential not only to history, but also to salvation history, for it is through the empire that the once-and-for-all intervention of Providence into the world of human society was brought about.

Two Suns

Such a view of the coming together, at the turning point of time, of religious and secular history must inevitably raise the question of the role of the Church in the complex pattern of interlocking political relationships that we have been tracing. As we have seen, the Donation of Constantine had first legitimized the papacy's holding of political power, and the ambitions, greed, and nepotism of successive popes had built upon this foundation, making of the Church a major political player in the medieval world.

Dante's own view of the corrupting influence of the Church's involvement in secular affairs is clear from his vehement attack on the simonist popes of *Inferno* XIX. The Donation of Constantine, which first opened the Church up to the dangers of wealth, and hence of *cupiditas*, lies at the root of the world's political ills (115–17). Dante's ideal Church is one that embraces apostolic poverty (90–6); it is not one which pursues power. With this in mind, Dante reserves a particular judgement for Boniface VIII, a pope whose engagement with political machinations and ventures aimed at furthering himself and his family were legendary, and whom Dante was inclined to blame personally for his exile from Florence. Although he was still alive – indeed, still pope – in 1300, the fictional date of the *Comedy*, Dante manages to convey that Boniface's eternal fate is already sealed, when the soul of Nicholas III dramatically mistakes the pilgrim for Boniface arriving before his time (53–4). And confirmation is provided by no less a soul than St Peter himself, who asserts – in an extraordinarily passionate outburst – that Boniface's corruption is such that the papacy 'in the sight of the Son of God is empty' (vaca / nella presenza del Figliuol di Dio; *Par.* XXVII, 23–4): if Italy lacks an emperor, it also – effectively – lacks a pope.

By the time he writes the invective against Italy in *Purgatorio* VI, the poet has started to connect his views on the temporal power of the Church with his emergent views on the role of the empire. On the one hand, the horse of state, in the absence of any plausible imperial authority, is riderless; on the other, it is subject to the attempts of a corrupt and power-hungry Church to pick up its reins and to steer it where it should not go (*Purg.* VI, 91–6).

It is left to the soul of Marco Lombardo to draw the political threads raised in the invective to a conclusion. In response to the pilgrim's naïve question as to why the world has gone so badly astray, Marco embarks on a discussion of free will, which concludes that, in the face of the overwhelming human fallibility in discerning what is good, there is a need for 'law to be set as a curb' (legge per fren porre), and for 'a king who should discern at least the tower of the true city' (rege ... che discernesse / de la vera città almen la torre; *Purg.* XVI, 94–6). In other words, if the world has gone astray this is only indirectly a consequence of sin, and more specifically the result of a failure of leadership. Marco goes on to use a striking image to illustrate this. Rome, he claims, the city which is the seat of both Church and empire, 'used to have two suns, which made plain the one way and the other, that of the world and that of God' (Soleva Roma ... / due soli aver, che l'una e l'altra strada / facean vedere, e del mondo e di Deo; 106–8). Humanity needs both political and spiritual enlightenment in order to live well in the here-and-now and to attain salvation in the hereafter; but these are distinct and separate goals, which require distinct and separate authorities to point towards them. Dante is here playing on the medieval truism that equated the papacy with the sun and the empire with the moon and stated that, just as the moon did not produce light of its own but merely reflected the light of the sun, so the empire did not have authority except insofar as it received it from the papacy, from whence the need for the emperor to be crowned by the pope in order to attain full legitimacy. Dante, however, destroys this hierarchical relationship by replacing the sun and the moon with two suns: equal authorities, each shining with equal brightness in its own sphere of authority.

This image of both limpid simplicity and dazzling audacity, seen in light of the providential role that Dante attaches to the empire, helps to explain the poet's almost fanatical support for the Italian campaign of Henry VII. If the world is to be put to rights, it needs a king who can discern the towers of the true city, and that king must needs be a Roman, one who follows in the footsteps of Augustus and Tiberius in doing God's work, aligning once again providential and secular history. Only with such political safeguards in place can the Church do what it is called to do – namely, to preach the Gospel and to save souls – while the world lives in peace and harmony. For a brief time, Dante truly believed that Henry might be that king.

Henry is, of course, still alive in 1300, but it is surely no coincidence that the seat which he will eventually come to occupy in the Empyrean is the first to be revealed to the pilgrim. Like Boniface, his place in the hereafter is guaranteed. But unlike Boniface, and despite the fact that he is unable, in the event, to 'set Italy straight' (drizzare Italia; *Par.* XXX, 137), his place is in Heaven, for his mission is 'holy' in intention, even if it is defective in execution.

A Party of One

I have chosen to end this account of Dante's politics in the *Comedy* with Henry – a character who appears in the poem only indirectly, and whose intervention on the political stage of medieval Italy was ultimately brief and inglorious – for an important reason. Henry's inclusion in the poem returns us – unexpectedly perhaps – to the theme of community which was the starting point for our exploration and which lies at the very heart of Dante's political thought. Between about 1309 and 1313, Dante does – briefly – elaborate a political programme: an ideal which he would like to see lived out in the world, and which he believes would, if carried off, guarantee human happiness in this life and point the way to the bliss of the world to come. It is an ideal that never loses its appeal for him,[7] but it is, nonetheless, one that fails. Henry does not unify Italy, let alone the world, and Boniface's papal successors, far from abandoning secular power, become ever more entrenched in the world of politics.

What, in the face of political failure, is a politically engaged poet to do? How can he speak about politics in a situation where he sees no hope of any political solution? A potential solution is provided in that same episode of the heaven of Mars where the good Florence of the past is held up as an example to the Florence of the present. Prophesying Dante's exile, Cacciaguida tells him that 'it shall be to your honour to have made a party by thyself' (a te fia bello / averti fatta parte per te stesso; *Par.* XVII, 68–9). The poet's ancestor is not here suggesting that Dante fight civic factionalism, the corruption of the Church, and the absence of an emperor by forming a political movement of his own. Rather, he is responding to Henry's failure, Boniface's corruption, and Florence's greed by suggesting an entirely different approach to politics, one already embodied in his enumeration of the good Florentines of two centuries earlier. Dante's becoming a party all of his own implies a rejection of party politics, and indeed of politics itself. Accepting that human beings are, as he has always believed, political animals, Dante must also come to accept that, as fallible, human, political animals, they are so inevitably tainted by *cupiditas* that they cannot hope to save themselves in a political context. Marco Lombardo tells the pilgrim: 'the world is blind and indeed you come from it' (lo mondo è cieco, e tu vien ben da lui; *Purg.* XVI, 66). Cacciaguida, however, takes this one step further: the world *is* blind, but precisely because it is blind, Dante must engage with it. He must engage with it not in order to present it with a programme for political reform, which seems doomed to fail, but in order to address his readers, appealing to them not as Guelfs or Ghibellines, not as supporters of pope or emperor, not as Florentines or Pisans, but as political animals, as individuals with an investment in and a commitment to life as part of a community. Dante writes his poem 'for the world's good, which lives ill' (in pro del mondo che mal vive; *Purg.* XXXII, 103), but with a view not to reforming the world in the here and now, not to recreating the Rome of Augustus under a new 'holy' Roman emperor, but in the hope of teaching his readers to live well as citizens and members of their communities, in order that they might eventually come to be citizens of the city which Beatrice reveals to him at the end of the *Paradiso*, of 'that Rome of which Christ is Roman' (quella Roma onde Cristo è romano; *Purg.* XXXII, 102).

Notes

1. These groupings are the fundamental building blocks of political life for Dante, as set out in the *Convivio*, where he explains that human beings are not designed to be solitary, but need to come together in communities of different sorts and on different scales (IV, iv, 2).
2. The dating of the *Monarchia* has been, and continues to be, hotly contested by scholars, although most now agree that it dates to the last five years or so of Dante's life.
3. Although later proved to be a forgery, the Donation of Constantine, which purported to authorize the handing-over by Constantine (emperor 306–37) of jurisdiction over the western part of the empire, with its capital in Rome, to the Church, was accepted as genuine throughout the medieval period.

4. Of particular interest are the three letters (those numbered V, VI, and VII in modern editions) that Dante wrote on the subject of Henry's Italian campaign. These acclaim Henry in no uncertain terms as a political saviour, a messianic figure, a second Christ, coming to save Italy from her (political) sins.

5. The first evidence we have of the *Inferno* circulating in its complete form dates from 1314, but it is likely that Dante was working on it from around 1306 onwards.

6. The reference here is to the codification of Roman law by the Emperor Justinian (emperor 527–65), which had given the Middle Ages a legal framework that was relevant and workable in the Christian context.

7. The idea is re-elaborated – though in a more theoretical than practical vein – in the *Monarchia*, a text that was almost certainly composed after Henry's death.

13

ZYGMUNT G. BARAŃSKI

Genesis, Dating, and Dante's 'Other Works'

Inside and Outside the *Commedia*

There is an unfortunate, albeit comprehensible, tendency in Dante studies to subsume the poet's other writings under the *Commedia*: to consider these not so much as self-sufficient texts but rather, if composed before the poetic masterpiece, as somehow 'preparatory' for it, or, if written after its inception, as affording legitimation for some of its more problematic aspects, whether formal or ideological. It is thus not surprising that, towards the end of the eighteenth century, these works should have been termed 'minor', a problematic designation that continues to be popular and which appears to set in stone their subordination to the 'major' *Commedia*. Such a delimitative attitude has critical consequences. In general terms, it tends to downplay the distinct character and originality of each of the 'other' writings ('other' is the more neutral epithet that is beginning to supplant 'minor').[1] More specifically, it fails adequately to appreciate the varied, and not infrequently unique links that the *Commedia* forges with a particular 'other work'. Indeed, if the stratified complexity of the relationship between the poem and the rest of Dante's oeuvre is ignored or minimized, then, as we shall see, this can result in important issues regarding the *Commedia*'s purpose and poetics being discussed in an unsatisfactory manner.

There are six main ways in which the *Commedia* and the 'other works' can be validly brought together. First and most interestingly, Dante overtly, and hence deliberately, alludes to and occasionally directly cites a text during the course of the *Commedia*. Notable examples are when a soul recites the opening of one of his *canzoni* or when the *Vita nova* is expressly evoked in the Earthly Paradise. Second, the poem refers to a work indirectly: whether intertextually or by reprising common narrative, thematic, and ideological elements. This is a tricky and contentious category which requires an act of interpretation for the link to be made evident, thereby raising questions not only about whether or not the poet actually intended to indicate the work under consideration, but also about the critical validity of the proposal itself. The question of the *Convivio*'s presence and role in the *Commedia* largely falls under this category, as do aspects of its relationship to the *Vita nova*. Third, a text is deemed to have primarily (or even exclusively) a metacritical and clarificatory function with respect to the poem as a whole or to certain of its features. Dante's eclogues, with their defence of the *Commedia*'s language, style, and subject matter, have traditionally been read in this key. Equally, the *Questio de aqua et terra* is judged to provide support for the poem's complex and original cosmological system and perspective. Fourth, certain works, in particular the *Rime* and *Convivio*, are deemed to serve as the linguistic and stylistic training ground for the *Commedia*'s plurilingual experimentation. Closely connected to this is the view that Dante first tested ideas in the 'other works', for instance on the vernacular, Latin, and language in general in *De vulgari eloquentia* (this approach dovetails with the sixth of my categories). Fifth, on a par with other types of historical, doctrinal, and documentary sources, the 'other works' are used as supplementary material with which to elucidate aspects of the *Commedia* – for example, recourse is made to a passage from *Monarchia* to explain a matter of politics or history raised by the poem. When the 'other works' are utilized in this manner, this is normally done without intending to suggest that, from within the poem, Dante was either openly or obliquely making reference to the extract (or extracts) quoted. Finally, the 'other works' are employed to help cast light on the *Commedia*'s tortuous and protracted composition. Thus, the unfinished status of both *De vulgari* and *Convivio* is seen in terms of pressing new interests to which Dante gave expression by starting to pen the poem.

In assessing the nature of the relationship between the *Commedia* and the 'other works', it is important to remember that only the first three forms of textual integration are authorially sanctioned (and much of the present chapter necessarily focuses on them, given that they all play an active role in the poem, and hence in its systems of signification). The remaining three modes are the products of the critical interests and efforts of the *Commedia*'s readers and, as such, are 'external' to the poem itself. Nonetheless, the six categories are not mutually exclusive. The *Commedia* can be flexibly and, at times, concurrently brought into contact with the 'other works' in light of all, most, or just some of the six types. The results are enlightening. Thus, whether singly or as a group, the 'other works' provide spyholes onto the poem that open vistas of meaning which otherwise would be difficult to discern. Indeed, in the last analysis, they are 'other' because, from within the *Commedia*, they serve as a deliberate reminder that, first, Dante's poetic and intellectual career ought not be understood wholly in terms of the poem – a very real danger given its definitive character and its totalizing, 'encyclopaedic', and salvific aims – and second, that the *Commedia* needs to be assessed in terms not just of the literary tradition at large, but also, and more intimately, as part of a personal poetic history and evolution. Consequently, throughout his writings, Dante presented his artistic, cultural, and human development as a progressive and organic, if far from untroubled, process in which different moments illuminate, at times revise, and ultimately integrate with each other. This presentation is a literary construct and, as should become apparent, it can (deliberately) jar with the historical realities of Dante's career. In addition, as is common when Dante deals with his own artistic status and his own works, the ensuing mix intermingles narrative demands, biographical imperatives, and metaliterary explanations. To put it somewhat differently, his presentation assimilates the two authorial figures present in the *Commedia*, the pilgrim and the poet, that are normally kept separate, while also conflating them with the historical author, Dante Alighieri – a powerful synthesis intent on establishing his literary exceptionality.

The 'New Life' of 'Comedy'

Soon after realizing that the shade he has just encountered in the menacing wilderness is the great Roman poet Virgil, the pilgrim declares: 'You are my master and my author; you are he alone from whom I took the beautiful style that has brought me honour' (Tu se' lo mio maestro e 'l mio autore, / tu se solo colui da cu' io tolsi / lo bello stilo che m' ha fatto onore; *Inf.* I, 85–7).[2] At the very outset of the *Commedia*, Dante defines his protagonist, and by extension himself, by alluding to his literary accomplishments. Although no works are specified, in the Spring of 1300, such achievements could only refer to his career as an experimental lyric poet and author of the *Vita nova*. Subsequently, in light of Virgil's retelling in *Inferno* II of how Beatrice, the dead beloved of the 'little book' (libello; *Vn* I, 1 [1, 1]),[3] had descended to Limbo to encourage him to come to the aid of her wayward 'faithful one' (fedele; 97) – a quintessential erotic lyric conceit (see *Vn* III, 9 [1, 20]) – Dante-character is further and more narrowly defined as a writer not just of love literature but of love literature exclusively dedicated to Beatrice. Indeed, among contemporary readers familiar with the *Vita nova* who, for the first time, were perusing the strikingly original new poem by Dante Alighieri, such a description would have been reinforced by the justifiable assumption that they were at last reading the work in celebration of Beatrice that, more than a decade earlier, the poet had promised at the close of the *Vita nova* (on which more anon): 'and if my life is long enough, I hope to say things about her that have never been said about any woman' (XLII, 2 [31, 2]).

At the same time, especially after the broad sweep of the preceding canto, *Inferno* II offers a conspicuously lopsided, and hence problematic, account of the poet's career; and one that is likely to have struck his early Florentine readers – *Inferno*'s most immediate audience – as such. Virgil's presentation ends up by marginalizing, if not actually denying, most of what Dante had written after 1294, namely after he had completed the *Vita nova*. Yet, this was not poetry that could be easily dismissed. Indeed, some of the verses Dante composed during his last years in Florence had unmistakably 'public' ends, since they addressed ethical and doctrinal issues that had an obvious bearing on the civic life of his city. It was poetry, therefore, that was addressed to a broad audience and which neatly meshed with Dante's growing active involvement in Florentine politics. In addition, this poetry also recorded a crisis in the relationship between Beatrice and her lover as his interests began to move beyond her to embrace new moral and philosophical concerns, as well as alternative models of love and femininity, as embodied in the figures of the *donna petra*, the sensually cruel lady of stone, and the indifferent *pargoletta*, the young girl.

Dante's reflections on his artistic past in the opening *canti* of the *Commedia* are complex and perplexing, especially if they are meant to serve as an introduction to his protagonist and to his own career as a writer. Rather than straightforwardly tell a unified story of a poetic vocation, *Inferno* I and II suggest something rather more tortuous and tricky. Together, the cantos end up by both foregrounding and downplaying elements of a (lyric) literary itinerary that had been noteworthy for its range and originality: 'the novelty that is alight through your form [that of the canzone "Love you see well that this lady"], / a thing never conceived before at any time' (*Rime* 65–6). Yet, the fact that, in sketching the portrait of his younger Florentine artistic self, Dante characterizes himself exclusively as *scriba Beatricis* only at a second, albeit immediately contiguous, moment would suggest that he wants his readers to be in no doubt about the radical selection that he is making, while also ensuring that they do not forget the actual range of his poetic achievements. His apparently contradictory approach raises a host of challenging questions regarding his views about his past achievements – did some of them in fact not merit being 'honoured', as would appear to be the case with his exchange of scurrilous sonnets with Forese Donati which seems to be linked to the 'dark wood' in *Purgatorio* XXIII, 115–9? – and the nature of their import for the *Commedia*, where the 'comic-realist' expressionism of the *tenzone* with Forese is most decidedly at work. And yet these are questions that scholars have normally preferred to bypass or ignore.

The standard view maintains not only that Dante's treatment at the beginning of the *Commedia* is free of complications, and so that there is nothing especially challenging when he summons his literary past, but also that his aim is to indicate a largely seamless continuity between the poem and his earlier writings. In particular, the 'beautiful style' of *Inferno* I and the conjuring of the *Vita nova* in the following canto are treated independently, as if no ties might unite them or tensions separate them, a perspective that is reductive and counterintuitive, especially in an author as purposeful as Dante. It is thus customary to restrict the 'bello stilo' to unspecified 'moral and doctrinal' canzoni in line with the assumption that only these fall into the category of the 'tragic' 'high style', of which Virgil was deemed the supreme master and to which the phrase appears to allude – an astonishing claim given that most of what Dante wrote up to 1300, with the *Vita nova* clearly to the fore, belongs to this 'mode' of writing. Furthermore, the only work for which we have evidence that it did in fact bring 'honour' to Dante while he was still in Florence is in fact the *libello*. Equally delimitative is the deeply entrenched idea that, after the philosophical seductions of the 'gentle lady' of the *Convivio*, by restoring Beatrice to a position of prominence in the *Commedia*, the poem marks an orthodox and unproblematic return to the religious and erotic purview of the *Vita nova*, as well as to its core salvific concerns. The *Commedia* and the 'little book' thus resemble two paired panels of an artistic and ideological diptych that narratively explores the ties between God and humanity, as well as those linking human beings, by concentrating on the interactions between this world and the next, the universalizing setting common to both works. The *Commedia* thus describes the continuation of an experience whose effective beginnings are recorded not in its pages but in the *libello*. In simple terms, the poem's composition is crucially dependent on Dante returning to the vein that he had begun to mine in the *Vita nova*.

That the two major texts involving Beatrice ought to be considered together and that they are to a degree complementary is, in itself, unremark-able, as the stress granted to the 'woman of virtue' (donna di virtù; 76) in *Inferno* II makes obvious. Nevertheless, rather than merely indicating a comfortable co-existence between the *Vita nova* and the *Commedia*, the evidence, and not solely in the poem's opening, points to something more troubling and involved: yes, a degree of continuity between the two, but also signs of rift and disassociation. If, on the one hand, by alluding to Beatrice's eyes (55 and 116), beauty (53), and blessedness (53 and 124), Virgil's description is in keeping with her treatment in the *Vita nova*, on the other, the woman he meets could not be more different from her incarnation in the *libello*. Descending to Hell, which, tellingly, reverses her ascent to Paradise described in *Vita nova* XXIII [14], Beatrice is no longer a nebulous, passively humble, beautiful woman known only through her effects. She is instead a psychologically complex and authoritatively active individual – 'I am Beatrice who makes you go' (I' son Beatrice che ti faccio andare; 70) –

who, most strikingly, after being reduced to silence in the *libello*, speaks with a powerful and distinctive voice.

Dante underscores this vital difference by dedicating two lines to defining her voice (56–7). He also embeds her speeches within Virgil's discourse, while inserting Mary's and Lucy's words into hers, a highly recherché rhetorical construction that draws attention to the new loquacious Beatrice. Something has dramatically shifted in the interval between the promise made at the end of the *Vita nova* and the Spring of 1300. Moreover, Virgil's account leaves no doubt about the reasons for this crisis. Lucy asks a question which contains its own answer: 'Beatrice, true praise of God, why do you not succour him who [had once] loved you so much that he [had] left for you the vulgar crowd?' (Beatrice, loda di Dio vera, / ché non soccorri quei che t'amò tanto, / ch'uscì per te de la volgare schiera?; 103–5). The doom-laden finality of those two past historics – 'amò' and 'uscì' – which shockingly reveal that Dante-character had at some point stopped loving his *donna*, and hence had stopped writing about her, explains how and why he had ended up in the dark wood and why Beatrice can now only reach him through the good offices of a series of go-betweens. In light of what the pilgrim himself admits in *Inferno* I, it is possible to be more precise about the nature of his error: it is the poetry that he had composed on non-Beatrician themes that lies at the root of the problem. This verse may have brought him 'honour' in strictly earthly terms, but it had also dangerously separated him from his beloved, and hence from her divinely ordained salvific properties, thereby placing his soul at serious risk of eternal damnation. In this regard, by 'rejecting' his post-*Vita nova* writings, *Inferno* II does mark the return of the pilgrim and of the poet, and by extension of the *Commedia*, to Beatrice, and so to the *libello*. At the same time, the *beata*'s drastic transformation cannot but call into question any suggestion of a cosy relationship between the 'little book' and the *Commedia*. Things, on account of the protagonist's sinfulness, have changed irremediably, and so require a new start, whether moral or literary.

Indeed, already in the opening canto, the pilgrim deliberately distances himself from the poetry that he had composed after the *libello*. He conventionally and dutifully acknowledges Virgil's status as his culture's supreme authoritative poet; however, another past historic introduces an unexpected, albeit highly significant, personal admission: 'you [Virgil] are he alone from whom I took [*tolsi*] the beautiful style' (86–7). Dante recognizes that, in the past, he had 'imitated' Virgil's 'tragic' *stilus*, but that now the 'bello stilo' belongs to a literary experience that he has consciously left behind, and which, therefore, is inappropriate for the new poem that we have just begun to read.[4] Indeed, the implication is that realizing the inadequacy of the Virgilian 'manner' is in part connected to the pilgrim's 'coming to himself' (mi ritrovai; 2) in the 'savage wood' (selva selvaggia; 5). Yet, doesn't the *Vita nova* too belong to the 'high' register? How can Dante be rejecting the 'little book' at the very moment when, as the following canto appears to establish, he is returning to its divinely sanctioned concerns? It is certain that, as the reappearance of Beatrice corroborates, any misgivings cannot affect the *Vita nova*'s key ideological issues: salvation, the exemplary and providential nature of Beatrice's relationship to the protagonist, and her own miraculous status – all features that *Inferno* II explicitly affirms and restores as central to the pilgrim's life and otherworldly experience. The problem thus lies elsewhere. It must involve the *libello*'s status as literature, namely, its status as an instance of the 'bello stilo', which are, of course, the narrow terms in which the lost traveller introduces himself to Virgil.

In *Inferno* II, Beatrice is restored to Dante's poetry; however, she and her inconstant lover continue to remain far apart. It is only once the pilgrim has renounced sin, repented, and cleansed himself spiritually that, in the Earthly Paradise, he is fit to be reunited with her. Their reunion is not simply an acutely personal event, but also the moment when the *Commedia*, in the wake of *Inferno* II's intimations, is explicitly conjoined with the *Vita nova* – and, of course, Dantists treat this process too as unproblematic. Yet, there is little that is harmonious about their encounter, a state of affairs that cannot but have a bearing on the associations between the two Beatrician texts. In contrast to her former passivity, the woman is angry, incisive, and unrelentingly reproachful; while the pilgrim's shame and turmoil have little in common with his highly stylized emotionalism in the 'little book'. There is in fact nothing in the *Vita nova* that even remotely comes close to the tense, painful, complex drama of their otherworldly meeting. At the same time, nowhere in the *Commedia* is the *Vita nova* as insistently and overtly evoked as in *Purgatorio* XXX and XXXI. Beatrice thrice and at length refers to several of the *libello*'s key events (XXX, 109–35; XXXI, 22–30; and XXXI, 43–63), and even openly speaks of her lover's 'new life' (vita nova; XXX, 115). Most arrestingly, Beatrice's Edenic 'resurrection' calques aspects of the 'straying fantasy' (XXIII, 8 [14, 8]) of her death: angelic singers, angels associated with a cloud, and her being draped in a white veil. Yet, despite their connections, Beatrice's arrival in *Purgatorio* XXX represents a direct reversal of her departure, so that the *Commedia* absorbs, revises, and supersedes the *Vita nova*'s defining event. The canto and the one following are calculatedly constructed in opposition to chapter XXIII. For instance, Dante-character no longer sees dishevelled and terrifying faces, traditional harbingers of doom (XXIII, 4 [14, 4]), but 'ministers and messengers of eternal life' (ministri e messaggier di vita etterna; XXX, 18). More significantly, although in both episodes he feels shame (*Vn* XXIII, 13 and 19 [14, 13 and 19]; *Purg.* XXX, 78 and especially XXXI, 64) for having given credence to what was not real, the causes of the pilgrim's reaction could not be more different. In the former he is embarrassed because he has been tricked by a fantasy; in the latter he is deeply ashamed for having betrayed Beatrice by allowing himself to be taken in by 'deceptive things' (cose fallaci; XXXI, 56).

The pilgrim thus admits that he had not assimilated the exemplary lessons which he himself had presented in the *Vita nova*, a disturbing disclosure that suggests that the 'little book' may be flawed as a work of salvation. Indeed, it is Beatrice who most devastatingly criticizes it. Her three speeches depict a new version, which differs in key ways from the original, of the principal events portrayed in the *libello*. She rewrites the story of their relationship from her perspective – a view that is entirely absent in the *Vita nova* – and her main scope is to leave no doubt that Dante-character was solely responsible for failing to love her properly. He was not, as the 'little book' claims, a quasi-innocent at the mercy of forces stronger than himself – a situation that, revealingly, is reprised by Francesca in *Inferno* V. Nor did he just betray her once, as he had claimed in the *libello*; rather his infidelities were many and he wilfully ignored her interventions on his behalf (XXX, 133–5).

We are thus faced with two irreconcilable renderings of the same story, only one of which can be true. In acknowledging the 'truth' (vero; XXXI, 5) of Beatrice's account, the pilgrim confesses both to having offended his beloved and to having written bad, because dishonest, literature. This becomes especially apparent if one compares the *libello*'s treatment of the 'gentle lady' who distracted the grieving lover (XXXV–XXXVIII [24–7]) with Beatrice's reconsideration of the same event. In the *Vita nova*, the woman embodies an idealized portrait of 'gentleness' and 'compassion' (XXXV, 2–3 [24, 2–3]; and cp. XXXVI, 1–2 [25, 1–2]; XXXVIII, 1 [27, 1]). Conversely, Beatrice underscores her 'falsehood' (XXX, 130–2); she is a 'ditch' (*fossa*) and 'chain' (*catena*; XXXI, 25) preventing progress; she is a 'siren' (serena; 45) and a wounding 'blow' (*colpo*; 59). The 'gentle lady' is in fact the archetypal temptress. She is not, as Beatrice makes plain, her close companion, regardless of what the *Vita nova* had maintained. This is the nub of Beatrice's criticism of the *libello*: book and author lack a proper sense of discrimination. They dress up what is morally ugly as if it were a thing of beauty. By adopting the elegantly refined 'tragic' register, the *Vita nova* cannot deal with the complexity of existence. Most worryingly, it cannot deal with the intricacy and reality of evil. The 'bello stilo' is thus both morally and artistically flawed, and so, as the pilgrim announces at the very outset of his adventure, it needs to be rejected. Tellingly, in Eden, Beatrice speaks in a manner that is diametrically opposite to the 'beautiful style'. She employs a wide-ranging, Scripturally laced, 'comic' register heavily dependent on concrete, practical imagery, thereby offering the poet a plurilingual and 'realistic' model that he can 'imitate' when composing the *Commedia*.

As is normal, Dante's trenchant critique of his earlier writing, as with his delimiting assessments of the works of other writers, is aimed at vindicating the *Commedia* and establishing its literary uniqueness. Returning to Beatrice was ideologically the correct choice to make. However, returning to the style of the *Vita nova* was not an option. Dante makes clear what was both good and bad about the *libello* and the verses that he had written for Beatrice. In addition, the various erotic lyric registers that he had employed to speak of her, despite their limitations, were important stages in his arriving at the 'totalizing' style of the *Commedia*, hence their return at various points in the poem, yet always 'corrected' by being integrated with other languages and genres. Equally, if, on the one hand, what Dante had written after 1294/5 was morally problematic and a betrayal of Beatrice, on the other, the rich formal experience of this verse, as with what he had written up to and including the *Vita nova*, constituted a vital prerequisite for composing the *Commedia* – hence the reason why, at the start of the poem, he alludes to his full artistic career in Florence, while also discriminating between its different moments. With characteristic brevity and nuance, Dante evaluates his past and points to his future as both a man and a poet.

Convivio, what Convivio?

The textual tension that Dante scholarship generally perceives as underpinning Beatrice's criticism of the pilgrim's past behaviour is centred not on the *Commedia*'s relationship to the *Vita nova* but on that to the *Convivio*. To put it simply, his betrayal is equated with his having abandoned Beatrice for Lady Philosophy as embodied by the 'gentle lady', and hence theology for secular thought. The 'almost commentary' (*Conv*. I, iii, 2) thus confirms that, as Beatrice charges, Dante had followed the erroneous 'doctrine' (dottrina; *Purg*. XXXIII, 86) of an earthbound 'school' (scuola; 85). There are three main drawbacks with this position. First, the extent to which the *Convivio* is actually ideologically unorthodox is to say the least questionable. Second, and more germane for the present discussion, introducing *Convivio* into the *Commedia*'s diegesis is invalid. As every reader of the poem knows, Dante-character's 'voyage' (viaggio; *Inf*. I, 91) takes place during the Spring of 1300. Consequently, the *Convivio*, which was probably written between 1303 and 1306/7, must lie outside the poem's narrative ambit, since, at the time of the pilgrim's otherworldly adventure, it did not exist. Thus, if we are to respect the narrative logic of the fictional world created by Dante, when Beatrice levies her charges, it is not possible to equate *Convivio* with the 'bad seed' (mal seme; *Purg.* XXX, 119) which causes the pilgrim to weep bitter tears of contrition. Moreover, if we are to defer to the *Commedia*'s 'letter' and to Dante's fundamental desire to ground his story in history (and if we start tampering with the poem's 'literal sense', we then create a host of problems for its allegorical status ...), we need to seek for 'errors' (error*i*; XXXI, 44), as both the *Commedia*'s opening and the Earthly Paradise verify, that belong to the years 1290–1300. The text of the poem is transparent on this point. All Beatrice's attacks against her lover unambiguously refer to a time before their present meeting. Verb tenses – like the voice of God – do not lie.

Finally, and just as crucially, in light of the manuscript evidence, it is almost certain that Dante had no intention of making *Convivio* public, thereby, raising extremely serious questions regarding the work's status in relation to the *Commedia*. This does not mean that we cannot have recourse to the 'exposition' (*Conv.* I, ii, 1) when endeavouring to understand aspects of and shifts in Dante's thought in the poem, or to establish his intellectual formation and sympathies in the years immediately after his exile, and hence evaluate *Convivio* as 'preparatory' for the *Commedia*; and I shall return to this issue in due course. At the same time, what is almost certainly not legitimate is to claim that, from within the poem, Dante expects us to recognize that he is actively dialoguing with his unfinished and abandoned commentary either at the narrative level or through other allusive strategies. Thus, if we identify, as is actually possible, borrowings from the *Convivio* in the linguistic make-up of the poem, how should we react to these? If we are not meant to perceive them as quotations, we should note them, consider them in light of the *Commedia*'s composition, and then, as Virgil urges his ward to do as they travel through the afterlife, move on.

Lyric Autocitation

Dantists, however, have rather too often been doggedly reluctant to move on. Indeed, they have asserted that, in the *Commedia*, the poet is publicly recanting, or at best revising, views that he had expressed in the *Convivio* as a means to avowing the poem's and his own re-found ideological and sentimental orthodoxy – a perspective that especially in North American scholarship is termed Dante's 'palinodic' approach to his past errors. One episode in particular is deemed emblematically to capture this process. Soon after their arrival in Purgatory, the two travellers meet a group of souls who have just landed on its shores, among whom is the Florentine musician Casella, a long-time friend of the poet's. The pilgrim invites Casella to sing. In response, the latter intones one of Dante's post-*Vita nova*, and hence post-Beatrice, *canzoni*, 'Amor che ne la mente mi ragiona' (Love that discourses to me in my mind; *Purg.* II, 112). All the listeners are mesmerized by the 'sweetness' (dolcezza; 114) of the singing and can think of nothing else (117), until their reverie is broken by Cato's timely attack on their 'negligence' (negligenza; 121) for not hurrying to begin their atonement. The standard view is that, beyond its immediate narrative context, Cato's criticism is a considered rejection of the *Convivio*, where the canzone takes pride of place in the third book. Indeed, his censure increases in consequence when it is linked to the souls' earlier communal singing of Psalm 113 (46–7). The sacred song offers a model of spiritually appropriate writing in contrast to the intellectual and religious deficiencies of *Convivio* and 'Amor che ne la mente'. A not dissimilar argument is proposed for the presence in *Paradiso* VIII of the opening line of another of the *canzoni* included in *Convivio*, 'Voi che 'ntendendo il terzo ciel movete' (You who by understanding move the third heaven; 37). In book II, where the poem is analysed, Dante associates the heaven of Venus with the angelic order of the Thrones, while, in the final canticle, he links it to that of the 'celestial princes [Principalities]' (principi celesti; 34). The change is viewed as another deliberate correction and open dismissal of *Convivio*. Yet, if the 'almost commentary' lies squarely outside the *Commedia*'s remit, then, the palinodic explanation normally put forward for Dante citing himself is necessarily inadequate.

It is striking that, when he quotes himself, the poet should make recourse to three of his *canzoni* – the third, 'Donne ch'avete intelletto d'Amore' (Ladies who have intelligence of Love), appears in *Purgatorio* XXIV, 51. According to medieval literary theory, the canzone represented the most sophisticated metrical form, and hence the most 'honourable' poetry that Dante had composed prior to the *Commedia*. More significantly, the three autocitations integrate neatly with the poet's ongoing assessment of his lyric career, which is the key feature of his engagement with his artistic past in the poem. The quotations thus ought to be evaluated from this same perspective, while also being considered in light of their placement in the *Commedia* and as comprising a single system. And that the *canzoni* do indeed constitute such a structure is apparent from the fact that each is connected to an expressly autobiographical moment, which permits Dante to grant historical substance to the idealized account that he was constructing of his path to the *Commedia*. In addition, each marks an important, though not necessarily positive, new stage in this development.

'Amor che ne la mente' is a poem that determinedly declares its author's love for a new woman who is not Beatrice. It thus offers the first concrete proof in the *Commedia* of what had caused the poet's alienation from Beatrice and of the kind of poetry that, at the beginning of *Inferno*, he had suggested was problematic, and hence had decided to forswear. On the one hand, by introducing the canzone, Dante fittingly, albeit indirectly, recognizes and confesses his earlier fault, the necessary prerequisite for embarking on his purgatorial journey. On the other hand, however, Casella's decision to recite that same poem of betrayal 'to console' (consolare; 109) his friend as he is about to set out on a spiritually cleansing experience that will lead him back to Beatrice is jarringly inappropriate. Casella's mistake and his listeners' total absorption in the song points to the seductiveness of sin and how far the pilgrim and his fellow-penitents are still from their final goal of spiritual purity. Cato is absolutely right to stress that the canzone, whether seen in terms of Dante's life and poetic career or of the souls' behaviour, is 'the slough that doesn't allow God to be made manifest to you' (lo scoglio / ch'esser non lascia a voi Dio manifesto; 122–3). The poem is deficient both in its content – it is the record of an abandonment and a major moral transgression – and in its form, given that its 'sweetness', an archetypal characteristic of the vernacular love lyric, is the source of sinful distraction. What makes Dante's error especially pernicious is that the new woman is presented as if she were Beatrice – most troublingly when the poet announces that 'In her aspect things appear that show the joys of Paradise' (55–6) – and is celebrated in the same style that he had employed to praise his rightfully divine beloved. Furthermore, the evocation of Psalm 113 is a reminder that, in the canzone, the poet had regularly misapplied Scriptural references and religious language.

His past lack of discrimination is shocking; but it also points to the flaw at the heart of love poetry, especially that composed in the 'beautiful style', namely, its inability properly to discriminate between different objects of desire, as Virgil explains in *Purgatorio* XVII–XVIII. 'Amor che ne la mente' thus prepares for Beatrice's denunciations in Eden. Ultimately, what emerges from Dante's reconsideration of his canzone in *Purgatorio* II is that, however much 'Love that discourses' might mark a new development in his personal and literary career, not all novelty is necessarily positive. It is only the exceptional *Commedia*, which can suitably imitate biblical *sermo humilis* while originally integrating this with other literary registers, including the lyric, and which succeeds in replicating Scripture's salvific ends, that is able to make 'God manifest'.

'Voi che 'ntendendo', too, stresses its novelty (3 and 10); however, once more, its *novitas* is morally and artistically dangerous. The canzone records the start of the process that will lead to 'Amor che ne la mente', since it tells, again in the 'high style', of the struggle in the lover's heart between Beatrice and the new woman, whose victory, not least because she is inappropriately sacralized, is pretty much assured by the end of the fourth stanza. The flaws of 'You who by understanding' are the same as the ones that damn 'Love that discourses'; and, as occurs with the latter, so the former too is contrasted to a biblical and liturgical song: 'and among those [the blessed] that appeared in front sounded a *"Hosanna"'* (e dentro a quei che più innanzi appariro / sonava *'Osanna'*; *Par.* VIII, 28–9). In addition, given the canzone's close ties to *Vita nova*'s last sonnet, it also highlights the almost immediate failure of the *libello*. Lines 14–19 and 27–9 reprise the situation described in 'Beyond the sphere' (*Vn* XLI, 10–13 [30, 10–13]) of the poet's sigh rising up to Paradise to gaze on Beatrice in her glory. Now, however, the poet's 'gentle thought' (l. 15) is overwhelmed by the appearance of another woman. 'Voi che 'ntendendo' is not primarily an account of an erotic duplicity, but of how good love turns to bad. The lover's behaviour thus stands in contrast to the actions of the blessed in Venus, who, after indulging in sinful passions, managed to redirect their love to pious ends. Fortunately, like them, by asserting the necessary spiritual and intellectual control over his love, which, as the canzone documents, he had been unable to achieve in the aftermath of Beatrice's demise, Dante too, as the *Commedia* recounts, was subsequently able to find a way to return to his beloved. Thus, *Paradiso* VIII reverses the key moment of 'Voi che 'ntendendo': rather than his eyes focusing on the wrong woman (33–9) – a standard trope for the act of falling in love – the pilgrim's 'eyes … *are* offered in reverence' (occhi … si *sono* offerti … reverenti; 40–1) to Beatrice.

The incipit of 'Voi che 'ntendendo' is intoned by Charles Martel, the Angevin heir to the thrones of Hungary, Provence, and Naples, whom Dante supposedly met in Florence in 1294. Charles makes clear that their relationship represented the type of right loving that the poet ought to have pursued after Beatrice's death (55–7), a point which Casella had already articulated (*Purg.* II, 88–90). An altruistic poetry dedicated to friendship would not have led Dante astray. Yet, he was morally and intellectually too weak to sustain such relationships. Again employing an irrefutably instructive past historic – 'm'amasti' (*Par.* VIII, 55) – Charles makes evident that the poet 'had loved' him but had then ceased doing so. Instead, like 'the ancients peoples in their ancient error' (le genti antiche ne l'antico errore; 6), who expressed their mistakes about love in the 'high style' – Dante alludes to Virgil's *Aeneid* in line 9 – the poet had gone on to compose a deeply flawed 'tragic' canzone about the effects on him of uncontrollable 'mad love' (folle amore; 2). In the *Commedia*, Dante's judgement on 'Voi che 'ntendendo' is definitive and bleak. Contrary to what some scholars have claimed, the fact that the canzone is cited in Paradise does not mean that it takes on positive hues – the opposite is in fact true.

Only 'Donne ch'avete' escapes, and then up to a point, the kind of stern judgement with which Dante censures his other two *canzoni*. The Lucchese poet Bonagiunta degli Orbicciani cites the poem as the defining highpoint of the pilgrim's literary career up to Spring 1300: 'But say if I see here him who brought forth the new rhymes, beginning "Ladies who have intelligence of Love"' (Ma dì s'i' veggio qui colui che fore / trasse le nove rime, cominciando / 'Donne ch'avete intelletto d'amore'; *Purg.* XXIV, 49–51).[5] Bonagiunta's appreciation involves not just the canzone in itself, but also its status as the *Vita nova*'s defining and emblematic text (*Vn* XVIII–XIX [10, 3–33]) – the text in which Dante had established the new 'praise style' (stilo de la ... loda; XXVI, 4 [17, 4]) through which he celebrated in a selfless manner, akin to the tribute that ought to be directed towards God, his love for Beatrice. 'Donne ch'avete' confirms that, at his best, Dante was an innovative and refined poet who deserved, as Bonagiunta acknowledges, to be honoured, not least because he had succeeded in introducing a salvific Christian dimension into the love lyric. In this regard, given the canzone's religious impetus, it is no coincidence that no sacred song is intoned in *Purgatorio* XXIV. By equally emphasizing Beatrice, salvation, and correct loving, the *Commedia* accepts and augments the ideological and providential purview of the canzone and the *libello*. Conversely, it categorically rejects their stylistic, and hence representational, solutions. In strictly literary terms, 'Donne ch'avete' is indistinguishable from the two erroneous *canzoni*, a defect that results in Beatrice being identical to the temptress. This is why the repentant pilgrim refuses to allow himself to be defined in terms of 'Ladies who have intelligence', but instead portrays himself – his insistent use of the present tense reiterates the point – as now a divinely inspired writer, the future author of the *Commedia*, who, with due discrimination, appropriately verbalizes what God reveals: 'I am one who, when Love breathes into me, take note, and in the manner that He dictates within go on to grant it form' (I' mi son un che, quando / Amor mi spira, noto, e a quel modo / ch'e' ditta dentro vo significando; 52–4).

It is obvious that, when, in the *Commedia*, Dante reconsiders his previous career as a writer, his intent is to present himself essentially as a lyric love poet, and to categorize the 'sacred poem' and himself in light of and as a departure from this tradition and experience. If Dante had wanted to achieve a different or a more varied focus, then, he could have cited one or more of his openly doctrinal *canzoni*. Strictly doctrinal elements are at best marginal in the three unashamedly erotic poems that he did quote; and this fact in itself affirms how inappropriate it is, when analysing their function in the *Commedia*, to deflect attention on to the *Convivio* and to 'over-philosophize' the poet's treatment of his past. His perspective is determinedly literary. Equally, his assessment is overarching and absolute, as is evident from the fact that the order in which he introduces the *canzoni* is not chronological but exemplary, as well as subordinate to the needs of the *Commedia*. Through his selection, Dante exemplifies the best and the worst, in moral terms, of his earlier poetry, as well as the transition from the former to the latter, while also underscoring their common reliance on the 'beautiful style'.

As regards his other lyric stylistic experiences, Dante alludes to them in less direct ways. For instance, his scurrilous, linguistically heterogenous, and syntactically involved sonnet exchange in the 'low style' with Forese Donati lies behind his meeting with his friend in *Purgatorio* XXIII and the bitter recriminations Sinon and master Adam launch against each other in *Inferno* XXX. Similarly, the experimental, rhetorically rich, and intellectually complex *petrose* poems for the 'stony-hearted' lady are discernible in the evocation of the petrifying Gorgon Medusa in *Inferno* IX and in some of Beatrice's condemnatory stylistic choices and accusations that characterize her Edenic diatribe. In illustrating the *Commedia*'s providentially sanctioned uniqueness, Dante presents a clear-sighted assessment of his literary past – a past whose limitations are many but which, nonetheless, had succeeded in establishing, albeit briefly, the potential of the relationship between salvation and literature, and which did offer, on account of its stylistic eclecticism, the first intimations of the *Commedia*'s all-embracing plurilingualism. Yet, however harshly Dante may have judged his lyric writings, the fact remains that, in the *Commedia*, he only cites directly three textual traditions: the Bible, the *Aeneid*, and his own *canzoni*. Yes, his verses are deficient when evaluated against the 'sacred poem'; however, they still deserve to be treated on a par with what is best in literature, so that, together with their two illustrious predecessors, they can serve as the principal pillars on which Dante constructed his unparalleled masterpiece.

The Other 'Other Works'

Although, as with *Convivio*, *De vulgari eloquentia* is unfinished and has a manuscript transmission that raises questions about whether or not Dante actually intended to make it public, there are nonetheless elements in the treatise and in the *Commedia* that suggest that the poet may have wanted to establish a discernible contrastive dialogue between the two works. In terms of medieval poetics, *De vulgari* is Dante's most conservative work. The idea of literature that it propounds is exceedingly codified and artificial, being based on a rigid application of the doctrine of three distinct literary 'styles' (the so-called theory of the *genera dicendi*, the highly popular 'modes of speech'). More than anything, the treatise concentrates on the 'tragic' 'high style' as applied to the canzone. Yet, in its last paragraph (II, xiv, 2), and without any prior preparation, *De vulgari* exposes the limitations of the *genera* for defining literature, and instead alludes to a different, more flexible system: 'everything we touch upon in poetry can be treated either positively or negatively'. By presenting literature in broad ethical terms, Dante undermined the idea that the three *stili* cannot share the same subject matter; that they cannot cross-fertilize each other; that literature is made up of neatly packaged segments; and that any single categorization can exhaust its possibilities.

Just as significantly, he rejected the notion that the 'illustrious vernacular' – the constructed and refined supraregional form of Italian that lies at the core of *De vulgari* – was the language best suited for poetry. Dante's critique of the doctrine of the *genera*, and of the elegant 'high style' in particular, chimes with his criticisms in the *Commedia* of his *canzoni* – the vernacular embodiment of the 'tragic' register – and of his pre-1300 lyric verse generally. However faintly, in the final brief paragraph of *De vulgari*, Dante was starting to trace the first lines of the eclectic 'comic' plurilingualism of his great poem. It is the startling manner in which this unsettling digression is introduced and the fact that the treatise is then dramatically abandoned in mid sentence that imply a calculated operation, one of whose functions might be to create a meaningful link with the *Commedia*. In this respect, when Dante concludes *Inferno* XX, one of the most classicizing, and hence 'high', cantos, with the adverb *introcque* – 'He thus spoke to me, and in the meantime we were walking on' (Sì mi parlava, e andavamo introcque; 130) – a Florentine colloquialism condemned for its crudity in *De vulgari* (I, xiii, 2), it is tempting to conclude that, once again, he was intentionally highlighting the distance between his old and new poetics.

Equally, having Adam explain that the language he spoke was not God-given but fashioned by himself, and so perishable (*Par.* XXVI, 124–32), a view that directly challenges what is stated in *Dve* I, vii, 4–7, has antithetically illustrative implications. The 'illustrious vernacular' was meant to 'imitate' Hebrew's original universalism, thereby in part rectifying the destructive effects of Babel's linguistic fragmentation. To vindicate his use of the vernacular in the *Commedia* as a medium for undertaking a task of universal and providential import, Dante has Adam assert the corruptibility of all language. Furthermore, by employing the vernacular rather than an artificial elitist language like Latin or the *vulgaris illustris*, the poet ensured that, in theory at least, he was 'speaking' to everyone about salvation in the type of language that was natural to all of them. Even if Dante had not intended that readers of the *Commedia* be aware of *De vulgari*, recognizing the radical implications of the shift documented in the treatise's close, allows us to appreciate one of the key moments that prepare for the composition of the 'sacred poem'.

I focus on the *Commedia*'s genesis in the following subsection. However, before that, a rapid glance at the works that Dante penned once he had started writing the poem. Given the *Commedia*'s divinely sanctioned reformist and plurilingual ends, its status was absolute. Everything else Dante wrote after 1306/7, still the most convincing date for the start of the poem, was necessarily subordinate to and at the service of the *Commedia*. While the texts Dante composed before beginning the poem are wholly self-sufficient, it is difficult to contend the same for *Monarchia*,[6] the eclogues (1319–21), and the *Questio* (1320),[7] which, while they can certainly be read autonomously, and recently scholars have justifiably insisted on this point, were also written with the *Commedia* in mind. In light of the poem's acute experimentation and its radical ideological claims, it was an immediate source of controversy. It is therefore no coincidence that it should be the *Commedia*'s most debatable features which are addressed in the 'other works' that Dante composed towards the end of his life. Thus, the eclogues offer a response to the criticism of the poem's language and form expressed in two Latin poems by Giovanni del Virgilio, a professor of rhetoric at the University of Bologna, while revealing a mature mastery of classical genre and Virgil's oeuvre. *Monarchia* offers a defence of the *Commedia*'s views of history, politics, semiotics, and Scriptural interpretation. Finally, the *Questio* confirms the range of Dante's philosophical, scientific, and theological knowledge, and hence asserts the legitimacy of the poem's doctrinal ambitions. It is precisely because these texts play a *post factum* explicatory role in relation to the *Commedia* that Dante does not evoke them in the poem.

Genesis and Dating

With its tightly organized structure, the *Commedia* has the appearance of a text under strict authorial control. Yet, this impression runs counter to what we can (hypothetically) reconstruct about the poem's genesis, formation, and composition. Thus, its coming into being was laborious and problematic. It is enough to recall that Dante spent the last fifteen or so years of his life mostly writing a poem of less than 15,000 lines. In any case, it is probably misleading to think of the *Commedia*'s genesis and formation in relation only to those years. Around 1294, in the *Vita nova*'s close, Dante declared that he was actively 'studying' so as to be able to write a new work 'worthy' of the 'blessed' Beatrice (XLII, 1–2 [31, 1–2]). Such a text could not but have had an eschatological theme; indeed, given its sacred subject, it is not unlikely that it would have been limited to a vision of Heaven. Regardless of this, as I have already adumbrated, the final chapter of the *libello* can be considered as the first trace of the *Commedia* in Dante's oeuvre. It is impossible, however, to establish when Dante decided to broaden his perspective to include all three realms of the afterlife. Nonetheless, it is suggestive that, in his life of Dante, Boccaccio should report that the poet composed the first seven cantos of *Inferno* while still in Florence, and thus before his exile in late 1301. Indeed, Boccaccio notes that evidence for the 'double beginning' of the *Commedia* is present in the momentous phrase 'I say, continuing' (Io dico, seguitando) with which *Inferno* VIII opens.[8]

While no philological evidence exists to support the idea of a Florentine version of the poem, the opening cantos do offer some traces of discrepancies between them and the remainder of the canticle: for instance, they bear the likely imprint of an earlier moral organization based on the seven capital vices rather than on the Aristotelian-Ciceronian system that largely structures Dante's Hell. Furthermore, according to a fourteenth-century apochryphal letter supposedly written by a friar Ilaro, Dante's original idea had been to write a poem about the afterlife in Latin, which, on the basis of the lines that are quoted from this mysterious text, would very likely have been restricted to Paradise – a scope that fits rather well with the close of the *libello*.[9]

Whatever the validity of such claims – and they ought to be treated with caution – they do hint at the tremendous effort that lay behind the writing of the *Commedia*, and at the not inconceivable possibility that, before beginning to compose the version of the poem that we read today, Dante may have been experimenting both linguistically and with the genre of otherworldly visions and voyages. On account of its all-embracing aspirations, the *Commedia* is dramatically different from any other extant work belonging to this literary tradition, and, thankfully, some evidence exists of how Dante arrived at composing a new type of 'encyclopaedic' eschatological poem.

Scholars generally acknowledge that the early years of his exile had a fundamental impact on Dante's thinking. They significantly broadened his intellectual interests – an intellectual revolution that touched every area of his experience and knowledge. Most significantly, it granted him that acute awareness of existence as richly varied and divinely ordered which is at the core of the *Commedia*'s universalizing poetic and ideological purview. Thanks largely to *Convivio* and *De vulgari*, we are able to track how this vital shift occurred and how Dante first developed some of the poem's key components. For instance, both works confirm that the poet ceased to focus his attention essentially on Florence, and instead started to consider the national and international ramifications of contemporary politics, while complementing this change of perspective with an increasingly sophisticated ethical, philosophical, and religious vision. Especially in book IV of the *Convivio*, Dante began to develop a providential model of society that envisaged the world peacefully and justly ruled by an emperor (iv–v). Indeed, according to Dante, Rome confirmed the sacred character and reality of a universal monarchy (iv, 10–13; v, 4), not least because its history had been divinely ordained (v, 4–20).

Concurrently, the poet was also developing a sense of his own key role in God's plans for humanity (v, 2), an awareness that also signified a return to the *Vita nova*'s claims that his life was exemplary, except that now Dante no longer restricted his attention to love nor wrote exclusively for an elite audience. At the same time, his views on literature and language were changing too, as the close of the *De vulgari* documents, while chapters xxiv–xxviii of book IV of the *Convivio* reveal that Dante had acquired a much fuller understanding of classical epic literature, beginning with Virgil and the *Aeneid*. In general, what is most striking about Dante's new way of thinking is its synthesizing force. *Convivio* and *De vulgari* offer an excellent idea of how the poet attempted to integrate literature, philosophy, theology, exegesis, science, linguistics, cosmology, ethics, history, autobiography, etc. into a single overarching textual system that would be accessible to an ever larger audience. However, neither work, for all their fundamental transitional functions, could formally accommodate the ambition of Dante's thinking. The poet was thus faced with the conundrum of finding a literary form that could encompass the all-embracing range of his ideas and sense of the vibrancy of reality. Given the segregated character of medieval literature as evidenced by the theory of the discrete 'styles', no obvious genre existed that could satisfactorily include Dante's new intellectual, moral, and literary ambitions. It was only when he decided to go against established literary convention and grasped the possibilities that mingling the *genera* and drawing on the full resources of his native language could offer that Dante was ready to commence the *Commedia*.

Most scholars today, despite several recent alternative proposals, continue to concur that Dante began the *Inferno* in 1306–7 and the *Purgatorio* in 1308–9. It is not unlikely that he revised the former between 1312–14 and the latter around 1314–15, circulating the *Inferno* in 1314 and the *Purgatorio* in 1315–16, which would mean that the *Paradiso* was written between 1315–16 and 1321.

In the Empyrean, as Beatrice is about to hand over responsibility for the pilgrim to St Bernard, the poet makes a last remarkable claim about his literary career. He declares that 'From the first day I saw her face in this life, until this vision, the pursuit [of depicting Beatrice] in my song has not been interrupted' (Dal primo giorno ch'i' vidi il suo viso / in questa vita, infino a questa vista, / non m'è il seguire al mio cantar preciso'; *Par.* XXX,

28–30). What he says is untrue, as even the account of his artistic development in the *Commedia* makes clear. As he had done in the opening cantos of *Inferno*, at the end of the poem, Dante stresses his dedication to Beatrice while implicitly recalling his non-Beatrician writings. His aim, once more, is to elucidate the *Commedia*'s uniqueness not simply in light of the rest of his oeuvre, but of literature in general: his poem surpasses any previous literary endeavour, going beyond what any author has had to depict – and Beatrice stands as the emblem of his own and the *Commedia*'s singularity (13–27). In the poem, the 'other works' and the historical realities of Dante's career are entirely bent to its needs, an operation that ought to be judged on its own terms and not used as the basis for evaluating the works in themselves. It should never be forgotten that, if Dante had never written the *Commedia*, his inappropriately labelled 'minor' works, many of which constitute substantial new departures in the Western literary canon, would have been more than enough to ensure his fame. Yet, from within the all-encompassing 'absolute' logic of the 'sacred poem' either they do not merit so much as a mention or they are ruthlessly criticized. As Beatrice makes the pilgrim and us aware, the path of the *Vita nova* leads to the 'dark wood', while that of the *Commedia* truly leads to a 'new life'.[10]

Notes

1. This chapter does not offer a critical evaluation of the 'other works'. Its interconnected aims are to examine the presence and relevance of the remainder of Dante's oeuvre in the *Commedia*; to offer a brief account of the poem's genesis and composition; and to discuss its dating.
2. All translations are my own.
3. Dante's designation of the *Vita nova* as a 'little book' is both a literal description of its length and a form of authorial modesty. The *libello* is in reality a work of extraordinary cultural, poetic, and ideological complexity, a worthy precursor of the *Commedia*.
4. As these are matters that largely lie beyond the remit of the present chapter, I am unable to address why, perplexingly, Dante should celebrate Virgil and, from the very start of *Inferno* I, formally display his debts to the *Aeneid*, while concurrently revealing that the Latin poet – or at least his 'beautiful style' – cannot guide him in composing the *Commedia*.
5. The meeting between the two poets is among the most complex and debated episodes in the *Commedia*, ranging from autobiography to literary history and from the status of the poem to prophecy. My discussion here, by concentrating on the canzone's function as a self-citation, necessarily omits most of what is fascinating about the encounter on the terrace of gluttony. In particular, I avoid addressing the question of the nature, range, and worth of the so-called 'sweet new style' (dolce stil novo; *Purg.* XXIV, 57), although any criticism of 'Donne ch'avete' cannot but affect this too.

6. The dating of the *Monarchia* is controversial. Indeed, some have maintained that it was composed before the *Commedia*. However, most scholars agree that Dante wrote it while he was penning the poem, either in 1312–13 or more likely in 1317–18.

7. On account of the continuing disagreements about their authenticity, I do not consider the so-called Epistle to Cangrande nor the early *Fiore* and *Detto d'amore* (1286–7).

8. See G. Boccaccio, *Trattatello in laude di Dante*, ed. P. G. Ricci (Milan: Mondadori, 1974), pp. 423–538 (paragraphs 179–82).

9. See H. W. Storey and B. Arduini, 'Edizione diplomatico-interpretativa della lettera di frate Ilaro (Laur. XXIX 8, c. 67r)', *Dante Studies*, 124 (2006), 77–89.

10. I should like to thank Annalisa Cipollone and Laurence Hooper for allowing me to read sections of their forthcoming books. I am also grateful to Ted Cachey, Ambrogio Camozzi, Simon Gilson, Claire Honess, Tristan Kay, Paola Nasti, and Lino Pertile for their comments on earlier versions of this chapter.

14

PRUE SHAW

Transmission History

Nothing written in Dante's own hand has survived. Our knowledge of his masterpiece comes from the more than eight hundred extant manuscript copies of the *Commedia*: the richest manuscript tradition for any medieval vernacular work. (There are six hundred or so complete copies of the poem; another two hundred contain just one *cantica* or are otherwise incomplete.) For purposes of comparison, around eighty manuscripts survive of the *Canterbury Tales* (*c.*1387–1400), around two hundred of the *Roman de la rose* (*c.*1230 and 1275), both works hugely popular in their time. The *Commedia* was the medieval equivalent of a runaway best-seller. The very high number of surviving copies is comparable to a modern print-run of many millions; the wastage rate – the percentage of copies which do not survive – has been calculated at between 80 and 90 per cent. The textual scholar working on the transmission history of the poem shares the same goal – to restore a text as close as possible to the author's original – as scholars working on other medieval vernacular texts, and has the same need for a sound method for evaluating the available evidence. But the sheer scale of the task facing an editor of the *Commedia* makes it a unique case.

Eight hundred copies of the poem, no two of them identical. How do we work back from the surviving evidence to Dante's lost original, or something as close to that original as our scholarly expertise and acumen allow? In this chapter, I attempt to set out the problem, to outline the history of engagement with it over the course of seven centuries, and to describe the current state of play in this area of Dante scholarship.

The transmission of a text is a process that occurs over time: we can usefully start with some dates. Dante died in 1321. The oldest securely dated manuscript of the *Commedia*, the Landiano manuscript (La) now in the Biblioteca Comunale of Piacenza, dates from 1336.[1] There is a tantalizing fifteen-year interval in which there was an explosion of interest in the poem but no copies of it survive. A proliferation of commentaries and glosses in these years throws much light on matters of fact and interpretation, but in the absence of copies of the poem itself, our knowledge of its transmission history in these crucial missing early years is of necessity indirect or speculative.

No fewer than five commentaries on the poem were written in this fifteen-year interval. The poet's youngest son Jacopo composed a sketchy one within six months of his father's death, in early 1322. Two Bolognese intellectuals, Graziolo Bambaglioli and Iacomo della Lana, quickly followed. Graziolo's Latin commentary on *Inferno* dates from 1324; Lana's extensive vernacular commentary on the whole poem was composed between 1324 and 1328. Early in the next decade the Carmelite friar Guido da Pisa wrote a Latin commentary on *Inferno* whose first draft is pre-1333; and the anonymous Florentine author of the *Ottimo commento* on the whole poem was working around 1334. (The conventional title of this commentary reflects the seal of approval later accorded it by the Accademia della Crusca for the excellence of its content and the quality of its vernacular language). There are smaller collections of glosses on *Inferno*, the so-called *Chiose palatine*, composed between 1325 and 1333; and those conventionally attributed to an *Anonimo lombardo*, whose initiator was working before 1326. Collectively these commentaries and glosses give glimpses into the earliest phase of the *Commedia*'s transmission history, showing that there were already errors and variant readings in circulation, and that alert copyists and commentators were well aware of this and were anxious (like any modern editor) to present the best possible text.

Jacopo's *Chiose* give us our first documented case of a corrupt reading. At *Inferno* XXVII, 54, the line 'tra tirannia si vive e stato franco' is glossed by Jacopo as though it read *si vive in stato franco*. But Dante is telling Guido da Montefeltro that Cesena is in a politically intermediate state 'between tyranny and liberty', not a city 'in a state of liberty' – a clear error. The process of textual degeneration in the *Commedia* almost certainly predates Dante's death for those portions of the poem already released to the public (*Inferno* 1314, *Purgatorio* 1315–16; some scholars believe smaller groups of *canti* were released earlier in batches as composition progressed).

Dante's older son Pietro, in his thoughtful commentary begun twenty years after his father's death, alerts us to an error widely in circulation when he paraphrases the line 'ma chi parlava ad ire parea mosso' (but the person who spoke seemed moved to going; *Inf.* XXIV, 69): 'the person who spoke seemed moved, don't say "to anger", as many texts say wrongly, but say "to go", that is, in motion'. Many texts have the corrupt reading *ad ira* (to anger); the correct reading, he says, is *ad ire* (to go). The two readings are equally plausible in context. This, in a nutshell, is the problem: two possible

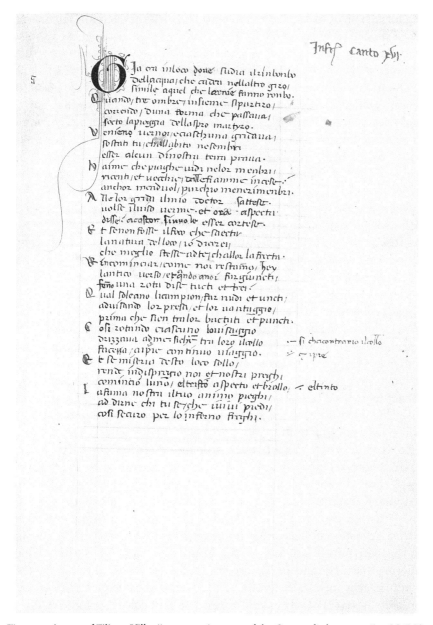

Figure 4. A page of Filippo Villani's manuscript copy of the *Commedia* known as LauSC (MS, Florence, Biblioteca Medicea Laurenziana, Pl. 26, sin. 1), showing a heavily worked-over text. For a full account of the interventions of the correcting hands here, see the *Commedia* DVD-Rom and follow the links > Editorial Material > IV. Ms Transcription Notes > LauSC. By permission of the Ministero per i Beni culturali e ambientali.

readings, both of which make perfect sense. What do we think Dante wrote? Most modern scholars think *ad ire* to be the better reading, even though, remarkably, it is not known from any early surviving manuscript – a striking instance of the value of the commentary tradition for the textual scholar.

Questions of this kind arise over the whole 14,233 lines of the poem. But why is textual corruption in manuscript traditions omnipresent? For our purposes anything which alters the words Dante wrote counts as corruption (a more neutral term would be scribal innovation). Where do these alternative or competing readings come from? There is no evidence of authorial variants for the *Commedia*, though such variants have sometimes been hypothesized.

Texts become corrupt because there are two things scribes unfailingly do: they alter textual substance, and they alter linguistic form. They alter textual substance in two ways: by innovating inadvertently as they copy, unwittingly introducing variants and errors; or by intervening deliberately to improve the text, correcting what are, or seem to them to be, obvious mistakes. An obvious mistake might be to call the German theologian Albert the Great, 'Alberto ... di Bologna' instead of 'Alberto ... di Cologna' (*Par.* X, 98–9); or to add the unlikely name Merlino to the list of ancient writers celebrated early in *Inferno* (IV, 141) in place of the obscure Lino whose unfamiliar name was an early casualty of the copying process, and, remarkably, survives intact in only one manuscript.[2] But most innovations or errors are far more insidious: often they make perfect sense in context and are very plausible. Many of them will be distributed throughout the tradition in a way which does not lend itself to easy analysis.

It is true that the metrical scheme of the *Commedia* acts as a constraint on textual volatility: it might almost have been devised by Dante to function as a brake on the wilder excesses of scribal ignorance, carelessness, and over-confidence. The mandatory syllable count within the line, the non-negotiability of the intricate *terza rima* rhyme scheme, inhibit scribal innovation to some extent. It is startling to find Cristoforo Landino, in his prestigious 1481 print edition, misquoting the first line of the poem: 'Nel mezzo del camino di nostra vita', clearly metrically faulty with its twelve syllables (the error is present in several early manuscripts);[3] it is unusual to find an uncorrected error which falls at the end of the line and fails to observe rhyme, as when the scribe of manuscript Rb writes *porse* instead of *puose* in the sequence – *dolorose-puose-cose* – at *Inferno* III, 19. But in spite of the inbuilt metrical constraints, the degree of textual variation in surviving copies of the *Commedia* can seem little short of astonishing.

The second thing copyists unfailingly do involves linguistic form: they adapt the text they are copying to their own language habits and preferences. In medieval Italy there was no standard form of Italian and regional varieties were very distinctive. The northern manuscript Urb opens: 'Nel meggio del cammin di nostra vita'; *meggio* is simply a northern form of *mezzo*. A Tuscan copyist copying from a northern manuscript will write *mezzo* even if his exemplar has *meggio*. But this linguistic flexibility and lack of fixity can be a source of confusion and error: copyists may fail to recognize or correctly interpret some forms. At *Inferno* V, 64, 65, and 67 ('Elena vedi ... vedi 'l grande Achille ... Vedi Paris, Tristano ... '), present tense *vedi* ('you see') in some northern manuscripts is written *vidi*, a form which a Tuscan reader will interpret as a past tense ('I saw'), altering the dynamics of the narrative. Even within central Italy, manuscripts copied in western Tuscany (Pisa, Lucca) will have a quite marked linguistic colouring which is very different from Florentine.

From the outset, geographical and regional factors are a crucial dimension of the transmission history of the *Commedia*, and pose fundamental questions for the textual scholar. The precise relationship between the relatively small number of surviving northern manuscripts of the poem and the much larger number of Tuscan manuscripts is one such key question. The earliest copies of the poem were northern: Dante had lived in Verona and Ravenna for many years before he died. The Tuscan tradition has as its point of origin a copy of the poem assembled by Jacopo which he is thought to have taken to Florence circa 1325. (We can be sure he did not have access to a notional master-copy belonging to his father.) Dante's birthplace quickly became the epicentre for the production of copies. One professional scribe reputedly provided dowries for his daughters by copying the poem one hundred times.

A separate and particularly delicate question touching on geography is what form of language Dante actually wrote. How permeable was his native Florentine to other regional forms of speech and pronunciation during his twenty years of exile in northern Italy? A related and important consideration is that Tuscan copyists may re-Tuscanize the language, but their language will not necessarily be that of Dante and his time. Linguists assume that Dante's Florentine is that of the last decade of the Duecento, some forty-odd years before the earliest surviving Tuscan manuscript, the magnificent Trivulziano 1080 (Triv), dated 1337.

Erosion and oil stain are two compelling images for the process and effects of textual degradation through successive generations of manuscript copying, evoking as they do both the loss for the reader and the problems for an editor that such degradation entails. Erosion – a wearing away, a flattening of distinctive features – translates in linguistic terms into *banalizzazione*, the loss or blurring of everything which is freshest and most original and distinctive in the poet's language. An oil stain spreads outwards from an initial spill: just so an initial error may have a knock-on effect, seeping into and causing further errors in the surrounding text. The final result may be that a passage becomes not just flat but unintelligible, as when *Inferno* XVI, 34–6 – 'Questi, l'orme di cui pestar mi vedi, / tutto che nudo e dipelato vada, / fu di grado maggior che tu non credi' (This man, in whose footsteps you see me tread, for all that he goes naked and hairless, was of higher rank than you believe) – becomes, in the famous Holkham Hall manuscript now in the Bodleian library in Oxford, 'Queste lorme di cui tu pestar mi vedi / tucto che nudo et dipelato vada / fur di grado maggior che tu non credi'. Here the initial error of making *questi* agree with *orme* (*queste l'orme*: 'these the footsteps', rather than *questi, l'orme di cui*: 'this man, whose footsteps') is compounded when the singular verb *fu* is changed to a plural *fur* to agree with this new subject. The lines now make no sense at all.

Textual corruption, and an awareness of textual corruption, go hand in hand from the very beginning of the *Commedia*'s transmission history. The words of a scribe working in 1330, six years before our earliest surviving copy of the poem, are revealing. He describes the care with which he has sought out good readings from several manuscripts: 'on account of the lack of skill and experience of those who write in the vernacular, the book is much disfigured by corrupt and false readings. But I, drawing on various other copies, rejecting readings that are false and bringing together those that are true or seemed suited to the meaning, faithfully executed this copy as soberly as I could'. These words, written just nine years after Dante's death, strikingly bear witness both to an awareness of widespread corruption in the text, and to one copyist's attempts to counteract it. This is the earliest copyist of whom we have knowledge, albeit indirect – and he is actively and enthusiastically seeking out alternative readings and evaluating them: in modern terms, editing. (In technical terms he is contaminating, on which more below.)

The manuscript to which this note was appended was copied in 1330–1 and does not survive. We can reconstruct it from the careful collation made of it in 1548 by the Florentine humanist Luca Martini, who meticulously recorded, in the margins of his copy of the Aldine printed text of 1515, the many readings where the manuscript he was examining diverged from his printed collation copy (Martini's collation is referred to with the sigil Mart). He copied the scribe's account of his search for good readings onto a blank page at the end of the Aldine volume.[4]

La, the earliest securely dated surviving manuscript, offers an excellent image of the state of the text fifteen years after Dante's death. The whole text of the poem in the Landiano manuscript has been revised, with readings erased and replaced by other readings: some but not all of the erased readings are recoverable; some but not all of the amended readings are improvements.

How do we make sense of the textual evidence provided by Mart and La, not to mention the many hundreds of later copies of the poem? What conceptual model does an editor work with when seeking to understand the myriad alternative readings attested in the surviving tradition, and to choose between them?

The presence of scribal error lies at the heart of philological methodology. The act of copying embodies a vertical transmission model: each new copy is made from an existing copy of the text, forming an unbroken chain which ultimately leads back to the original. Precisely because copyists make errors, we can create a genealogical tree (or stemma) of manuscript relationships based on shared errors. But, crucially, those errors must be significant ones. Trivial errors, the myriad small errors copyists are liable to make independently of one another – 'convergent error' in English or 'polygenetic error' in Italian – will have no evidential force. Scholars using stemmatic methodology to illuminate the textual transmission of the *Commedia* will need to decide which errors are significant and therefore form a solid basis for reliable deductions. There is no consensus about what constitutes a significant error.

La is a graphic example of how a vertical transmission model is compromised by horizontal transmission (contamination) – that is, by the introduction of readings laterally, from a source other than the primary source of a given copy. Contamination subverts the relatively simple model of vertical transmission that enables us to plot manuscript relations with some confidence. When contamination is rampant, as it is in the *Commedia* – from the very earliest times, as the evidence of Mart and La so clearly shows – the difficulties may seem insurmountable. Paradoxically, from the very beginning, the keenest, most proactive admirers of Dante's genius, in spite of (or rather because of) their eagerness to have the best possible version of his poem, make the task of establishing an authoritative text incomparably more difficult.

Not all the earliest copies of the poem are contaminated. Of the small number securely dated before 1340, three magnificent exemplars show no obvious traces of contamination, though all three have occasional minimal corrections to the text: Ash, the Pisan manuscript known as the 'antichissimo', the 'oldest', which may indeed date from 1334; Triv, securely dated 1337, copied by one of the most famous of Tuscan scribes, Francesco di Ser Nardo; and Rb, copied in Bologna by a maestro Galvano towards the end of the decade. (All three can be viewed in their entirety – the full text, images, and transcriptions – on the *Commedia* DVD-Rom, where close analysis reveals that Rb is in fact contaminated, but only in the opening and closing cantos of the poem.) These very precious early manuscripts neatly illustrate the main geographical areas of scribal activity, and the characteristic linguistic forms associated respectively with western Tuscany, Florence, and northern Italy.

By the time we reach the turn of the century, sixty years later, we are dealing with some three hundred surviving manuscripts. Within this rich panorama of scribal activity, two figures stand out for their passionate commitment to Dante and the *Commedia*: Giovanni Boccaccio, working in the third quarter of the century; and Filippo Villani, working in its final decade. Their tireless activities over many years – copying the poem and seeking out variants, working on a commentary and a biography – are a vital part of its transmission history, not just because of their high intrinsic interest, but because they play a determining role in the unfolding story of modern scholarly attempts to establish a reliable text of the poem. Villani's editorial endeavours underlie the work of the nineteenth-century German scholar Karl Witte, the founding father of Dante manuscript studies for the modern age; Boccaccio's provide the theoretical underpinning of the most authoritative twentieth-century edition of the poem, that of Giorgio Petrocchi.

Boccaccio copied the *Commedia* three times, using as his exemplar ms. Vat 3199 (Vat), the manuscript he had ordered from a Florentine scriptorium for his friend Petrarch, probably in 1351. Vat is a manuscript of key importance in the transmission history of the poem, being not just the source of Boccaccio's copies (To, Ri, Chig), but the basis, as we shall see, of the two most influential early printed editions. But far from copying this illustrious exemplar faithfully, Boccaccio consulted other copies, and incorporated into his own copies plausible variants from these other manuscripts. Nor was this a once-and-for-all procedure: he continued actively to seek out and introduce new readings in the later copies. As a result, his second and third copies differ both from his first copy and from one another. Boccaccio's contaminatory activity is on such a scale that when Petrocchi was asked by the Società Dantesca Italiana to prepare a critical edition of the poem for the 1965 centenary of the poet's birth, he decided to base his edition only on manuscripts securely datable, in his view, before 1355 – before (as he believed) Boccaccio's editorial endeavours had irremediably contaminated the tradition beyond any possibility of rational analysis.

Villani's copy of the poem in his own hand (LauSC), written at the turn of the century (*c*.1401), heavily corrected and worked over, with many abrasions and rewritings, was long regarded, in spite of its relatively late date, as one of the most valuable and reliable of all the surviving manuscripts. It is one of the four manuscripts on which Witte based his ground-breaking 1862 edition. More recently, a renewed claim for its importance was made in 2001 by Federico Sanguineti, who claimed (but offered no proof) that the *scriptio prior* of LauSC is an authentic uncontaminated copy of a very old manuscript, rather than the heavily contaminated composite text that fine-grained analysis of the variants shows it in reality to be.

Boccaccio and Villani's editorial procedures were pragmatic rather than theoretical: they replaced one reading with another they thought better in the copy they were working on. Their *strumenti di lavoro* were the pen in their hand and their own judgement. Only in the nineteenth century was a methodology established for evaluating manuscript variants more objectively, eliminating (or at least minimizing) the subjective element. We can briefly survey key moments in the transmission history of the poem in the intervening centuries, before considering attempts in the last one hundred and fifty years to apply the stemmatic methodology that puts the establishing of a critical text on a more objective footing.

Not much interest was shown in the text of the poem in the Quattrocento. Little changed with the invention of printing. The earliest printed editions of the poem (Foligno, Mantua, Venice [all 1472], Venice [1477], Naples [1477, 1478], Milan [1478]) are mostly based each on a single manuscript whose text is uncritically reproduced. The Landino commentary to his 1481 edition was to be hugely influential, but its text, as we have seen, was poor.

The Cinquecento, by contrast, was a period of intense interest in the text of the poem. The century is bookended by two important editions, both widely influential, seen as authoritative in their time, and often reprinted.

The Aldine edition, first printed in 1502, was prepared by the eminent man of letters Pietro Bembo; the 1595 edition was prepared by the Accademia della Crusca.[5] The Aldine edition was still essentially the reproduction of a single authoritative manuscript, Boccaccio's exemplar Vat, which Bembo's father owned, though Bembo did consult other manuscripts. It was reprinted in 1515 and became the standard printed edition for the century, republished many times, several times in tandem with Cristoforo Landino's authoritative commentary, even when text and commentary do not match.

In the middle years of the century there was a resurgence of interest in Florence in establishing the text of the *Commedia*. Martini, who two years later collated Mart, tells us that in 1546 a group of five Florentine scholars met at San Gavino in Mugello to compare the readings of seven early manuscripts. This was a landmark moment: a collective enterprise to assemble and

collate textual data. Sadly, many of the very early manuscripts they examined
do not survive; nor, alas, does a complete record of their activity.

The edition published in 1595 by the Accademia della Crusca was
produced in tandem with the Academy's famous dictionary, whose first
edition was published a few years later. The academicians made extensive
efforts to establish a good text of the *Commedia*, consulting some hun-
dred-odd manuscripts, whose readings appear as occasional marginal
variants in the printed text; but that text nonetheless still remains
anchored to Bembo and Vat. The Crusca edition became the vulgate
text for the following centuries.

Only in the nineteenth century is the dominance of Vat challenged, with
the heroic efforts of two distinguished Dante scholars, Karl Witte and
Edward Moore. Both studied hundreds of manuscripts of the poem; both
were familiar with the now well-established stemmatic methodology. Their
pioneering work vastly broadened the manuscript base underlying their
respective editions. Witte's 1862 edition is based on four manuscripts, but
his choice of those four drew on his wide knowledge of many more. Moore's
extensive researches, presented in his epoch-making volume *Contributions
to the Textual Criticism of the Divina Commedia* (1889), included
a collation of the whole of the *Inferno* in the seventeen manuscripts found
in Oxford and Cambridge. Moore's conclusion on the methodological front
was that the tradition was so contaminated that he believed it would never be
possible to produce a genealogical tree of manuscript relations. He made
a practical suggestion: a way forward might be to work with 'test passages'.
His edition of the text, published in Oxford in 1894, superseded that of Witte
and remained authoritative for several decades.[6]

When the Società Dantesca Italiana was founded in 1888 its stated goal
was to establish authoritative texts for all of Dante's works. In 1891, at the
invitation of three senior *dantisti* linked with the Società, a youthful Michele
Barbi produced a list of lines in the *Commedia* which he believed would
prove crucial for establishing manuscript relationships: the so-called 400 *loci*
(in actual fact, 396 lines of text). The *loci* were not chosen arbitrarily, but, as
Barbi himself emphasized, were the result of much practical experience
working with the rich manuscript resources of the Florentine libraries and
pondering on the significance of certain variant readings. When the list was
published, an open invitation was issued to other interested scholars to check
these lines in any manuscripts of the poem to which they had access, and to
send in a record of the readings at these various points. Special forms were
printed to facilitate the task. The hope was to accumulate a mass of material
drawn from a large number of manuscripts scattered over a vast geographical
area – far beyond the possibilities of any individual scholar to examine and

record. This would constitute an invaluable data bank of textual material and serve as a basis for a detailed analysis of manuscript relations, and, in the fullness of time, an authoritative edition of Dante's poem to be prepared under the aegis of the Società.

The response to Barbi's invitation was disappointing. A handful of scholars examined a handful of manuscripts and reported their findings. Thirty years later, in the early 1920s, when Giuseppe Vandelli and Mario Casella independently produced new scholarly editions of the poem, they had largely to rely on their own labours. Vandelli's edition, which was published to mark the 1921 centenary of Dante's death and was to be influential for more than forty years, was the fruit of many years of investigation into individual manuscript variants, but Vandelli did not produce a theory of manuscript relationships; like Witte and Moore before him, he thought it was not possible to do so. Rather, he attempted for each individual reading to explain how the variants were related to, and derived from, an original reading which might account for them. In effect he applied stemmatic methods to individual readings on a case-by-case basis.[7]

Casella's edition was less influential than Vandelli's, but methodologically his contribution was fundamental, in that he articulated a first tentative theory of manuscript relationships. His grouping of manuscripts into two families (α and β) paved the way for all future studies of the transmission history of the poem.[8] Petrocchi's edition is based on a two-branched stemma, though his α and β families are very differently constituted from Casella's; and scholars since Petrocchi have continued to hypothesize a two-branched tree, although there is no consensus about its exact configuration.

In Petrocchi's view, as we have seen, the scale of contamination in and after the Boccaccio copies is new and non-negotiable. Petrocchi based his edition on twenty-four complete manuscripts and three fragmentary copies, renouncing any attempt systematically to utilize later manuscripts (though he was confident they contained no good readings not present in the earlier tradition). This editorial strategy was not simply a pragmatic response to the vast size of the surviving tradition; on the contrary – he insisted – it was imposed by the transmission history of the text itself. Petrocchi's edition marked a historic step forward in Dante studies, both for its theoretical take on the complexities of the textual tradition and the text which resulted from his approach: not simply *La Commedia* (the poem as Dante wrote it), but *La Commedia secondo l'antica vulgata* (the poem as it circulated in the three and a half decades after the poet's death). Crucially, that is, Petrocchi did not claim to be reconstructing Dante's original; and his title reflected his scrupulous insistence that no edition could be called genuinely critical or definitive which had not examined all the manuscript evidence.

In the fifty years since Petrocchi's edition was published, scholarly work on the transmission history of the *Commedia* has proceeded on many fronts. Recent scholarship suggests that of the three hundred or so surviving Trecento manuscripts of the poem, many more than the twenty-seven used by Petrocchi were copied before 1355 (the true figure appears to be over eighty). The contribution of codicologists and paleographers to the debate has been crucial. In this new and more complex panorama, the significance of Boccaccio's role seems less clear than Petrocchi believed to be the case.

On the theoretical front, scholars have debated, and continue to debate, the shape of the stemma, and the relative weight to be given to particular families or to individual manuscripts within it. The question of whether it is possible to reconstruct Dante's original remains open: two recent editions claim to supersede Petrocchi by presenting a text which is very close to that original.

The 1995 edition of the *Commedia* by Antonio Lanza argued that since it was impossible to examine and analyse all the manuscript evidence, the only rational course of action left to an editor was to choose the best manuscript available and to prepare an edition in conformity with the practice recommended in an influential contribution to the theoretical debate by the eminent French philologist Joseph Bédier. On Bédier's view, the most useful thing an editor could do was to give an accurate and scholarly edition of the 'best' surviving witness, so that the reader would see a version of the text which in that limited sense at least was authentic. The 'best manuscript' chosen by Lanza as the basis for his edition was Triv, whose Florentine character and exceptionally careful scribe in his view justify this choice. With this new text, Lanza claims, we have 'a Dante who has not been "italianized" (or, worse, "bembo-ized"), but a municipal and much more medieval Dante: in a word, the true "Florentine" Dante'. The text is said to be 'close, very close, to Dante's original text'.[9]

This same claim was made – but on entirely different grounds, and of a very different text – in the edition of the poem edited by Federico Sanguineti in 2001.[10] Sanguineti questioned Petrocchi's methodology in a far more radical way than Lanza, claiming that by applying stemmatic methodology rigorously, it could be shown that Petrocchi had simply got it wrong. The number and choice of manuscripts on which a critical edition should be based, the exact relationships among those manuscripts, and the weighting of different readings in the light of those relationships, were all called into question. Sanguineti's edition explicitly sought to displace the Petrocchi edition as the standard critical text, with a detailed and intricate argument about the nature of the poem's transmission history and the character of the text that could be reconstructed from a proper understanding of it. This text, far from being merely 'secondo l'antica vulgata', was – like Lanza's, but for very different reasons – declared to be a critical edition very close to Dante's original.

Sanguineti's idea was to take Barbi's 400 *loci* and examine them in all surviving manuscripts, and to see what results such an analysis might yield. His conclusion was that just seven manuscripts were necessary and sufficient for a critical edition of the *Commedia*. An edition based on these seven manuscripts, far from being in some sense provisional (as Petrocchi's 'secondo l'antica vulgata' formulation explicitly acknowledged), would instead be very close to the authorial original. The isolated β manuscript Urb – the sole representative of the β family, in his view – although it dates from 1352, is extremely close to Dante's original, and its readings, unless they are manifestly erroneous, are always to be preferred over those of the remaining manuscripts. Even its northern linguistic patina requires only moderate intervention.

Sanguineti's stemma has the visual appeal of an elegant and minimalist diagram. Nothing in it hints at the two evocative images Petrocchi used to describe the effects of contamination in the textual tradition of the *Commedia*: the tangled web and the seeping oil-stain. To judge at least by the visual representation he provided, Sanguineti believes the manuscript relationships to be clear-cut and unambiguous.

Sanguineti's edition had a mixed reception: the response of some philologists was very critical. Scholars questioned the reasoning which lay behind the drastic winnowing of the extant manuscripts to a mere seven, pointing out the inadvisability of basing a stemma for a text of this length on a very small number of readings. They expressed reservations both about the configuration of the stemma (the positions of Rb and LauSC), and the use made of it in constituting the text. The choice of many of the Urb readings incorporated into the text left many unconvinced – some of those readings seemed clearly inferior or wrong. The automatic privileging of Urb, sole representative of one branch, ignores a basic tenet of stemmatic methodology: with a two-branched tree, each branch is worth 50 per cent, and textual choices must be argued case by case. Nor does Sanguineti acknowledge that some Urb readings will have been introduced in the β sub-archetype of which it is the only representative. (A case in point: the last line of Urb reads 'L'amor che move il cielo e l'altre stelle'; *cielo* instead of *sole* (sun) could have been introduced in β, in Urb, or in some intermediary copy: isolated Urb readings which seem plausible cannot be accepted uncritically as original.)

But Sanguineti's edition, notwithstanding its problematic aspects, galvanized Dante scholars: some of the most interesting work being done today on the textual transmission of the poem was directly sparked by engaging with his challenging claims. Paolo Trovato believes that Sanguineti is right in privileging the northern manuscripts of the poem, though his configuration of the stemma is very different from Sanguineti's; and, along with a team of young scholars based in Ferrara, Trovato continues to work with the Barbi *loci*, supplemented by another 100-odd errors which he believes are securely monogenetic, that is, from a single source.[11] Giorgio Inglese is much closer to Petrocchi in his view of the tradition: his stemma fine-tunes Petrocchi's, emphasizing that the congruence of Triv and Urb is the key to reconstructing Dante's original. Both these distinguished scholars have produced a steady stream of important articles in recent years. Trovato's projected edition of the *Commedia* is yet to appear. Inglese has published single volumes for *Inferno* (2007), *Purgatorio* (2011), and *Paradiso* (2016) which contain a wealth of interesting observations on individual readings and on theoretical questions.[12]

There is widespread agreement that Urb, though relatively late (1352) and relatively isolated, is the least corrupt surviving manuscript in terms of textual substance. Scholars whose editorial approaches and procedures are very different agree on this. Yet their views on where Urb fits into the broader picture, and the use they make of Urb in establishing a text, are at odds. We are brought back to *iudicium*, to the role of personal judgement in evaluating the evidence about the transmission history of the poem. Even within the structured context provided by stemmatic methodology, *iudicium* still looms large.

An attempt to remove *iudicium* from the equation entirely was made in the electronic *Commedia* project, a UK-based and funded project headed by the author of this chapter, working with a small team of research assistants, in collaboration with a scholar widely experienced in working with computers and manuscripts. The aim of the project was twofold: specifically, to utilize information technology to test Sanguineti's hypothesis about manuscript relationships; more generally, to explore the use of computers in analysing and understanding complex manuscript traditions. The Sanguineti seven manuscripts were transcribed and collated in their entirety, presenting notable technical challenges in the registering of altered and amended readings. (In the case of LauSC, there were sometimes as many as four layers of readings.) The files were then fed through cladistic programmes designed by evolutionary biologists to produce genealogical trees on the basis of shared genetic innovations. No judgements were made at any point about the value of readings, about errors, significant or otherwise. The neutral notion of scribal innovation replaced the value-laden one of error or corruption.

Though limited in its scope to just seven manuscripts, the project produced three interesting results that could not easily have been achieved with such precision by any other means: it clarified the contested position of Rb; it showed the heavily contaminated character of the *scriptio prior* in LauSC; and it gave identical phylograms or diagrams of manuscript relationships for *Inferno* and *Purgatorio*, and a near-identical one for *Paradiso*. (The separate release of the three *cantiche* to the public in theory makes it possible or even likely that they might have different transmission histories.) It goes without saying that it would be extremely interesting to add other key manuscripts to this computer analysis, though the time and costs involved in such an enterprise are daunting; but it also needs to be emphasized that, although computers can help the textual scholar, the expertise of the philologist will always be necessary for correctly understanding and interpreting the results a computer analysis gives.

Notes

1. The manuscript sigils used in this article are those widely adopted by textual scholars working on the *Commedia*. See Dante Alighieri, *La Commedia secondo l'antica vulgata*, ed. G. Petrocchi, 4 vols. (Milan: Mondadori, 1966–67; 2nd edn., Florence: Le Lettere, 1994), 1, 57–8. Ms. Ash in the Biblioteca Medicea Laurenziana in Florence may be two years older than La, but experts disagree about its dating.
2. *Alberto [...] di Bolongna* in ms. Po; *Merlino* in ms. Canon. Ital. 97 in the Bodleian Library in Oxford; *e lino* only in ms. Urb.
3. S. Bertelli, *La tradizione della 'Commedia' dai manoscritti al testo. I. I codici trecenteschi (entro l'antica vulgata) conservati a Firenze* (Florence: Olschki, 2011), pp. 340 [Plut. 90 sup. 125], 343 [Plut. 90 inf. 42], 345 [Acq. e doni 86], 354 [Strozzi 150], 358 [Strozzi 152], 385 [Ricc. 1012].
4. The original is viewable on the *Commedia* DVD-Rom: Dante Alighieri, *Commedia. A Digital Edition*, ed. P. Shaw (Birmingham: Scholarly Digital Editions and Florence: SISMEL-Edizioni del Galluzzo, 2010), and website (sd-editions.com) at Mart Image/Text page 247v, where one can also see a virtual recreation of the lost 1330 manuscript by following the links: Home page > Image/Text > Mart > Form to show > Martini's Collation.
5. *Le terze rime di Dante. Lo 'nferno e 'l Purgatorio e 'l Paradiso di Dante Alaghieri* (Venice: Aldo Manuzio, 1502); *La Divina Commedia di Dante Alighieri Nobile Fiorentino: ridotta a miglior lezione dagli Accademici della Crusca* (Florence: Domenico Manzani, 1595; anastatic reprint Turin: Loescher and Florence: Accademia della Crusca, 2012).
6. C. Witte, *La Divina Commedia di Dante Allighieri, ricorretta sopra quattro dei più autorevoli testi a penna* (Berlin: R. Decker, 1862); E. Moore, *Contributions to the Textual Criticism of the Divina Commedia* (Cambridge University Press, 1889); *Tutte le opere di Dante Alighieri*, ed. E. Moore (Oxford: Stamperia dell'Università, 1894).

7. *Le Opere di Dante. Testo critico della Società Dantesca Italiana*, ed. M. Barbi, E. G. Parodi, E. Pellegrini, E. Pistelli, P. Rajna, E. Rostagno, G. Vandelli (Florence: Bemporad, 1921).

8. M. Casella, 'Studi sul testo della *Divina Commedia*', *Studi Danteschi*, 8 (1924), 5–85; *La Divina Commedia*, ed. M. Casella (Bologna: Zanichelli, 1923).

9. Dante Alighieri, *La Commedìa. Nuovo testo critico secondo i più antichi manoscritti fiorentini*, ed. A. Lanza (Anzio: De Rubeis, 1995), p. xiii.

10. Dante Alighieri, *Comedìa*, ed. F. Sanguineti (Florence: Edizioni del Galluzzo, 2001); Dante Alighieri, *Comedìa. Appendice bibliografica 1988–2000*, ed. F. Sanguineti (Florence: Edizioni del Galluzzo, 2005).

11. P. Trovato (ed.), *Nuove prospettive sulla tradizione della 'Commedia'* (Florence: Cesati, 2007); E. Tonello and P. Trovato (eds.), *Nuove prospettive sulla tradizione della Commedia, Seconda serie (Studi 2008–2013)* (Padua: Libreriauniversitaria. it, 2013).

12. Dante Alighieri, *Commedia*, ed. G. Inglese, 3 vols. (Rome: Carocci, 2007–16).

15

ANNA PEGORETTI

Early Reception until 1481

The earliest biography of Leonardo da Vinci, by the so-called 'Anonimo Gaddiano' (pre-1540), tells of the great Renaissance artist being asked by a group of honourable Florentine men to explain 'a passage by Dante'.[1] The anecdote presents Leonardo as attempting to shift the exegetical responsibility on to Michelangelo and being mocked by the latter in what is an early instance of a crafted dramatization of the rivalry between the two artists. However, it also reveals several features of Dante's reception in the Italian Renaissance. First of all, we note the centrality of the *Commedia*, which is referred to as the Dantean work *par excellence* (usually called 'the Dante'). Second, the poem is presented as a topic of everyday conversation in the streets of Florence. Third, the passage highlights the difficulties of a text that had required explanation since its first appearance. Finally, the anecdote indicates that Dante's influence had crossed the boundaries of the literary to have an impact on the visual arts.

These features offer an indication of the complexity and variety of the reception of the *Commedia* in the fourteenth and fifteenth centuries. Few works in Western literature have influenced such a broad range of readers (and listeners) as Dante's poem. At the same time, its afterlife has been characterized by periods of notable contestation and resistance as well as unalloyed celebration. Following the *Commedia*'s publication, Dante's main group of readers emerged amongst the 'new people' with their 'rapid gains' (La gente nuova e i sùbiti guadagni; *Inf.* XIV, 73), so fiercely condemned by the poet as the main cause of Florence's decadence. His political vision of a Rome-centred Christian polity, peacefully governed by an emperor and spiritually guided by the pope, had already been doomed during his lifetime by the transfer of the Holy See to Avignon and by the death of the Holy Roman emperor Henry VII. The poem's prophetic claims would be neutralized by most commentators, while its encyclopaedic range was about to be replaced by a specialized interest in classical antiquity. The vernacular, so powerfully and influentially forged by Dante himself, was increasingly becoming overshadowed by a resurgence of classical Latin. Indeed, the poet had had to defend his decision to write a poem in the vernacular against strictures of the proto-humanist scholar Giovanni del Virgilio. In the first two centuries of its afterlife, the only uncontested feature of the poem was its metre, the *terza rima*, which was developed in different ways by generations of poets.

The present chapter explores this complex history as it unfolds from the second decade of the fourteenth century until 1481 – the date that marks the publication of the most important Renaissance commentary by Cristoforo Landino – highlighting the dynamics of the *Commedia*'s transmission and reception across different social strata, media, and cultural and political environments.

The Earliest Reception

Around 1313, the Florentine notary Francesco da Barberino, at that time living in Mantua, mentions in his *Documenti d'Amore* a '*Comedia*' by 'Dante Arigherii', which, 'among many other things', talks about Hell.[2] Perhaps the earliest explicit allusion to Dante's *Inferno*, this reference is all the more remarkable since it mentions the first *cantica* as a 'comedy'. However, it is very likely that Francesco knew some cantos of the *Inferno* before this date. Equally, echoes of the poem in the inscriptions of Simone Martini's *Majesty* in the Palazzo Pubblico in Siena (1315–21), which for the first time imitate Dante's *terza rima*, offer a further early example of the poem's dissemination and its influence on the visual arts. Together with the few lines of *Inferno* III, 94–6, that a Bolognese notary copied in the margins of a legal document in 1317, these allusions to the *Commedia* provide evidence of its partial circulation, either in *cantiche* or groups of cantos, before its completion just before Dante's death in September 1321. Notwithstanding, the Latin poetic correspondence between Dante and Giovanni del Virgilio (the *Eclogues*) in 1319–20 reveals the debate that the poem had triggered among intellectuals about Dante's decision to write in the vernacular.

In April 1322, Dante's son Iacopo presented a versified summary (the *Divisione*) of the *Commedia* to Guido Novello da Polenta, a member of the family under whose patronage Dante had spent his last years in Ravenna, and who had recently been appointed governor of Bologna (he also offered him a copy of the whole poem, or alternatively of his commentary, which can also be dated to the same year). Iacopo's *Division* enjoyed considerable success and inaugurated a tradition of similar summaries of the poem that normally utilize *terza rima* to help the reader navigate and memorize the text. This tradition can be related, at least in its schematizing aims, to the diagrams of the otherworld sketched in a number of the earliest manuscripts of the *Commedia*, which anticipate the figures included in almost any modern edition of the poem. Their goal is to provide an overall view of the realms of the afterlife, of their moral order, and of the structure of the text, whose partitions are strictly related to the topography of the other world.

Even though the *Commedia* was a contemporary vernacular poem, not included in the medieval literary canon (which privileged exclusively Latin classical texts), exegetical activity around it began very early. The poem itself stresses the need for commentary, hinting time and again at its difficulties (for instance, at the beginning of *Paradiso* II), and invites the reader to consider its hidden meanings (*Inf.* IX, 61–3). Dante's ambition to write a poem worthy of commentary and of being considered on a par with, if not actually superior to, classical canonical texts, such as the *Aeneid*, is strikingly apparent when the reader is ordered to stay 'on your bench' (sovra 'l tuo banco; *Par.* X, 22). Dante depicts his ideal reader as someone sitting at a scholar's bench, where medieval intellectuals would read large folio books (over 40cm high) with ample margins for commentary and glosses – books to be studied thoroughly in the institutional setting of a scholastic library. Some sort of proto-glosses to the first two *cantiche* probably date back to Dante's lifetime. Among the possible extant candidates is the corpus of Latin glosses to *Inferno* and *Purgatorio* known as the 'Anonymous Lombard' (pre–1326), which is part of a substantial body of anonymous annotations, both in Latin and in the vernacular (*chiose palatine, filippine, ambrosiane, cassinesi*, etc.). In a way that paradigmatically exemplifies an underlying mechanism of late-medieval commentary traditions, the poem's exegesis progressively grew, becoming a flexible storehouse of interpretations, which were relentlessly quoted or summarized, very often without declaring sources, and tailored to specific contexts, audiences, and purposes. Hence, each commentary must not be assessed exclusively in relation to the *Commedia*, but also in relation to the wider tradition of the poem, to its cultural and political context, and to a range of exegetical practices.

The earliest systematic commentaries were composed in north-east Italy, with Bologna playing an especially significant role. Iacopo's commentary on the *Inferno* was written in Ravenna. The first Latin one, also on the first *cantica*, was penned in Bologna by a prominent political figure of the commune, Graziolo de' Bambaglioli, in 1324. The earliest commentary on the whole poem was written in the vernacular in 1324–8, possibly in Venice, by the Bolognese Iacomo della Lana. These three works establish some long-lasting interpretations of the *Commedia*, such as the reading of Virgil as an allegory of human reason and Beatrice as a symbol of theology. Despite its rudimentary character, Iacopo's commentary presents the *Commedia* as an encyclopaedic work that allegorically describes mankind according to a moral hierarchy. The idea of the poem as an encyclopaedia is richly developed by Iacomo della Lana, whose lengthy commentary was immensely successful and was translated into Latin by the middle of the century. In analysing the *Commedia*, Iacomo deploys an impressive array of juridical, philosophical, and theological sources alongside scholastic techniques, such as the identification and explanation of specific problems (*quaestiones*), which reveal his acquaintance with the Bolognese university environment. In the early years of its reception, the *Commedia* also raised tensions among intellectuals gravitating on Bologna. The university master Cecco d'Ascoli adopted the *terza rima* in his didactic poem *L'Acerba* while consistently attacking Dante's philosophical positions. Even more remarkably, Graziolo was the dedicatee of a treatise which fiercely condemned Dante's *Monarchia*, written around 1329 by the Dominican friar Guido Vernani.

The cultural and social impact of the reception of the *Commedia* was even more noteworthy in Tuscany and in Florence, where the poem found a large and diversified audience. Thus, the fact that younger Dominican friars in the city were prohibited in 1335 from reading the poem testifies to its popularity in the order's Florentine house of Santa Maria Novella, where Nardo di Cione was commissioned to paint a fresco of the topography of Dante's Hell (1354–7). A landmark in the poem's reception among mendicant friars is represented by the exegetical activity of the Carmelite Guido da Pisa, who composed a versified vernacular introduction to the poem, the *Dichiarazione*, and a Latin commentary on the *Inferno* that he completed during the second half of the 1330s and which includes a Latin paraphrase of the *cantica*. Guido's commentary stands out for its doctrinal sophistication, its critical and linguistic sensitivity, its classicizing interests, and its unique reading of the *Commedia*. While the majority of commentators considered the poem as an allegory, namely, a fictional representation of moral concepts, of humanity, and of the Christian tension towards God, Guido read it as a prophetic text.

If interest in the *Commedia* in religious circles is a striking feature of its reception, in Florence, such readers are overwhelmed by a substantial lay audience that included intellectuals, merchants, notaries, and members of the other professions. The poem's popularity had a significant impact on the production of copies, whose high numbers and levels of standardization – nonetheless characterized by a refined execution – are unprecedented in the history of medieval book production. In Florence there also flourished a particular type of commentary, which is well exemplified by the so-called *Ottimo commento* (*c.*1334) – termed 'best' in 1612 by linguistic purists impressed by the authenticity of its Florentine vernacular – and by its partial re-elaboration which is now attributed to the *Amico dell'Ottimo* (*c*.1337–41). These anonymous commentaries were conceived as compilations of earlier interpretations, whose variety – despite the fact that the *Commedia* had been circulating for only twenty or so years – was such that a degree of ordering and rationalization was deemed necessary. Andrea Lancia, a notary and a prolific translator into the Florentine vernacular of classical texts, was very close to the milieu of these anonymous exegetes, and his commentary (1341–3) displays most of the same features as their works, such as a new focus on the literal meaning of the text, on the historicity of characters, and on presenting information in narrative form reminiscent of short stories.

Moreover, these commentaries are all characterized by their use of classical sources, which are merged with anecdotes about Dante's life and views during his time in Florence and, most notably, with references to the poet's other works. This way of 'reading Dante with Dante' involves the earliest allusions to the *Convivio*, as well as Lancia's isolated mention of the so-called *Epistle to Cangrande* as Dantean, before Filippo Villani's own reference to this work at the end of the century. Lancia's translation of parts of the Latin commentary by Dante's son, Pietro Alighieri, confirm the rapid success of this work, written in the early 1340s in Verona, where Pietro worked as a judge. His rich interpretive framework draws on the popular medieval exegesis of Aeneas' otherworldly journey in the sixth book of Virgil's *Aeneid*. According to this reading, the journeys undertaken by both Aeneas and Dante symbolize humanity's intellectual growth. Pietro substantially reworked the first draft of his commentary in two subsequent versions (post–1357). The revised versions reveal a better acquaintance with Dante's other works, including *Monarchia*, *Convivio*, and *Questio de aqua et terra*, which otherwise remained unknown until the sixteenth century. Pietro's work as a commentator is characterized by a profound interest in classical texts, by extensive references to Aristotelian works, and by his sound knowledge of civil and canon law. In addition, he defended his father's religious orthodoxy, and his commentary stands out as probably the most distinguished among the early readings of the poem.

Dissemination, Imitation, Exegesis: The Early Life of a Bestseller

By the middle of the fourteenth century, the *Commedia* had become immensely popular throughout most of the Italian peninsula and was disseminated in a variety of ways and through a range of means, to the point that 'there is no such a thing as direct, unmediated access to Dante'.[3] The poem was copied in large numbers and in every type of script and layout, while manuscript illustrators developed a dedicated iconography to accompany the text that often served to interpret it. The *Commedia*'s widespread influence on the visual arts testifies to the complexity of its reception. Indeed, the poem reached a broad-based public that almost certainly included illiterate city dwellers, as confirmed by allusions to it in popular preaching. This oral transmission was especially bolstered by a growing tradition of public lectures on the *Commedia*. One such event (about which we know very little) was Pietro Alighieri's versified summary of the poem that allegedly he declaimed in Verona's central square on a feast day in the late 1340s.[4] Preachers continued to quote Dante's poem in their sermons well into the next century, as confirmed by the testimony of illustrious witnesses such as Lorenzo de' Medici and Erasmus of Rotterdam.

In fact, the *Commedia* may have reached Naples in this way as early as the 1320s, since quotations from *Paradiso* have been noted in the sermons of the Augustinian friar Agostino d'Ancona. There is even the possibility that the *Commedia* arrived in Cambridge in this manner thanks to the Sicilian friar Rogerius de Platea (or de Heraclea), who may have taught there around 1350 and who drew on Dante in his sermons. In Naples, around 1370, the nobleman Guglielmo Maramauro provided a vernacular commentary on the *Inferno* (the other two *cantiche* are lost), which, although marred by exegetical flaws, highlights the difficulties in making a Tuscan text accessible to a non-Tuscan audience. In line with the prevalent bilingualism of late-medieval Italy, the first *cantica* had been paraphrased into Latin by Guido da Pisa, while commentaries were translated from the vernacular into Latin and vice versa. At the same time, the genre of carefully structured poems in *terza rima* had become commonplace. The most noteworthy example is Boccaccio's dream vision, the *Amorosa visione* (1342–3), although various other late-fourteenth- and fifteenth-century poems were written in close imitation both of the *Commedia*'s structure and content, such as Federico Frezzi's *Quadriregio* (1394–1403). More generally, Dante's poetic language led to a remarkable broadening of the vocabulary of the Tuscan vernacular and an enrichment of its expressive potential. Consequently, Tuscan quickly penetrated throughout the Italian peninsula as the standard literary language.

The exegesis of the *Commedia* has no parallel in any medieval vernacular literature, bringing to light the poem's extraordinary doctrinal richness, while providing a range of interpretations of Dante's account of the afterlife. The classical and Christian representation of the afterlife, which offered moral instruction and encouraged reflection on the soul's eternal destiny, offered commentators a framework that helped them explain the grandiose depiction of the *Commedia* as eminently ethical, in line with the standard contemporary moralizing interpretation of literature. At the same time, a number of manuscript miniature illustrations accompanying the opening canto represent Dante-character as sleeping or receiving a visionary experience, thereby promoting an understanding of the poem as the account of a dream – in keeping with a literal reading of 'so full of sleep was I' (tant'era pien di sonno; *Inf.* I, II) – or of a vision. Such a vision or dream-vision could be interpreted by readers as pure fiction, or as the result of a cognitive experience that the poet enjoyed and then decided to tell in the form of a long narrative fiction. Interestingly, the reality of Dante's journey through the otherworld was a kind of non-issue, at least amongst learned readers: for them what was more important were the verisimilitude of his account and its moral message, conveyed through a most powerful and imaginative narrative.

Building the Canon: Boccaccio between Dante and Petrarch

Around 1352, Giovanni Boccaccio sent to the most influential writer and intellectual of his time, Francesco Petrarca, a copy of the *Commedia*,[5] accompanied by a dedicatory Latin poem *Ytalie iam certus honos* (Already certain honour of Italy), which praises Dante's achievements. Despite his constant echoing of Dante in his vernacular poetry, and his use of the *terza rima* in the dream vision the *Triumphi* (1340–74), Petrarch did not share Boccaccio's public enthusiasm for his predecessor, whose presence loomed large over Italian vernacular literature. His carefully constructed self-positioning in relation to Dante is obvious in a famous letter he sent to Boccaccio in 1359 (*Familiares* XXI, 15), in which he dismissively stated that he had not owned a copy of the *Commedia* before his friend's gift, so as not to be influenced by a poem which he considered to be far too popularizing. Furthermore, he restricted Dante's achievements to the realm of the vernacular, while stating his own desire for excellence in Latin and for recognition among an elite audience. Petrarch's aim seems to have been to re-dimension and curb Dante's cultural prestige, while concealing his own debts to his predecessor, thereby creating a space in which to place himself and his own work.

In the complex dialectic between Petrarch and Dante, Boccaccio, destined to be third among the so-called 'three crowns' of Italian literature, became the mediator who defined the future transmission of their works. In both its structure – with its one hundred *novelle* imitating the one hundred *canti* – and its subtitle – 'otherwise known as Prince Galahalt' – with a clear reference to the episode of Paolo and Francesca, and their 'Galeotto book'

(Galeotto fu 'l libro; *Inf.* V, 137), – the *Decameron* clearly signals its close engagement with the *Commedia*. Moreover, several manuscripts testify to Boccaccio's activity as a copyist and editor of Dante's works. Alongside a philological attention to establish a reliable text of the poem, his editorial strategies were aimed at elevating Dante to the same authoritative status as that granted to classical authors – strategies such as the use of parchment and a single-column layout for the text, thereby leaving space for glosses. In addition, Boccaccio gave special prominence to the *Commedia* when he copied it together with other Dantean vernacular works to form an authorial collection which resembled manuscripts of Virgil's works, and which, as convention required, was introduced by a life of the poet, his so-called *Trattatello in laude di Dante*. Boccaccio's editorial commitment to Dante and his role as mediator between Dante and Petrarch culminated in the monumental Chigiano manuscript, later divided into two items (now Vatican Mss. Chigi L.VI.213 and L.V.176), possibly by Boccaccio himself. The second one contains only the *Commedia*, but was originally part of a larger collection that included the *Vita nova* and fifteen *canzoni* alongside an early redaction of Petrarch's *Canzoniere*. Such a compilation clearly aimed to establish a canon of Italian literature, centred on the reconciliation between Dante and Petrarch.

Boccaccio's authority as a *dantista* was officially sanctioned when the Florentine government decided to appoint him as public lecturer on the *Commedia* in 1373. His unfinished lectures, known as *Esposizioni*, probably inaugurated the practice of the so-called *lectura Dantis*, the interpretation and reading of the poem canto by canto, that continues to flourish today. Lectures were held on weekdays in the chapel of Santo Stefano in Badia, but were interrupted at *Inferno* XVII, 17, because of Boccaccio's illness. In many ways, the *Esposizioni* synthesize Boccaccio's main concerns regarding Dante and the status of poetry. He neatly separates the literal and the allegorical explanation of the text (the latter, however, is not always provided), creating an exegetical structure that permits close reading, stylistic analysis, and the recounting of stories that benefit from their author's remarkable abilities as narrator. The result is a mix in which quasi-*novelle* – most famously, the account of Francesca and Paolo's death – are framed by a commentary that employs advanced scholastic interpretive techniques and pays considerable attention to linguistic and literary matters.

From earlier commentators, Boccaccio inherits his attention to the doctrinal content of the poem and to the ethical value of literature. More powerfully than anyone had done before him, he applies to the *Commedia* a set of ideas in defence of poetry mainly elaborated first in the proto-humanist circles of Paduan intellectuals such as Albertino Mussato, and then authoritatively developed by Petrarch (*Familiares* X, 4) and expounded by Boccaccio both in the *Trattatello* and in the last two books of his *Genealogies of Pagan Gods*. According to this perspective, shared too by friars with classicizing interests, such as Guido da Pisa, poetry can effectively convey moral, theological, and Christian truths under the veil of allegorical fiction. Boccaccio used the *Commedia* as a powerful weapon in the battle against detractors of poetry and literature, placing the poem at the very centre of the debate on the value of fiction that raged throughout the fourteenth century as well as the early part of the next. From the pulpit of a church, Boccaccio justified Dante dealing with vital spiritual matters by stating that ancient poets were 'the first to theologize'. Indeed, Christian poets, whose position is superior to that of their pagan predecessors, are even more reliable, inasmuch as 'they did not hide in their fabulous speech anything false, especially where they narrated things dealing with God and the Christian faith'.[6]

The Italian and European Reception of the *Commedia*

In replying to an anonymous author who accused him of having disseminated the *Commedia* among the 'unworthy masses', Boccaccio expressed regret for his action.[7] However, the impact of his *lectura Dantis* cannot be overstated. Public lectures on the *Commedia* continued to be given in Florence for more than a century, to be then revived by the Florentine Academy in the 1540s and 1550s. Moreover, this practice spread to other cities, where the exegetical commitment to Dante's poem was often intertwined with political factors. The university master of arts and chancellor of Pisa, Francesco da Buti, read 'the Dante' probably in 1385 (the written version of his lectures was completed by 1396). Buti provided the first vernacular word-by-word commentary of the entire poem, according to a scholastic critical model usually applied to classical texts. The same technique, this time in Latin, was employed by another university master, Benvenuto da Imola, who was among Boccaccio's most avid listeners in Florence, and who read the *Commedia* in Bologna and Ferrara between 1375 and 1383. Benvenuto wrote the most impressive of the Trecento commentaries, one which relies on an unprecedented range of first-hand sources, on sound rhetorical expertise, and on a philological attention to textual variants. In his prologue, Benvenuto engages in a lengthy discussion about the genre of the *Commedia* and its title, in which he demonstrates the ground-breaking novelty of a poem that stretched to breaking point the conventional boundaries of medieval literary genre.

By the end of the fourteenth century, Dante's *Commedia* had begun to influence writers beyond Italy. Geoffrey Chaucer famously retells the story of

Ugolino in the *Monk's Tale* (part of *The Canterbury Tales*), while his *House of Fame* is a tripartite vision that includes several allusions to the *Commedia*. Christine de Pizan, Italian by birth but who wrote in French, claimed direct knowledge of Dante's poem, which informs her allegorical dream-vision *Livre du chemin de long estude* (1402–3), as well as her *Cité des dames* (1405). In fifteenth-century Spain, the *Commedia* was translated no less than seven times, into both Castilian and Catalan. Important evidence of the European interest in Dante is provided by the complete Latin translation and commentary that the bishop Giovanni Bertoldi da Serravalle – who attended Benvenuto's lectures in Ferrara – completed at the time of the Council of Constance (1414–18), at the invitation of an Italian cardinal and two important English prelates.

The role of the *Commedia* in the struggle for political power in Italy emerges in the vernacular commentary on the *Inferno* that, in 1438, the humanist Guiniforte Barzizza was commissioned to write by the Duke of Milan, Filippo Maria Visconti, at a time of bitter tensions with Florence. Barzizza's highly limited and literal exegesis betrays his humanistic unease towards vernacular medieval literature. His commentary stems directly from the partisan interests of his *signore*, whose appropriation of the Florentine literary tradition constituted a political gesture as much as a cultural one. It is equally possible to consider the ambitious illuminated manuscript prepared for Alphonso of Aragon at the Neapolitan court during the 1440s as having a similar function.[8]

The *Commedia* in Fifteenth-century Florence: Between Humanism and Civic Pride

While beyond Florence the *Commedia* was read almost exclusively by the intellectual and political elite, in Dante's native city the poem had circulated widely ever since the first years of its dissemination. At the beginning of the fifteenth century, copies were present in the private libraries of many members of the Florentine *borghesia*. In addition, evidence has survived of its use by teachers of grammar, such as Nofri di Giovanni da Poggitazzi and Bartolomeo Nerucci, a former pupil of Francesco da Buti. In Florence, Dante was also an object of civic pride, even though the city had become the leading centre of humanism, which advocated the revival of classical Latin and an elitist conception of literature. Consequently, some humanists expressed reservations about Dante's choice of language and his ties to the classical tradition, as emerges in Leonardo Bruni's *Dialogues to Pier Paolo Vergerio* (c.1404–6). The protagonist of the *Dialogues* is the fiercest opponent of Dante, Niccolò Niccoli, who considered the *Commedia* as little more than a wrapping for fish. Dante's expertise in classical literature was questioned, and his medieval cultural formation was censured as antithetical to the ideal figure of the poet as someone well versed in Latin and rhetoric, and highly selective in choosing poetic genre and subject matter.

Despite the reservations, Dante continued to play a key role in Florence, both because of the *Commedia*'s popularity and because of his fundamental position in the construction of the city's municipal identity. The generation of humanists prior to Bruni and Niccoli, including the chancellor of the Republic Coluccio Salutati and Filippo Villani, cultivated the idea of a Florentine literary canon, which featured the great fourteenth-century vernacular authors as heirs of the classical tradition. Such a genealogy is most clearly evident in Villani's historical Latin work on *The Origin of the City of Florence and its Illustrious Citizens* (1381–97). It was also depicted in a now lost series of portraits of eminent figures in the municipal building of Palazzo Vecchio, designed by Salutati to promote poets as representatives of the highest level of civic rhetoric. Interestingly, in his role as the second humanist Florentine chancellor (1427–44), Bruni gradually adjusted his interpretation of Dante along similar lines. Despite oscillations about the value of the vernacular, both Salutati and Villani expended their scholarly expertise on the *Commedia*. The latter also lectured on the poem from 1391 until his death. In its length and overwhelming emphasis on allegorization, Villani's introduction and interpretation of the first canto suggest that the commentary tradition had reached an impasse. However, Villani's work also highlights his commitment to the defence of Dante and of poetry in general against the resurgent attacks against both by leading ecclesiastics.

The *Commedia* naturally found devoted support among the staunch advocates of vernacular culture, such as Giovanni Gherardi da Prato – who lectured on the poem (1417–25) and was apparently the first to label Dante, Petrarch, and Boccaccio as the 'three crowns' of Florentine literature – and a near contemporary, Cino Rinuccini, who termed the poem a *summa* of knowledge. Moreover, Dante's masterpiece was increasingly perceived as a standard poetic linguistic model and as an endless reservoir of words and images, even for Latin poets such as Ugolino Verino. Parodic rewritings were also produced by minor poets such as Stefano Finiguerri 'il Za' and most prominently by Lorenzo de' Medici in his youthful *Simposio*.

The political dimension of the reception of the *Commedia* became especially evident in the years of conflict between the oligarchy governing the Florentine Republic and the rising Medici faction. The appointment of the pro-oligarchy figure Francesco Filelfo as lecturer on Dante (1431–4) in the prestigious setting of the city's cathedral raised bitter controversies, which led to Filelfo being attacked and to his flight at the time of the definitive return of Cosimo de' Medici to the city in 1434. In Medicean Florence, the vernacular acquired an undisputed status as a legitimate literary language. The cult of Dante reached its climax, and the obsession with the *Commedia*, which characterized much of the afterlife of Dante's *oeuvre*, was tempered by an interest in the so-called 'minor works'. His *Rime* feature in the opening of the anthology that the most important Florentine poet of the time, Angelo Poliziano, together with Lorenzo de' Medici prepared in 1477, the so-called *Raccolta aragonese*. The introductory epistle clearly sets the co-ordinates of a vernacular literary canon, where Dante and Petrarch feature – with a direct reference to *Purgatorio* XVI, 107 – as 'two wonderful suns' (due mirabili soli),[9] according to a harmonizing poetic agenda already pursued by Poliziano's and Lorenzo's mentor, Cristoforo Landino. The *Commedia*, however, remained centre stage, and continued to attract large numbers of readers. Among these, the notary Piero Bonaccorsi and Antonio Manetti were the initiators of the peculiarly Florentine interest in the topography of the poem's otherworld, which is also apparent in Landino's commentary. The merchant and politician Matteo Palmieri is the author of a lengthy poem in *terza rima* entitled *Città di Dio* (1464–6), which closely imitates the *Commedia* both structurally and thematically. What is more, this work presents a clearly Platonic interpretation of Dante's poem – already outlined in Palmieri's earlier dialogue *Vita civile* (1434–6). Particularly revealing is its reading of the pilgrim's loss in the dark wood as a symbolic representation of the corruption to which the soul is doomed when it descends to earth.

The Platonic interpretation of the poem emerges from the Florentine philosophical environment dominated by Marsilio Ficino, and which found its most authoritative interpretation in Landino's commentary (1481), where Dante is presented as a Platonic poet, a prophet, and an emblem of Florentine civic life. Landino's work, which relies significantly on previous exegesis, is remarkable for its erudition, its classical and linguistic expertise, its philosophical knowledge, and its capacity to synthesize the tradition of earlier encyclopaedic commentaries. It deals with many of the concerns that characterize the *Commedia*'s fourteenth-century reception. The poem is presented as on a par with classical texts, to the extent that, according to an interpretation that relies on Pietro Alighieri, its structure is the same as Virgil's *Aeneid*, inasmuch as the pilgrim's and Aeneas' journeys allegorically represent human life. Dante is celebrated as the author who resuscitated poetry, and who, as a poet-theologian, acts as a mediator between God and men. Boccaccio's perspective is thus filtered through the lens of Ficino's notion of poetry as a means of divine illumination.

The presentation to the Medici of the dedicatory copy of the *Commedia* with the commentary by Landino[10] constitutes the climax of the reception of the poem in the fifteenth century. This sumptuous large-format book was in part a response to the first printed editions of the *Commedia*, which were produced outside Florence, including the first edition (*princeps*) printed in Foligno in 1472, and most prominently the one promoted by Martino Paolo Nibia in 1478 in the rival city of Milan, which featured the Bolognese commentary by Iacomo della Lana. The extant copies of the first edition of Landino's commentary include a variable number of engravings based on drawings by the most famous Florentine artist of the time, Sandro Botticelli. In the prologue to his commentary, which includes the vernacular translation of a letter by Ficino, Landino promoted the image of a Dante who, after his death in exile, is finally reunited with his hometown. Laurentian Florence is depicted as a new Athens, where learning, literature, the arts, and prosperity flourish. The troubling reality of Dante's exile had been repeatedly confronted by Florentines ever since Boccaccio's call for a return of the poet's remains from Ravenna at the beginning of his biography. To mark the centenary of Dante's birth in 1465, the Laurentian government commissioned Domenico di Michelino to paint a celebratory canvas which was symbolically placed in the city's cathedral. The iconography of the *Allegory of the Commedia,* which presents Dante with a copy of the poem before the three realms of the afterlife and with Florence on his left, implies the poet's return to his city, which appears as divinely sanctioned. Placed at the opposite side to Hell, Florence is blessed by the light and wisdom of the heaven of the Sun, which shines over Brunelleschi's dome. A few years later, in Landino's prologue, Dante symbolically returns to his city courtesy of the commentary, which itself is immediately disseminated across Italy as the new standard of Dante's exegesis. At the end of the fifteenth century and amidst the splendid blossoming of Medicean Florence, the fortune of the *Commedia* had reached a climax and guaranteed to its author a magisterial authoritative status.

Notes

1. C. Vecce, *Leonardo* (Rome: Salerno, 2006), pp. 362–3.
2. Francesco da Barberino, *I documenti d'Amore*, ed. F. Egidi, 4 vols. (Rome: Presso la Società, 1905), II, 375.
3. S. Gilson, '"La divinità di Dante": The Problematics of Dante's Critical Reception from the Fourteenth to the Sixteenth Centuries' in R. Antonelli *et al.* (eds.), *Dante oggi*, 3 vols. (Rome: Viella, 2011), I, 581–603 (p. 587).
4. The poet Moggio Moggi (*c.*1330–88) refers to the event in one of his poems; see M. Moggi, *Carmi ed epistole*, ed. P. Garbini (Padua: Antenore, 1996), pp. xix–xx, and 20–8.

5. This copy has been identified in Vatican ms. Lat. 3199, later used by the humanist Pietro Bembo to prepare his milestone edition of the poem printed by the Venetian publisher Aldus Manutius in 1502.

6. *Boccaccio's Expositions on Dante's Comedy*, ed. and trans. M. Papio (Toronto University Press, 2009), p. 65.

7. G. Boccaccio, *Rime*, ed. R. Leporatti (Florence: Sismel-Edizioni del Galluzzo, 2013), pp. 7–10.

8. British Library, ms. Yates Thompson 36.

9. A. Poliziano, 'Epistola' to the *Raccolta aragonese*, ed. E. Garin, in *Prosatori latini del Quattrocento*, ed. C. Varese (Milan and Naples: Ricciardi, 1952), pp. 985–90 (p. 989).

10. Florence, Biblioteca Nazionale Centrale, ms. Banco Rari 341.

16

FABIO CAMILLETTI

Later Reception from 1481 to the Present

1481–1766: A 'Wild and Gloomy Poem'

'Cousin Francis', [Miss Vernon] said ... 'I have encountered this morning a difficult passage in the Divina Commedia of Dante; will you have the goodness to step to the library and give me your assistance? and when you have unearthed for me the meaning of the obscure Florentine, we will join the rest at Birkenwood-bank, and see their luck at unearthing the badger' ... Rashleigh made an effort to accompany us. 'I am something better skilled', he said, 'at tracking the sense of Dante through the metaphors and elisions of his wild and gloomy poem, than at hunting the poor inoffensive hermit yonder out of his cave'.[1]

The fleeting mention of the *Commedia* in Walter Scott's *Rob Roy* (1817) perfectly captures how Dante's poem was received between the end of the eighteenth century and the beginning of the nineteenth, when it exited the cabinet of medieval curiosities – as a historical object of study for erudite scholars – and entered the canon of world literature. In 1817, the *Commedia* was so familiar to the reader that its title might be left in Italian; Miss Vernon may name Dante 'the obscure Florentine' almost by definition, implicitly opposing Dante's Florence – the medieval commune plagued by civil wars, the city of Giotto and Cimabue – to the Florence of the Renaissance, which had monopolized the imaginary of the Grand Tour. In Scott's passage, Dante can be an acceptable reading for young girls, a fashionable topic for conversation, and even an occasion for gallant interactions interspersed between country games. At the same time, he is described as an 'obscure' poet, the author of a 'wild and gloomy' work, whose main characteristics are 'metaphors and elisions', namely, the traditional stock of the literary sublime.

For centuries, precisely these features – obscurity and gloominess, wildness and difficulty – had excluded Dante from the Italian (and, more broadly, Western) lyric canon, whose boundaries and strict compartmentalization in terms of genres had been fixed in the Renaissance by Pietro Bembo. An unclassifiable work, with no identifiable precursor nor direct follower, the *Commedia* eschewed the rigorous normativity of Bembo's purist classicism as far as genre, language, and style were concerned. No surprise, then, if in the age of classicism – largely corresponding to the sixteenth century – Dante remained a relatively marginal presence, notwithstanding the textual studies produced by the Florentine Academy and, later, by the Accademia della Crusca, and by scholars such as Benedetto Varchi and Vincenzo Borghini. During the same period, the *Commedia* was a major source for Ludovico Ariosto's *Orlando furioso* (1516–32) and Torquato Tasso's *Gerusalemme liberata* (1581), and was also translated into Spanish (1515) and French (1596). However, the dominant position of Petrarchism prevented any substantial evaluation of Dante and the *Commedia* on a European scale.

The seventeenth century corresponds to the lowest point in the history of Dante's fame. Alongside aesthetic and literary biases, this was a consequence of political and religious factors. On the one hand, the *Commedia* was trapped within the broader confrontation between classicism and the baroque. Whereas the former condemned its 'obscurity' and 'wildness' as forms of linguistic and stylistic unruliness, the latter, in its constant pursuit for novelty, saw Dante's poem as the relic of a past age that was irrelevant for the present. On the other hand, as a potentially anti-clerical work, taking a firm stance as regards the separation between secular and religious powers, the *Commedia* could not be easily welcomed during the decades witnessing the theorization and affirmation of absolute monarchy and the strict censorship, in Catholic countries, of the Counter-Reformation. As a consequence, at the height of Counter-Reformation repression, the reading of the *Commedia* – after the *Monarchia* had been banned in the mid-sixteenth century – was severely discouraged by the Church. All these elements contributed to the limited circulation and popularity of the *Commedia*. Only three editions appeared between 1613 and 1629, and, tellingly, they were all printed in the Republic of Venice, where the Church's control over publishing was restricted. At the same time, outside Italy, interest in Dante continued to be scarce or non-existent. Isolated exceptions were protestant countries, such as England – where Dante stimulated the interest of a poet of the calibre of John Milton – and Germany, where occasional translations of single groups of tercets began to appear from the early seventeenth century.

The anti-baroque reaction of the Academy or Arcadia, between the last decade of the seventeenth century and the beginning of the eighteenth, was not particularly favourable to Dante either. The appraisal of Dante in Gian Vincenzo Gravina's *Della ragion poetica* (1708) is largely limited to moral and historical elements. Gravina considered Dante a medieval equivalent of Homer and an effective ethical writer. However, overall, he excluded him as a model for imitation, given the dominant Aristotelian–Horatian normativity pervading Italy's contemporary literary scene, which was reflected in Gravina's treatise. Nonetheless, Dante's poem could be considered an effective and thought-provoking historical document, as is the case in the works of Giovan Battista Vico and Ludovico Antonio Muratori, who triggered a renewed interest in the history of the Italian Middle Ages through his editorship of *Rerum Italicarum Scriptores* (1723–51; Writers on Italian Matters) and *Antiquitates Italicae Medii Aevi* (1738–43; Italian Antiquities of the Middle Ages). Such interest in Dante and medieval Italian literature corresponded to a broader European trend towards the historicization of national literary narratives, eliciting a new perspective on the Middle Ages as the cradle of individual national identities. It is in light of these developments that the first complete publication of Dante's *oeuvre* – in five volumes and printed in Venice between 1739 and 1741 – ought to be considered, as well as the 1757–8 edition, also published in Venice, accompanied by Giuseppe Bencivenni Pelli's account of Dante's life and history of the Alighieri family. Notwithstanding its many mistakes, Pelli's account was to be the century's most comprehensive biography of Dante, as well as a fundamental source for the historical assessment of the *Commedia*.

However, from a literary viewpoint, Dante continued to face classicism's harsh condemnation, as well as the ideological biases of Enlightenment thinkers against the age of feudalism and religious 'obscurantism'. Although an Arcadian scholar such as Giovanni Mario Crescimbeni did propose some isolated passages as stylistic models, the *Commedia* was normally viewed as a 'barbaric' and chaotic work, flaunting rules of good taste, and characterized by verbal excess and an unbridled imagination. The most emblematic example of this tendency is Voltaire, whose disparaging treatment of Dante, most notably in the *Dictionnaire philosophique* (1764), underpinned and popularized the Enlightenment appreciation of Dante as a primitive writer: 'The Italians call him divine', Voltaire wrote, 'but it is a mysterious divinity; few men understand his oracles, and although there are commentators, that may be an additional reason why he is little comprehended ... What ... is the taste of this poem? An exceedingly wild one, but it contains verses so happy and piquant that it has not lain dormant for four centuries and never will be laid aside'.[2] Voltaire's comments, as well as the harsh judgement on Dante pronounced by the Jesuit Saverio Bettinelli in his *Lettere virgiliane* (1757), triggered the reaction of Gasparo Gozzi and Giuseppe Baretti, resulting in a literary quarrel that would deeply influence the reception of Dante by authors – such as Vincenzo Monti and Ugo Foscolo – writing at the historical turn between neoclassicism and romanticism.

1767–1830: Romanticism, the Gothic, and the Lure of Italy

In 1790, in his collection *The Marriage of Heaven and Hell*, William Blake made the claim that '[t]he reason Milton wrote in fetters when he wrote of Angels and God, and at liberty when of Devils and Hell, is because he was a true Poet and of the Devil's party without knowing it'.[3] The same remark, during those same years, could have been perfectly applied to Dante and his *Inferno*. Indeed, the beginning of Dante's modern fame can be dated between the 1760s and the late 1820s, namely, when the modern theorization of the sublime, the vogue of the Gothic, and the advent of romantic (or more broadly anti-classicist) movements across Europe, afforded new perspectives upon the 'wildness' and 'gloominess' of the *Commedia*, and of the *Inferno* in particular. This was a transnational phenomenon that occurred through and thanks to the cultural exchanges of the age of revolutions, and, despite national differences, Dante's reception followed a generally homogeneous pattern across Europe.

In a first phase, between the 1760s and the 1780s, the *Commedia* was translated into the principal European languages, conforming to an emerging interest in the poem among the broader public. However, the translations were not normally characterized by their editorial care, and were often restricted to the *Inferno*. Between 1767 and 1799 Leberecht Bachenschwanz translated the entire *Commedia* into German; in 1776 Julien-Jacques Moutonnet de Clairfons rendered the *Inferno* into French, as did Charles Rogers into English in 1782; a new French translation of the *Inferno* by Antoine de Rivarol appeared in 1783; finally, in 1785, Henry Boyd began his translation of the whole poem into English.

The second phase can be dated from the early 1790s to circa 1818, when the lecture on Dante by Samuel Taylor Coleridge and an article by Foscolo in the *Edinburgh Review* created the conditions for the poet's broader reception across the various romantic movements in Europe. This period witnessed an increasing growth of references to Dante's work on the part of European intellectuals, testifying to the emerging role of the *Commedia* within the canon of world literature. Pivotal in this regard were the essay 'On the Divine Comedy' published by August Wilhelm Schlegel in 1791 and the note penned by his brother Friedrich which appeared in 1798 in the periodical *Athenäum*. In these texts, Dante was presented as the most illustrious model for the syncretistic cultural project undertaken by the romantic circle of Jena. Concurrently, in England, John Flaxman illustrated the whole poem (1792–3), re-reading Dante through the paradigms of artistic primitivism. August Wilhelm Schlegel's acquaintance with Madame de Staël's circle at Coppet intersected with the activity of Jean Charles Léonard Simonde de

Sismondi and Pierre-Louis Ginguené, whose works on medieval Italian history and literature would play a central role in the reception of Dante in France and beyond. However, during this phase, Dante appears to have been more referenced than read. In most cases, authors mentioned in general terms the episodes of Ugolino and of Francesca, and attention was normally focused on the *Inferno*. Thus, de Staël, whose novel *Corinne, ou l'Italie* (1807) alludes to just those two passages, defined Dante as a 'modern Homer' who had drawn his inspiration from the depths of Hell. Nonetheless, this new fashion encouraged a new bout of translations, resulting in the need for scholarly editions with accompanying introductions and commentaries. Such is the case with the French translation by Artaud de Montor of 1811–13, a reference work for the whole romantic generation; with the German translation published by Karl-Ludwig Kannegiesser beginning in 1814; and especially with the English translation by Henry Francis Cary published in 1806 (*Inferno*), 1814 (*Purgatorio*), and 1818 (*Paradiso*). Cary's work, which appeared in the United States in 1822, paved the way for the independent and local reception of Dante and the *Commedia* in the English-speaking world.

The third phase, from 1818 to the end of the 1820s, saw Dante being definitively established as a central presence in the European canon, thanks especially to the contributions of Coleridge and Foscolo, but also to those of the second generation of British romantics (Byron, Keats, and Shelley), of Parisian romantic circles, and of the Florentine Gabinetto Vieusseux. Additionally, influential translations were published, such as the German ones by Karl Streckfuss (1824–6) – thanks to which Goethe probably first came into contact with the *Commedia* – and Prince John of Saxony, using the pseudonym of Philalethes, of 1828–33, as well as Antoine Deschamps' 1829 French translation. Most of all, the *Commedia* became a popular and highly fashionable source for the visual arts. After Flaxman and Henry Fuseli, there followed Jean-Auguste-Dominique Ingres' and Joshua Reynolds' paintings inspired by Ugolino and Francesca, Blake's illustrations of 1824–7, and Eugène Delacroix's *La barque de Dante* (1822).

Basically, the romantic reception of Dante privileged those features of the *Commedia* that the baroque and Enlightenment had condemned. The 'irregularity' of Dante's poem made it, for the Schlegel brothers, the perfect model for 'universal' poetry, bridging literature, philosophy, theology, and science. For Friedrich, the *Commedia* was the sole example of 'transcendental poetry', using allegory and mysticism to express the sublime. Revealingly, the recuperation of Dante happens concurrently with the flourishing of the Gothic genre, from Horace Walpole's *The Castle of Otranto* (1764) to Mary Shelley's *Frankenstein* (1818 and 1831), and the modern reconfiguration of the sublime, originating in Edmund Burke's *A Philosophical Enquiry into the Origin of Our Ideas of the Sublime and Beautiful* (1757). A quintessentially sublime work, moving from the depths of Hell to the depiction of the light of Paradise, Dante's *Commedia* matches the pre-romantic and romantic taste for all that is horrid and prone to excess, revealing a world in which anthropophagy and torture, abuse and betrayal, turbid sexuality and unruly behaviour are described through an elliptical and overtly 'primitive' style. Dante's poem is an implicit model for experiments in literary subversion. This strain of the *Commedia*'s reception is most evident in the popularity of the Ugolino episode. Extensively translated as a self-standing text, it was also an apt subject for painting, as evidenced by Reynolds' and Fuseli's two eponymous artworks (1773 and 1806). In both, Ugolino serves as an emblem of vehement and contradictory passions, in line with contemporary reflection on the limits of the visual arts when compared to literature, which was triggered by Gotthold Ephraim Lessing's *Laocoon* (1766). Furthermore, Ugolino was treated as an example of Christian sublime in de Staël's *Corinne* and François-René de Chateaubriand's *Génie du Christianisme* (1802).

Dante's *Commedia* also connected with the lure of Italy characteristic of the Grand Tour imaginary, marking the shift from an idea of Italy as a land of ancient ruins and the cradle of the Renaissance to the appraisal of the Italian Middle Ages as the earliest seed of Italian identity and of the impulse towards independence. Heralded by Sismondi's work on early Italian republics, first published in 1807, the ideal of the Italian medieval commune triggered a different perspective on Italian cities and on Florence specifically. In this regard, Dante acted as a symbol of medieval Italy, as well as of Italy's national identity: a symbol that strongly resonated with the claims for independence animating Italy during the years of the Bourbon Restoration – claims that many foreign travellers viewed with sympathy. Furthermore, Dante was appropriated by neo-Catholicism trends characterizing some manifestations of romanticism, from the circle of Jena – August Wilhelm Schlegel and Ludwig Tieck viewed the *Commedia* as the *summa* of an age when art and religion were still intertwined – to Chateaubriand who praised Dante's poem as the emblem of the totalizing faith of medieval Europe.

Finally, romantic readers were fascinated by the representation of passions in the *Commedia*. In a period that witnessed the rediscovery, and in many ways the reinvention, of medieval courtly love, considered as the wellspring of European identity, Dante's poem provided two powerful models for conceptualizing desire: the idea of love as a destructive passion in the episode of Francesca; and the heavenly love for Beatrice. Whereas the cult of Beatrice reached a peak in popularity in the second half of the nineteenth century, thanks to the Pre-Raphaelites, the preoccupation with Francesca spans the whole romantic age. Translated by Byron in 1816, illustrated by Ingres in 1819 and by Ary Scheffer in 1822, the pilgrim's meeting with Francesca inspired, among others, Silvio Pellico's tragedy *Francesca da Rimini* (1815) and Leigh Hunt's narrative poem *The Story of Rimini* (1816).

1831–1913: Nationalism, Historicism, and the Impossibility of a 'Modern' *Comedy*

The nineteenth century marked the consolidation of Dante's vital presence in the Western canon, alongside Homer, Shakespeare, Cervantes, and Goethe. Scholarly work and historical inquiry came together to make the *Commedia* available to a broad readership, thanks to editions and translations disseminating the work worldwide, including Sweden (1842–53), Russia (1843), Portugal (1886), Brazil (1888), and Argentina (1894). At the same time, the long nineteenth century, after the pan-European enthusiasm of the romantic age, saw Dante's fame becoming polarized between Italy and the Anglo-American world. Although Dante remained an important reference for writers and artists worldwide, the influence of the *Commedia* progressively became a largely Anglo-Italian affair.

The Risorgimento played a fundamental role in this regard. Dante had already become part of nationalist aspirations during the eighteenth century, as occurred in the writings of Giuseppe Parini and Vincenzo Monti, and in Foscolo's systematic use of quotations from the *Commedia* in his patriotic novel *Ultime lettere di Jacopo Ortis* (1799, 1801, and 1816). During the Bourbon Restoration, Dante was discussed in the cultural circles of romantic Milan and of the Gabinetto Vieusseux, and a famous patriotic poem by Giacomo Leopardi took its inspiration from a projected monument to Dante which was to be erected in Florence. Dante was viewed both as a precursor of Italy's national identity and as the 'founder' of the Italian language, a role that he was assigned as a result of the vogue of *trecentismo*, namely, the return to fourteenth-century writers as models of style. The image of Dante as the 'father' of Italy's national language permeated the influential 1837 commentary on the *Commedia* by Niccolò Tommaseo. Dante entered the Risorgimento imaginary beyond Italy too. In England, his status as an exile provided a framework for Italian *émigrés* with which to interpret and narrativize their own experiences. In 1865, the celebrations for the sixth centenary of Dante's birth became an occasion for the newly unified Italy to cement its identity by establishing Dante as the 'father' of the nation. 1888 witnessed the birth, in Florence, of the Società Dantesca Italiana.

The long nineteenth century also corresponds to the foundation of Dante studies as a modern academic discipline. In France, the university lectures of 1833–4 on Italian literature by Claude Fauriel paved the way for a new and scholarly understanding of Dante with a particular emphasis on theology, the first and most important outcome of which was the study *Dante et la philosophie catholique au XIIIème siècle* (1839) by Frédéric Ozanam. In England, a similar role was played by Thomas Carlyle's lectures of 1838–40 that paired Dante and Shakespeare as examples of 'the hero as poet'. However, the actual birth of English-language Dante studies occurred in the 1860s with Henry Clark Barlow's textual-critical studies, the founding of the Oxford Dante Society in 1876, the publication of the so-called 'Oxford Dante' (1894) edited by Edward Moore, Paget Toynbee's *Dictionary of Proper Names and Notable Matters in the Works of Dante* (1898), and Edmund Gardner's studies on the poet's thought. In 1899–1901, the Temple Classics edition and translation of the *Commedia* by Philip Henry Wicksteed and Hermann Oelsner appeared. This edition would prove to be highly influential on modernist poets, including T. S. Eliot and Ezra Pound. In the United States, the 1867 version of the *Inferno* by Thomas W. Parsons, the translation of the *Commedia* by Henry W. Longfellow (1865–7), and the contributions of James R. Lowell and of Charles E. Norton paved the way for the foundation of the Dante Society of America in 1880 and for the establishment of a distinctly American tradition of Dante studies.

Italian scholarship was monopolized by Francesco De Sanctis' reading of Dante that utilized the legacy of romantic criticism to interpret the conjunction between theology and history in the *Commedia*, and by the so-called *scuola storica* of Giosuè Carducci and Pio Rajna, which challenged De Sanctis in the name of a scientific, text-based, and historicist understanding of the poem and its context. The 'historical school' paved the way for the later work of Michele Barbi, whose methodology was firmly grounded in a philological approach. In Germany, after romanticism, Dante's influence on contemporary literature waned, but he became a major focus for literary scholarship: Karl Witte's textual-critical studies, begun in the 1820s, culminated in 1865 in his monumental edition of the *Commedia*; and the same year witnessed the establishment of the Deutsche Dante-Gesellschaft. The end of the century saw the publication of Franz Xaver Kraus's *Dante: Sein Leben und Werk, sein Verhältnis zur Kunst und Politik*; while, in 1908, Karl Vossler published his influential work *Die göttliche Komödie*.

The historical (and historicist) work of late nineteenth-century Dante scholarship resulted in a more sophisticated appreciation of the *Commedia* than the romantic one. Rather than a 'primitive' work nourishing the modern artist's neo-medieval nostalgia, the historicization of Dante's poem as a 'document' for understanding medieval history, philosophy, and poetry triggered artists' reflection on the cultural fissure separating the medieval mind, which could still envisage a 'universal' and all-encompassing poem, from the modern one, characterized by a loss of experience and the sense of the impossibility of grasping the real in its totality. Not by chance, therefore, did Ulysses become, after Ugolino and Francesca, one of the *Commedia*'s key figures haunting nineteenth-century sensibilities, from Alfred Tennyson's *Ulysses* (1833) to Giovanni Pascoli's *L'ultimo viaggio* (1904). Ulysses, the pilgrim's failed counterpart, whose journey to the southern hemisphere was an emblem of flawed human striving towards knowledge and experience, epitomized the 'folly' of the modern poet and the feeling of displacement caused by an ultimately ungraspable world. Even the esoteric interpretations of the *Commedia* proposed by Gabriele Rossetti, Eugène Aroux, Pascoli, and Luigi Valli can be seen as unconvincing yet revealing answers to the complexity of a poem whose understanding lay beyond contemporary sensibilities, and whose richly intertwined levels of meaning – literal, moral, allegorical, and anagogical – ultimately result in its inaccessibility for moderns. The *Commedia* is a fundamentally 'other' and totalizing work, standing as an antithetical paragon of the dispersed knowledge of the modern age which literature was no longer able to grasp. Perhaps the awareness of Dante's alterity also underlaid attempts at conveying the 'totality' of his poetic experience by means and media other than the literary – an aspiration that was part of the search, characteristic of the whole *fin de siècle*, for a 'total' form of art. Notable examples include: the Pre-Raphaelite ideal of bridging literature, the visual arts, and craftsmanship; illustrated editions of the poem, from that by Gustave Doré (1861–8) to the painted *Commedia* edited in 1900 by the photographic studio Alinari; theatrical and balletic adaptations (Piotr Tchaikovsky in 1876 and Gabriele d'Annunzio in 1901 and 1914); and, finally, cinema – short films on Ugolino, Francesca, and Pia de' Tolomei (1908–09), and the first *Inferno* by Francesco Bertolini, Giuseppe de Liguoro, and Adolfo Padovan in 1911.

1914–: The Inferno of the Twentieth Century and Beyond

'A crowd flowed over London Bridge, so many, / I had not thought death had undone so many'. Towards the end of the first part of *The Waste Land* (1922), T. S. Eliot translates almost literally (and declares it in his notes) *Inferno* III, 55–7.[4] In Eliot's poem, Dante is ubiquitous – even its title recalls the 'paese guasto' of *Inferno* XIV, 94. Fragments from the *Commedia* are interspersed within a complex system of more or less dissimulated quotations from the Eastern and Western literary traditions, some of which the poet elucidates in his annotations. Eliot, who would write a highly influential essay on Dante (1929), thus provided personal answers to the aporias of Victorian readings of the poem: Dante could be an object of study and, at the same time, an author whose intrinsic power could be reactivated in an age of disenchantment by means of estrangement. Such an effect is achieved, in the passage above, by drastically transforming the Dantean echo, originally referring to the 'uncommitted', into a crowd of the dead that, in 1922 London, evoked rather more literal resonances. Thus, the First World War and its traumatic memory pervasively haunt *The Waste Land*, as well as James Joyce's *Ulysses* (also published in 1922) and Pound's *Cantos* (begun in 1915 and published starting in 1925), both of which were deeply influenced by the *Commedia*, especially as regards linguistic and stylistic freedom.

Works such as these, to which should be added the writings of W. B. Yeats and Virginia Woolf, herald a new way of reading and reshaping the *Commedia* that would pervade the twentieth century after the experiences of two world wars, the crimes of totalitarian regimes, and the rise and fall of ideologies. Twentieth-century authors cease to see Dante's work as an inimitable model of syncretistic, prophetic, and transcendental poetry. Instead, they draw on its linguistic experimentation (most notably in Joyce's *Finnegans Wake* of 1939), its alternation between first-person mode and universalizing claim, and its striving to represent the ineffable to express the 'unsayable' of their own time. The *Commedia* offers a framework to be freely de-structured (and re-structured) in order to interpret the traumas of history. In the years of Stalinist purges, the Russian poet and essayist Osip Mandel'štam wrote his *Conversation about Dante* (1933), taking Ulysses as a paradigm of human freedom and the figure of Dante the exile as a model for negotiating political disillusion. Ulysses is also a central figure in Primo Levi's *Se questo è un uomo* (1947), an antidote against the dehumanization brought about by Nazi concentration camps. In Pier Paolo Pasolini's unfinished *La divina Mimesis* (1975), but planned since 1963, Dante's descent to Hell becomes the structure with which to frame and narrativize the slow decay of Italy after the disillusionments of the post-war period and the rise of neo-capitalism. Throughout the twentieth century, the *Inferno*'s structure of crime and punishment, which raises ethical questions about order and unruliness, is powerfully employed to frame and express situations of marginality in terms of desire and sexual identity (for example by gay authors such as Frank Bidart, Robert Duncan, Robin Blaser, and Derek Jarman), of race (by the Afro-American film-maker Spencer Williams in his *Go Down, Death* [1944] and by the black revolutionary Amiri Baraka, who entitled his autobiographical novel of 1965 *The System of Dante's Hell*), of errancy (as in Seamus Heaney's 1979 collection *Field Work* or Derek Walcott's *Omeros* of

1990), and of seclusion (as in Ron Jenkins' play *To See the Stars*, performed in a women's prison in Connecticut and later in several other places of confinement around the world). The last such experiment is Giorgio Pressburger's novel *Nel regno oscuro* (2008), witnessing a significant shift from Hell as a place of punishment for the guilty to a space of suffering and an appeal to remember the victims of history. Pressburger's autobiographical narrator, accompanied by Sigmund Freud, enters a Hell where the victims of twentieth-century tragedies tell their stories, and their descent culminates in the contemplation of the Shoah as the most inexpressible evil. In 2013, Pressburger published a sequel to his novel, progressing from *Inferno* to *Purgatorio* and *Paradiso*. The result is *Storia umana e inumana*, in which Freud is replaced by Simone Weil performing the role of Beatrice.

The multiple strains of twentieth- and twenty-first-century scholarship on the *Commedia* are too numerous to be replayed here. The most significant centres remain Italy, where the long-lasting influence of historicism and philological approaches has at times been integrated with methodological suggestions deriving from Russian formalism, French structuralism, and the so-called *critica stilistica*; the United Kingdom, whose tradition of Dante studies has opened new research pathways in a wide variety of fields, including Dante's textual history and reception, his experimentation, and the relationship between his *oeuvre* and medieval forms of knowledge, including philosophy, theology, and the other 'sciences'; and the United States, where the legacy of Charles S. Singleton's studies on allegory has given birth to a broad scholarly tradition in which attention to the multiple levels of meaning in the *Commedia* has suggestively intersected with reader-oriented criticism, deconstruction, and New Historicism. The interpretations of a few scholars have moved beyond the academic sphere to produce new modes of reading. Thus, Erich Auerbach's essays on the 'secular world' in the *Commedia* (1929), as well as his chapter on Dante's realism in *Mimesis* (1946), alongside Gianfranco Contini's affirmation of a 'realist' and 'plurilingual' Dante, together with the distinction between 'Dante character' and 'Dante the poet', play a key role in the use of the *Commedia* by late-twentieth -century film-makers such as Pasolini, Federico Fellini, and Michelangelo Antonioni, endeavouring to renegotiate notions of realism.

In recent years, but following a trend that was already apparent in the late nineteenth century, the *Commedia* has significantly entered into popular culture: cinema (directors explicitly influenced by Dante include Peter Greenaway and David Lynch); pop music; crime fiction (Matthew Pearl's 2003 novel *The Dante Club*; Giulio Leoni's series on Dante detective published since 2004; Dan Brown's 2013 *Inferno*); videogames (*Dante's Inferno*, 2010); and multimedia projects, such as *Inferno 2033*, combining cinema, videogaming, and elements drawn from graphic novels (since 2013). The worldwide success of public readings of the *Commedia* by the writer Vittorio Sermonti and the Academy Award winner Roberto Benigni confirm the enduring vitality of Dante's poem in today's world.

Notes

1. W. Scott, *Rob Roy*, in *The Prose Works*, 8 vols. (Paris: Galignani, 1827–34), I, p. 498.
2. Quoted in M. Caesar (ed.), *Dante: The Critical Heritage, 1314(?)–1870* (London and New York: Taylor & Francis, 1989), pp. 375–7.
3. W. Blake, *Selected Poetry and Prose*, ed. D. Fuller (New York: Pearson, 2000), p. 129.
4. T. S. Eliot, *The Waste Land and Other Poems* (Orlando: Harvest, 2014), p. 60.

FURTHER READING

1   Narrative Structure

Auerbach, Erich, *Dante, Poet of the Secular World* (Chicago University Press, 1961).
Barański, Zygmunt G., 'The Poetics of Meter: Terza Rima, "Canto," "Canzon," "Cantica"' in T. J. Cachey Jr. (ed.), *Dante Now* (University of Notre Dame Press, 1995), pp. 3–41.
Barolini, Teodolinda, *The Undivine Comedy. Detheologizing Dante* (Princeton University Press, 1992)
    'Medieval Multiculturalism and Dante's Theology of Hell' in J. Francese (ed.), *The Craft and the Fury. Essays in Memory of Glauco Cambon* (West Lafayette, IN: Bordighera Press, 2000), pp. 82–102.
Cogan, Marc, *The Design in the Wax. The Structure of the 'Divine Comedy' and Its Meaning* (University of Notre Dame Press, 1999)
Corbett, George and Heather Webb (eds.), *Vertical Readings in Dante's 'Comedy'* (Cambridge: Open Book Publishers, 2015).
Croce, Benedetto, *The Poetry of Dante* (New York: Henry Holt & Co., 1922).
Ferrante, Joan, 'A Poetics of Chaos and Harmony' in R. Jacoff (ed.), *The Cambridge Companion to Dante* (Cambridge University Press, 2007), pp. 181–99
Hollander, Robert, 'Two Notes on Dante: *Inferno* VII and VIII: Dante's Treatment of Wrath and the Ordering of *Inferno*', *The Italianist*, 34 (2014), 107–17.
Pertile, Lino, 'A Desire of Paradise: Dante and Mysticism' in A. A. Iannucci (ed.), *Dante* (University of Toronto Press, 1997), pp. 148–66.
    '"Trasmutabile per tutte guise": Dante in the *Comedy*' in S. Fortuna *et al.* (eds.), *Dante's Plurilingualism: Authority, Knowledge, Subjectivity* (Oxford: Legenda, 2010), pp. 164–78.
Russo, Vittorio, *Il romanzo teologico. Sondaggi sulla 'Commedia' di Dante* (Naples: Liguori, 1984), pp. 13–53.
Singleton, Charles S., 'The Poet's Number at the Center', *MLN*, 71 (1966), 1–10.

2   Dante-poet, Dante-character, Dante Alighieri

Ascoli, Albert R., *Dante and the Making of a Modern Author* (Cambridge University Press, 2008).

Auerbach, Erich, 'Dante's Addresses to the Reader', *Romance Philology*, 7 (1954), 268–78.

Barolini, Teodolinda, *The Undivine Comedy: Detheologizing Dante* (Princeton University Press, 1992).

Contini, Gianfranco, *Un'idea di Dante* (Turin: Einaudi, 1976).

Dronke, Peter, *Poetic Individuality in the Middle Ages* (Oxford: Clarendon Press, 1970).

Ferrara, Sabrina, *La parola dell'esilio. Autore e lettori nelle opere di Dante in esilio* (Florence: Cesati, 2016).

Foster, Kenelm, *The Two Dantes and Other Studies* (London: Darton, Longman, and Todd, 1977).

Freccero, John, 'Allegory and Autobiography' in R. Jacoff (ed.), *The Cambridge Companion to Dante* (Cambridge University Press, 2007), pp. 161–80.

Hollander Robert: *Allegory in Dante's 'Commedia'* (Princeton University Press, 1969).

Iannucci, Amilcare A. (ed.), *Dante e la 'bella scola' della poesia* (Ravenna: Longo, 1993).

Jacoff, Rachel, 'Dante, Geremia e la problematica profetica' in G. Barblan (ed.), *Dante e la Bibbia* (Florence: Olschki, 1988), pp. 113–23.

Ledda, Giuseppe, *La guerra della lingua. Ineffabilità, retorica e narrativa nella 'Commedia' di Dante* (Ravenna: Longo, 2002).

La Bibbia di Dante (Turin: Claudiana, 2015).

Mazzotta, Giuseppe, *Dante, Poet of the Desert* (Princeton University Press, 1979).

Pertile, Lino: *La puttana e il gigante: Dal 'Cantico dei Cantici' al Paradiso Terrestre di Dante* (Ravenna: Longo, 1998).

Picone, Michelangelo, 'Ovid and the "exul Inmeritus"' in T. Barolini and W. Storey (eds.), *Dante for the New Millennium* (New York: Fordham University Press, 2003), pp. 289–307.

Santagata, Marco, *Dante. The Story of His Life* (Cambridge, MA: Belknap Press, 2016).

Singleton, Charles S., *Dante Studies. 1. Elements of Structure* (Cambridge, MA: Harvard University Press, 1954).

Spitzer, Leo, 'Note on the Poetic and Empirical "I" in Medieval Authors', *Traditio*, 4 (1946), 414–22.

'The Addresses to the Reader in the *Commedia*', *Italica*, 32 (1955), 143–65.

Tavoni, Mirko, *Qualche idea su Dante* (Bologna: il Mulino, 2016).

3 Characterization

Auerbach, Erich, 'Figura' (1938) in *Scenes from the Drama of European Literature* (Minneapolis: University of Minnesota Press, 1984), pp. 11–76.

Barnes, John C. and Jennifer Petrie (eds.), *Word and Drama in Dante* (Dublin: Irish Academic Press, 1993).

Barolini, Teodolinda, *Dante's Poets* (Princeton University Press, 1984).

Caesar, Michael, (ed.), *Dante: The Critical Heritage, 1314(?)–1870* (London: Routledge, 1989).

Croce, Benedetto, *The Poetry of Dante* (Mamaroneck, NY: Appel, 1971).

Curtius, Ernst Robert, 'Dante' in *European Literature and the Latin Middle Ages* (New York: Harper & Row, 1963), pp. 348–79.

Freccero, John, *Dante: The Poetics of Conversion* (Cambridge, MA: Harvard University Press, 1986).

Frow, John, *Character and Person* (Oxford University Press, 2014).

Genette, Gérard, *Fiction and Diction* (Ithaca, NY: Cornell University Press, 1993).

Greene, Thomas, 'Dramas of Selfhood in the *Comedy*' in T. G. Bergin (ed.), *From Time to Eternity: Essays on Dante's 'Comedy'* (New Haven, CT: Yale University Press, 1967), pp. 103–36.

Hollander, Robert, *Allegory in Dante's 'Commedia'* (Princeton University Press, 1969).

Kirkham, Victoria, 'A Canon of Women in Dante's *Commedia*', *Annali d'italianistica*, 7 (1989), 16–41.

Lansing, Richard (ed.), *Dante: The Critical Complex*, 8 vols. (London: Routledge, 2003), VII: *Dante and Interpretation*.

Simons, Dorothy L., 'The Individual Human *Dramatis Personae* of the *Divine Comedy*', *Modern Philology*, 16 (1918), 371–80.

Singleton, Charles S., *Dante Studies. II. The Journey to Beatrice* (Baltimore, MD: Johns Hopkins University Press, 1977).

Yates, Frances A., 'Transformations of Dante's Ugolino', *Journal of the Warburg and Courtauld Institutes*, 14 (1951), 92–117.

4   Moral Structure

Barański, Zygmunt G., *Dante e i segni* (Naples: Liguori, 2000).

Barolini, Teodolinda, 'Medieval multiculturalism and Dante's theology of Hell' in *Dante and the Origins of Italian Literary Culture* (New York: Fordham University Press, 2006), pp. 102–21.

Boyde, Patrick, *Perception and Passion in Dante's 'Comedy'* (Cambridge University Press, 1993).

Human Vices and Human Worth in Dante's 'Comedy' (Cambridge University Press, 2000).

Busnelli, Giovanni, *L'ordinamento morale del Purgatorio dantesco* (Rome: Civiltà cattolica, 1908).

Cachey, Theodore J. Jr., 'Cartographic Dante', *Italica*, 87 (2010), 325–54.

Cogan, Marc, *The Design in the Wax. The Structure of the 'Divine Comedy' and Its Meaning* (University of Notre Dame Press, 1999).

Corbett, George, *Dante and Epicurus* (Oxford: Legenda, 2013).

'The Christian Ethics of Dante's Purgatory', *Medium Ævum*, 83 (2014), 266–87.

Delcorno, Carlo, 'Dare ordine al male (*Inferno* XI)', *Lettere italiane*, 63 (2011), 181–207.

Falzone, Paolo, 'Dante e la nozione aristotelica di bestialità' in G. Crimi and L. Marcozzi (eds.), *Dante e il mondo animale* (Rome: Carocci, 2013), pp. 62–78.

Gilson, Simon A., 'Sincretismo e scolastica in Dante', *Studi e problemi di critica testuale*, 90/1 (2015), 317–40.

Hollander, Robert, *Dante: A Life in Works* (New Haven, CT: Yale University Press, 2001), pp. 104–14.

Moore, Edward 'The Classification of Sins in the *Inferno* and *Purgatorio*' in *Studies in Dante. Second Series* (Oxford: Clarendon Press, 1899), pp. 152–209.

Parodi, Ernesto G., 'La costruzione e l'ordinamento del Paradiso dantesco' in *Poesia e storia nella 'Divina Commedia'* (Venice: Neri Pozza, 1965), pp. 363–586.

Pinto, Raffaele, 'Indizi del disegno primitivo dell'*Inferno* (e della *Commedia*): *Inf.* VII–XI', *Tenzone*, 12 (2011), 105–52.

Reade, W. H. W., *The Moral System of Dante's Inferno* (Oxford: Clarendon Press, 1909).

Scott, John A., 'Dante's Other World: Moral Order' in *Understanding Dante* (University of Notre Dame Press, 2004), pp. 191–212.

Vazzana, Steno, 'Dov'è la "matta bestialitade". (Ancora sulla struttura aristotelica dell'*Inferno*)', *L'Alighieri*, 38 (1997), 95–108.

Witte, Karl, 'The Ethical Systems of the *Inferno* and the *Purgatorio*' in *Essays on Dante* (Boston, MA: Houghton Mifflin, 1898), pp. 117–52.

5   Title, Genre, Metaliterary Aspects

Agamben, Giorgio, 'Comedy' in *The End of the Poem. Studies in Poetics* (Stanford University Press, 1999), pp. 1–22.

Ascoli, Albert R., *Dante and the Making of a Modern Author* (Cambridge University Press, 2008).

Auerbach, Erich, *'Figura'* in *Scenes from the Drama of European Literature* (New York: Meridian Books, 1959), pp. 11–76.

Barański, Zygmunt G., 'The "Marvellous" and the "Comic". Towards a Reading of *Inferno* XVI', *Lectura Dantis*, 7 (1990), 72–95.

'"Primo tra cotanto senno": Dante and the Latin Comic Tradition', *Italian Studies*, 46 (1991), 1–31.

'The Poetics of Meter: Terza Rima, "Canto," "Canzone," "Cantica"' in T. J. Cachey Jr. (ed.), *Dante Now* (University of Notre Dame Press, 1995), pp. 3–41.

'*Magister satiricus*. Preliminary Notes on Dante, Horace, and the Middle Ages' in J. C. Barnes and M. Zaccarello (eds.), *Language and Style in Dante* (Dublin: Four Courts Press, 2013), pp. 13–61.

Barolini, Teodolinda, *Dante's Poets* (Princeton University Press, 1984).

The Undivine Comedy: Detheologizing Dante (Princeton University Press, 1992).

Cachey, Theodore, J. Jr., 'Dante's Journey between Truth and Fiction: Geryon Revisited' in M. Picone (ed.), *Atti del Seminario Dantesco Internazionale 2000* (Florence: Cesati, 2001), pp. 75–92.

'Cartographic Dante', *Italica*, 87 (2010) 325–54.

Franke, William, 'The Place of the Proper Name in Topographies of the *Paradiso*', *Speculum*, 87 (2012), 1089–124.

Freccero, John, 'The Significance of Terza Rima' in *Dante. The Poetics of Conversion* (Cambridge, MA: Harvard University Press), pp. 258–71.

Hollander, Robert, 'Dante *theologus-poeta*', *Dante Studies*, 94 (1976), 91–136.

Kleiner, John, *Mismapping the Underworld: Daring and Error in Dante's 'Comedy'* (Stanford University Press, 1994).

Leone, Anne C., 'Communal and Economic Implications of Blood in Dante', *Italian Studies*, 71 (2016), 265–86.

Minnis, A. J. and A. B. Scott (eds.), *Medieval Literary Theory and Criticism c.1100–c.1375* (Oxford: Clarendon Press, 1988).

Minnis, Alastair and Ian Johnson (eds.), *The Cambridge History of Literary Criticism. II. The Middle Ages* (Cambridge University Press, 2005), pp. 561–665.

Pertile, Lino, 'Cantica nella tradizione medievale in Dante', *Rivista di storia e letteratura religiosa*, 27 (1991), 389–412.

Singleton, Charles. S. 'The Irreducible Dove', *Comparative Literature*, 9 (1957), 124–35.

'The Vistas in Retrospect', *MLN*, 81 (1966), 55–80.

Tambling, Jeremy, 'Monstrous Tyranny, Men of Blood: Dante and *Inferno* XII', *MLR*, 98 (2003), 881–97.

Tavoni, Mirko, 'Perché il poema di Dante è una *commedia*?' in *Qualche idea su Dante* (Bologna: il Mulino, 2015), pp. 335–69.

Villa, Claudia, '*Comoedia: laus in canticis dicta?* Schede per Dante: *Paradiso*, XXV.1 e *Inferno*, XVIII', *Rivista di studi danteschi*, 1 (2001), 325–31.

6   Language and Style

Ambrosini, R., Franca Brambilla Ageno, *et al.*, 'Strutture del volgare di Dante' in *ED*, VI, 113–497.

Baldelli, Ignazio, 'Lingua e stile delle opere in volgare di Dante' in *ED*, VI, 55–112.

Barański, Zygmunt G. '"Significar per verba": Notes on Dante and Plurilingualism', *The Italianist*, 6 (1986), 5–16.

(ed.), '*Libri poetarum in quattuor species dividuntur*': Essays on Dante and 'Genre', supplement 2 to *The Italianist*, 15 (1995).

Barnes, John C. and Michelangelo Zaccarello, (ed.), *Language and Style in Dante* (Dublin: Four Courts Press, 2013).

Brownlee, Kevin, 'Why the Angels Speak Italian: Dante as Vernacular *Poeta* in *Paradiso* XXV', *Poetics Today*, 5 (1984), 597–610.

Cella, Roberta, *I gallicismi nei testi dell'italiano antico (dalle origini alla fine del sec. XIV)* (Florence: Accademia della Crusca, 2003).

Contini, Gianfranco, *Un'idea di Dante* (Turin: Einaudi, 1976).

D'Amico, Marta, *La sintassi della frase complessa nella 'Commedia' di Dante* (Pisa: ETS, 2017).

Deen Schildgen, Brenda, 'Dante's Neologisms in the *Paradiso* and the Latin Rhetorical Tradition', *Dante Studies*, 107 (1989), 101–19.

De Mauro, Tullio, *La fabbrica delle parole. Il lessico e problemi di lessicologia* (Turin: Utet Libreria, 2005).

De Ventura, Paolo, *Dramma e dialogo nella 'Commedia' di Dante. Il linguaggio della mimesi per un resoconto dell'aldilà* (Naples: Liguori, 2007).

Librandi, Rita, 'Dante e la lingua della scienza' in M. Tavoni (ed.), *Dante e la lingua italiana* [*Letture classensi*, 41] (Ravenna: Longo, 2013), pp. 61–87.

Manni, Paola, *La lingua di Dante* (Bologna: il Mulino, 2013).

Patota, Giuseppe, *La grande bellezza dell'italiano. Dante, Petrarca, Boccaccio* (Rome and Bari: Laterza, 2015).

Robey, David, *Sound and Structure in the Divine Comedy* (Oxford University Press, 2000).

Tavoni, Mirko, 'Dante' in *Enciclopedia dell'Italiano*, 2 vols. (Rome: Istituto della Enciclopedia Italiana, 2010), I, 321–37.

'Che cosa erano il volgare e il latino per Dante' in *Dante e la lingua italiana*, pp. 9–27.

'DanteSearch: istruzioni per l'uso. Interrogazione morfologica e sintattica delle opere volgari e latine di Dante' in M. D'Amico (ed.), *Sintassi dell'italiano antico e sintassi di Dante* (Pisa: Felici, 2015), pp. 59–79.

'Linguistic Italy' in Z. G. Barański and L. Pertile (eds.), *Dante in Context* (Cambridge University Press, 2015), pp. 243–59.

Qualche idea su Dante (Bologna: il Mulino, 2015).

7 Allegories of the Corpus

Armour, Peter, *Dante's Griffin and the History of the World: A Study of the Earthly Paradise* (Oxford: Clarendon Press, 1989).

Ascoli, Albert R., *Dante and the Making of a Modern Author* (Cambridge University Press, 2008).

Auerbach, Erich, 'Figura' in *Scenes from the Drama of European Literature* (New York: Meridian Books, 1959), pp. 11–76.

Barański, Zygmunt G., 'The "Marvellous" and the "Comic": Towards a Reading of *Inferno* XVI', *Lectura Dantis*, 7 (1990), 72–95.

'La letteratura allegorica e didattica: La *Commedia*' in F. Brioschi and C. di Girolamo (eds.), *Manuale di letteratura italiana*, 4 vols. (Turin: Bollati Boringhieri, 1993–6), I, 492–500.

'Dante's Signs: An Introduction to Medieval Semiotics and Dante' in J. C. Barnes and C. Ó Cuilleanáin (eds.), *Dante and the Medieval World* (Dublin: Irish Academic Press, 1995), pp. 139–80.

Barnes, John C. and Jennifer Petrie (eds.), *Dante and the Human Body* (Dublin: Four Court Press, 2007).

Barolini, Teodolinda, *The Undivine 'Comedy': Detheologizing Dante* (Princeton University Press, 1992).

De Ventura, Paolo, 'Dante, Dupin, e l'epistola a CanGrande' in V. Placella (ed.), *Dante oltre il medioevo* (Rome: Pioda Imaging, 2012), pp. 59–79.

Durling, Robert M., 'Introduction' in *Paradiso*, ed. and trans. by R. M. Durling and R. L. Martinez (Oxford University Press, 2011), pp. 3–19.

Franke, William, *Dante's Interpretive Journey* (University of Chicago Press, 1996).

Freccero, John, *Dante: The Poetics of Conversion* (Cambridge, MA, Harvard University Press, 1988).

Hollander, Robert, *Allegory in Dante's 'Comedy'* (Princeton University Press, 1969).

Gragnolati, Manuele, *Experiencing the Afterlife: Soul and Body in Dante and Medieval Culture* (University of Notre Dame Press, 2005).

Martinez, Ronald L., 'Allegory' in R. Lansing (ed.), *The Dante Encyclopedia* (New York: Garland Publishing, 2000), pp. 24–34.

Mazzotta, Giuseppe, *Dante, Poet of the Desert* (Princeton University Press, 1979).

Moevs, Christian, *The Metaphysics of Dante's 'Comedy'* (Oxford University Press, 2005).
Picone, Michelangelo (ed.), *Dante e le forme dell'allegoresi* (Ravenna: Longo, 1987).
Scott, John A., 'Dante's Allegory of the Theologians' in T. O'Neill (ed.), *The Shared Horizon* (Dublin: Irish Academic Press, 1990), pp. 27–40.

8 Classical Culture

Auerbach, Erich, 'Sermo humilis' in *Literary Language and Its Public in Late Latin Antiquity and in the Middle Ages* (Princeton University Press, 1965), pp. 25–66.
Barański, Zygmunt G. (ed.), *'Libri poetarum in quattuor species dividuntur'*. Essays on Dante and *'Genre'*, Supplement 2, *The Italianist*, 13 (1995).
   'Magister satiricus. Preliminary Notes on Dante, Horace and the Middle Ages' in J. C. Barnes and M. Zaccarello (eds.), *Language and Style in Dante* (Dublin: Four Courts Press, 2013), pp. 13–61.
Barolini, Teodolinda, *Dante's Poets* (Princeton University Press, 1984).
Brownlee, Kevin, 'Dante and the Classical Poets' in R. Jacoff (ed.), *Cambridge Companion to Dante* (Cambridge University Press, 1993), pp. 100–19.
Clay, Diskin, 'The Metamorphosis of Ovid in Dante's *Divine Comedy*' in J. F. Miller and C. Newlands (eds.), *A Handbook to the Reception of Ovid* (London: Blackwell, 2014), pp. 174–86.
Davis, Charles Till, *Dante and the Idea of Rome* (Oxford University Press, 1957).
Ginsberg, Warren, 'Dante, Ovid, and the Transformation of Metamorphosis', *Traditio*, 46 (1991), 205–33.
Heslin, Peter, 'Statius in Dante's *Commedia*' in W. J. Dominik *et al.* (eds.), *Brill's Companion to Statius* (Leiden: Brill, 2015), pp. 512–26.
Hollander, Robert, 'The Tragedy of Divination in *Inferno* XX' in *Studies in Dante* (Ravenna: Longo, 1980), pp. 131–218.
Iannucci, Amilcare A. (ed.), *Dante e la 'bella scola' della poesia* (Ravenna: Longo, 1993).
Jacoff, Rachel and Jeffrey T. Schnapp (eds.), *The Poetry of Allusion: Virgil and Ovid in Dante's 'Commedia'* (Stanford University Press, 1991).
Leo, Ulrich, 'The Unfinished *Convivio* and Dante's Rereading of the *Aeneid*', *Mediaeval Studies*, 13 (1951), 41–64.
Mazzotta, Giuseppe, *Dante, Poet of the Desert* (Princeton University Press, 1979).

9 Vernacular Literature and Culture

Alfie, Fabian, *Dante's Tenzone with Forese Donati* (University of Toronto Press, 2011).
Barański, Zygmunt G., 'La lezione esegetica di *Inferno* I: Allegoria, storia e letteratura nella *Commedia*' in M. Picone (ed.), *Dante e le forme dell'allegoresi* (Ravenna: Longo, 1987), pp. 79–97.
   '"'Nfiata labbia" and "dolce stil novo"': A Note on Dante, Ethics, and the Technical Vocabulary of Literature' in D. De Robertis and L. Coglievina (eds.), *Sotto il segno di Dante* (Florence: Le Lettere, 1998), pp. 17–35.

'"Per similitudine di abito scientifico": Dante, Cavalcanti and the Sources of Medieval "Philosophical" Poetry' in P. Antonello and S. Gilson (eds.), *Literature and Science in Italian Culture from Dante to the Present Day* (Oxford: Legenda, 2004), pp. 14–52.

Barolini, Teodolinda, *Dante's Poets* (Princeton University Press, 1984).

Dante and the Origins of Italian Literary Culture (New York: Fordham University Press, 2007).

Brownlee, Kevin, 'The Conflicted Genealogy of Cultural Authority: Italian Responses to French Cultural Dominance: Il *Tesoretto*, Il *Fiore*, and La *Commedia*' in V. Finucci and K. Brownlee (eds.), in *Generation and Degeneration* (Durham, NC and London: Duke University Press, 2001), pp. 262–86.

Cherchi, Paolo, 'Vernacular Literatures' in Z. G. Barański and L. Pertile (eds.), *Dante in Context* (Cambridge University Press, 2015), pp. 371–88.

Contini, Gianfranco, *Un'idea di Dante* (Turin: Einaudi, 1970), pp. 33–62, 245–83.

Cornish, Alison, *Vernacular Translation in Dante's Italy* (Cambridge University Press, 2011).

Honess, Claire, 'Dante and Political Poetry in the Vernacular', *Journal of the Institute of Romance Studies*, 6 (1998), 21–42.

Kay, Tristan, *Dante's Lyric Redemption: Eros, Salvation, Vernacular Tradition* (Oxford University Press, 2016).

Lombardi, Elena, *The Wings of the Doves: Love and Desire in Dante and Medieval Culture* (Montreal: McGill-Queens University Press, 2012).

Maddox, Donald, 'The Arthurian Intertexts of *Inferno* V', *Dante Studies*, 114 (1996), 113–27.

Pertile, Lino, 'Il nodo di Bonagiunta, le penne di Dante e il Dolce Stil Novo', *Lettere italiane*, 46 (1994), 44–75.

Picone, Michelangelo, '*Paradiso* IX: Dante, Folchetto e la diaspora trobadorica', *Medioevo romanzo*, 8 (1981–3), 47–89.

'Giulleria e poesia nella *Commedia*: una lettura intertestuale di Inferno XXI–XXII', *Letture Classensi*, 18 (1989), 11–30.

Rea, Roberto, 'Guinizzelli *Praised and Explained* (da *[O] caro padre meo* al XXVI del *Purgatorio*)', *The Italianist*, 30 (2010), 1–17.

Sowell, Madison U., 'Brunetto's *Tesoro* in Dante's *Inferno*', *Lectura Dantis*, 7 (1990), 60–71.

Steinberg, Justin, *Accounting for Dante: Urban Readers and Writers in Late Medieval Italy* (University of Notre Dame Press, 2007).

Took, John, 'Dante and the *Roman de la rose*', *Italian Studies*, 37 (1982), 1–25.

10   Religious Culture

Ardissino, Erminia, *Tempo liturgico e tempo storico nella 'Commedia' di Dante* (Città del Vaticano: Libreria Editrice Vaticana, 2009).

Barański, Zygmunt G., *Dante e i segni* (Naples: Liguori, 2000).

Barblan, Giovanni (ed.), *Dante e la Bibbia* (Florence: Olschki, 1988).

Barnes, John C., 'Vestiges of the Liturgy in Dante's Verse' in J. C. Barnes and C. Ó Cuilleanáin (eds.), *Dante and the Middle Ages* (Dublin: Irish Academic Press, 1995), pp. 231–70.

Benfell, V. Stanley, *The Biblical Dante* (University of Toronto Press, 2011).

Brilli, Elisa, *Firenze e il profeta. Dante fra teologia e politica* (Rome: Carocci, 2012).

Corbari, Eliana, *Vernacular Theology: Dominican Sermons and Audience in Late Medieval Italy* (Berlin: De Gruyter, 2013).

Dameron, George W., *Florence and Its Church in the Age of Dante* (Philadelphia: University of Pennsylvania Press, 2005).

Delcorno, Carlo, 'Cadenze e figure della predicazione nel viaggio dantesco', *Lettere italiane*, 37 (1985), 299–320.

Ferzoco, George, 'Dante and the Context of Medieval Preaching' in C. E. Honess and M. Treherne (eds.), *Reviewing Dante's Theology*, 2 vols. (Bern: Lang, 2013), II, 187–210.

Gragnolati, Manuele, *Experiencing the Afterlife. Soul and Body in Dante and Medieval Culture* (University of Notre Dame Press, 2005).

Hawkins, Peter S., *Dante's Testaments. Essays in Scriptural Imagination* (Bloomington, IN: Stanford University Press, 1999).

'Religious culture' in Z. G. Barański and L. Pertile (eds.), *Dante in Context* (Cambridge University Press, 2015), pp. 319–40.

Ledda, Giuseppe (ed.), *La Bibbia di Dante* (Ravenna: Centro Dantesco dei Frati Minori Conventuali, 2011).

Preghiera e liturgia nella Commedia (Ravenna: Centro Dantesco dei Frati Minori Conventuali, 2013).

Maldina, Nicolò, 'L'*oratio super Pater Noster* di Dante tra esegesi e vocazione liturgica. per *Purgatorio* XI, 1–24', *L'Alighieri*, 53 (2012), 89–108.

Martinez, Ronald L., 'The Poetics of Advent Liturgies: Dante's *Vita Nova* and *Purgatorio*' in M. Picone *et al.* (eds.), *Le culture di Dante* (Florence: Cesati, 2004), pp. 271–304.

'Dante and the Poem of the Liturgy' in *Reviewing Dante's Theology*, II, 89–155.

McInerny, Ralph, *Dante and the Blessed Virgin* (University of Notre Dame Press, 2010).

Nasti, Paola, 'Dante and Ecclesiology' in *Reviewing Dante's Theology*, II, 43–88.

11 Doctrine

Barański, Zygmunt G., *Dante e i segni* (Naples: Liguori, 2000).

'Dante and Doctrine (and Theology)' in C. E. Honess and M. Treherne (eds.), *Reviewing Dante's Theology*, 2 vols. (Oxford: Lang, 2013), I, 9–63.

'(Un)orthodox Dante' in *Reviewing Dante's Theology*, II, 252–330.

Bianchi, Luca, 'Moral Philosophy' in *Dante in Context*, pp. 159–72.

Black, Robert, 'Classical Antiquity' in Z. G. Barański and L. Pertile (eds.), *Dante in Context* (Cambridge University Press, 2015), pp. 297–318.

Botterill, Steven, *Dante and the Mystical Tradition: Bernard of Clairvaux in the 'Commedia'* (Cambridge University Press, 1994).

Boyde, Patrick, *Dante Philomythes and Philosopher* (Cambridge University Press, 1981).

Perception and Passion in Dante's 'Comedy' (Cambridge University Press, 1993).

Human Vices and Human Worth in Dante's 'Comedy' (Cambridge University Press, 2000).

Cornish, Alison, *Reading Dante's Stars* (New Haven, CT and London: Yale University Press, 2000).

Foster, Kenelm, *The Two Dantes and Other Studies* (London: Darton, Longman and Todd, 1977).

Grant, Edward, 'Natural Philosophy' in *Dante in Context*, pp. 173–88.

Gilson, Etienne, *Dante the Philosopher* (London: Sheed and Ward, 1948).

Gilson, Simon A., 'Dante and Christian Aristotelianism' in *Reviewing Dante's Theology*, I, 65–110.

'Sincretismo e scolastica in Dante', *Studi e problemi di critica testuale*, 90/1 (2015), 317–40.

Hawkins, Peter, *Dante's Testaments. Essays in Scriptural Imagination* (Stanford University Press, 1999).

'Divide and Conquer: Augustine in the *Divine Comedy*', *PMLA*, 406 (1991), 471–82.

Hollander, Robert, 'Dante's *Paradiso* as Philosophical Poetry', *Italica*, 86/4 (2009), 571–82.

Mazzotta, Giuseppe, *Dante's Vision and the Circle of Knowledge* (Princeton University Press, 1992).

Moevs, Christian, *The Metaphysics of the 'Comedy'* (Oxford University Press, 2005).

Montemaggi, Vittorio and Matthew Treherne (eds.), *Dante's 'Commedia'. Theology as Poetry* (University of Notre Dame Press, 2010).

Nardi, Bruno, *Dante e la cultura medievale*, revised edn (Bari: Laterza, 1983).

Saggi di filosofia dantesca, 2nd edn (Florence: La Nuova Italia, 1967).

Saggi e note di critica dantesca; Nel mondo di Dante (Rome: Istituto Grafico Tiberino, 1944).

Dal 'Convivio' alla 'Commedia', 2nd edn (Rome: Istituto Storico Italiano per il Medio Evo, 1992).

Nel mondo di Dante (Rome: Edizioni di Storia e Letteratura, 1944).

Nasti, Paola, *Favole d'amore e 'saver profondo'. La tradizione salomonica in Dante* (Ravenna: Longo, 2007).

Pertile, Lino, *La puttana e il gigante: Dal Cantico dei Cantici al Paradiso Terrestre di Dante* (Ravenna: Longo, 1998).

La punta del disio. Semantica del desiderio nella 'Commedia' (Florence: Cadmo, 2005).

12 Politics

Armour, Peter, *Dante's Griffin and the History of the World: A Study of the Earthly Paradise* (Oxford: Clarendon Press, 1989).

Davis, Charles Till, 'Dante and the Empire' in R. Jacoff (ed.), *The Cambridge Companion to Dante* (Cambridge University Press, 2007), pp. 257–69.

Dante and the Idea of Rome (Oxford: Clarendon Press, 1957).

Farnell, Stewart, *The Political Ideas of the 'Divine Comedy'* (Lanham: University Press of America, 1985).

Ferrante, Joan M., *The Political Vision of the 'Divine Comedy'* (Princeton University Press, 1984).

'Dante and Politics' in A. A. Iannucci (ed.), *Dante* (Toronto University Press, 1997), pp. 181–97.

Honess, Claire E., *From Florence to the Heavenly City: The Poetry of Citizenship in Dante* (Oxford: Legenda, 2006).

'Dante and the Theology of Politics' in C. E. Honess and M. Treherne (eds.), *Reviewing Dante's Theology*, 2 vols. (Oxford: Peter Lang, 2013), II, 157–85.

and Matthew Treherne (eds.), *'Se mai continga . . .': Exile, Politics, and Theology in Dante* (Ravenna: Longo, 2013).

Hyde, Kenneth, 'The Social and Political Ideal of the *Comedy*' in E. Haywood, (ed.), *Dante Readings* (Dublin: Irish Academic Press, 1987), pp. 47–71.

Keen, Catherine, *Dante and the City* (Stroud: Tempus, 2003).

Limentani, Uberto, 'Dante's Political Thought' in U. Limentani (ed.), *The Mind of Dante* (Cambridge University Press, 1965), pp. 113–37.

Mancusi-Ungaro, Donna, *Dante and the Empire* (New York: Lang, 1987).

Mazzotta, Giuseppe, *Dante Poet of the Desert* (Princeton University Press, 1979).

Dante's Vision and the Circle of Knowledge (Princeton University Press, 1993).

Najemy, John M., 'Dante and Florence' in *The Cambridge Companion to Dante*, pp. 236–56.

Schnapp, Jeffrey, *The Transfiguration of History at the Center of Dante's Paradise* (Princeton University Press, 1986).

Scott, John A., *Dante's Political Purgatory* (Philadelphia, PA: University of Pennsylvania Press, 1996).

Steinberg, Justin, *Dante and the Limits of the Law* (University of Chicago Press, 2013).

Woodhouse, John R. (ed.), *Dante and Governance* (Oxford: Clarendon Press, 1997).

13   Genesis, Dating, and Dante's 'Other Works'

Ascoli, Albert R., *Dante and the Making of a Modern Author* (Cambridge University Press, 2008).

Barański, Zygmunt G., 'The "New Life" of "Comedy": The *Commedia* and the *Vita Nuova*', *Dante Studies*, 113 (1995), 1–29.

'"'Nfiata labbia" and "dolce stil novo": A Note on Dante, Ethics, and the Technical Vocabulary of Literature' in D. De Robertis and L. Coglievina (eds.), *Sotto il segno di Dante* (Florence: Le Lettere, 1998), pp. 17–35.

Barolini, Teodolinda, *Dante's Poets* (Princeton University Press, 1984).

Bartuschat, Johannes, 'Le rime' in M. Picone and J. Bartuschat (eds.), *Le opere minori di Dante nella prospettiva della 'Commedia'*, pp. 17–40 [=*Letture classensi*, 38 (2009)].

Boyde, Patrick, *Dante's Style in his Lyric Poetry* (Cambridge University Press, 1971).

Cipollone, Annalisa, 'Dante and Bonagiunta', *Journal of the Institute of Romance Studies*, 6 (1998), 61–80.

Combs-Schilling, Jonathan, 'Tityrus in Limbo: Figures of the Author in Dante's Eclogues', *Dante Studies*, 133 (2015), 1–26.

Durling, Robert M. and Ronald L. Martinez, *Time and the Crystal. Studies in Dante's 'Rime petrose'* (Berkeley, CA: University of California Press, 1990).

Freccero, John, 'Casella's Song (*Purg.* II, 112)', *Dante Studies*, 91 (1973), 73–80.

Hollander, Robert, '*Purgatorio* II: Cato's Rebuke and Dante's *scoglio*', *Italica*, 52 (1975), 348–63.

'*Purgatorio* II: The New Song and the Old', *Lectura Dantis Virginiana*, 6 (1990), 28–45.

Jacoff, Rachel, 'The Post-palinodic Smile: *Paradiso* VIII and IX', *Dante Studies*, 98 (1980), 111–22.

Kay, Tristan, *Dante's Lyric Redemption: Eros, Salvation, Vernacular Tradition* (Oxford University Press, 2016).

Leo, Ulrich, 'The Unfinished *Convivio* and Dante's Rereading of the *Aeneid*', *Mediaeval Studies*, 13 (1951), 41–64.

Pertile, Lino, 'Dante's *Comedy* beyond the *Stilnovo*', *Lectura Dantis Virginiana*, 13 (1993), 47–77.

'Works' in Z. G. Barański and Lino Pertile (eds.), *Dante in Context* (Cambridge University Press, 2015), pp. 475–508.

Scott, John A., 'The Unfinished *Convivio* as a Pathway to the *Comedy*', *Dante Studies*, 113 (1995), 31–56.

14 Transmission History

Barański, Zygmunt G., 'Textual Transmission' in Z. G. Barański and L. Pertile (eds.), *Dante in Context* (Cambridge University Press, 2015), pp. 509–17.

Bellomo, Saverio, *Dizionario dei commentatori danteschi* (Florence: Olschki, 2004).

Filologia e critica dantesca, rev. ed. (Brescia: La Scuola, 2012).

Bertelli, Sandro, *La 'Commedia' all'antica* (Florence: Mandragora, 2007).

La tradizione della 'Commedia' dai manoscritti al testo, 2 vols. (Florence: Olschki, 2011–16).

Boschi Rotiroti, Marisa, *Codicologia dantesca della 'Commedia'* (Rome: Viella, 2004).

Chiavacci Leonardi, Anna Maria, 'Il libro di Dante dalle prime copie manoscritte all'edizione della Crusca' in R. Rusconi (ed.), *Pagine di Dante* (Perugia: Electa-Editori Umbri Associati, 1989).

Chiesa, Paolo, *Elementi di critica testuale* (Bologna: Patron, 2012).

Ciociola, Claudio, 'Dante' in E. Malato (ed.), *Storia della letteratura italiana. X. La tradizione dei testi* (Rome: Salerno, 2001), pp. 137–99.

Folena, Gianfranco, 'La tradizione delle opere di Dante Alighieri' in *Atti del Congresso Internazionale di Studi Danteschi*, 2 vols. (Florence: Sansoni, 1965), I, 1–78.

Inglese, Giorgio, *Come si legge un'edizione critica*, 2nd ed. (Rome: Carocci, 2015).

Manni, Paola, *La lingua di Dante* (Bologna: il Mulino, 2013).

Padoan, Giorgio, *Il lungo cammino del 'poema sacro'* (Florence: Olschki, 1993).

Roddewig, Marcella, *Dante Alighieri. Die göttliche Komödie: vergleichende Bestandsaufnahme der Commedia-Handschriften* (Stuttgart: Hiersemann Verlag, 1984).

Serianni, Luca, 'Sul colorito linguistico della *Commedia*', *Letteratura italiana antica*, 8 (2007), 141–50.

Stussi, Alfredo (ed.), *Fondamenti di critica testuale* (Bologna: il Mulino, 1998).

Trovato, Paolo, *Everything You Always Wanted to Know about Lachmann's Method* (Padua: Libreriauniversitaria.it, 2014).

and Vincenzo Guidi, 'Sugli stemmi bipartiti. Decimazione, asimmetria e calcolo delle probabilità', *Filologia italiana*, 1 (2004), 9–48.

Vandelli, Giuseppe, *Per il testo della 'Divina Commedia'*, ed. R. Abardo (Florence: Le Lettere, 1989).

Veglia, Marco, 'Sul testo della *Commedia* (da Casella a Sanguineti)', *Studi e problemi di critica testuale*, 66 (2003), 65–120.

Viel, Riccardo, 'Sulla tradizione manoscritta della *Commedia*: metodo e prassi in centocinquant'anni di ricerca' in R. Antonelli *et al.* (eds.), *Dante oggi*, 3 vols. (Rome: Viella, 2011), I, 459–518.

15 Early Reception until 1481

Armstrong, Guyda, 'Boccaccio and Dante' in G. Armstrong *et al.* (eds.), *The Cambridge Companion to Boccaccio* (Cambridge University Press, 2015), pp. 121–38.

Azzetta, Luca and Andrea Mazzucchi (eds.), *Boccaccio editore e interprete di Dante* (Rome: Salerno, 2014), pp. 73–111.

Barański, Zygmunt G., 'The Early Reception (1290s–1481)' in Z. G. Barański and L. Pertile (eds.), *Dante in Context* (Cambridge University Press, 2015), pp. 518–37.

and Theodore J. Cachey Jr. (eds.), *Petrarch and Dante: Anti-Dantism, Metaphysics, Tradition* (University of Notre Dame Press, 2009).

Brieger, Peter H., Millard Meiss, and Charles S. Singleton, *Illuminated Manuscripts of the Divine Comedy*, 2 vols. (Princeton University Press, 1969).

Brownlee, Kevin, 'Literary Genealogy and the Problem of the Father: Christine de Pizan and Dante' in T. J. Cachey Jr. (ed.), *Dante Now* (University of Notre Dame Press, 2013), pp. 205–35.

Caesar, Michael, *Dante: The Critical Heritage* (London and New York: Routledge, 1995).

Eisner, Martin, *Boccaccio and the Invention of Italian Literature* (Cambridge University Press, 2013).

Gilson, Simon A., 'Reading the *Convivio* from Trecento Florence to Dante's Cinquecento Commentators', *Italian Studies*, 64 (2009), 266–95.

Havely, Nick, *Dante's British Public: Readers and Texts, from the Fourteenth Century to the Present* (Oxford University Press, 2014).

Hollander, Robert, 'Dante and his Commentators' in R. Jacoff (ed.), *The Cambridge Companion to Dante* (Cambridge University Press, 2007), pp. 270–80.

Malato, Enrico *et al.* (eds.), *Censimento dei commenti danteschi*, 3 vols. (Rome: Salerno, 2011–14).

Nasti, Paola and Claudia Rossignoli (eds.), *Interpreting Dante: Essays on the Traditions of Dante Commentary* (University of Notre Dame Press, 2013).

Parker, Deborah (ed.), *Dante and the Art of the Italian Renaissance* [=*Lectura Dantis*, 22–3 (1998)].

Richardson, Brian, 'Editing Dante's *Commedia*, 1472–1629', in *Dante Now*, pp. 237–62.

Steinberg, Justin, *Accounting for Dante: Urban Readers and Writers in Late Medieval Italy* (University of Notre Dame Press, 2007).

16 Later Reception from 1481 to the Present

Audeh, Aida and Nick Havely (eds.), *Dante in the Long Nineteenth Century. Nationality, Identity, and Appropriation* (Oxford University Press, 2012).

Barański, Zygmunt G., 'Reflecting on Dante in America', *Annali d'italianistica*, 8 (1990), 58–86.

Botterill, Stephen, 'Dante Studies in the British Isles since 1980', *Dante Studies*, 111 (1993), 245–61.

Braida, Antonella, *Dante and the Romantics* (Basingstoke: Macmillan, 2004).

 and Luisa Calè (eds.), *Dante on View: The Reception of Dante in the Visual and Performing Arts* (Aldershot: Ashgate, 2007).

Capaci, Bruno (ed.), *Dante oscuro e barbaro. Commenti e dispute (secc. XVII e XVIII)* (Rome: Carocci, 2010).

Dionisotti, Carlo, 'Varia fortuna di Dante' in *Geografia e storia della letteratura italiana* (Turin: Einaudi, 1967), pp. 255–303.

Ellis, Steve, *Dante and English Poetry: Shelley to T. S. Eliot* (Cambridge University Press, 1983).

Friederich, Werner P., *Dante's Fame Abroad 1350–1850* (Rome: Edizioni di Storia e Letteratura, 1950).

Gragnolati, Manuele, Fabio Camilletti and Fabian Lampart (eds.), *Metamorphosing Dante. Appropriations, Manipulations, and Rewritings in the Twentieth and Twenty-First Centuries* (Vienna and Berlin: Turia + Kant, 2011).

Havely, Nick, (ed.), *Dante's Modern Afterlife: Reception and Response from Blake to Heaney* (Basingstoke: Macmillan, 1998).

 (ed.), *Dante in the Nineteenth Century. Reception, Canonicity, Popularization* (Oxford: Peter Lang, 2011).

 Dante's British Public: Readers and Texts, from the Fourteenth Century to the Present (Oxford University Press, 2014).

Hawkins, Peter and Rachel Jacoff (eds.), *The Poets' Dante: Twentieth-century Responses* (New York: Farrar, Straus & Giroux, 2001).

Haywood, Eric G. (ed.), *Dante Metamorphoses: Episodes in a Literary Afterlife* (Dublin: Four Court Press, 2003).

Iannucci, Amilcare, A. (ed.), *Dante, Cinema, and Television* (University of Toronto Press, 2004).

Levillain, Henriette (ed.), *Dante et ses lecteurs du Moyen Âge au XXe siècle* (Poitiers: La Licorne, 2001).

Looney, Dennis, *Freedom Readers: The African American Reception of Dante Alighieri and the 'Divine Comedy'* (University of Notre Dame Press, 2011)

Milbank, Alison, *Dante and the Victorians* (Manchester University Press, 1998).

Pite, Ralph, *The Circle of Our Vision. Dante's Presence in English Romantic Poetry* (Oxford: Clarendon Press, 1994).

Pitwood, Michael, *Dante and the French Romantics* (Geneva: Droz, 1985).

Pozzato, Maria Pia (ed.), *L'idea deforme. Interpretazioni esoteriche di Dante* (Milan: Bompiani, 1989).

GENERAL INDEX

Abel, 131
academies
  Accademia della Crusca, 230, 237–8, 260
  Florentine Academy, 253, 260
Acheron, 14, 62, 67, 130, 137
Achilles, 130, 134, 233
Adam, 14, 17–18, 24, 51, 188, 223
Aeneas, 30, 38–41, 102, 130, 137, 139, 201, 249, 256
affectivity, 20, 189
Agapetus, pope, 76
Agathon, 24
Agostino d'Ancona, 250
Alan of Lille, 174, 178, 185, 191
  Anticlaudianus, 114–15, 125, 146, 191
  De planctu Naturae, 146, 191
Albert of Hapsburg, Holy Roman emperor, 202
Albert the Great, 189, 232
Albertano da Brescia, 60
Alberto Della Scala, 84
alchemy, 12, 66
Alderotti, Taddeo, 149
Aldobrandeschi, Omberto, 71–2, 247–8
allegory, 1, 19, 43, 51, 67, 71–2, 110–25, 157, 160, 217, 247–8, 263, 269
  allegoresis, 111, 113
  allegoria in factis, 111–12, 115–16, 118–19, 125
  allegoria in verbis, 112, 116, 125
Alphonso of Aragon, 254
Amico dell'Ottimo, 249
Anaxagoras, 134
Anchises, 39
Andreas Cappellanus, 107
angelology, 174, 188, 190
angels, 4, 15–17, 22–4, 44, 48, 62, 73, 103, 105, 163, 166, 188, 190, 214

Anonimo Genovese, 108
Anonimo lombardo, 230
Anselm, Saint, 189
Antaeus, 13, 22
Ante-Inferno, 7, 14
Ante-Purgatory, 7, 14, 62, 70–1, 74, 77, 166
Antiphon, 24
Antonioni, Michelangelo, 269
Apollo, 39–40, 124
Aquinas, Thomas, 52, 65, 75–6, 103, 158, 168, 172, 188–9, 191
  Summa theologiae, 171
Arduini, Beatrice, 228
Arezzo, 32
Argenti, Filippo, 10–11, 24–5, 154
Ariosto, Ludovico
  Orlando furioso, 260
Aristotle, 65, 67–8, 128, 130, 134–6, 174, 177, 180–1, 195
  De anima, 135, 183
  De generatione animalium, 184
  Metaphysics, 67
  Nicomachean Ethics, 11, 64, 67, 127, 149, 177, 183
  Physics, 65, 67, 127, 135, 177–8
  Politics, 65–6
Aroux, Eugène, 267
Arthur, King, 155
astronomy, 73, 75, 97, 101, 108, 173, 181
Auerbach, Erich, 44, 46, 60, 93, 114, 269
Augustine, Saint, 69, 122, 128, 133, 182, 187, 194
  City of God, 69, 128, 182
  Confessions, 122, 126
  On Christian Doctrine, 71, 126, 133
Augustus, Roman emperor, 113, 194, 201, 203, 205–6

INDEX OF REFERENCES TO DANTE'S WORKS

Purg (cont.)
V, 107, 166
V, 117, 106
V, 130–1, 164
V, 133, 164
V–VI, 71
VI, 136, 181
VI, 46–8, 57
VI, 75, 24
VI, 76–151, 16
VI, 82–4, 202
VI, 83, 202
VI, 88–9, 202
VI, 88–90, 68
VI, 91–6, 204
VI, 97, 202
VI, 112–4, 202
VI, 118, 137
VI, 145–7, 200
VI, 151–2, 200
VI-VII, 156
VII, 10–13, 104
VII, 37–51, 55
VII, 39, 70
VII, 82–4, 166
VII–VIII, 71
VIII, 32
VIII, 19–21, 113
VIII, 25, 23
VIII, 64–66, 24
VIII, 85–93, 71
VIII, 106, 23
IX, 13, 16
IX, 32
IX, 49, 70
IX, 70–145, 71
IX, 85, 137
IX, 104, 23
IX, 130, 162
IX, 132, 71
IX, 136, 138
IX, 139, 163
IX, 139–44, 162
IX–XXVII, 68
X, 138
X, 34–45, 166
X, 35–6, 166
X, 44, 166
X, 55–69, 39
X–XXVII, 70
XI, 1–3, 165
XI, 22–4, 165
XI, 58–72, 72

XI, 79–108, 179
XI, 81, 106
XI, 82–108, 72
XI, 94–6, 140
XI, 97–9, 140
XI, 109–42, 72
XI, 156, 165
XIII, 106–29, 9
XIII, 128, 164
XIV, 86–7, 182
XIV, 103, 107
XIV, 124, 107
XV, 181
XVI, 19–21, 163
XVI, 23–5, 52
XVI, 36–7, 53
XVI, 47–8, 53
XVI, 52, 149
XVI, 62, 30
XVI, 66, 206
XVI, 85–90, 187
XVI, 94–6, 204
XVI, 97, 54, 202
XVI, 104–5, 182
XVI, 106–8, 204
XVI, 107, 256
XVI, 107–8, 76
XVI, 124, 53
XVI, 137, 107
XVI, 141–5, 53
XVII, 63, 69, 146
XVII, 70–139, 14
XVII, 91–2, 69
XVII, 91–139, 16
XVII, 93, 69
XVII, 94–6, 70
XVII, 96, 70
XVII, 104–5, 15
XVII, 104–14, 65
XVII, 106–14, 70
XVII, 115–7, 70
XVII, 118–20, 70
XVII, 121–3, 70
XVII, 136–9, 70
XVII–XVIII, 124, 178, 219
XVIII, 2, 182
XVIII, 146
XVIII, 1, 182
XVIII, 12, 14, 182
XVIII, 18, 146, 183
XVIII, 19–33, 183
XVIII, 22, 23, 49, 51, 57, 183
XVIII, 28–30, 183